Southern Ladies, New Women

NEW PERSPECTIVES ON THE HISTORY OF THE SOUTH

UNIVERSITY PRESS OF FLORIDA / STATE UNIVERSITY SYSTEM

Florida A&M University, Tallahassee
Florida Atlantic University, Boca Raton
Florida Gulf Coast University, Ft. Myers
Florida International University, Miami
Florida State University, Tallahassee
University of Central Florida, Orlando
University of Florida, Gainesville
University of North Florida, Jacksonville
University of South Florida, Tampa
University of West Florida, Pensacola

Southern Ladies, New Women

RACE, REGION, AND CLUBWOMEN
IN SOUTH CAROLINA, 1890-1930

JOAN MARIE JOHNSON

UNIVERSITY PRESS OF FLORIDA
Gainesville · Tallahassee · Tampa · Boca Raton
Pensacola · Orlando · Miami · Jacksonville · Ft. Myers

Copyright 2004 by Joan Marie Johnson
Printed in the United States of America
All rights reserved

First cloth printing, 2004

First paperback printing, 2005

Library of Congress Cataloging-in-Publication Data
Johnson, Joan Marie.
Southern ladies, new women : race, region, and clubwomen
in South Carolina, 1890–1930 / Joan Marie Johnson;
foreword by John David Smith, series editor.
p. cm. – (New perspectives on the history of the South)
Includes bibliographical references and index.
ISBN 0-8130-2782-9 (cloth : alk. paper); ISBN 0-8130-2955-4 (pbk.)
1. Women—South Carolina—Societies and clubs—History.
2. African American women—South Carolina—Societies and clubs—History.
3. Women social reformers—South Carolina—History. 4. Social problems—
South Carolina—History. 5. South Carolina—History—1865–
I. Title. II. Series.
HQ1905.S6J64 2004
305.4'06'0757—dc22   2004053718

The University Press of Florida is the scholarly publishing agency for
the State University System of Florida, comprising Florida A&M University,
Florida Atlantic University, Florida Gulf Coast University, Florida International
University, Florida State University, University of Central Florida,
University of Florida, University of North Florida, University
of South Florida, and University of West Florida.

University Press of Florida
15 Northwest 15th Street
Gainesville, FL 32611-2079
http://www.upf.com

*Dedicated to
Elise, Sophie, Darci, and Don*

Contents

List of Illustrations viii

Series Foreword ix

Acknowledgments xiii

1. Southern Ladies, New Women 1

2. "As Intensely Southern As I Am": Black and White Clubwomen, the United Daughters of the Confederacy, and Southern Identity 24

3. "Less Said Soonest Mended": The Parallel Lives of Black and White Clubwomen 60

4. "Unity in Diversity": South Carolina Clubwomen, the South, and the Nation 89

5. Reluctant Reformers, Resistant Legislators: White Clubwomen and Social Reform 129

6. "Exalting the Cause of Virtue": Black and White Clubwomen and Juvenile Reformatories 168

Conclusion. "This Wonderful Dream Nation!": Contesting Confederate Culture 202

Notes 209

Bibliography 259

Index 277

Illustrations

1. Louisa Poppenheim   85

2. Louisa Poppenheim, president
of the South Carolina Federation of Women's Clubs   85

3. Mary and Louisa Poppenheim published the *Keystone*   86

4. Marion Wilkinson and other women
in the International Council of Women of the Darker Races   87

5. Marion Birnie Wilkinson Home for Girls   87

6. Marion Birnie Wilkinson, president
of the South Carolina Federation of Colored Women's Clubs   88

Foreword

Joan Marie Johnson's pathbreaking *Southern Ladies, New Women: Race, Region, and Clubwomen in South Carolina, 1890–1930* joins an increasing number of books that use class, gender, and race to illumine the complexities of Southern history, historical memory, and identity. Women's clubs, North and South, black and white, were important gendered components of the Progressive Era. By World War I their membership totaled over one million nationally.

Elite and middle-class women joined clubs to establish and promote female solidarity, to exchange intellectual interests, and to lobby and then initiate reform. They studied literature, discussed historical and current events, and pushed for social and political change. Clubwomen campaigned for the construction of libraries, kindergartens, schools, and reformatories. But they also led the fight to improve conditions for laborers, to clean up the cities, and to promote public health.

Examining minutely the women's club movement among blacks and whites in South Carolina, Johnson underscores the clubwomen's "abilities both to fuse Southern identity construction with social reform work and to reconcile tradition with progress." Drawing upon a rich arsenal of sources, including minutes, newspapers, private papers, official publications, and oral history interviews, she compares the contributions, goals, and strategies of three organizations. These include the white South Carolina Federation of Women's Clubs (SCFWC) founded in 1898, the South Carolina Federation of Colored Women's Clubs (SCFCWC) launched in 1909, and the South Carolina state division of the United Daughters of the Confederacy (UDC) organized in 1896. Though the SCFWC and the UDC shared many members and ideals, the UDC aimed its social reform narrowly at Confederate veterans and their widows while the women's clubs had much broader social agendas. Each of the groups is significant, however, in the varied ways they intertwined race, gender, reform, and the conceptualization and popularization of a distinctly Southern historical memory and sectional identity.

Though it began as a literary club, the SCFWC, like other organizations of women's clubs throughout the nation, supported Progressive Era reforms. In addition to fostering civics, education, and philanthropy, the group endorsed labor legislation and aid for delinquent children, the feebleminded, and tuberculosis patients. Johnson makes clear how white South Carolina women, enmeshed in the ultra-conservative, male-dominated culture of the Palmetto State, walked a fine line between "traditional gender ideals" and the "new possibilities for activism." Though club members differed on the merits of joining the campaign for woman suffrage, they challenged conventional roles "by demanding an interventionist government responsive to social reform." Much like white clubwomen elsewhere in the South, SCFWC members "moved cautiously by defending the Confederacy, chivalry, and segregation, while quietly expanding their opportunities in the public sphere and promoting higher education for women."

Members of the SCFWC, paralleling their sisters in the UDC, celebrated and commemorated the Old South, the Confederacy, and the Reconstruction-era Ku Klux Klan, perpetuating the image and values of the Lost Cause. In advancing education reforms and sponsoring public ceremonies, the South Carolina clubwomen constructed what they considered a "true" historical memory of the antebellum South and the Confederacy. According to Johnson, they "embraced a past in which the Confederate cause was just, slavery benign, and slaves racially inferior." The women thus contributed significantly in shaping "the culture of the newly segregated South; segregation thus became natural and timeless."

Black women, however, who labored under many burdens, including their gender, their race, their region, and legalized Jim Crow, confronted the white women's glorification of the Lost Cause head on. African American clubwomen organized to disprove allegations that black women were inherently immoral, to promote self-education, and to sponsor welfare among their people. Like their white peers, they also studied and discussed historical and literary topics. Unlike the whites, black women integrated such distinguished authors as W.E.B. Du Bois, Paul Laurence Dunbar, and Charles Waddell Chesnutt into what became their celebration of African American culture and their demand for the recognition of black humanity and citizenship. According to Johnson, black women "negotiated an alternate understanding of African American, Southern, and American identities that belied stereotypes of inferiority."

Johnson frames the women's groups within the broad cultural, economic, intellectual, and political history of the New South. For example, she notes that both the SCFWC and the UDC organized after white South Carolinians disenfranchised African American men and passed discriminatory Jim Crow laws. "Clubwomen and other proponents of the Confederate Celebration," Johnson writes, "while not engaging in either violence or vitriolic language, did help legitimize the Lost Cause around Southern honor and gender ideals; they upheld segregation through their telling of history, especially to children in schools." White women studied blacks as historical or sociological "problems," not as subjects of philanthropy or uplift. Although unwilling to accept black clubwomen as peers, they discussed the race question "because it implied inferiority on the part of blacks and reinforced the white paternalism of whites that predominated their discourse on slavery."

In response, black women used their special history—the role of African Americans in overthrowing slavery—to fashion a past more American than Southern. Black clubwomen celebrated African American heroes and heroines like Frederick Douglass, Booker T. Washington, Phyllis Wheatley, and Marian Anderson. In 1919 club members began a subscription campaign to raise funds for a monument to black veterans of World War I. Black women also took the lead in the 1920s in launching South Carolina's interracial movement. Though largely ignored by white clubwomen, their black counterparts nonetheless fought tirelessly in condemning segregation and lynching. "Ultimately, however," Johnson concludes, "most of their projects concentrated on aiding those in the black community who were in need, especially girls, rather than on agitating for an end to discrimination."

As elite and middle-class reformers, as Southerners, and, most important, as women, South Carolina's black and white clubwomen of the early twentieth century championed similar projects, employed similar strategies, and experienced similar frustrations. Despite shared agendas and apparent parallels between the two groups, deep historical and racial forces divided them. As Johnson's well-crafted study suggests, white clubwomen created a Southern identity through Confederate culture; black clubwomen challenged this culture but struggled to establish their respectability. Both found their contributions to Southern reform circumscribed by the color line.

John David Smith
Series Editor

Acknowledgments

When I finished my dissertation, Anne Firor Scott told me that the best way to turn it into a book was to set it aside and begin writing again. Although I did not take her advice, this book has indeed taken several years and much rewriting. I would like to thank the many people who supported this work throughout that process.

I could never have completed the research without the aid of diligent and patient librarians and archivists, notably those in the interlibrary loan departments of UCLA, Miami University of Ohio, the University of Cincinnati, and Northeastern Illinois University. Archivists have assisted me in my research throughout the Carolinas, at the South Carolina Historical Society, the Charleston Library Society, Avery Research Center for the Study of African American History and Culture, the Laurens County Library, and the Darlington County Historical Society. Archivists were also helpful at the special collections departments at Duke University, the University of South Carolina Caroliniana Library, the American Jewish Archives at Hebrew Union College in Cincinnati, and Winthrop University. I am particularly grateful to Gina Price White at Winthrop University for her unflagging aid. Morgan Davis at the General Federation of Women's Clubs archives provided me with the first names of several married women.

I am most appreciative to the residents of Orangeburg, Columbia, and Spartanburg who agreed to meet with me to discuss the early days of the South Carolina Federation of Colored Women's Clubs and Marion Wilkinson, including Geraldine Zimmerman, Louise Robinson, Emma Casselberry, Lavonia Atkinson, Charlie May Campbell, and Robert Evans. I am also grateful to Barbara Jenkins of South Carolina State University, who gave me a tour of Orangeburg and led me to various sources on Marion Wilkinson and the Sunlight Club.

The University of California–Los Angeles, Miami University, and the

University of Cincinnati provided generous financial support for research and travel. A Women's Studies Research Grant from Special Collections at Duke University assisted in research on the Poppenheims, and a Starkoff fellowship from the American Jewish Archives at Hebrew Union College in Cincinnati donated funds for research on South Carolina Jewish women's clubs. The Institute for Southern Studies at the University of South Carolina offered encouragement and a much-needed parking pass for the campus. The Southern Association of Women's Historians has been a source of much needed support, and I have appreciated the friendships made within this group. Meredith Morris-Babb has been a generous and supportive editor at the University Press of Florida. I am grateful to her for her enthusiasm for this project.

I also wish to thank John Boles and the anonymous reviewers at the *Journal of Southern History*. Chapter 2 of this book appeared in a slightly different form in that publication. Portions of chapters 5 and 6 appeared in a different form in *Before the New Deal: Social Welfare in the South, 1830–1930*, edited by Elna C. Green, copyright 1999 by the University of Georgia Press and reprinted by permission.

Various scholars and friends have offered indispensable support and insight to me during this study. I thank especially Anne Firor Scott for introducing me to Southern women's history while I was an undergraduate at Duke; Brenda Stevenson, my advisor at UCLA, who pushed me to think more critically about black and white Southern women; Ellen DuBois, who offered keen insight into women's history; and Jan Reiff and Valerie Matsumoto, who encouraged my work. Colleagues and friends have heard me talk about the project and read various versions of conference papers, articles, and chapters. I thank Fitzhugh Brundage, Kathleen Clark, Catherine Clinton, Cita Cook, Chrissy Cortina, Arleen DeVera, Erika Wright Ellis, Glenda Gilmore, Shirley Lim, Rebecca Montgomery, Francesca Morgan, Anastasia Sims, and Marjorie Spruill. In Cincinnati, I had the support of Kirsten Gardner, Mary Frederickson, Charlotte Goldy, Wayne Durrill, Joanne Meyerowitz, and Barbara Ramusack. My appreciation to Glenda Gilmore for telling me about Marion Wilkinson early in my research and to George C. Rogers and Connie Schulz at the University of South Carolina for their advice. I want particularly to thank Joan Cashin for her unfailing confidence in my work; Carol Berkin and Sandra Treadway, who made the book immeasurably stronger with their comments; and Karen Cox, who has been a loyal friend as well as colleague, and heroically read the manuscript at the last moment.

This book could not have been written without the many friends and family members who have encouraged me and listened to me talk about South Carolina women for years. Raising young children, teaching, and writing have been challenging at times, and their friendship enabled me to persevere. I thank especially Cincinnati friends Nancy and Terry Koritz, Carolyn and David Livingston, Lisa and John Thaler, Lynn and Mark Tinsey, and Tony and Ronna Ueber. In Evanston I am buoyed up by "Salon" members Sheila McGuire, Joan Emrich, Connie Hanson, Karen Angotti, and Janet Henry. Various family and friends hosted me during my travels to the South for research, including friends Jennifer and Jose Torres, in Durham; my sister-in-law and brother-in-law Gina and Alvin Wells, in Durham; my aunt and uncle Camy and Robert Scalera, at Pawley's Island; the Vallone family, while on vacation at Kiawah Island; my sister-in-law and brother-in-law Meghan and Jeff Johnson, in Los Angeles; Kathleen Clark, in Atlanta; and especially my mother-in-law, Anne M. Johnson, in Columbia, with whom I stayed many nights. Their support, along with that of my siblings, Andrew, Monica, and Anne Marie Infosino, and my parents, Joseph and Dorothy Infosino, sustained me throughout this process more than they know.

My daughters, Darci, Sophie, and Elise, were born during the revision process; their smiles heartened me. Everything I do, I do for them. Finally, I thank my husband, Don. He supports my history habit, makes me laugh, and makes me think. For his love and generosity, I am profoundly grateful.

Chapter 1

Southern Ladies, New Women

The notion of a distinctive Southern identity promoted by South Carolina clubwomen is the subject of this book. Did black and white clubwomen across the state believe that they were different because they were Southern? And if so, did it matter? Did it affect their agenda? Evidence from South Carolina suggests that it mattered deeply. In 1910 Louisa Poppenheim encouraged the readers of the *Keystone*, the periodical for Southern clubwomen, to attend the national General Federation of Women's Clubs meeting. Not only would Southern delegates bring their record of achievement, but they would also "in their persons, and by their deportment, character and manners express types of an old and established civilization." According to Poppenheim, the South had "given to American life brave, honest, courtly, highminded men and courteous, modest, unselfish and truth-speaking women." These ideals, she proclaimed, "are the most cherished possessions of the South.... These ideals Southern women are taking to the Biennial, and these ideals will make themselves felt in the future development of the club movement in America."[1] To Poppenheim, no matter how much they had in common with Northern clubwomen, they remained foremost Southern.

At the turn of the century thousands of black and white Southern women joined a national trend and established women's clubs in small towns and cities. In many ways these clubwomen were similar to those in the North: they studied literature and history for self-improvement and took on social reform projects, ranging from building libraries to lobbying for better sanitation. But women's clubs in the South were distinctive. The movement blossomed about ten to twenty years later than it had in the North, and Southern clubwomen faced greater opposition from those who believed that clubs threatened women's traditional gender roles.

More important, in South Carolina, their Southern identity suffused their work. The peculiar entwined history of race and gender in the region influenced not only the activities of black and white South Carolina clubwomen but also relations with Northern clubwomen and with each other.[2]

Most historians analyze white Southern clubwomen primarily in terms of their participation in Progressive-era social reform by emphasizing similarities to their sisters in the North. However, most significant about white clubwomen in South Carolina was not their "progressive" behavior as reformers but rather their abilities both to fuse Southern identity construction with social reform work and to reconcile tradition with progress. Louisa Poppenheim exhorted clubwomen to draw motivation from their study of the past for social reform; she argued that "inspiration for the future can be secured through the contemplation of that past."

Decades after the South's defeat in the Civil War, its citizens still struggled to understand what it meant to be Southern. For many white women, the answer could be found in the Lost Cause, the movement to honor the Confederacy. They believed that inventing an honorable Confederate tradition was necessary to reconstruct the region. The United Daughters of the Confederacy (UDC) dedicated itself to building Confederate monuments, writing and regulating history, and extending their social work to only Confederate veterans, widows, and their children. Recently, scholars focusing on history and memory have begun to highlight the role of the UDC in this movement; these historians provide a new understanding of women's importance to the Lost Cause, and sweep aside Gaines Foster's contention that the ascendancy of the UDC to the leadership of the Lost Cause in the 1890s suggested its loss of centrality to Southern society. Rather, women assuaged defeat by celebrating white men's "masculine" roles as protectors of white women.[3]

The records of the South Carolina Federation of Women's Clubs (SCFWC) and its member clubs show that a sense of place, pervading much of their literary and reform work, provided a little-noticed link between white women's clubs and the "Confederate Celebration." The Lost Cause, and consequently the past, pervaded their work and Southern society to a significant degree. Clubwomen studied Southern history and literature at club meetings, and then attempted to transmit their vision of history through education reform, public ceremonies, and other forms of outreach to the public. From memories of their own families' experiences, they worked to create a collective memory of the antebellum South and Confederacy, and to make that historical memory the "true" history. Expanding our study of women and the Lost Cause beyond the UDC and into women's clubs provides a crucial understanding of the pervasiveness of the Lost Cause in Southern society. Although this link took place primarily in literary clubs, even civics clubs sometimes expressed the motivation for their reform work in Lost Cause rhetoric. Women's central role as proponents of the Lost Cause becomes even more evident if clubwomen are incorporated alongside the Daughters, because the UDC and federated women's clubs were two of the largest women's associations in the South in the early twentieth century.[4]

As proponents of the Lost Cause white clubwomen embraced a past in which the Confederate cause was just, slavery benign, and slaves racially inferior. By promoting this particular story of Southern history through their literary studies and historical teachings, white women significantly shaped the culture of the newly segregated South; segregation thus became natural and timeless.[5]

Control over historical memory is a powerful tool. African Americans had to fight not only social and economic oppression but also the Lost Cause itself. Black clubwomen sought to create a place for themselves and their families in South Carolina. As clubwomen, they too studied history and literature, although they included W.E.B. Du Bois and other African American authors. Like their white counterparts, black clubwomen took their message to the public through schools and libraries. They negotiated an alternate understanding of African American, Southern, and American identities that belied stereotypes of inferiority. African American clubwomen confronted the Lost Cause, struggled against Jim Crow laws, and demanded recognition of their citizenship. Historical memory thus simultaneously both oppressed and freed African Americans.

It was significant that sectional identity affected how both black and white South Carolina clubwomen perceived their ability to participate in national organizations—the General Federation of Women's Clubs and the National Association of Colored Women. When clubwomen met with their sisters from the North, they wore their Southern identity on their sleeves and fought a persistent feeling of inferiority. At the same time black and white South Carolina clubwomen worked more closely with their Northern black and white counterparts than with each other in South Carolina. Southern black women led notable overtures across the racial divide, but with little result. If their regional identity differentiated them from Northern clubwomen, their Southernness also separated them from each other because it was so interwoven with racial identity. Although some identities—class, gender, region—surged and receded in importance, race remained salient always.[6]

Finally, South Carolina clubwomen's focus on Southern identity was fraught with incongruity: because they were Southern, they desired to participate in social reform; because they were Southern, their ability to affect change was severely limited. The contest over memory and identity reveals that the approved version of Southern history had the potential to shape the future of the New South. Like women across the nation, Southern women justified their new work in the public sphere as municipal housekeeping—that is, their maternal impulse led them to work for cleaner and safer communities for their children. But in South Carolina pride in identity also provided the impetus for white clubwomen to build libraries, kindergartens, and reformatories and to improve education, health services, and city streets and sanitation. This club work was significantly different from that of the UDC, which limited its social reform agenda to a narrow focus on the needs of veterans and their widows. Clubwomen felt compelled by the glory of the Southern past to address socioeconomic needs in the postwar South. As black clubwomen identified and met social and economic needs of blacks, their strategies to uplift the race showed their resistance to Jim Crow and their fight to shape a New South that recognized their citizenship. By comparing their efforts, in this history I show that black and white clubwomen often did similar work for different reasons.[7]

Furthermore, this focus on Southern identity also potentially limited reform work because, in part, many white clubwomen had difficulty criticizing the South. Women's emphasis on remembering the past shaped the contours of their social reform work and sometimes undercut crusades to change the South. Their social activism was limited by both their own female ideology and resistance from male legislators.

South Carolina clubwomen understood that they were forging new gender roles by expanding opportunities for women. The relationship between clubwomen and the UDC reveals how white Southern women negotiated their image as "protected" women with their role during and after the Civil War as "protectors" of the South. Expectations that women exhibit maternal behavior provided a means through which South Carolina women not only swept municipalities clean through social reform efforts but also taught themselves, their children, and the public about the meaning of Southern history. They redefined citizenship to include themselves in this new role. Despite its potential political power, men generally regarded women's work for memory and identity with less suspicion than their social reform work. Although women were expanding their roles outside the home, they ultimately did not challenge white male patriarchy; as a whole the Lost Cause celebrated manly men and womanly women.[8] Clubwomen's social reform agenda, which more directly challenged male political power by calling for an interventionist government, experienced far greater opposition than their memorial work. Although women's use of Lost Cause rhetoric helped legitimize their new roles, they used such language, not as a conscious strategy to gain authority, but because they deeply believed in its validity.

African American women were unconstrained by the same ideals of the need for "protection" surrounding white women; moreover, they did not benefit from the same assumptions of morality that chivalry could provide white women. Examining how South Carolina black clubwomen fought for reform in such a society reveals the influence of region on their struggle to fight gender and race oppression simultaneously. Their focus on young girls and "respectability" demonstrates the possibilities and the limits of their racial uplift agenda.

South Carolina clubwomen thus differed from their Northern sisters in meaningful ways. This study reveals the profound influence of the region's unique history on white Southern clubwomen's work, white women's subsequent role in creating a collective memory of that history, and the overwhelming significance of race in the establishment of that memory. At the same time, it illustrates how black clubwomen's efforts for social reform to uplift their race were shaped by their contestation of white constructions of racial difference and power and their own claims to Southern and American identity.

This book breaks new ground by providing a comprehensive comparative analysis of black and white women's clubs in South Carolina. It examines the South Carolina Federation of Women's Clubs (SCFWC), an umbrella organization for white women's clubs, the South Carolina Federation of Colored Women's Clubs (SCFCWC), a parallel, yet distinct federation, and the South Carolina state division of the United Daughters of the Confederacy (UDC). My research includes the minutes, correspondence, publications, newspapers, and personal papers of individuals, local clubs, and state organizations. Although there is copious documentation for white clubwomen, there are few extant written records of black women's clubs, and I conducted oral interviews to gain additional information for the SCFCWC. This remains a comparative study, however, because these women led parallel lives—lives that were stunningly similar, but worlds apart.

Louisa Poppenheim and her counterpart in the SCFCWC, Marion Birnie Wilkinson, were extremely influential and left extensive records of their work. Thus they receive a greater share of attention. However, I have balanced their prominence with evidence from many local clubs and other state leaders.

As the first state to secede from the union and a leader in southern nationalism, South Carolina is a natural site for study. Clubwomen's emphasis on Southern identity can be found not only in Charleston, a city steeped in tradition, but also in the New South milltowns of the upcountry. Recent histories of women in the Progressive-era South have focused on states such as North Carolina and Texas, states that were comparatively progressive and less entrenched in Southern nationalism.[9] Whether the Confederate celebration pervaded women's work in other deep South states as it did South Carolina remains to be seen. Although I focus on South Carolina, my exploration of race, gender, reform, and Southern identity reveals the profound consequences of women's work on the culture of segregation and race relations in the South and the nation and helps better clarify these issues in contemporary America.

The rest of this chapter explores the beginnings of women's clubs in South Carolina and how black and white clubwomen understood what it meant to be a woman in the South. Chapter two turns to the contest over memory and identity in the South. It analyzes the literary and historical work done by both black and white women's clubs as they fought to shape what story would be told of Southern, black, and American history. Chapter three explores how the identity clubwomen created affected race relations in the South; it argues that the focus on history and memory was crucial to creating—and contesting—a culture of segregation in the South. Chapter four shows how a sense of place also heightened tensions between Southern clubwomen and the national associations for black and white women's clubs to which they belonged. The final two chapters demonstrate how the struggle over identity influenced social reform work. Chapter five shows how pride in the South not only motivated white women but also restrained them, especially in their unwillingness to criticize the region. Furthermore, opposition from legislators, the press, and the beneficiaries of their social welfare outreach intersected with their own reluctance to transgress boundaries, which inevitably limited their ability to enact change. Chapter six explores the different kinds of resistance to their reform agenda that black clubwomen encountered as they fought for respectability and citizenship.

NEW WOMEN, NEW SOUTH

The Civil War left the Southern economy in shambles; the postbellum South lacked both industry and infrastructure. A group of editors and businessmen responded by espousing calls for a "New South," in which they sought economic prosperity primarily through industrialization, embodied in new cotton mills built in the Carolinas and Georgia. The call for a new economy divided Southerners. In an effort to make sense of their defeat in the Civil War, many Southerners rejected industrialization and instead embraced the Lost Cause. However, the practical division between the old and the new, the past and the future, was not so clear cut. New South spokesmen tempered their rhetoric by paying tribute to regional traditions and repeatedly assuring listeners of their loyalty to the South. Lost Cause adherents, especially women, glorified the Old South and the Confederacy while simultaneously hoping a new economy would revitalize the region.[10] Furthermore, changes in the economy and race relations seemed to turn Southern society upside down. Some farmers joined the Populist party in protest of economic conditions, while others left the country to seek work in the new mill towns. Some blacks, excluded from working at the mills and sinking deeper into debt as sharecroppers and tenants, also looked to the Populist party. Blacks hoped for advancement through improved educational opportunities, even while politicians enacted Jim Crow laws and disfranchised African Americans.

In the midst of this political, social, and economic flux, black and white Southern women's roles also underwent dramatic change. The Civil War forced white women to assume the duties of husbands or fathers away at war, while postwar industrialization brought middle- and upper-class women increased leisure time.[11] More women had access to higher education, and white women increasingly worked for wages, as both cotton mill operatives and teachers.[12] These socioeconomic changes, in addition to women's long history of benevolent work through church associations, fostered an explosion of women's public activity. Anne Firor Scott has effectively traced women's involvement from Civil War Soldier's Aid Societies, Home Missionary Societies, and the Woman's Christian Temperance Union (WCTU) in the 1870s and 1880s, women's clubs and settlement homes in the 1890s, to various Progressive era reforms under the rubric of "municipal housekeeping," in the early twentieth century. Although a handful of women first publicly called for the vote at Seneca Falls in 1848, the number of suffragists increased greatly in the early twentieth century. In the South, strict conformity to the racial and gender social hierarchy forced women participating in these new roles to stress their femininity while they sought greater opportunity.[13]

The women's club movement began with literary clubs in the late 1860s in the Northeast. When the General Federation of Women's Clubs was founded in 1890, there were already almost 500 clubs and more than 100,000 members across the nation. This number exceeded a million women by World War I.[14] The South Carolina Federation of Women's Clubs formed in 1898, when Ludie Merriam Coleman, president of the Once a Week Club of Seneca, issued an invitation to white women's clubs throughout the state to convene. When she attempted to have the announcement printed in the *Seneca Free Press*, "The shocked editor refused to print it." Nonetheless, thirty-two delegates representing nineteen clubs gathered at Gresham's Eating House, and after a dinner of shrimp salad, soft shell crabs, broiled spring chicken, and other delicacies, wrote the founding charter.[15] The SCFWC grew rapidly. Within a year, it reported twenty-six clubs and almost one thousand members. At its thirtieth anniversary, the federation included 202 clubs and 14,739 clubwomen. Early on, clubs from the upcountry, with its growing New South cities and mill towns, dominated the leadership. This geographic division is significant. The federation's focus on Southern identity therefore came just as strongly from the New South upcountry as from the traditional city of Charleston, located in the low country.[16]

Like the first clubs in the North, all charter clubs were literary, although federation leaders encouraged members to take part in the Progressive reform movement sweeping the nation.[17] In 1898, the SCFWC formed committees on philanthropy and civics, horticulture and village improvement, press, library, and education. Throughout the years the public welfare department expanded and fought for labor legislation, institutional aid for delinquent children, the feeble-minded, and tuberculosis patients, and improved conditions in the penal system for men, women, and children. Despite the growth in social reform, many clubs retained their literary focus.[18]

Many members of the SCFWC also belonged to the United Daughters of the Confederacy, which was founded in the 1890s with the express purpose of honoring the Confederacy through education, memorialization, and historical preservation. The Charleston chapter was the third to join the national association, and the South Carolina state division was organized in 1896. As in other Southern states, the UDC boasted more members than the federation of women's clubs, with more than 8,000 in South Carolina in 1913 and more than 60,000 in the organization as a whole.[19]

African Americans participated in the women's club movement in substantial numbers. Excluded from white women's clubs, they built upon their own tradition of benevolence and formed their own local, state, and national organizations. The National Association of Colored Women (NACW) was founded in 1896, and like the GFWC the NACW grew quickly, with 50,000 members by 1914. Clubs formed to defend charges that black women were immoral, to improve their education, and to provide much needed welfare for their communities. African American clubs significantly saw their role as uplifting the race through outreach and education programs.[20] Their motto, "Lifting As We Climb," also reveals the tensions that sometimes resulted when relatively elite women reached out to their poorer brethren, in both black and white communities.

The South Carolina Federation of Colored Women's Clubs was a relative latecomer to the NACW. In 1909, Marion Birnie Wilkinson, Sara B. Henderson, Lizella A. Jenkins Moorer, all of Orangeburg, Celia Dial Saxon of Columbia, Susie Dart Butler of Charleston, and others founded the federation at Sidney Park Church, in Columbia.[21] The SCFCWC grew to 2,500 members by 1922. Forty years after its founding, first president Marion Wilkinson wrote, "I talk federation all day and dream Federation all night."[22]

In 1962, Emily Albertha Johnston Murray recalled the founding of the SCFCWC, which she attributed to the need for organized racial uplift work. "We felt the need of united and systematic effort and hop[ed] to furnish evidence of moral, mental, and material progress made by our people," said Murray, quoting from the federation constitution. The federation was primarily concerned with women, children, and the home. Its goals included black women's own self-improvement, protection for working children and women, "civic and political rights" for African Americans, and "interracial understanding." By the 1920s the SCFCWC broadened the scope of its program to include economic prosperity, professions, and business.[23]

The most influential white clubwoman in the state was Louisa Bouknight Poppenheim, born in Charleston in 1868. Poppenheim, second president of the SCFWC and an officer in the GFWC, devoted herself to women's clubs. She was a charter member of the Century Club, the Civic Club, the Intercollegiate Club, the Charleston City Federation of Clubs, and a member of the UDC, the South Carolina Audubon Society (led by her sister, Christie), the Southeast branch of the Vassar Alumnae Association, the Ladies' Memorial Association, the Woman's Exchange, the Daughters of the American Revolution, and the YWCA.[24] Louisa's older sister Mary, also a clubwoman, was president of the state division of the UDC before becoming president-general of the national organization in 1917.

The sisters exerted considerable influence on South Carolina clubwomen through a monthly journal, the *Keystone*, which they owned and edited for fourteen years.[25] Throughout the years, the *Keystone* published short stories, poetry, recipes, reports from other organizations, and book reviews, in addition to columns from each state association, the national General Federation of Woman's Clubs (GFWC), and the national UDC. The *Keystone* was an important medium of communication for Southern women. As the official organ of the state federations of five Southern states and the state divisions of the UDC for South Carolina, Virginia, and North Carolina, the *Keystone* represented 28,384 women in 1913.[26] From the beginning the journal was a Poppenheim family affair: Mary was associate editor, Louisa managed the club column, and younger sister Christie edited college news. Louisa then bought the journal in December 1900, and she and Mary edited it. The Poppenheim home was the center of production for the *Keystone*. When the sheets came back from the printer, family members and the servants aided in collating and mailing. The journal reflected their strong ideas about Southern identity and womanhood. When a Massachusetts newspaper suggested that the General Federation of Women's Clubs adopt the *Keystone* for its official organ, the Poppenheims demurred, claiming "our plan of life is entirely a sectional one. We know our South, we are part of it, and we claim to represent it."[27]

While eldest sister Mary, who was quite serious, fussed and worried over her younger sisters, Louisa was more social and out-going. Both, however, took their leadership role in women's clubs quite seriously and intimidated other club members with their intelligence and sense of purpose. An "Ode to the Century Club on Her 21st Birthday" claimed, "Then rose the grave Miss [Louisa] P. with the 'Constitution Book'; and when she knocked her gavel down How all the Century shook!"[28] Despite the differences in personality, they lived together their entire lives, sharing their dedication to women's organizations and leaving no trace of any quarrels between them.

In their economic and social status, the Poppenheims were representative of many Southern white clubwomen. Their father, Christopher Poppenheim, was the son of a South Carolina doctor and rice planter, descended from Bavarian and Irish eighteenth-century immigrants. Their maternal grandfather was a cotton planter, also with pre–Revolutionary

War ancestors. After the Civil War, Christopher left his father's plantation and opened a successful dry goods store in Charleston. As members of an old Carolina family, the Poppenheims associated with upper-class Charleston society, although they were not one of the most elite families.[29]

Like Louisa and Mary, women's clubs members and officers in South Carolina ranged from middle to upper class and typically married businessmen, professionals, and professors.[30] In Columbia, "the bride of a University professor said to another, there is no literary club here." Pauline Owings founded the New Century club, whose members, along with those in Columbia's other prestigious literary club, the Current Literature, were married to professors at University of South Carolina, doctors, and various white-collar workers, including traveling salesmen, bookkeepers, and directors of insurance and railroad companies. The Current Literature club even had the wives of two governors, Dorcas (Robert) Cooper and Leila (Richard) Manning. In Rock Hill, an upcountry town where Winthrop College was located, records show that only one member of the Over the Teacups Club married a farmer; the others married professors, attorneys, bankers, wholesale grocers, and a mill president and cotton merchant. Clubwomen were the wives of men more likely to be proponents of the new economy, that is, mill owners or managers, cotton brokers, or merchants, rather than planters. For example, the father of Margaret Smythe McKissick, a former president of the federation, owned the renowned Pelzer Cotton Mill. These close ties to the mills would prove significant when clubwomen considered the child labor problem.[31] Beyond the professional status of these women's husbands, biographical sketches of many club leaders at the time focused on their ancestry and service to the Confederacy. Although club members generally had similar social status, at least one South Carolinian saw women's clubs as an opportunity where "Mrs. Nobody has a chance to exchange ideas with Mrs. Somebody" and possibly improve her social position.[32]

Clubwomen were also relatively well educated. At least eighteen leaders in the SCFWC had attended college, and an additional sixteen had gone to a female seminary or equivalent institution.[33] Euphemia McClintock, who served on the education committee as president of the College for Women in Columbia, had graduated from the Woman's College of Baltimore and done graduate work at Harvard, the University of Chicago, and in Paris; Minnie Melton Burney, president of the federation from 1908 through 1909, had graduated from the Columbia College for Women and completed postgraduate work at Wellesley.[34] Louisa, Mary, and both of their younger sisters all had graduated from Vassar College. They later organized an Intercollegiate Club for fellow college graduates in the state to provide fellowship and to stimulate more girls to attend college.[35]

Higher education provided these leaders with confidence in their intellectual capabilities, gave them leadership experience, and encouraged friendship with like-minded women. Female professors served as role models; not only were they intelligent women, but they were also paragons of community service. Mary got her introduction to women's rights at Vassar, where despite her mother's warning "to avoid having anything to do with a party that savors of woman's rights," as a student she prophesied to her friends that she "would be a second Susan B Anthony coming to W[ashington] to hand a petition for woman's rights to the president."[36] Back at home in Charleston, Mary found herself more comfortable leading the UDC and women's clubs than the suffrage movement, but her schooling did help prepare her for activism. Such a prestigious education also elevated the Poppenheims' stature. Other clubwomen were awed by Mary and Louisa's intelligence and presence. When a Perehelion Club member met Mary for the first time, she wrote, "I positively drank her in. She is a woman who could never die by degrees. She is so completely vitalized in mind, feeling, nerve and sinew, that a lack of vigor in one direction would instantly be supplied from the others with electrical decision. Her whole heart is in her work."[37]

The high education level for club leaders was especially significant because the benefits of college education for women were the source of much debate at the time, particularly in the South where educators had to stress that college did not unsex women. According to an article by Nina Honer of Converse College, a women's college in Columbia, there were "defects" in Southern girls' schools. Schools, she wrote, "will make of the girl a self-reliant, strong, self-supporting, yet womanly women."[38] Clubwoman and former *Keystone* editor Ida Lining remonstrated Southern women for not taking advantage of college scholarships. She argued that women needed to spend more time and money cultivating their minds than cultivating dress or amusements.[39] She realized that for women to be taken seriously, they had to take themselves seriously. Their message was clear: women were intelligent, women were capable of higher learning, but yes, women were still womanly.

A driving force in the federation, Louisa was intelligent and strong-minded. She was raised by her mother to be loyal to the South and to traditional Southern manners; she pulled her hair back in a bun and wore her gloves and hat until her death in 1957. Strong-willed as well as bound to tradition in manners, she continued to drive the wrong way on her street, even after it became a one-way street; she claimed that she had always driven in that direction.[40] Despite her adherence to custom, however, she worked hard to change the opportunities available to women. Active in women's clubs for almost sixty years, Poppenheim left her stamp on women's organizations in the state and the region. Her influence cannot be underestimated. A colleague in the DAR thanked her for her service, "Without your consent to serve as the leader and *mouthpiece* we could not have accomplished our aim. . . . We had to have *you* as the one person in whom all had confidence. And moreover your long experience in club work assured that your suggestions would be accepted and that no one would try to thwart any details you backed."[41]

Although there is no evidence to suggest that she and Louisa Poppenheim ever met, Marion Birnie Wilkinson was the most influential African American clubwoman in the state. A large, light-skinned woman, she was born in Charleston around 1873 but lived her married life in Orangeburg. Her father, Richard Birnie, and his brother Charles were cotton shipping agents, and Richard was wealthy enough to own two homes, both worth $2,100, in 1880.[42] Both the Birnies and the Frosts, her mother's family, were descendants of antebellum free black families, and her father was a member of Charleston's elite Amateur Literary and Fraternal organization.

Marion married South Carolina State College President Robert Shaw Wilkinson in 1897. He was born February 18, 1865, to Charles and Lavinia A. Robinson Wilkinson and named for Robert Gould Shaw, commander of the Fifty-fourth Massachusetts regiment. His father, formerly in the fruit and meat business, worked as a janitor in A. Toomer Porter's church and academy. Orphaned at the age of sixteen, Robert worked various odd jobs to support himself, including stints as a janitor, railroad and hotel waiter, porter, newspaper clerk, and a postal clerk. He eventually earned a doctoral degree and became president of South Carolina State College, the only state college for African Americans. A bank director, he also served as president of the South Carolina Negro Business League and promoted "education, self help, saving, [and] land ownership" as a means for blacks to better themselves.[43]

Marion Wilkinson was president of the Sunlight Club and the SCFCWC and an officer in the National Association of Colored Women. In addition to chairing South Carolina State College's YWCA Advisory Board and leading the state Commission on Interracial Cooperation, she was also an officer in the International Council of Women of the Darker Races and a member of both the County Executive Committee of the Red Cross and the Board of Trustees of Voorhees College, Denmark, South Carolina.[44] As the wife of a college president, along with her many other leadership roles, "Mother Birnie" was loved and respected by students and African Americans across the state. Benjamin Mays, president of Morehouse College, described her as "South Carolina's outstanding Negro woman; indeed, in programs designed to help the poor and improve race relations, in my opinion, she was *the* leading woman in South Carolina."[45]

Marrying an educated professional placed Marion Wilkinson in an elite group of blacks in South Carolina. The vast majority of employed African American men and women males worked the land or were classed as laborers, servants, domestics, or laundresses.[46] With few exceptions, the original twenty-eight members of the Sunlight Club, founded by Wilkinson in 1909, were the wives of professionals, businessmen, and educators. Four were married to South Carolina State College professors, two to owners of a sawmill (a large and prestigious black business in Orangeburg), two to attorneys, and one each to a doctor and a minister.[47]

In comparison to Orangeburg, Charleston had a long tradition of an elite black society, which was made up primarily of antebellum free black families and known for its emphasis on skin color because of the city's large number of mulattos.[48] The Phyllis Wheatley Club (which used a variant spelling from that of its namesake, eighteenth-century African American poet Phillis Wheatley) was the leading women's club in Charleston. Jeannette Keebler Cox, whose husband Benjamin Cox became the first black president of Avery Normal Institute, founded it primarily with other teachers from Avery. Born in Tennessee to a seamstress and a barber, who studied law and eventually became a Tennessee legislator, Jeannette Cox came to Avery from Albany, Georgia, where she had been a member of a women's club. Although Charleston had a City Federation of Women's Clubs, of which Cox was a member, there was no club with the stated purpose of "culture and self improvement." Cox recalled that her original idea was to invite members from different groups within the African American population in Charleston to combat the "lack of unity" plaguing the community. Despite her noble intentions, she alludes, without explanation, to "several instances in which we had a few explosions and in the process, some of the members escaped as uncontrollable gases" until "finally we were resolved into a club whose members were representative of one group."[49] That group, despite Cox's original more inclusive intentions, was a who's who of Charleston's so-called black aristocracy, including at least twelve members who taught at Avery. Other members were married to professionals and ministers, and many had free black ancestry and belonged to the most prestigious churches and associations.[50]

Jeannette Cox worked to push the club beyond color differences and other sources of tension. Dark-skinned members Sarah Oglesby and Geneva Singleton believed that Cox did her best to chip away at color prejudices. Oglesby admired Cox for being "very open-minded. . . . She didn't see some of the things we accepted . . . she didn't see the caste system."[51] Yet clubs remained exclusive. Mamie Garvin Fields, whose husband was a member of the Bricklayers Union, was a federation leader and public school teacher from Charleston. Like her mother, she was educated at Claflin University, and her father was a carpenter. She joined the City Federation in 1916, although she was not a member of an individual club. According to Fields, "Joining the City didn't mean you could join a club. Many people in the community were not invited to join the individual clubs; regardless to your ability, your education, your readiness to serve, you were excluded. The City Federation couldn't progress until women started new clubs." Because of these exclusionary practices, ten years later, Fields and two friends founded the Modern Priscilla Club with more open membership policies.[52]

Education was equally crucial to black women's ability to expand their public role. Many black clubwomen were educators themselves, including at least thirty-four federation members from a sample of 128 clubwomen from leading cities in the state. Some of these teachers graduated from a high school or a normal school, while others attended college. Florence Alberta Clyde, a member of the Phyllis Wheatley Club in Charleston, was typical. She graduated from Avery and then attended summer school on and off throughout the 1920s and 1930s at Columbia University, University of Pennsylvania, and South Carolina State College to earn her teaching certificate. Celia Dial Saxon, wife of a professor, began teaching after her graduation from South Carolina State Normal School. She later took chautauqua courses to further her education.[53]

Marion graduated with high honors in 1888 from Avery Institute, where her father was a trustee.[54] Because of the dearth of black teachers in South Carolina, she then taught at her alma mater, as did many other Avery graduates. Like Louisa and Mary Poppenheim, Wilkinson's educational experience helped her to develop her ideals of community service. Teachers and administrators at Avery promoted a sense of service, related to noblesse oblige, in their students.[55] Asa Gordon, a professor at South

Carolina State College, claimed that Wilkinson spent most of her teaching salary on charity. Septima Clark recollected that when she graduated from Avery and began teaching her father was proud of her because he viewed teaching as a "life of service."[56] African American teachers were dedicated not only to promoting academics but also to bettering the community.

As the wife of a college president, Marion Wilkinson was well positioned to encourage education for black women. She was part of a network of many clubwomen in her state and across the nation who were either wives of college presidents or educators themselves. Their influence in clubwork and community service cannot be overemphasized. In the South, Margaret Murray Washington, wife of Booker T. Washington and member of the Tuskegee Women's Club, and Lugenia Burns Hope, wife of Atlanta University president John Hope and member of the Neighborhood Union, are two of the most prominent examples.[57] In South Carolina, five founding members of the Sunlight Club were married to faculty at State College, while in Charleston, the Phyllis Wheatley Club was closely tied to Avery.[58] As the Wilkinsons learned at Avery, they had a responsibility to share their education with others, through not only teaching but also service. Teachers and faculty wives disproportionately led women's clubs because the community viewed them as models of black achievement. Their level of education ensured them respect, even if not wealth.[59]

Louisa Poppenheim and Marion Wilkinson were extremely influential in the white and black federations, respectively. Each woman, active from the founding of the federations until her death, served as president and in many other capacities. Moreover, their activity in the national associations brought South Carolina into the larger movement and introduced South Carolina women to the possibilities of women's clubs. As leaders who dedicated their lives to clubwork, in many ways they were typical of the average clubwoman, who was also a well-respected community member. Whether married or single, they sought support from husbands, fathers, and well-placed men in the community. As members of local clubs and city, state, and national federations, elite South Carolina clubwomen came together to improve themselves and the communities in which they lived. They socialized, studied, reformed, lobbied—all the while cognizant of their regional identity. That identity shaped how others saw them and how they saw themselves, whether as "Southern Ladies" or "New Women."

NEW WOMEN, SOUTHERN LADIES

At the turn of the century, changes in women's roles threatened the long established social order in the South, based on a hierarchy of race and sex. To negotiate their way through this tumultuous terrain, clubwomen forged new definitions of Southern womanhood that encompassed both traditional ideals of the "Southern Lady" and more progressive norms of the "New Woman." South Carolina clubwomen balanced traditional gender ideals with new possibilities for activism.

White clubwomen who promoted expanded women's roles had to step gingerly in the explosive atmosphere of turn-of-the-century South Carolina. White supremacy in the new South was in many ways legitimated by a "web" of race and sex. "Chivalry" ensured that elite white women would be recognized for their purity; at the same time they were assumed to need protection of white men. This code justified the separation of the races, and in its most extreme form, the code resulted in white men lynching black men under the guise of protecting the sexual purity of white womanhood. In other words, chivalry "masked" racism as the source of such violence. Thus, the stability of the social system based on an intertwined racial and gendered hierarchy required white women to conform to traditional gender roles as "protected" women.[60] Many clubwomen throughout the South therefore moved cautiously by defending the Confederacy, chivalry, and segregation, while quietly expanding their opportunities in the public sphere and promoting higher education for women.[61]

White clubwomen saw themselves as "womanly" in the traditional sense; that is, they were delicate, modest, and gentle. They exhibited some deference to men; in fact, some early members of the Thursday Club of Greenville had to quit clubwork because their husbands did not want them to be "strong-minded women."[62] Yet, they also admired the strength of their mothers and other "Women of the Confederacy," who (they believed) bravely survived the war and remained loyal to the Southern cause. Confederate mothers' strength did not threaten men's dominance because it did not call for equality, but rather combined "feminism and femininity."[63]

Moreover, by explicitly linking themselves to the ideals of the Old South and the Confederacy, white South Carolina clubwomen alleviated some of society's fear of women's public activity.[64] The United Daughters of the Confederacy were crucial to reinforcing both male and female gender norms. According to historian Lee Ann Whites, through the UDC and similar groups, "Confederate men, rather than having fought the war in defense of their right to dominate those household dependents—the slaves—who were now lost to them, were reenvisioned as having loyally stood for the defense of those household dependents—their women and children—who in the postwar era continued to stand loyally by them."[65] Thus, women supported chivalry to help men find meaning in their defeat in the Civil War. The resulting emphasis on conformity to gender roles in the South translated into an understanding of Southern identity itself; to describe the section one had only to describe the Southern lady and gentleman. Moreover, because that identity was based in Southern tradition, women looked to the past to reformulate their gender identity.[66]

White women who accepted tenets of Southern chivalry were better able to avoid male disapproval of their work. Like their sisters in the North, they justified their interests in public affairs as mothers. Although a few may have adopted maternalist language as a conscious strategy to disarm their opponents, most clubwomen simply used the language that came naturally to them. They did not have to act the part of the lady—they were ladies. Although seeking to broaden their opportunities, they did not challenge the fundamental gender hierarchy, nor did they question the Southern economic system. Even so, when clubwomen attempted more far-reaching social reforms, especially those that required state funding or threatened the New South industrialization program, they encountered resistance from male politicians. This strategy succeeded in legitimizing women's clubs in general, but clubwomen were still unable to gain widespread support for their more radical social reform agenda.

Because white clubwomen supported greater opportunities for women and enlarged public roles through women's clubs, they were forced to defend themselves against charges of "manliness." Manliness encompassed neglect of housework, political aspiration, and other violations of gender roles. A report from the Perihelion Club delegates to the SCFWC convention provides one of the most typical statements of the charges leveled against women's clubs: "Some have erroneously construed our banding together as an incipient suffrage movement," the delegates wrote, "others have been fearful that we may either inadvertently or intentionally forget that modest estimate of our selves which has made us agreeable home-companions, and leaving the quiet dignity of our accustomed seclusion, launch out among the Amazons." That "modest estimate" of self was evident when a member of the Perhelion Club was elected second vice president in 1900. She commented that she was nowhere near the presidency. When a friend asked, "Suppose the President should take the measles, and the 1st Vice-President the mumps, what would you do?" She replied, "Then I should take the whooping-cough."[67]

Women also denied they were neglecting their own home as they helped reform others' homes. Former president Grover Cleveland wrote one of the most notable attacks, published in the *Ladies Home Journal*. According to Cleveland, the "club habit" fostered selfishness and neglect for the home. He suggested that women content themselves with influencing society indirectly through their roles as wives and mothers rather than directly through civic work. In response, Sarah Visanska told the Charleston City Federation that true women would not neglect their own homes even as they tried to improve others' homes.[68]

Women also were accused of becoming unsexed or manly by expanding their boundaries. The Poppenheims argued just the opposite. They claimed that womanliness was "the keynote of the club movement" and that clubwomen were not "fussy, mannish, or unfeminine creature[s]." They further explained that "clubwomen are proving each day that a woman can be seriously in earnest and yet be attractive; can be intellectual and cultured and yet be natural; in fact, can be a promoter of enterprise, causes, and philanthropies and yet be charmingly feminine."[69] This last statement reveals the bind in which they found themselves: they needed to redefine "womanly" to combine seriousness of purpose, intellect, and activism with attractiveness, charm, and femininity. Only by retaining the latter could they get away with assuming the former.

South Carolina women used various tactics to defend their new roles. Clubwomen understood that by retaining that femininity, they drew less attention and less attack. Federation president from 1905 through 1906, Mrs. Wilbur K. Sligh, told clubwomen that as long as their work remained unobtrusive, their friends would approve and their enemies would have little to argue about.[70] Clubwomen also used their class status to undergird their femininity. The Perihelion Club's report on the federation's third meeting noted that, "These conventions have no suggestion of unwomanliness . . . for the unrefined do not seek such places." Thus, refined women could get away with certain actions simply because of who they were. "White-gloved" women disarmed men who objected to women's activism simply by their appearance and their tone.[71]

The most damaging accusation against which white clubwomen had to defend themselves was that they sought political power and the right to vote. Woman suffrage received less support in the South than in the North. The conformity to gender roles demanded in a society highly segregated by race prevented many from endorsing such a radical demand, and South Carolina did not ratify the nineteenth amendment until 1969.[72]

When the SCFWC was first founded, white clubwomen were careful to distinguish themselves from suffragists. In a telling report to the *Keystone* in 1899, the Charleston city union claimed that they did not intend "to invade man's domain, revolutionize politics, and get into the police force"; instead, clubwomen sought to do social, literary, and philanthropic work. The strength of their community service would "overcome the long established prejudice against women's clubs, so firmly rooted in the Southern states." Despite their disavowals, clubwomen did "revolutionize politics" by demanding an interventionist government responsive to social reform. Within twenty years they had even "gotten into the police force" by forcing the city to hire a police matron. Their denials as to political aspiration were genuine; many clubwomen moved slowly to embrace new women's roles, reform, or suffrage.[73] Sarah Visanska argued it would be beneficial for the suffragists within clubs to moderate their actions so that they would not cause "outsiders" to associate all clubs with suffrage. "The ill-advised utterances of the politically inclined," she claimed, "have caused the outsider to believe that every woman's club tingles with the desire to grasp the ballot box, and with it, every political office within the gift of the nation." Visanska warned that suffragists were marking all women's clubs as political.[74]

When the movement gained momentum in South Carolina after 1910, references to suffrage in the *Keystone* and individual club minutes increased dramatically. Although many were founded with explicit agreements not to debate suffrage, clubs later began to broach the subject.[75] For example, the Thursday Club of Greenville declared three subjects taboo: suffrage, religious difference, and "any topic involving North versus South." But the Thursday Club of Columbia devoted its 1913–14 program to "The Woman Question"; the women discussed not only woman suffrage but also women's employment, obviously recognizing the link between increased women's public roles as wage earners and the potential for a public role as citizen and voter.[76] The Wednesday Club of Laurens featured woman suffrage as a current events topic, with seven different suffrage topics, and continued to debate suffrage the following month. When the nineteenth amendment eventually passed, the club voted to use the ballot to work toward better water, lights, streets, and school buildings.[77]

Several SCFWC officers were strong supporters of suffrage, including president Hannah Hemphill Coleman, Emily Evans, and sisters Mabel and Carrie Pollitzer. A Methodist who did not believe in dancing or card playing, Coleman nonetheless was president of the South Carolina Equal Suffrage League and presided over her local Civic Club and Music Club in Abbeville. Louisa Poppenheim claimed Coleman brought "youth energy, enthusiasm, and a splendid physique" to the club movement. The Pollitzers' youngest sibling, Anita, was the most active suffragist in the family and a long-time national officer for the National Woman's Party. Although Evans was born in New York, Coleman and the Pollitzers were native Southerners. Anita was even known for her Southern charm, which disarmed anti-suffragists who stereotyped the suffrage proponents as severe women.[78] The SCFWC as a whole was decidedly more conservative and did not endorse woman suffrage until 1917, when it had already established itself as a legitimate organization in the public's eye.

Never accorded the same privileges as white women, African American women fought a different battle as they, too, sought to remake their image in the early twentieth century. Viewed by many whites as immoral, they urged black women to be moral exemplars and focused on women's role in the home. At the same time, they recognized the need for many black women to work outside the homes for wages. They believed that women needed to uplift the race because men had been disenfranchised and were therefore politically powerless. More important, as long as whites viewed black women as lacking virtue, the race would never achieve equality with whites. African American women also balanced domesticity with a public role, but for different reasons.

Like white women, black women idealized a slightly adapted version of the Victorian true woman. They too strove to be good, true, pious, and cheerful. When African American clubwomen stressed the importance of home life and women's responsibility for establishing its moral atmosphere, they hoped to gain respect for the race. In a series she wrote for the *Palmetto Leader* South Carolina clubwoman Cora Gethers quoted from prominent clubwomen in the nation. "Industry, honesty and morality are the cardinal attributes to become acquainted with in forming an irreproachable character," she wrote, "and each and all of them must be dwelt upon in the home." Not only was the home to be the provider of a "healthy, moral atmosphere," but it was also "the citadel for the children's preservation and development. . . . Queen of the home is woman."[79] The South Carolina Federation exemplified this focus on the home as the bulwark of morality. Clubwomen founded the federation with the intent to simultaneously build stronger homes and uplift women and children.

Their emphasis on woman as queen of the home was significant, given that most black women historically had been forced to work outside their homes, whether in fields or in white homes. They were also vulnerable to sexual assault because whites presumed that they lacked virtue. Thus black women promoted morality and home life even for women who worked outside the home for wages. Of course, the women who dominated clubs were more easily able to achieve such an ideal than their lower class sisters. Despite these significant consequences, such an ideal placed black women on the same moral plane as white women. Long denied the privilege of domesticity, black women hoped it would empower them.

Studies of black women activists in women's clubs and other associations show that many black women reformers had to combine wage work, activism, marriage, and motherhood.[80] Although many leading black clubwomen in South Carolina worked for wages, most of them were teachers, and a significantly high proportion did not work outside of the home. Wilkinson taught prior to her marriage, worked at State College, and performed the duties of the president's wife. However, of the original twenty-eight women Wilkinson recruited as members of the Sunlight Club, only six can be identified as working for wages outside the home: three teachers, Etta Butler Rowe (who was married to a doctor), Lizelia A. J. Moorer (married to an attorney), and Ethel Judson; Bessie Judson, a hairdresser; and Mamie Lawton and Ella McDuffie, both domestics.[81] This number is fairly low; in 1930, 44 percent of married black women were gainfully employed, while only 15 percent of white women worked for wages.[82] Of those who did work for wages, a significantly high number were teachers. In Charleston, of the original nineteen members of the Phyllis Wheatley Literary Club, seven taught at Avery Institute.

Despite the low number of wage-earning members, the SCFCWC recognized that some clubwomen did work, as did many of the women they sought to aid. The federation included protection of working women and children in its statement of purpose. They supported day nurseries, ran employment agencies (for men and women), and educated themselves on the professions, farms, businesses, and personal finance.[83]

Historian Deborah Gray White argues persuasively that when they called for black women to lead the effort to uplift the race, tension erupted with black men whose ability to lead was therefore in question, especially at the same time men's political power was broken by white supremacy.[84] Despite this conflict black clubwomen received positive press within their own communities. In South Carolina, when the *Palmetto Leader* claimed that the Sunlight Club had "practically taken over the charity work of

Orangeburg for colored people," it was with appreciation, not apprehension.[85] The newspaper carried only positive articles dealing with clubs. The needs of the race, coupled with women's history of wage labor and a strategy of uplift that emphasized the home, limited the need for them to defend themselves to other blacks against overstepping the boundaries of acceptable womanly behavior. No evidence survives of tension over clubwork between clubwomen and male relatives in South Carolina. Their defense of their own morality, necessary to refute charges from whites of immorality, also reminded black men of their womanliness.

Given their relative freedom from gender tensions, it should not be surprising that African American women starred in the early history of the suffrage movement in South Carolina. In the 1860s and 1870s, Charlotte (Lottie), Frances, and Louisa Rollins led the South Carolina Woman's Rights Association. Lottie attended a national woman suffrage association meeting and addressed the Republican-dominated South Carolina House of Representatives.[86] The Rollins sisters' outstanding work may have influenced Marion Wilkinson, who grew up in Charleston. Wilkinson supported woman suffrage and argued for the inclusion of suffrage in a statement made by black women when the interracial movement began in 1920. Because Wilkinson was so influential among clubwomen in her state, her support for suffrage would have spoken loudly to her sisters in the federation. Other clubwomen, such as Collin Robinson Embley, a charter member of the Sunlight Club, became suffragists because of Northern white women who taught at Claflin.[87] After the nineteenth amendment passed, black women in South Carolina lined up to register to vote, only to be turned down by the same white registrars who effectively disfranchised their husbands and fathers.[88]

In a state with a majority black population, neither black nor white clubwomen could escape the limitations that the specter of black women voting placed upon any desire they might have had to work for enfranchisement. They therefore had to focus instead on expanding women's roles through women's clubs. Clubs provided a window of opportunity for Southern women to become more active outside their homes. Most clubs, especially in the early years, began as literary clubs. Their study of Southern history or African American literature enabled them to influence their communities as they shaped the telling of history and the making of identity.

Chapter 2

"As Intensely Southern As I Am"

Black and White Clubwomen, the United Daughters of the Confederacy, and Southern Identity

When General Sherman marched through the South during closing months of the Civil War, Southern families scrambled to get out of the way of his path of destruction. Among them was Louisa Poppenheim's family; her mother, Mary Elinor Poppenheim, preserved a record of her traumatic experiences in her journal. When word of Sherman's approach reached Charleston, the Poppenheim family sought safety at Mary Elinor's father's plantation, north of Columbia on the Saluda River. En route, they learned that Columbia was already burning, so they attempted to go around the city. Sherman's soldiers approached them while they were seeking refuge in Liberty Hill. In her journal, Mary Elinor described her fears:

> February 22, 1865—I go to the commanding officer and ask for assistance; he promises protection. Christie [her husband] and myself go upstairs; my trunks broken open, and everything scattered in confusion over the floor. Oh! what a scene, impossible to describe! Money, jewelry, and clothing of every description taken by these demons! . . .
> February 26—Yankees still plundering, and the negroes following them. . . . A sleepless night of suspense, expecting every hour to have the torch set to the house we were in.
> February 27—The wicked Yankees! How they torment the people! The brutal wretches! How they insult helpless women!

This episode was even more disturbing because Union soldiers doubted her husband's claims that he was not in the Confederate army and repeatedly threatened to take him prisoner.[1] Mary Elinor Poppenheim's dramatic narrative of how the family suffered personally during the war was similar to stories told by thousands of families throughout the postbellum South. Her continued devotion to the Confederacy surely influenced Mary and Louisa Poppenheim as they began their work as clubwomen and as members of the United Daughters of the Confederacy (UDC). Like the Poppenheims, many white South Carolina women with long lines of Southern ancestry belonged to both women's clubs and the UDC. The Civil War turned upside down the lives of white women, especially the wives of plantation owners. Fifty years later they and their daughters were still reeling. Women's club records reveal that the Confederacy continued to evoke an emotionally intense reaction from Southern women.

Southern identity affected black and white elite South Carolina clubwomen differently as each sought to tell the story of Southern and American history. Historians have recognized that clubwomen's interest in history and literature, the self-study component of their clubs, was important because it provided an opportunity for education and growth for women. But the content of what they studied is also critical.

White clubwomen and the UDC attempted to promote the values and order they found in the past. The advent of modernization brought about a national movement, in which Southern women took part, to understand the present through use of the past.[2] They created Southern identity by inventing and preserving traditions and collective memory. Clubwomen used their collective memory of the past, especially of the antebellum South and the Confederacy, to fashion a history, which in turn shaped their identity as Southerners. Historians have recently begun to unravel this connection between social or historical memory and identity formation. Fitzhugh Brundage reminds us, "Groups invariably fashion their own image of the world and their place in it by establishing an accepted version of the past, a sort of genealogy of identity." Furthermore, individuals situate themselves and their sense of self within a group identity; often this allows for justifications of inherited hierarchies.[3] Through telling stories about the Civil War, clubwomen assuaged their own families' suffering as well as the Confederate defeat; through stories of an idyllic antebellum South, they justified their own past as plantation owners and defended the plantation system as a whole. More important, before they could draw on the values of the past, they had to invent a suitable version of that past. Their preservation of the "true history" of the war—that is, the South's interpretation of the war—served to "invent tradition" through reinterpreting the Confederate past. The emphasis on "true history" allowed women to transform the past from grim defeat to near-victory.[4] The women celebrated the values of bravery and loyalty that the Confederate soldiers symbolized and heralded the racial order of the antebellum South.

The invention of tradition is meaningful because it provides a sense of continuity and stability in a changing world.[5] At the turn of the century Southerners still faced lingering postwar disorder: damage to property and land, loss of slave labor, and trials of Reconstruction politics. Moreover, the New South faced premodern disorder: business interests' promotion of industrialism, the Populist challenge, and Progressive era reforms. Further political and social change loomed.[6] In the 1890s, the Lost Cause flourished at the same time that Jim Crow laws were enacted in all the Southern states. The codification of segregation occurred, not from a newfound belief in white supremacy, but rather from a new need to enact or enforce such supremacy in response to perceived threats from Populism, industrialization, and economic strife.[7] In addition, the evident progress of African Americans caused fear among those who denied the possibility of such progress. Whites described blacks as uppity or insolent and decried the fact that they no longer knew their place.[8] Furthermore, challenges to long-established gender roles frightened Southerners, who justified segregation on the need to protect white women from black men.[9] Men in changed economic circumstances who were unable to support families and women in changed social circumstances who entered the public world through clubs and other associations, including suffrage leagues, threatened traditional assumptions of the male as "protector" and the female as "protected." The Lost Cause, defending slavery and its undergirding racial hierarchy, bolstered segregation.

Clubwomen's attention to history and identity is compelling because clubwomen did more than study within the confines of the club. Through education outreach and libraries, they also attempted to transmit celebrated ideals of Southern, American, and racial identity to children and the general public. Their cultural work—the program of building identity through the study of Southern history and literature—as well as their social work shaped the New South. The racial underpinnings of the history they read and promulgated ultimately made white clubwomen part of the effort to create a culture of segregation just as black clubwomen simultaneously fought to combat that very culture.

Furthermore, women created new public roles as citizens for themselves through their Lost Cause memorial work. Even before they were able to vote, women were raising funds, lobbying the legislature, giving speeches, and writing articles. They literally changed the landscape of Southern towns with Confederate monuments, created legal holidays celebrating Confederate heroes, and influenced school curriculums.[10] Historian Fitzhugh Brundage argues that men were less interested in historical work; either they were too close to defeat to memorialize it, or they did not realize its potential for power. Therefore, the men, unthreatened by women's memorial work, generally allowed women this opportunity to gain a public presence and political power. Like the women in Brundage's study, South Carolina women used the power they drew from their role as gatekeepers to the past to support reactionary causes such as white supremacy as well as liberal social reform.[11]

Yet, it must be understood that women did not embrace the Lost Cause and its incumbent promotion of Southern memory, history, and identity because they saw an opportunity to gain a more powerful role in society. Rather, their support evidenced their deep belief in the Lost Cause. Their own identity was intertwined with Southern history, the meanings of their own memories of the antebellum South and the War tied to a collective memory of the past. Historian Karen Cox quotes UDC president-general Rassie White in a speech given to the 1913 UDC convention: "Long ago I discovered it was not a hobby with any of us, but is and has been from the very beginning, a serious work."[12] Such work came naturally to these daughters of Confederate veterans.

Women were drawn to memorial and historical work in part because they directed much of their work to children; they were concerned with the transmission of identity to the next generation. As women and as mothers, this teaching was a natural fit. "A Southern Woman," writing for the *Keystone*, argued that if Southern values were to be preserved, "it is from the daughters of the South that the inspiration must come. They make the home and the social circle." Women directly sought to reach children through schools, libraries, monuments, and essay contests, and the UDC even organized chapters of the Children of the Confederacy.[13]

White women understood well that monuments, rituals, and texts legitimized collective memories and that the history encompassed in these was a powerful tool for ordering the present.[14] While they looked to the past to build a New South, that exhaustive construction effort demonstrates clearly that the past could not simply be remembered; rather, a collective memory had to be reinvented, reshaped, reconstructed. The Southern nation clubwomen and the Daughters imagined was simple: whites dominated a subordinate, though nominally free, black population.[15] The women participated in, and enjoyed the advantages of, the social order created through black disenfranchisement and Jim Crow laws enacted as a solution to the "Negro problem."

The SCFWC and the UDC both organized after the process of disenfranchisement and legalization of segregation had already begun in South Carolina. A state constitutional convention in 1895 disenfranchised most African American voters, and segregation laws quickly followed. However, new laws were continuously being passed throughout the first decades of the twentieth century, and clubwomen's work overlaps the full implementation of such laws. Although, as women, the SCFWC and UDC did not make Jim Crow laws, they fostered the acceptance of segregation as timeless, natural, and just.[16] White women succeeded at making a culture of segregation because they operated at the local level, through everyday events, and ordinary people. The Lost Cause pervaded Southern culture and, like minstrelsy, as argued by historian Thomas Holt, "established a tradition, a system of signs, symbols, and layered racial codes that penetrated deep into American culture."[17] White South Carolina clubwomen can therefore be considered responsible for the segregated South in the same way that historians have begun to discover the role of women in the Ku Klux Klan and in Nazi Germany as "legitimators" and as "cultural organizers" of these movements. Clubwomen and other proponents of the Confederate Celebration, while not engaging in either violence or vitriolic language, did help legitimize the Lost Cause around Southern honor and gender ideals; they upheld segregation through their telling of history, especially to children in schools.[18]

Despite their best efforts, white clubwomen and the UDC did not monopolize Southern history. African American clubwomen negotiated a different black Southern and American identity. African American women were forced to respond to the efforts of white women to define the South around slavery, the Confederacy, and white supremacy. Repudiating the Lost Cause, black women promoted an alternative history, culture, and identity for themselves. It is, however, a mistake to view this identity as created only in response to the Lost Cause; black identity was also grounded in African Americans' own sense of history and pride. Tellingly, blacks often stressed their American citizenship and contribution to the nation, rather than "answering" the Lost Cause with an alternative version of Southern history. Furthermore, it is important to recognize that, although they lived in the horrors of the Jim Crow South, the elite women of the SCFWC were themselves educated and comparatively well-off; in fact, they saw themselves as race leaders rather than victims of segregation. This sense of pride and accomplishment shines through their telling of African American history.[19]

African Americans understood the threat that the UDC and other proponents of the Lost Cause posed. Justifying and honoring the memory of the Confederacy promoted a false memory of the success of slavery in regulating race relations and a refusal to reorder the racial hierarchy, despite the thirteenth, fourteenth, and fifteenth amendments. This view enabled both the North and the South to ignore crucial questions concerning black emancipation.[20] First the Ku Klux Klan and then mob lynchings proved that whites were more than willing to use violence to enforce white supremacy, despite legislated emancipation. African Americans linked their continuing impoverishment and disenfranchisement to white Southerners' recalcitrance symbolized by the Lost Cause. Black clubwomen across the South and particularly in South Carolina therefore understood that they had to define African American identity for themselves through their study of history, literature, and culture. Like white women's clubs, black women's clubs also prioritized social welfare efforts, such as building juvenile reformatories, improving schools, and establishing day care centers and kindergartens. But their first purpose, as listed in the federation constitution, was the education of black women. Clubs across the state read and studied history and literature. Some clubs, such as the Book Lover's Club of Charleston, focused primarily on literary study.

Through literary clubs, black clubwomen armed themselves with the knowledge of black talent and a proud African heritage. They celebrated race men, such as Frederick Douglass, Booker T. Washington, and W.E.B. Du Bois, and race women from Phillis Wheatley to Marian Anderson. In their historical studies, they stressed black achievement in the abolitionist movement and service as Union soldiers in the Civil War. In so doing, they placed more emphasis on an American than on a peculiarly Southern identity. Furthermore, they understood the importance of having black teachers and black literature in the classrooms, so that their children could grow up proud and strong, rather than weak and inferior.

Documents and oral histories from the South Carolina Federation of

Colored Women's Clubs (SCFCWC) as well as other local sources reveal that African Americans rejected the Lost Cause and that black clubwomen read and told a different history from their white counterparts. After studying history and literature themselves, they took their message to the community and promoted their own "true histories" to others, especially children, through schools and libraries. Black and white clubwomen therefore utilized the same basic methods—the study of history and literature within clubs, and the promotion of such history and literature in schools and libraries—to tell completely different stories. African American clubwomen did not have the resources, or even perhaps the interest, to build the types of public monuments that white women built to the Confederacy, but even white clubwomen left that work to their colleagues in the UDC.[21] Although their efforts would not be enough to break down the walls of segregation and discrimination, black clubwomen fought Jim Crow with words as well as action.

White women's clubs in early twentieth-century South Carolina were literally made up of women and daughters of the Confederacy; that is, many club members had either lived through the War or been born shortly thereafter. Many also belonged to the United Daughters of the Confederacy. In South Carolina, the links between women's clubs and the UDC are most evident in the lives of Mary and Louisa Poppenheim, sisters from Charleston, and editors of the *Keystone*, the official organ for several state federations of women's clubs and divisions of the UDC. Mary Poppenheim was the state president and eventually national president-general of the UDC, while Louisa was SCFWC president and an officer in the national General Federation. Yet each was also active in the other organization by holding committee chairmanships and attending national conventions.[22] A survey of leaders and local membership shows that elsewhere in the state, many prominent women held offices in both associations, and membership rolls overlapped. These included, for example, Martha Orr Patterson, president of the SCFWC and second vice president of the SCUDC; Eloise Wright, treasurer of the SCFWC and third vice president of the SCUDC; and Daisy White, president of the Johnston UDC chapter and New Century Club. Known as "Johnston's Club Organizer" and dedicated to temperance and church work in addition to her club and the UDC, White was responsible for making Jefferson Davis's birthday a legal holiday in South Carolina.[23] Of thirty significant leaders in the SCFWC whose membership status in the UDC is known, twenty-five were members of both associations, a percentage probably somewhat higher than a more complete sample would yield.

On the local level, there was also significant overlap. In Rock Hill, of thirty-one local UDC officers, sixteen are identifiable as club members. One of those, Janie Smith, was the official poet of the Ann White chapter of the UDC in Rock Hill, and her poem to South Carolina is in the files of her club, the Perihelion Club. Furthermore, because most leaders were born in the state or the region, it was likely that they would qualify for membership in the UDC.[24] Although this connection may have been more meaningful in South Carolina, a state in the forefront of Southern nationalism as the first to secede, other cities and states in the South were also home to many other women active in both organizations.[25]

The Poppenheims recognized and facilitated a close relationship between the two organizations by publishing editorials, articles, and news in the *Keystone* aimed at both groups. Although no subscription lists are available, both organizations supported the journal. In only one known instance did the UDC in Virginia publicly complain that "there was very little of interest to the Daughters" in the *Keystone*. A Mrs. Randolph responded by arguing that the UDC should be obliged to contribute more information for publication; furthermore, she contended that information on clubwork was beneficial to Daughters as well because it "after all, in the South, was along many lines that the U. D. C. would do well to follow." Privately, a letter to Mary Poppenheim from Mrs. Joseph White indicates further dissension. White wrote that Daughters complained that articles on clubs outweighed those on the UDC and refused to subscribe to the journal.[26] These two examples reflect the fact that the *Keystone*, founded at the same time as the SCFWC, immediately became the federation's official organ. The state UDC division adopted the journal four years later. Perhaps because of this chronology, club columns preceded UDC columns in their position within the journal. Thus, if anything, the focus on Southern identity found within the journal is even more striking, as it was weighted more toward clubwomen than toward Daughters in its origination and layout.

Examples of cooperation between the UDC and clubs went far beyond the courtesies and greeting each organization routinely gave to one another. In Columbia they shared physical space. The City Federation of Women's Clubs sponsored a Woman's Building, which included a relic room for the UDC and the DAR, a Timrod Library, and meeting rooms for clubwomen, Daughters, and other women. In Laurens, they met regularly. The Wednesday Club suspended reading reciprocity papers from the federation bureau and instead instituted reciprocity meetings in which UDC and DAR members read poems and papers to their club. They also supported each other's projects. The Amelia Pride Club of Rock Hill appointed Anna Fewell to confer with the UDC concerning sending relief to Cuba, and the Current Literature Club of Columbia appointed a girl to sell coins for the Confederate Memorial at Stone Mountain.[27]

For many, although not all, women in South Carolina this overlap between women's clubs and the UDC was significant. Undoubtedly, they belonged to a network of active women in their communities, and some were members of many women's groups, including church societies, the WCTU, and the Daughters of the American Revolution. Although some women joined a wide range of associations because membership reflected propriety (it was "the thing to do") or politesse (they were asked by friends or colleagues), women's overlap in leadership as well as membership and dedication to both clubs and the UDC signaled a more important fit between the two. The agenda of clubs and the UDC reinforced each other.

Most clubs in the SCFWC originated as self-improvement or literary study clubs, and they naturally gravitated toward the history of the region for their studies. They looked back longingly at the Old South and recognized, according to the Wednesday Club of Laurens, that "the *Old South* is gone forever but memory serves to dwell on the happy, prosperous, wonderful conditions which characterized our dear Southland."[28]

The pages of the *Keystone*, civic speeches, and local club meeting minutes reveal how members of the SCFWC defined Southern identity. Clubwomen and Daughters alike emphasized the values learned from the Lost Cause: honor and chivalry. In their retelling, Confederate soldiers not only bravely defended state's rights but also protected the South's values of chivalry, community, and family from invasion by the uncivilized North. Clubwomen had to battle histories written by Northerners who called Confederates "rebels" and the "War between the States" the "Civil War." Clubwomen approached their studies with a zealousness of purpose because the suffering they and their families had experienced during the war was meaningless unless explained in light of the "true history" of the cause.

Individual clubwomen found meaning in their study, evident when the Up-to-Date club of Chester noted that they had studied the history of the Civil War in anticipation of the Confederate veteran reunion. Their report, indicating the depth of feeling sustaining the program, claimed, "Each description was vivid and the eloquence was nothing marred, if these daughters of southern sires, found sometimes their voices tremulous and their eyes moist, as they pictured the superb valor and self-sacrifice of those ragged, war-torn veterans, who even in defeat won the laurels of unsurpassed courage."[29]

Several representative examples from local women's clubs illustrate white clubwomen's passion for the South.[30] These local club minutes reveal an even greater interest in the region than the federation's official records do, an emphasis that suggests its grass roots and perhaps subconscious nature for many clubwomen. Countless clubs studied South Carolina and Southern history, often with a special emphasis on slavery or the Civil War. The Over the Teacups Club in Darlington studied the state and the region three times in thirteen years. In addition to glowing histories of male Southern political and Confederate heroes, this club also read Southern women such as Mary Chesnut's *Diary from Dixie*, in which she described "scars left by Sherman on the Southern mind and heart," and a letter written by Jefferson Davis's wife, Varina, during Union occupation. On one occasion, when the club member responsible for the day's program was absent, members quickly substituted a poem to the Confederate Dead. Those in attendance at the January 14, 1907, meeting might well have wondered if they had walked into a UDC meeting: after a sad program on Father Ryan (the poet of the Confederacy), they had refreshments in the dining room decorated in Confederate colors and heard a poem in tribute to Robert E. Lee for his birthday.[31] Up the road in Rock Hill, during the study of South Carolina in 1897–1898, the Amelia Pride Club had a superintendent of schools address the club on slavery and heard talks on Booker T. Washington, the story of the Confederate flag, and Daniel Emmett, the author of "Dixie." The secretary described "Dixie" as "that song that appeals to the patriotic sentiment and has taken a deep hold upon the affection of our people."[32] These choices indicate the breadth of study, the sentimental appeal of history, and the importance of regulating the history of race in clubwomen's studies. They also indicate that clubs' interest in sectional history did not abate over time. Like the Amelia Pride Club, the Perihelion Club returned to topics on the South several times, and that club even heard the same paper on the Civil War read by Mary Roddey on two separate occasions, after which the secretary noted that the club "particularly" enjoyed this paper, "even on the second reading."

Clubwomen explicitly fostered their consciousness as Southern women through programs of self-education. The Perihelion club not only chose John C. Calhoun, Jefferson Davis, Robert E. Lee, Sidney Lanier, Thomas Nelson Page, the Ku Klux Klan, and "How Southern Women Helped the Lost Cause," as topics for 1899–1900, but it also requested four members to give personal reminiscences of the "War Between the States." If these were typical of published accounts of the war written by

Southern white women, they stressed the bravery of Confederate soldiers, the loyalty of family slaves, and the personal deprivations suffered by Southern families at the hands of unscrupulous Union soldiers.[33] Members also contributed their memories of "Gentlemen of the Old South," during a presentation on the same at the New Century Club.[34] When club members shared their own personal stories, they helped clubwomen move from individual memories to a collective memory and inscribed their own experiences into the history they promoted. Clubwomen did not draw the same distinctions that professional historians make between memory and history. What they remembered (that is, what they chose to remember and chose to forget) was the history that shaped their identity as Southerners.

These personal reminiscences reveal that many clubwomen had much at stake in honoring the Lost Cause for which their family fought. In the case of the Poppenheims, although both were lifelong members of the Rebecca Motte chapter of the Daughters of the American Revolution, pride in their Confederate heritage was more significant to their identity. Louisa and Mary's father, Christopher Poppenheim, was a sergeant in Company A, Hampton Legion, Hood's Brigade, Longstreet's Corps, who had joined the Confederate forces on May 30, 1861, at the first call for troops. Despite an injury sustained at the battle of Sharpsburg in 1862, he remained with the legion until 1864 and then served "special duty" at the quartermaster's department in Charleston. He was not the only member of the family to fight for the Confederacy. Their mother's eldest brother, Lieut. J. R. Bouknight, was mortally wounded in battle; five of her cousins served; and even her youngest brother, J. H. Bouknight, although too young to enlist, "served the Confederacy with the Citadel Cadets, the boy soldiers of South Carolina."[35] Like many other Southern women during the war, their mother did her part for the cause by organizing the Bethany Hospital and Soldier's Aid Association, in Edgefield County, with her sister, Louisa Bouknight.[36]

Mary Elinor Poppenheim's loyalty to the Confederacy did not fade, as is evident when she considered traveling to Savannah to see Jefferson Davis, "our ex-pres.," in 1886. She at first refused to travel; to Mary and Louisa she explained, "I don't think my feelings will allow me, for I feel as if Davis had been buried with our sainted dead over whose grave a seal had been placed, and to see him would only awaken memories too sacred to hold in this busy bustling world." Eventually, she decided to accompany the rest of the family because she believed that the crowds gathered to see him would "let him know that he still lives in the hearts of true Southern people as strong as he did twenty years ago."³⁷ Mary Elinor succeeded beyond her best hopes in passing to her daughters her feelings as a "true Southerner." Mary included her mother's memories of the war when she coedited *South Carolina Women in the Confederacy*, a collection of reminiscences of the war published by the SCUDC. The state legislature purchased three hundred copies of the book at a price of $500 to distribute to schools and libraries.³⁸

Like the Poppenheims, many clubwomen came from families loyal to the Confederacy. Minnie Melton Burney, president of the SCFWC in 1908–1909, was related to Jefferson Davis; her father was a colonel, and her three uncles were majors in the Confederate army. She showed her loyalty to memory by presiding over the Wade Hampton UDC chapter in Columbia. Mary Clifford, president of both her local women's club and UDC chapter and a state officer, saw her father's "Scofield Car Shops" allegedly "burned by a negro in 1859, thus destroying an industry which would have been of much service to the Confederacy. 'The Finishing Shop' of this plant . . . was used as a hospital for Confederate soldiers." Eloise Welch Wright, an officer in the SCFWC and the state UDC, published the letters that her father, a Confederate surgeon, had written from the front. She had five uncles who also served the Confederacy. Honoring the Confederacy came naturally to clubwomen, revealed deep meaning, and helped assuage the pain of wartime suffering.³⁹ Devotion to the Confederacy and the South was not limited to UDC meetings; such sentiment pervaded women's daily lives and their clubs.

Clubs across the state celebrated the Lost Cause. Although Mary and Louisa were powerful, they were not omnipresent. The members of each of these clubs voted to study the region because it meant something important to many of them. The pervasive emphasis on Southern history cannot be attributed to only one or two zealots. Yet, the Poppenheims were instrumental in saturating clubs with regional history, especially through the *Keystone*. As chairman of the Reciprocity Committee, first Mary and then Louisa promoted the reciprocity bureau, in which clubs exchanged papers with one another. The *Keystone* kept these papers for the SCFWC and listed several dealing with Southern history and literature.⁴⁰ The *Keystone* also printed stories, such as "The Story of the Confederate Flag" and "The Effect of the War on Southern Literature." They promoted songs, such as "The Bonnie Blue Flag," as a way for women to learn and transmit history, and the magazine even printed a recipe for Confederate fruitcake.⁴¹

The Poppenheims also fostered a focus on Southern history through

Mary's offices in the UDC. Her love for history grew out of her studies in American history at Vassar College, especially under Professor Lucy Salmon. Salmon founded the Vassar Alumnae Historical Association, which promoted the preservation of historic materials at Vassar as well as in local communities, and Mary followed her example in South Carolina.[42] Mary created the historical committee of the state UDC, and as its chair she advocated studying local history. She supported the state historical commission's establishment of a state archives and participated in the national UDC committee that urged all Southern states to adopt the practice. Both sisters reminded readers that local history should be preserved, "for we owe it to our past; it is due our posterity."[43] In the state UDC, Mary created a historical circular that suggested topics of study and preservation for South Carolina UDC chapters, and she edited *South Carolina Women in the Confederacy*. Mary Poppenheim, through her offices in the UDC and through the *Keystone*, made history the focus of her UDC agenda.[44]

Promoting Southern history was linked to studying sectional literature because Daughters and clubwomen both believed that only native authors could accurately portray its history, describe its contemporary citizens, and capture the values and character of the region. Louisa Poppenheim, imploring the readers of the *Keystone* to support Southern literature, reminded them, "No country can hold its own in literature which does not foster its native talent." She then provided readers with reviews of books written by Southerners, in which she highlighted their knowledge of local conditions.[45] The journal also attempted to foster the work of *women* specifically by soliciting stories from its readers. In 1902, the editors implored, "We are a Southern periodical, aiming for what is highest and best in woman's work in our land." In exchange for promoting women authors, they expected support for a regional periodical. They continued, "As we have said before, 'to be vital we must express the life and thought of the women of today.' This we have tried to do with the co-operation of Southern women who have aided us with the idea that a Southern publication should receive recognition and support at home."[46] Ironically, the *Keystone*'s self-promotion as a regional periodical provides a nationalistic tone to the work of both the clubwomen and the Daughters represented therein.

The emphasis on true Southern literature was crucial because through literature Southerners and Northerners learned stereotypes and truths about each other. This knowledge is evident in a *Keystone* article, "Southern Life in American Fiction," by Virginia Hughes. Hughes first defined regional identity through its chivalric gender roles and then examined literature that contradicted these images. Most disturbing to Hughes was the inaccurate representation of African Americans in *Uncle Tom's Cabin*, which she compared unfavorably to Thomas Dixon's novels.[47] Clubwomen found Harriet Beecher Stowe's book dishonest as well as distasteful. The Amelia Pride Club, for example, criticized Stowe's work, and the secretary noted in the minutes, written in verse:

"Mrs. Mobley read a criticism
On Mrs. Harriet Beecher Stowe
As she helped to sway brother against brother,
We've no love on her to bestow.

As Mrs. Stowe and her literary contemporaries
Are now all gone
We hope *Uncle Tom's Cabin*
will be consigned to oblivion.[48]

Clubwomen thus had to focus intently on Southern literature; the benefits of "true histories" would be undercut unless read alongside "true fiction" of the South.

As study clubs, women's clubs were natural sites for promoting Southern literature. Along with Shakespeare and Dickens, clubwomen read Thomas Nelson Page and William Henry Timrod. This emphasis on things Southern did not wane over time. The Current Literature Club of Columbia continued its study of regional literature well into the 1920s. Thomas Nelson Page addressed the club in 1921. The secretary's description of Page echoes the attitude of clubwomen themselves: "When he came to speak of the writers of the Confederacy he did so with great feeling and showed himself as he is, intensely Southern pride of race and love of home animated every word of his delightful talk." Although other Americans were undoubtedly patriotic and loyal, that intense "pride of race and love of home" seemed to her to be unique to Southerners.[49] The Outlook Club mixed history and literature; its program included papers on statesmen from John Laurens and John C. Calhoun to Wade Hampton and poets and artists, such as William Henry Timrod. Women in the Old Homestead Club of Darlington felt especially privileged to have a member read "some beautiful, unpublished lines of Timrod, which were written to her mother years ago," and it was also revealed that a member "could boast of having slept in the bed that had been the personal property of Mr. Timrod."[50] The intimate nature of the connection that these clubwomen had with Southern authors no doubt made their studies more meaningful to them. The ways in which their personal memories coincided with collective memory of the region strengthened their sense of place.

Reading Southern authors, however, did not guarantee a positive view of the South. For example, the Poppenheims criticized Caroline Granger's article on Southern women's clubs in the *Annals*. Despite the fact that Granger was president of the Georgia Federation of Women's Clubs, in their opinion she inaccurately represented the section. They claimed that her article did not have enough "local color." Perhaps this was owing to the fact that, although the author lived in Georgia for twenty-five years, she was born in the North.[51] Mary P. Frost, in an article in the *Keystone* argued that Southern poets also did not accurately represent their region. She complained that they had ceased to emphasize the positive in the South. According to Frost, local poets such as Timrod, Sydney Lanier, and Father Ryan, before, during, and immediately after the war, duly praised the South. However, Frost complained that since defeat, Southerners no longer recognized achievements of the South. "It is strange to think," she wrote, "that in one generation there were poets enraptured with the love of country and people, and in the next, we speak of ourselves as incompetent, lacking vigor, nor worthy of admiration as others who inherit this broad land."[52]

Clubwomen's focus on Southern history and literature mirrored the literary program of the UDC in many ways. Daughters also studied history and literature and presented programs on both at meetings. Although women's clubs in South Carolina, like clubs across the nation, studied Shakespeare and Dickens, and although other clubs in the North and West studied their own local history, the intensity of the South Carolina clubs' focus on the South is overwhelming. Their emotional descriptions of Southern heroes and their seriousness of purpose in defending Southern history are far too striking to be dismissed.

For white clubwomen in South Carolina the "true history" of the South included defending the Confederate cause as just, its soldiers brave, its white women virtuous, and its slaves loyal. Moreover, the defense of the Confederate nation both implicitly and explicitly looked to the antebellum South as an ideal that included slavery as the best model for race relations. When the Outlook Club listened to a paper on antebellum Southern life, the secretary commented, "This paper interestingly described those leisurely days around which a certain halo lingers."⁵³ Such yearning for the past was not harmless, for it included nostalgia for the seemingly better race relations that occurred under slavery. Clubwomen's support for the Lost Cause therefore had critical implications for race relations in the early twentieth-century South. Most significant, clubwomen and Daughters used literature to disseminate their version of the history of slavery, one in which slaves were loyal and happy. Thus, clubs that studied the history and literature of the South reinforced their belief in white supremacy through their understanding of race relations during slavery and Reconstruction. The stories that they emphasized remind us that memory is a process of "construction rather than one of mere reproduction."⁵⁴ What clubwomen chose to remember about slavery and what they chose to forget—including the violence of slaveholders against slaves and the discontent of slaves evident in their rebellions—significantly helped shape race relations in the twentieth-century South.

In the history and literature read and written by clubwomen, slaves typically had been content in slavery. The Poppenheims included faithful slave stories, both reminiscences and fiction, in the *Keystone*. Louisa praised George Eggelston's portrayal of African Americans in her review of *A Carolina Cavalier*; she claimed that the character "Marlborough is the real Southern Negro, who knows of no greater distinction than to be the servant of his master."⁵⁵ Ludie Merriam Coleman, former president of the SCFWC, was known for her role in building a traveling library system in the state. She contributed several stories to the *Keystone*, which she wrote during her "idle hours" as a housewife. The stories feature slaves speaking negro dialect and promoting the happy plantation image. In one story, "Sam," a loyal slave tells of the benefits that he has received from his master and the sad fate of a disobedient slave, who, because of his outbursts, is traded to a mean master and dies running away from him.⁵⁶ These, the only African Americans who speak in the *Keystone*, have only the voice given to them by their white author. By promoting a positive image of race relations at home, Southerners persuaded many Northerners that they no longer needed to interfere in the fate of Southern blacks. Peaceful reconciliation between the two regions was predicated on the North's acquiescence to white supremacy in the South.

Locally, clubs reinforced the message of white supremacy through their papers and historical studies. For example, Mrs. Charles R. Hyde spoke to the Charleston City Federation on "The Instruction of the Negroes Prior to 1860." In her talk, she emphasized the positive influence whites had had on blacks in the antebellum South and detailed attempts to

Christianize blacks in the state. According to Hyde, white supervision mitigated the savage tendencies of the race. Dedicated to discussing African Americans, two meetings of the Old Homestead Club of Darlington typified the attitude of white clubwomen. On the first occasion, in 1908, they heard papers on "The Joys of Being a Negro" and "The History of Slavery," listened to negro songs, planned a debate entitled "Resolved; That Education Unfits the Negro for Menial Labor" (not held due to absences), and finally discussed the servant problem. Twenty years later, they read stories of the "old Plantation Negro," which "charmingly depicted the devotion and fidelity of these Negroes to their 'White Folks,'" and heard a paper on black superstitions and haunts, "in spite of their simple, childlike faith in God." Finally, club member "Mrs. Evans read a true, original story bringing out a pathetic contrast between the artlessness of one of her father's war-time slaves and the arrogance of his college bred son today."[57]

Clubwomen were more than willing to discuss childlike blacks who depended on their white masters—these African Americans posed little threat. The juxtaposition of discussions of the loyal slave with the servant problem and the arrogant college graduate clearly shows that clubwomen struggled to understand blacks in the postwar South, especially in comparison to their image of the faithful slaves of the plantation. The SCUDC also defended slavery by describing it as beneficial to slaves because of the uplifting and Christianizing contact with the masters' families. Their unwillingness to consider blacks as other than happy and loyal slaves reinforced the justness of the Confederate cause because the Confederacy fought for the right to retain slavery.

For clubwomen and the Daughters, true history included not only the benevolence of slavery and the justness of the Confederacy but also the horrors of Reconstruction, inflicted upon the South under the rule of inept black political leadership and ended only by the heroic work of the Ku Klux Klan. Their descriptions of Reconstruction echo those of white redeemers: under the "dark days" of Republican "misrule," whites had to endure various indignities until "white rule and civilization were restored" by Wade Hampton and the white Democratic redeemers.[58] To them, the Klan stood for Southern patriotism and the protection of white womanhood. By supporting the Klan they sanctioned its violence. Louisa Poppenheim promoted Thomas Dixon's portrayal of Reconstruction and the Klan in *The Klansman*, which was the basis for the film *Birth of a Nation*. She warmly praised Dixon in book reviews and ran an advertisement for *The Klansman* in the *Keystone*.[59]

Local clubs also supported the Klan. They read *The Klansman* and studied Dixon's life. In 1914, the Amelia Pride Club was pleased to have Jennie Hutchison, a charter member of the club and a member of the UDC, display items worn by her husband's father while a member of the Ku Klux Klan.[60] Likewise, in 1906 the New Century Club of Columbia heard an address and personal reminiscences on secession, and the following meeting featured a talk on South Carolina's part in the Confederate War and a presentation by Mrs. Childs who "recounted the workings and object of the Ku Klux Klan, and the great part it played in the reclaiming of power by the white people." Seventeen years later, the club again had a report on the Klan. For her presentation, Mrs. W. Davis interviewed a member, although the minutes do not reveal how she gained access to the Klan.[61] Studying the history of secession, the war, and then the Klan provided an understanding of the racial nature of the Civil War, belying Southern claims that it was based on states' rights rather than a defense of slavery. Implicit in their inclusion of the Klan on their literary agenda was their belief in its success at ending Reconstruction and restoring power to white men in the South.

The work of white clubwomen was all the more insidious because after studying these stories themselves, they then sought to tell the same story to others. They supported building Confederate monuments across the Southern landscape and ritual celebrations of Robert E. Lee, Jefferson Davis, and other heroes of the Lost Cause, events spearheaded by the UDC. More important, because reaching children was essential to ensuring the continuity of their program, they worked within the schools and libraries. For white clubwomen, the focus on "true history" was crucial in educating Confederate children. Clubwomen and the UDC obviously wanted to teach children that the South's behavior was justified. They sought to pass on the identity that they had worked to build among themselves. The SCFWC and the UDC alike emphasized the need for true history books in the schools and sponsored essay contests for children. This work was significant because its direction to the next generation ensured the continuity of tradition. Furthermore, middle- and upper-class clubwomen, descendants of slaveholders, promoted a history that linked white Southerners across class lines and elevated racial unity over economic solidarity. Thus, whatever their intentions, clubwomen were part of the effort to unite white Southerners.

Like clubwomen throughout the nation, the South Carolina Federation focused on children and education in their reform agenda. But this work was colored by their focus on sectional identity. As chair of the

SCFWC education committee in 1904, for example, Louisa Poppenheim recommended that clubwomen investigate school conditions—such as the number of pupils attending and teachers' salaries—investigations that mirrored activities of women's clubs throughout the nation. However, Louisa could never forget her regional identity. As a Southern woman, she also advocated asking what histories were being taught, a measure to ensure the preservation of the "true" history of the Civil War. She asked, "Instead of teaching Southern children 'Snow Bound,' 'Evangeline,' and 'Vision of Sir Launfall,' why are they not made familiar with our own Southern poets and the literature of our section?" Clearly, this work was the duty of clubwomen, a duty that the education committee, one of the most active in the federation, could not leave to the UDC alone. At the local level, mothers at the Over the Teacups Club in Darlington "resolved to see that their children studied true facts about our state," after a lecture by Col. Dargan on South Carolina history.[62] Their reaction to his lecture, concern for their children, fit perfectly with the SCFWC agenda of educational improvement.

Book reviews in the *Keystone* by Louisa Poppenheim helped clubwomen ascertain which books were appropriate or "true." For example, she censured Viola Conklin's *American Political History* because the author focused too much on slavery rather than on states' rights. In a review of F. E. Daniel's *Recollections of a Rebel Surgeon and Other Sketches*, Poppenheim warned, "How much better would be *Recollections of a Confederate Surgeon* or any adjective other than that one 'rebel,' which no Confederate deserves and which should never be associated with the Southern men who took part in the War between the States."[63] These examples are typical of her reviews, which take as their first standard of merit the author's portrayal of the South and her people.

One major effort undertaken by clubwomen throughout the nation was building libraries. In the South, libraries were ideal repositories for Lost Cause tracts. To ensure that libraries contained appropriate books, the Poppenheims printed in the *Keystone* a list of books approved by the UDC and thus recommended for donation. Further promoting its cause, the South Carolina Federation called for a special topical traveling library on Southern history and literature.[64] South Carolina's efforts echoed those of Alabama clubwoman Kate Morrissette, who believed that the traveling library, with biographies of Robert E. Lee and other appropriate works, was a vehicle for "placing impartial history in the hands of Southern youth to show them that in the valor and patriotism of our country they are coheirs."[65]

Anxious to have Confederate children avail themselves of such historical resources, both the SCFWC and the UDC sponsored scholarships and essays in the public schools. The Perihelion Club, for example, decided to follow up on the state federation's essay contest for South Carolina history and tradition with a similar contest in the local schools.[66] Like the SCFWC, the state UDC and local chapters also oversaw forty-one scholarships and prizes and medals worth $550 in 1917. The Florence UDC chapter protested against schoolchildren singing the "Battle Hymn of the Republic" and held a reception for teachers to establish a closer relationship with the Daughters and thus presumably to prevent such transgressions from occurring in the future.[67] Like Louisa, Mary Poppenheim recognized the value of cooperating with local schools in promoting true history. She attended the South Carolina State Teachers Association meeting in 1905 to plead for teachers to aid the UDC in studying local history.[68] She also suggested to the Daughters that they visit schools and decorate them with photographs of Southern authors and statesmen.[69]

Clubwomen also promoted local schools because they believed that Southern schools best taught Southern values. For example, a history of Charleston's schools in the *Keystone* extolled Elizabeth Wotten, one of Charleston's teachers, who was "a most ardent daughter of the South, a firm believer in States [sic] Rights; in her eyes South Carolina could do no wrong, if any of her pupils have been lukewarm in their allegiance to the South, the fault does not lie at her door, she did her utmost to teach them what was to her the only right view that could be taken."[70] Rather than judging Wotten's skills at teaching students to read, write, and multiply, they praised her Southern loyalty.

Women's clubs also followed the UDC tradition of celebrating Memorial Day and the birthdays of Jefferson Davis and Robert E. Lee. The Amelia Pride Club observed Robert E. Lee's birthday with a program devoted to him, as did the Perihelion Club. They did not allow clubwork to interfere with these occasions. The New Century Club of Columbia decided not to hold meetings on May 10 in order to attend local Memorial Day ceremonies, and the Century Club of Charleston postponed its June 3 meeting to observe ceremonies for Jefferson Davis.[71] These occasions were especially meaningful because they allowed Southern clubwomen to celebrate Confederate and American heroes simultaneously, reinforcing the defense of Confederates as patriots. For example, the Amelia Pride Club held a "patriotic" program in which they celebrated the birthdays of both George Washington and Robert E. Lee in February of 1919.[72] In the midst of World War I, this combined celebration in February on Washington's birthday reinforced for Southerners their tradition of patriotism even as they retained pride in a hero of the "Southern cause."

These ritual celebrations, some held for clubwomen themselves and others in public, reminded both black and white participants of their heroes and their history. The UDC also held ritual celebrations, which included solemn speeches, songs, and appropriate decorations. To aid Daughters in marking these holidays and other ceremonies, the South Carolina UDC Division yearbook listed "Red Letter Days for Historical Meetings and Exercises in Schools," including Secession Day and "Birthdays of Great Southerners," such as Nathan B. Forrest, leader of the Ku Klux Klan.[73] Clubwomen were also concerned with terminology; for example, the Amelia Pride Club debated the proper name for the War Between the States.[74] Although terminology may seem inconsequential, clubwomen treated it with great seriousness.

The UDC was the principle force behind building Confederate monuments, but clubwomen supported their progress. In Rock Hill, the Amelia Pride Club included in their reports accounts of monuments unveiled across the state and the region, including the Confederate monuments at Fort Mill, South Carolina, the Wade Hampton Statue in Columbia, the Calhoun statue in Washington, D.C., and the statue to South Carolina women in Columbia.[75]

African Americans in the South rejected the story that white women in women's clubs and the UDC told of slavery as benign, slaves as happy and loyal, and Reconstruction as a time when blacks were savage and immoral. African Americans consistently underscored the need to combat what they perceived as a pernicious retelling of history, even as historians and contemporary white observers often deemphasized the centrality of race to the Lost Cause. Specific examples of what blacks found so dangerous about the Lost Cause and why they rejected Confederate identity as Southern identity shed light on their subsequent attempts to create an alternate sense of place. Like white clubwomen, black women in the South Carolina Federation of Colored Women's Clubs (SCFCWC) studied history and literature.[76] Black and white women used many of the same tools—promoting history and literature both within clubs and in schools and libraries—but they had radically different goals. Black women had to confront Lost Cause teachings, yet they emphasized American history more than Southern history, an indication that they were not simply reacting to a white version of history.

At the turn of the century, prominent black male leaders tried to warn African Americans against the efforts of the UDC and others to rewrite the history of slavery and the war. Frederick Douglass and W.E.B. Du Bois perceived sectionalism as a growing danger and called for African Americans to combat a white supremacist history. Douglass fought for blacks to remember the Civil War and slavery at a time when many preferred to look ahead at progress rather than back to a bleak past. Historian David Blight argued that Douglass realized that "historical memory . . . was not merely an entity altered by the passage of time; it was the prize in a struggle between rival versions of the past, a question of will, of power, of persuasion."[77] Douglass wanted to celebrate emancipation rather than Union and Confederate soldiers and sectional reunion. Similarly, Du Bois understood that in admiring the Lost Cause, Americans accepted a deeply racist history of slavery, the war, and Reconstruction, and he warned that that telling of history was pernicious because it shaped policy and society in the present.[78]

In South Carolina, Columbia's black newspaper, the *Palmetto Leader*, noted the activities of "Confederate-Americans" who denounced Abraham Lincoln at the "Annual Meeting of the South Carolina Division of the [United Daughters of the] Confederacy." The *Palmetto Leader* also challenged the UDC's monopoly on defining true history. One editorial noted that the UDC had complained about "My Maryland," a play about a woman from Frederick, Maryland, who was shot while waving the Union flag, because it did not give a true portrait of the war. Blacks could sympathize, the editorial continued, because they "too have said many times 'what a pity it is that David Griffith did not present a true picture of the Negro while he was at it in his notorious and misnamed *Birth of a Nation*.'"[79] For black readers of the *Palmetto Leader*, Lost Cause and Confederate celebrations were attempts to impose race relations from the Old South into the postemancipation period. Douglass, Du Bois, and other African Americans protested the Lost Cause mythology's contemporary effects evident in race relations, education, and economic progress.

Black women joined male African American leaders in noting the persistence of Confederate ideology in the South. Susie King Taylor, a laundress, nurse, and teacher who accompanied the First South Carolina Volunteers, a black Union troop during the Civil War, focused her attention on Confederate-American women in the South. When she wrote her memoirs in 1900, she expressed anger with the "ex-Confederate Daughters," who had protested a performance of *Uncle Tom's Cabin*. Taylor defended Stowe's work against their claim that the book "exaggerated" negative aspects of slavery. She further ridiculed the reform efforts of white women in the UDC, particularly their professed concern for children's welfare, and pointedly asked, "Do these Confederate Daughters ever send petitions to prohibit the atrocious lynchings and wholesale murdering and torture of the negro? Do you ever hear of them fearing this would have a bad effect on the children?"[80] Taylor was one of many black women who recognized that lynching would continue if white women silently acquiesced in the myth that lynching defended white women from rape by black men.

Although African American clubwomen, particularly those who lived in the South, focused most of their time and energy on aiding blacks through services including kindergartens, nurseries, and other reform projects, they realized that combating Lost Cause ideology was also necessary if young people were to develop a strong sense of their abilities. If not the most significant component of the black clubwomen's agenda, literary and historical study was still critical to promoting black pride. Clubwomen understood it was also necessary to uplift the race. In South Carolina, many clubs divided their agenda between social reform projects and self-improvement. The constitution of the SCFCWC listed the promotion of education for black women first, followed by goals focused more explicitly on social and economic welfare and civil rights.[81] Black and white clubwomen lived parallel lives. One group celebrated the birthday of Robert E. Lee, the other the birthday of Frederick Douglass. One group read Thomas Nelson Page with tears in their eyes, while the other group read W.E.B. Du Bois with determination. One group vilified Harriet Beecher Stowe, and the other celebrated her birthday.[82]

Evidence from black women's clubs in South Carolina in the early 1900s, while limited, still suggests that local black women's clubs promoted African American history and literature as part of their literary programs. The Phyllis Wheatley Club in Charleston, for example, reported that it desired a greater variety of reading materials and therefore drew up a list of books about blacks or by black authors. Each member took the name of a book that she was expected to purchase, presumably for the use of all in the club as well as for herself. The entire program of one meeting was devoted to Africa's contribution to world civilization, and at other meetings the club read chapters of W.E.B. Du Bois's *Darkwater*, Phillis Wheatley's poetry, and the works of Paul Laurence Dunbar (in addition to Shakespeare). The Club purchased *The Negro in Our History*, which was intended for either club use or perhaps donation to the Avery Institute. They also received a request from the library for books, especially by Negro authors. Other expenditures included a donation to Carter G. Woodson, presumably in support of the Association for the Study of Negro History and Life, founded in 1915.[83]

In 1917, the club voted to discuss great men of the race by using Benjamin G. Brawley's *The Negro in Literature and Art* as the text. This book, written by a professor of English at Atlanta Baptist College, was an attempt to critique literature written by black authors while using the same standards applied to whites. For example, in the spirit of his objective standards, Brawley did not hesitate to criticize Phillis Wheatley for her childish verse, even as he praised her earnestness, piety, and imitation of Alexander Pope's style. In effect Brawley tried to "legitimize" the study of African American literature. One can imagine that his book therefore inspired deeper pride in black achievement in club members. Brawley critiqued Wheatley, Du Bois, Paul Dunbar, Charles Waddell Chesnutt, and William Stanley Braithwaite, among others. Moreover, Brawley's book introduced clubwomen to various writers for reading outside the club format.[84]

The Louise Fordham Holmes Literary and Art Club of Charleston not only read black authors but also white novelist Julia Mood Peterkin. Peterkin, who was known for her sympathetic portrayals of black plantation workers in the early twentieth century, was the wife of a plantation manager in South Carolina. In 1928 club member Esther Mazyck reviewed Peterkin's *Black April* for the club. A newspaper article described her review as a "most sympathetic interpretation of a White Southerner's conception of the lowly negro." Apparently, the club appreciated Peterkin's depiction of an all-black community, who spoke the Gullah language and practiced folklore, and if they resented the sexual promiscuity and negative characteristics of Peterkin's black characters, clubwomen did not record their unease.[85]

In Columbia, a group of young women formed the Brawley Book Club, named for the author, and committed themselves to a special study of black authors, such as Paul Robeson, to become more familiar with the "best minds of the ages."[86] The Booker T. Washington Literary and Social Club, in Georgetown, celebrated its tenth anniversary by playing the National Negro Anthem and conducting a program on the lives of Washington and Frederick Douglass. The Sunlight Club of Orangeburg celebrated Douglass's birthday with a special day in February.[87]

The South Carolina Federation of Colored Women's Clubs did its part to encourage clubs across the state to take up such study and advocated that individual clubs "strive to instill and encourage race pride through appreciation of Negro music and literature." The federation helped increase clubwomen's knowledge through speakers at their conventions, such as Carrie Thompson's address on "Negro Achievement." They also asked member clubs to remember National Negro History Week and Douglass Day.[88]

Nationally, the NACW recognized the importance of self-improvement and education, just as it encouraged clubwomen to celebrate Harriet Beecher Stowe's birthday and to study black history and literature. Mary Church Terrell led a celebration of the 100th anniversary of Stowe's birth in 1911 and called for the NACW to establish a scholarship in her name.[89] The *Palmetto Leader*, which covered SCFCWC activities extensively, also promoted black history and literature through a column on negro history and editorials, such as one advocating that every family start a library of negro literature in its home.[90]

Clearly, both black and white clubwomen focused much energy on history and literature. Continuing self-education was imperative for women who had achieved high educational levels. The Phyllis Wheatley was organized to give women the opportunity for "culture and self improvement."[91] By studying what they read the issues of most importance to them become clear. For white women, literature and history represented an opportunity to tell their version of the truth about Southern history, which included a defense of both the Confederacy and slavery. For black women, literature and history instead provided evidence of black achievement, pride, and place in the American nation. For both black and white women, the stories they learned were too important to remain within their own circle. Each also dedicated energy to promoting those truths to others, whether to children or to the general public.

Black clubwomen also understood the importance of public monuments and ceremonies. They promoted Frederick Douglass and other black heroes, celebrating Douglass's birthday alongside those of Lincoln and Washington every February. Although many white Americans in the North revered Lincoln as the Unifier—that is, the savior of the Union—African Americans idolized him as the Emancipator. Clubwoman Mamie Fields vividly recalled celebrations on the fourth of July, the only day of the year when blacks were allowed on the Battery (the Charleston riverfront). Although whites in Charleston still refused to celebrate the "Yankee" holiday, for blacks, festivities included more than eating and dancing. On July 4th, as on January 1, or Emancipation Day, children sang songs such as, "The Battle Hymn of the Republic" and "Lift Every Voice and Sing." They memorized the Emancipation Day proclamation, and they recited "pieces" about Lincoln and Frederick Douglass. As Fields described it, many of the children's parents or elders had been slaves and were actually celebrating their own freedom. The recitation of parts of Douglass's antislavery speeches was especially meaningful to them, and many had come to know the speeches by heart.[92]

Men and women participating in the annual race conference led by Rev. Richard Carroll also petitioned the state to erect a monument to black veterans of World War I in Columbia. In asking for such recognition and inaugurating a $100,000 drive, the conference attendees wanted to make public the sacrifice of those black men who "died for the liberty of humanity and peace of the world." They further asked for it to be built in the capitol city and for funds to be appropriated to match subscription funds. The reaction from the Columbia newspaper, the *State*, was to approve of the idea of a memorial while suggesting that it should take the form of a memorial building at State College in Orangeburg, thereby providing practical assistance to the community, rather than a simply offering a statue for viewing. Several months later, the legislature approved plans to appropriate funds for separate white and black memorials, the first to be erected at the University of South Carolina in Columbia and the latter at State College in Orangeburg. Each had to be raise "adequate" funds by popular subscription before the state would match them.[93]

In this case, the original demand for a memorial in the state capitol, presumably to be in sight of white passersby as well as black, became diluted into a memorial on the campus of State College, where few whites ever ventured. The message, therefore, that blacks were loyal soldiers, men, and Americans like their white counterparts and that they fought for the "liberty of humanity," which included humans of all colors, was too dangerous to display in the capitol city. Evidence of this was present at a parade of black veterans, where Dr. S. F. Hagood, a speaker, declared that blacks had proved themselves and would now be asking for "what belongs" to them, including a voice on juries and the employment of black policemen.[94] A monument at State College was a safer alternative. Although still acknowledging black participation in the war, the message of liberty would be overridden with the message intended in a segregated, separate memorial out of view of whites. Perhaps whites also believed that blacks would not be capable of raising the funds and that the memorial would never be built.

The *Palmetto Leader* supported the building of the WWI memorial because the editors believed that this memorial celebrated the battle for freedom and democracy at the heart of that war. This was in contrast to

Civil War memorials, which the newspaper castigated: "Why do we seek to keep alive those divisive forces which drove us asunder?" Recognizing the link between the Southern cause and race, the editorial continued, "If monuments make for the perpetuation of racial hatred then it is best for all of them, along with Stone Mountain, to be ground to powder and be cast into the midst of the sea."[95] White women who built Confederate monuments probably would have denied their "perpetuation of racial hatred" even as they supported the Klan.

Efforts directed at children were even more important than these public celebrations and monuments. Because women understood so well the need to teach children their own history, the classroom was a primary site where tensions between white and black versions of Southern history were most rampant in South Carolina. Here both black and white women fought to dictate school textbooks, lessons, and songs. In her memoirs, Mamie Fields recalled the experience of black Charleston children, who were taught predominately by white teachers in the segregated public schools until an NAACP campaign in 1919. Fields attended the Shaw School in Charleston as a young child. She resented the efforts of white teachers to teach black children the Lost Cause version of history:

> One thing they did drill into us was the Rebel tradition. They had a great many Rebel songs and poems. All had to learn "Under the Blue and Gray" and recite it once a week. The whole school did it, in all the classes. We stood to recite . . . then we would sing "Dixie," the whole school, in unison, "I wish I was in de lan' of cotton," in dialect, too. Then they were of fond of songs like "Swanee River," "My Old Kentucky Home," "Massa's in de Col' Col' Groun'." This is what they wanted to instill in us.

Fields was adamant that, although white Southern teachers might try to instill Confederate patriotism, blacks could seek alternative ideology at their own schools. "But you never heard these songs and poems at Claflin [a black college], which was established by Northerners," she boasted. "And you never heard them at Lala's [a local black woman's school]." Instead Lala taught them about slavery and abolitionists: "She taught us how strong our ancestors back in slavery were and what fine people they were. I guess today people would say she was teaching us 'black history.'" When Fields became a teacher herself, she stressed American citizenship and taught her students "America the Beautiful" and the Pledge of Allegiance because she explained, "My school was in the United States, after all, and not the Confederacy."[96]

African Americans rejected Lost Cause ideology by teaching black history and black pride, as well as American citizenship, emphasized in Emancipation Day celebrations. Because white women's clubs and the UDC influenced curriculum and textbooks in the public schools, black children were forced to learn a history of slavery that emphasized either the savagery or the childlike behavior of blacks and their consequent dependence upon paternalistic whites. White teachers enforced white supremacy through the use of books such as William Simms and Mary Simms Oliphant's *The History of South Carolina*, a widely used textbook that portrayed blacks as inferior and Reconstruction as a dark chapter in South Carolina history. The text explained that at the end of the war, "The State had a tremendous problem to face in the sudden freeing of thousands of irresponsible, uneducated, unmoral, and, in many cases, brutish Africans."[97] Black clubwomen therefore found it necessary to teach themselves and their children pride and dignity in their heritage. Clubwoman, educator, activist, and South Carolina native Mary McLeod Bethune argued, "If our people are to fight their way up out of bondage we must arm them with the sword and the shield and the buckler of pride—belief in themselves and their possibilities, based upon a sure knowledge of the achievements of the past."[98] They merged celebrations of Abraham Lincoln and Frederick Douglass, days that emphasized American citizenship and African American history.

Although most black public schools in the state had black teachers, African American students in Charleston had white teachers. Civil Rights activist and clubwoman Septima Clark recalled that she found the white teachers to be of poorer quality and lacking the same high expectations of black children that black teachers had. Thus clubwomen in Charleston joined the NAACP campaign to remove white teachers from the black public schools. Thomas Miller, former president of South Carolina State College, came to Charleston in 1919 and, together with the NAACP, started a campaign to replace them with black teachers.[99] Members of the Phyllis Wheatley Club and their husbands and fathers led the Charleston chapter of the NAACP, founded by eighteen men and eleven women in 1917. Members included Jeannette Cox, president of the Wheatley Club, and Susie Dart Butler, the most prominent clubwomen in Charleston, who was NAACP treasurer. Susie Dart was the daughter of John Lewis Dart, a Baptist pastor, and Edna P. Morrison, the granddaughter of the president of the Friendly Moralist Society, another prestigious black fraternal organization. Dart, educated at Avery Institute and Atlanta University, attended McDowell Millinery School in Boston before marrying

N. L. Butler and returning to Charleston where she opened a millinery shop in 1913. With a teacher from Atlanta, she founded the first kindergarten for black children in Charleston.[100] Undoubtedly, Butler, Cox, and other leaders in the Phyllis Wheatley, who were also teachers at Avery and NAACP members, joined this campaign as well.

The NAACP first approached the school board with a request for black teachers by emphasizing the bond necessary between child and teacher. The white school board, however, believed it in the interest of white supremacy to keep black children under the influence of white teachers. Charleston School Superintendent A. B. Rhett attributed what he perceived as good race relations to the fact that "colored children from a very early age were under the control and influence of white principals and teachers and were taught to look up to and respect white people."[101] According to Septima Clark, white Charlestonians dismissed the request, arguing that "mulattos . . . were the only ones who wanted Negro teachers for their children. The cooks and the laundresses, they declared, didn't want their children taught by Negro teachers." Whites had difficulty believing that their loyal servants would dare make such a demand and blamed it instead on the Charleston free black elite, who were associated with Avery and the NAACP. Miller therefore decided to start a communitywide petition drive to disprove them. Clark collected signatures, which she recalled as totaling more than ten thousand. "I remember the number," she writes in her memoir, "because of the fact that a white legislator known then as One-Eye Tillman had declared Mr. Miller would never be able to get 10,000 signatures in all Charleston."[102] When their petition was rejected, they went to the state assembly to gain a law that would make it illegal for a white person to teach in a public school for black children. Clubwomen, teachers, and other NAACP members gathered thousands of signatures on a petition, which they presented to the legislature. Legislators responded with two proposed bills, which never had to be passed, however, because two weeks later the Charleston school board reconsidered its position and agreed to allow black teachers in September 1920.[103]

The significance of this campaign cannot be overstated. Not only did thousands of blacks in Charleston come together to demand change, but they also went over the heads of the Charleston school board, to the state assembly, and forced them to back down. Ironically, of course, the state assembly could not reject their petition because it favored segregation. However, the substance of what blacks in Charleston were fighting for should not be lost in the significance of this campaign strategy in which blacks made the segregated school system work for themselves. That is, blacks understood that having black teachers would enable them to control to some degree what was being taught and to instill pride in children, even as it also provided respectable, relatively high-paying jobs for black women.

Locally, clubwomen in South Carolina sought to influence the history and literature taught in black schools. Because so many clubwomen were teachers, this was an obvious course of action, which was probably most often done unofficially through the teachers themselves. In some cities, there was an outstanding relationship between a particular school and club because of the prevalence of teachers from that school who were members of the club. The best examples of this relationship were the Sunlight Club in Orangeburg, which was closely associated with South Carolina State College and Claflin College, the Culture Club in Columbia, many of whose members were affiliated with Allen or Benedict colleges, and the Phyllis Wheatley Club in Charleston, tied to Avery Institute. In the first decade of the Phyllis Wheatley, at least fourteen members taught at Avery. The club took an active interest in the school, sponsored essay contests, and offered one graduate the opportunity to speak to the Avery Alumni Association on the club movement. At Claflin, Mamie Fields recalled two Sunlight Club members, Etta Rowe, who taught history, and L.A.J. Moorer, a librarian who began a Friends of Africa club.[104]

Black clubwomen extended their efforts to encourage black literature to the local libraries. In Charleston, Susie Dart Butler opened to local black residents her father's book collection, which eventually became part of the Charleston Public Library system. Butler undoubtedly ensured that black authors were represented on her shelves. The Phyllis Wheatley Club recorded their support for this project by requesting books, "especially by Negro authors," for the library in 1931. In Orangeburg, the Sunlight Club Community Center contained a library for local residents, which also included special mention of the black authors who could be found therein. The club noted that "the shelves of books by Negroes occupy a choice corner," a corner donated by Marion Wilkinson and her family.[105]

Black clubwomen took the pride in black history and literature to the public in other ways as well. For example, both the Phyllis Wheatley Club and the Sunlight Club also sponsored concerts by Marian Anderson. The Phyllis Wheatley Club proudly noted that her concert brought "culture and edification" to the mixed race audience that attended. At the same time, African American clubwomen were able to showcase black talent.[106]

Such local efforts echo the concern of the national network of black clubwomen to which Marion Wilkinson, state federation president, belonged. A member of the network of Southern black clubwomen and educators, she introduced many prominent figures and programs to South Carolina. The most well-known of these women included Lugenia Burns Hope, Mary McLeod Bethune, Charlotte Hawkins Brown, and Margaret Murray Washington. Lugenia Burns Hope, although born in Chicago, moved to Atlanta with her husband, John Hope, president of Atlanta University. She founded the Neighborhood Union, a women's club that performed services similar to a settlement house in education, health, and childcare. Mary McLeod Bethune was born in 1875 near Mayesville, South Carolina. She was educated at Scotia Seminary, Concord, North Carolina, and Moody Bible Institute, Chicago. After teaching at Lucy Laney's Haines Normal Institute in Atlanta, she founded the Daytona Educational and Industrial Training School for Negro Girls, in Daytona, Florida, which became Bethune-Cookman College in 1923. Bethune later was a member of the advisory committee of the National Youth Administration during the New Deal and founded the National Council of Negro Women in 1935. Charlotte Hawkins Brown, born in 1883, founded Palmer Memorial Institute in Sedalia, North Carolina, and published two books, *Mammy: An appeal to the Heart of the South* and *The Correct Thing to Do, to Say, and to Wear*. Margaret Murray Washington, born in 1865, was Booker T. Washington's second wife. She served as director of Girls' Industries and dean of Women Tuskegee and founded the Tuskegee Woman's Club with other faculty and faculty wives. She was instrumental in founding the National Federation of Afro-American Women, predecessor to the NACW, and then served as president of the NACW from 1912 to 1918.[107]

As a member of this network, Wilkinson was an integral member of the International Council of Women of the Darker Races (ICWDR), which grew out of the NACW's interest in pan-African issues. This group formed from leaders in the NACW because black women realized that, while educating themselves through their clubs was important, they also had to promote black literature and history in the schools to educate African American children. Founded in 1920 by Margaret Washington, the ICWDR counted most of the leaders in the NACW among its members, including Wilkinson, who was vice-president throughout the 1930s, Terrell, Hope, and Bethune.[108]

To facilitate improved educational opportunities, the ICWDR formed their own study groups for African American literature and history, and

Washington worked especially hard to include such works in school curriculums. In South Carolina, Marion Wilkinson informed Washington that she heartily agreed with Washington's plans for study and research committees. "I am deeply interested in this phase of our work and it makes a strong appeal to me," she wrote, "for I feel that it will be far reaching in results and in time will be the big idea of our organization."[109] The ICWDR also promoted a better understanding of the plight of women of color throughout the world through studying countries such as Haiti. With Wilkinson serving as a vice president, South Carolina clubs in the SCFCWC undoubtedly received the study guides from the ICWDR and supported her work throughout the state.

A history written shortly after the Council was founded explained that the Committee on Education's course of study was intended for "clubs, schools, and leaders in general." It described the effort to integrate black history and literature and the history of people of color throughout the world into the curriculum as imperative both for self-knowledge and for demonstration to whites. "For one to appreciate himself," the author stated, "he must know himself and certainly for another to appreciate him, there must be definite knowledge of his attainments and aspirations. Pride in one's self comes through racial consciousness." This would come through the exchange of information among people of different nations, such as countries in Africa, the Philippines, and Haiti. Moreover, it would correct the surprising lack of knowledge among black American children of leaders of their own race, such as Frederick Douglass. The author cited, for example, a member who visited a public school and found that only one child had heard of Douglass. Referring to black teachers, the author then asked, "If we, as teachers, do not think to do this, who will do it?" The ICWDR therefore existed to provide both the impetus and the information needed in order to aid teachers and local schools.[110]

In 1922, Margaret Washington wrote to Lugenia Hope and informed her that the first item on the ICWDR's agenda was to get Negro Literature and History in all the schools, North and South. "I think you will be surprised to know how many schools North and South, even our own schools, where our children are taught nothing except literature of the Caucasian race," she wrote. "We are not fighting any race, we are simply looking for our own."[111] The books she suggested reading included Hubert Shands's *White and Black*, Stephen Graham's *The Soul of John Brown*, history by Carter Woodson, and the *Southern Workman*.[112] While

Hope agreed with Washington's idea, she advocated caution and preparedness in approaching school officials to convince them of the merits of including such books. So did Janie Porter Barrett, founder of the Locust Street Settlement House, in Hampton, Virginia, who cautioned, "I think the move to get Negro Literature and History in the schools a splendid one. . . . But I fear we must plan carefully before moving."[113]

Marion Wilkinson also participated in a regional effort to promote black history and literature in the Women's Committee of the Commission on Interracial Cooperation (CIC). She chaired the committee on recommendations, which in addition to calling for better conditions on railroads and improved funding to black schools also drew attention to black history and literature. The committee recommended both "that a special effort be made to put books by Negro authors into the public libraries" and that black and white college students both needed better access to "well prepared literature concerning the history, growth, and accomplishment of the Negro race in America."[114] Presumably Wilkinson's participation in both the CIC and the ICWDR carried over into the state federation of women's clubs that she headed.

South Carolina black women's clubs were not unique in their study of black history and literature along with reform work and socializing. In Atlanta, The Chautauqua Circle was similar to the Phyllis Wheatley in its emphasis on literature. Started in 1912 by Henrietta Curtis Porter, the Circle frequently read black literature and history. Programs from 1913 to 1930 included "The Negro in Literature and Art, Race History, Negro Musicians of Note, The Influence of Slavery Upon Literature, Benjamin Brawley and His Racial Books, and the Educated Negro Before the Civil War.[115]

Through their local clubs, state women's clubs federation, the ICWDR, and the CIC, Wilkinson and other black clubwomen fought against the negative stereotypes of African Americans promulgated by white women through Lost Cause approved texts. They pushed for the study of black history and literature in not only black homes but also public schools. In so doing, they instead focused on black leaders and on Emancipation and their American citizenship. In one of the most bizarre and brilliant examples of African American rejection of the Lost Cause and concurrent celebration of emancipation, the *Palmetto Leader* even attempted to coopt the celebration of Robert E. Lee's birthday in the South, by advocating that African Americans join white Southerners in honoring him. An editorial praised Lee for his brilliance as a military strategist and described him as "the great soldier who surrendered to Grant at Appomattox in 1865, thereby causing a re-united nation and the freedom of four million slaves."[116] Such praise for Lee offered a stunning reversal of the UDC's idolization of him as a Confederate hero and created his alternative legacy, which focused on Emancipation.

Katherine Du Pre Lumpkin, raised in South Carolina by parents very much caught up in the Lost Cause, recognized that the Lost Cause ideology and its telling of history were bound to white supremacy. According to Lumpkin, the Lost Cause meant, "We must keep inviolate a way of life." Although some changes were acceptable, "it was inconceivable, however, that any change could be allowed that altered the very present fact of the relation of superior white to inferior Negro. This we came to understand remained for us as it had been for our fathers, the very cornerstone of the South." Lumpkin understood that the great preserver of tradition, the Lost Cause, preserved white supremacy too. "It too was sanctified by the Lost Cause," she wrote. "Indeed, more than any other fact of our present, it told us our cause had not been lost, not in its entirety." While she eventually was able to use these memories to break free and work for racial and economic justice, many white women were not.[117]

White clubwomen and Daughters saturated the air with Lost Cause ideology. The content of the history that they promoted in the Lost Cause had grave implications for race relations in the region. Although Southern white clubwomen most often attempted to ignore the presence and needs of African Americans in their community, when they did acknowledge African Americans, it was often in the past tense—that is, rather than dealing with blacks who lived among them, they preferred the image of happy and loyal slaves. Moreover, they reinforced a benevolent view of slavery and Southern race relations through defending the Confederate cause in the Civil War, which, although they justified it under the guise of "states' rights," was predicated on the Southern states' right to retain slavery. Finally, clubwomen and Daughters alike promoted the negative view of Reconstruction common in the South, which stressed the dangers of "negro rule." Together, these views of Southern history strengthened the dominance of whites and dependence of blacks. At the same time that white men hung black bodies from trees as a warning against "uppity" blacks who prospered economically or otherwise transgressed white expectations, white women worked to ensure that Emancipation did not change engrained and disabling beliefs in black inferiority.

The UDC is most known for their public monuments to the Confederacy. But the UDC and white clubwomen also subtly disseminated their understanding of race relations through the histories they promoted in schools. They also more explicitly expressed their views on race, by defending slavery and attacking Reconstruction through monuments to loyal slaves, book reviews, and club meetings. Thus, a broad range of Southern white women defended the Confederacy and slavery and attacked Reconstruction in their attempts to define Southern as white and black as inferior. Defeat in the Civil War and the consequent freeing of the slaves made it imperative that the memory of the Confederacy and the Southern identity that these women created enforce white supremacy. By promoting the image of blacks as loyal and happy slaves or subordinate servants, members of women's clubs and the United Daughters of the Confederacy in South Carolina participated in past and present solutions of the "Negro problem." Although as women, they were unable to vote in the political elections that disenfranchised African Americans and instituted Jim Crow laws, through their club work they were also responsible for creating a culture of segregation at the beginning of the century. They legitimized the Confederate defense of slavery, and they sanctioned the segregated system of the New South. Men had promoted disenfranchisement as the means to political stability, and women meanwhile had created a stable Southern community by unifying white Southerners through their program of fostering a white Southern identity. Unable, or unwilling, to challenge gender oppression, they ensured their own place in Southern society by reinforcing racial hierarchy through their literary program as well as through segregated social welfare reforms.

African Americans had to battle not only Jim Crow laws but also the exclusion and degradation promoted by white women's organizations, who did their part to ensure that Jim Crow laws were upheld by a culture of segregation in the South. Black clubwomen promoted a sense of pride in their race as they fought Lost Cause ideology. Although such efforts did not directly attack segregation, they helped build the sense of self necessary before more radical campaigns could be undertaken.

Black and white clubwomen therefore helped shape politics, ideology, and Southern identity in the early twentieth century. Examining their strategies for teaching history and black pride provides a reminder of the constant negotiation over public space and collective memory. Whose story is told, whose monument is raised, whose text is read—these questions remain contentious today.[118] Clubwomen expended so much energy on public history because they realized how much was at stake.

Perhaps the most noticeable effects of this struggle over history and memory are the ways in which black and white clubwomen worked separately, sometimes reaching out to one another, more often not. Women who told different stories about the South and about themselves failed miserably when it came to interracial cooperation.

Chapter 3

"Less Said Soonest Mended"

The Parallel Lives of Black and White Clubwomen

Sarah Patton Boyle, a white Virginian who took a stand against segregation in the 1950s, recalled a meeting she had with a black publisher named Mr. Sellers. When she asked him if he was from the North, he replied, "Oh, no, I'm a Southerner." Boyle recounts her astonishment: "If he had thrown a cup of water in my face, I couldn't have been more surprised. A Southerner! Never had I heard a Negro thus designated. Southerners were white. Sellers was a Southern Negro, not a Southerner."[1] Black Southern women had to force white Southerners to see them, to recognize them as neighbors and fellow Southerners. The regional history and literature that white South Carolina clubwomen studied in the early twentieth century centered around the happy plantation, Confederate glory, and the Ku Klux Klan. Through this telling of history, white women helped naturalize segregation and marginalize blacks. But African Americans refused to remain invisible. They rejected Lost Cause versions of history, and they asserted themselves into Southern Progressive era reform. They even made overtures to white women for cooperation. Despite the similarity of their interests, black and white clubwomen rarely communicated. South Carolina women's clubs, like those throughout the region, were rigidly divided by color. Moments of contact between the races were made and missed. Cooperation occurred mostly behind the scenes and was undermined in part by white clubwomen's Lost Cause rhetoric.

Notwithstanding the odds, black women attempted to bridge the gap. Despite the rebuffs they encountered, the act of asking for cooperation can be understood as not only a request for aid but also a demand for recognition, particularly by black clubwomen as fellow Southerners. Black Southern clubwomen attempted to gain the support and aid of white women through the Women's Section of the Commission on Interracial Cooperation (CIC), formed following World War I and subsequent race riots. By the 1920s, a significant barrier to interracial cooperation between women disappeared; passage of the woman suffrage amendment ended a debate that always seemed to come back to race. By this time, too, disfranchisement and segregation were firmly entrenched; these fixtures allowed race "liberals" to attempt to mitigate racial injustice without threatening segregation itself. Finally, the South had achieved a greater measure of reconciliation with the North through its united support for the First World War. This cooperation dampened the intensity of Lost Cause rhetoric.[2]

Black clubwomen understood that interracial cooperation, though limited, could help them gain badly needed state support for their community. Furthermore, as Karen Cox points out, African Americans understood the difficulty of criticizing white women in the South and their role in the Lost Cause.[3] Rather, it behooved African American women to swallow their pride, ignore racial insults, and attempt to work with white women.

Moments of cooperation reveal the possibilities as well as the pitfalls of race and Southern progressive reform. The relationship between black and white clubwomen included moments in which white women consciously chose to ignore or to study African Americans; on rare occasions they cooperated with black women. Nonetheless, black women initiated interracial cooperation through the founding of the CIC and the South Carolina state branch. Not surprisingly, in South Carolina black clubwomen were for the most part rebuffed by their colleagues in the white federation of women's clubs; white women from various church organizations did, however, respond to the overtures of the CIC.

White clubwomen rarely mentioned race or African Americans in either their rhetoric or their activity reports. Yet, this absence of race, paired with the select ways in which race became salient, illuminates their understanding of racial hierarchy. The first solution to dealing with African Americans in the early twentieth century seemed to be denial. For whites it was simpler not to deal with them: to ignore, to exclude, to segregate. In the antebellum South, white women were often responsible for the welfare of slaves through the distribution of clothing, food, and medicine. Removed from this obligation following the Civil War, they exerted little effort to aid the black population. Clubwomen simultaneously praised loyal plantation slaves and excluded their children from benefits and services. This contradiction is significant. Clubwomen carefully had to balance their rhetoric—too much sentiment for the old mammy might raise eyebrows about conditions in the Jim Crow South, while too much vitriol calling for segregation might call into question the myth of the happy plantation.[4] The easiest solution was to do little for blacks living nearby.

White South Carolina clubwomen worked virtually exclusively for white beneficiaries; their free kindergartens, playgrounds, and other educational assistance were provided for whites only. Other Southern progressive reformers did the same.[5] References throughout the *Keystone*, South Carolina Federation of Women's Clubs (SCFWC) yearbooks, correspondence, and reports indicate that white clubwomen consciously chose to exclude blacks from social reform benefits. For example, in 1918, Louisa Poppenheim, as chair of the Committee on Matron in the Police Station and County Jail, reminded the federation that securing a matron in the jail had become even more crucial because more white women were detained due to the presence of soldiers at local military bases for World War I. She enlisted the aid of state Senator Niels Christensen Jr., who reported to her that there had been approximately fifteen hundred female prisoners during the past year, one-third of whom were white. Armed with this information, Poppenheim requested that the federation cooperate in securing matrons "for these 500 white women prisoners."[6] Although aware of the plight of twice as many black female prisoners, she chose to extend aid to white prisoners only. Officials undoubtedly would have been more receptive to funding a white matron than both a white and a black matron, yet this prioritization was typical for the SCFWC.

At times, moreover, white women were willing to sacrifice making improvements for whites if blacks would also have access to them. In Rock Hill, the Castalian Club wanted to form a public library, which they viewed as "the nucleus of a public education." However, they refused to bring a Carnegie Library there when they realized that the Carnegie Foundation stipulated that both blacks and whites have access to the libraries it funded.[7] White clubwomen refused to aid blacks at considerable risk to their attempts to improve social and economic conditions of the state as a whole. Thus their reluctance to aid blacks overrode even their social reform agenda for a prosperous New South.

Their general unwillingness to aid blacks came primarily from their understanding of black racial inferiority, inscribed in the Southern history and literature they promoted. They also feared that black access to education following emancipation would enable blacks to eclipse poor whites in economic prosperity. In South Carolina, a leading cotton mill state, white clubwomen specifically believed that black children would attend school while poor white children worked in the mills.[8] Thus, suspicion of black progress at the expense of whites could handicap reformers, as with the Castalian Club's library work, or it could motivate clubwomen to work for child labor laws and education reform for white children only.

Furthermore, South Carolina clubwomen may have been more reluctant than their sisters in the upper South to aid blacks because of the history of race relations there. Like other states in the black belt, South Carolina had a majority black population from the early eighteenth century through the 1930 census. Additionally, the state had long been under the political influence of powerful planters, and, as the first to secede from the Union, South Carolina was deeply concerned with protecting slavery and the social order it imposed on blacks and whites. Perhaps the loss in the war was therefore felt more keenly, and South Carolinians, though no more "racist" than others in their section, more rigidly defended their racial mores and harked back to the antebellum past. Louis Harlan, in his history of inequality in public school funding, argued that South Carolinians were more candid than other Southerners about their discrimination. "The white majority in South Carolina, with some exceptions," he wrote, "ignored the democratic principles which troubled the sleep of some other Southerners who discriminated against Negroes."[9]

Finally, the makeup of women in the SCFWC may have been more conservative than in other states. Historian Elna Green found that antisuffragists, who were more likely to use racist rhetoric, were also more likely to be members of the UDC and literary women's clubs, more numerous in the black belt, and more often married to planters or mill owners than suffragists were. These characteristics certainly fit many South Carolina Federation leaders and members, only a minority of whom were suffragists. South Carolina clubwomen's conservatism perhaps made them less open to the interracial movement.[10]

Historians have long realized that the very proximity of blacks and whites made segregation so necessary: because they lived so close together, a false separation had to be enforced.[11] Clubwomen could not always ignore or exclude blacks living among them. In their literature and history programs, they studied black culture and discussed the "Negro problem."

They sometimes chose to extend aid to black beneficiaries, when they believed it to be in the best interest of white South Carolinians. In keeping with their praise for loyal slaves, white women usually characterized blacks as childlike and harmless, though inferior; sometimes, however, they resorted to more vicious attacks.

When clubwomen studied aspects of their culture that were heavily influenced by blacks, such as folklore or music, they promoted stereotypes of colorful, childish African Americans. The New Century Club, in a discussion of Southern folklore, "conceded that the Folklore of the South was connected principally with the negro." To learn more about the songs and stories that had become a part of Southern tradition, although sung and told by blacks, the club brought in "experts," such as Dr. Whaling of the University of South Carolina, who spoke on stories told by "old Southern Negroes" similar to those recounted by Joel Chandler, and E.T.H. Shaffer, who discussed Gullah stories.[12]

In these discussions, blacks were nonthreatening. The stories and white mimicry of the "negro dialect" often "provoked laughter" and entertained clubwomen. The Poppenheims shared in the enjoyment of black culture as harmless entertainment. During the Southeastern Council meeting held in Charleston in 1926, Louisa held a dinner at her home, where black servants entertained clubwomen. "A delightful feature of Miss Poppenheim's dinner was the real 'Charleston,' danced by a negro girl," reported the newspaper, "the music for the dance being given by the hand claps of the butler, the maid, and the cook."[13]

Southern white experts likewise buttressed claims that they knew blacks best and had no need of interference from Northerners. Louisa Poppenheim directly expressed this belief when she advocated that clubwomen study Southern folklore because "this subject should especially appeal to our Southern women as we have such intimate knowledge of the negro and his traditions." In her book reviews, Louisa judged whether books accurately portrayed the region and, more important, the "negro question." For example, she contended that Clifton Johnson did "not altogether grasp the negro question," while Thomas Nelson Page's *The Negro: The Southerner's Problem* drew warm praise.[14]

Many clubs discussed studied topics or listened to papers on "The State of the Negro," "The Negro Question," "The Negro Race in South Carolina," "What Columbia is Doing for the Negro," "The most desirable education for the Southern negro of the present day," and, "Does the negro develop under the influence of education?"[15] As with other reform topics, clubwomen embraced the subject as a sociological study, but for the most part they did not actively pursue reform programs to address these issues. Clubwomen felt comfortable studying but not aiding blacks because that might allow them to rise from their presumed degraded status. Although white women did not acknowledge African American clubwomen as colleagues, they could discuss the "Negro problem" because it implied inferiority on the part of blacks and reinforced the white paternalism that predominated their discourse on slavery.

Acknowledging the presence of African Americans as a problem also provided a scapegoat for the lack of progress of their state. For example, the library department amended its report in 1907 to acknowledge that the high percentage of South Carolina illiteracy was owing to the large black population.[16] Using a rather twisted logic, white Southerners also blamed African Americans for draining the state's financial resources. When *Good Housekeeping* magazine did a study on rural life, they asked the General Federation of Women's Clubs to read the thousands of letters they received describing rural life. Louisa Poppenheim read the letters from the South and reported that "the presence of the negro is a grave problem for Southern rural life—an ignorant and inferior race living separate and yet dependent, means a heavy responsibility for the white man. This race in many communities outnumbers the white population, and while contributing little to the support of the State, the State provides with education and bears the extra expense of furnishing separate buildings and separate teachers."[17] Louisa argued that African Americans were at fault for provoking whites to enforce segregation. The Poppenheims had already stressed the burden of segregation in an earlier editorial. In 1903 they compared educational progress in various states and proclaimed it "so interesting" to note that South Carolina had so few adult [white] males to pay taxes per one hundred students in school. According to the editorial, South Carolina had fifty-one males whereas other Northern states cited had more than one hundred. As the Poppenheims saw it, white men were responsible for paying for the education of African Americans.[18] Implicit is the belief that without its black population, the region would not lag behind.

In their study of black folk culture and the Negro problem, white clubwomen always depicted blacks as dependent upon whites. Their casting of blacks generally fell into one of two types: childlike, reminiscent of clubwomen's view of slavery, or as savage, reflecting their version of Reconstruction history. In either case, blacks were inferior to whites.

In viewing blacks as childlike, white clubwomen emphasized black dependence on whites for training in morals and blacks' natural inability to perform anything other than manual labor.[19] Louisa Poppenheim used Booker T. Washington's writings to bolster her belief that African Americans were incapable of the same progress as whites. In a book review in the *Keystone* of Washington's *Future of the American Negro*, Poppenheim praised him for asserting that the negro belongs in the South and that "the Southern white man is his best friend." She applauded his assertion that blacks needed education, not the ballot, and that their education should be industrial, not classical. At the same time, she condemned a biography of Frederick Douglass written by Charles Chesnutt. She accused him of misrepresenting the debate over slavery and of trying to heroicize Douglass rather than Booker T. Washington, who she saw as a more appropriate role model.[20] Like most white Southerners, Poppenheim believed Douglass talked too much about justice. Clubwomen embraced Washington as the leader of the black community instead because they did not think he threatened white supremacy. Locally, clubs supported this view of Washington, evident in the Amelia Pride Club's approval of his "refus[al] to dabble in politics."[21]

Clubwomen embraced Washington's philosophy of industrial education. Louisa Poppenheim had high praise for her region, where "the white man is trying to make the black man a useful part of the State by teaching him carpentry, bricklaying, and such trades, and in allowing him to do this kind of work by his side, a condition which does not exist in other sections of the country where labor unions control labor conditions."[22] The federation supported industrial rather than classical education for black children. At their annual meeting in 1904, the SCFWC education committee reported, "The corresponding secretary discussed negro education and outlined a plan by which the negroes could be taught cooking, sewing, and other domestic arts instead of so much reading and writing."[23] Clubwoman Rossa Cooley also promoted industrial education to the federation. Cooley was a Vassar graduate, originally from New York, and a member of the Clover Club in Beaufort. After teaching at Hampton, in Virginia, Cooley came to South Carolina, took over the Penn School, and instituted Hampton industrial education techniques. According to her, young blacks there carried their interest in book learning to an extreme, which she countered with the teaching methods she learned at Hampton.[24] Following this line of thinking, we can only assume that, when presented at the Century Club the paper discussing whether blacks "develop under the influence of education" might have argued that development depended on the type of education.

Despite their desire to ignore the needs of African Americans in their community, white clubwomen not only studied the Negro problem, but on occasion they felt obligated to extend their services to blacks. World War I was a turning point for some, who encouraged war work among blacks in their communities. The chair of the committee on war work suggested clubs in the SCFWC speak to negro churches and societies because, she argued, "we must prove to them that *this war is their war.*"[25] Following the war Louisa Poppenheim, as chair of the municipal playground commission in Charleston, led one notable movement to extend aid to blacks by establishing a black playground. The *News and Courier* claimed it was the first in the state. Although the superintendent of parks oversaw the playground, African Americans, including many clubwomen, raised $266 and contributed trained workers. Their contribution indicates that the idea for the playground probably came from blacks and that black women may have been pushing for cooperation, or at least aid, for years before white women became receptive to their demands.[26] By working on their own agenda, black clubwomen were therefore ready when and if white women decided to cooperate.

Beyond these few examples that took place during or after World War I, for the most part white South Carolina clubwomen chose to assist blacks only the few times when it appeared necessary to save whites. For example, when in 1912 the GFWC began to promote aid for tuberculosis victims, the Poppenheims advocated such work in the *Keystone*. However, the Poppenheims focused on the necessity of TB work in the South specifically because of the presence of blacks in their states. "TB germs are easily transmitted from gentle black mammies to white babies," they reasoned, "and so the protection of the black nurse may save its white charge." They attributed the high rates of TB in African Americans to their "carelessness and ignorance."[27] They addressed African American needs for better health care, not to display a disinterested benevolence, but rather to safeguard the white community. Yet even in this area, some white clubs were reluctant to aid blacks. The Over the Teacups Club of Rock Hill, for example, hesitated to act as a body. When asked for a contribution to a TB hospital for blacks, they decided to allow individual members to donate rather than giving as a club.[28]

Other cases of this self-serving aid were predicated on the same concern for the homes of white women in which black women worked, such as advocating the promotion of cleanliness in servants' homes and the training of servants. For example, the Amelia Pride Club of Rock Hill held a "Training School," which they referred to in parentheses as a "Better Servants School," for local black women in 1938. Clubwomen, giving instruction in cooking and serving, noted with pride the eagerness of black women to attend the school.[29] Clubwomen were encouraged by Booker T. Washington in their willingness to train domestic servants. In a speech he delivered in Columbia, Washington argued that "there is not a white family in South Carolina that should not be vitally interested in the improvement of the negro women—especially in the improvement of the negro cook, the negro nurse." When it came to eating the food prepared by black hands, white clubwomen succumbed to their own interests and reached out to train black women.[30]

Their willingness to train domestic servants highlights white dependence on black help—servants, nurses, and midwives. Clubwomen were forced to extend some services to African Americans, if only to ensure white health and safety, and in the case of training domestic servants, whites sought peace of mind. The federation also advocated the regulation of midwives because, as Julia Irby, chair of the health department of the federation claimed, "any old colored woman is allowed to attend our women during a most critical period in her life." Six years later, the SCFWC had established a program to train black midwives for their black patients, while white women were encouraged to have professional care. Yet, the federation still prioritized the needs of white women and noted that white women who were unable to obtain professional care would at least have trained black midwives.[31] It is significant that in each case white clubwomen only helped blacks when they were in position of serving whites; thus, whites reinforced the hierarchical relationship between them.

White Southerners who viewed blacks as incapable of high learning believed African Americans lacked civilization. Mary Poppenheim, in an address on domestic service, expressed the common belief that without white influence, blacks reverted to immorality and savagery. She complained that "the old time, well trained negro . . . taken into the house at an early age . . . grew up under the influence of social amenities, order, and cleanliness, which are unknown in the negro houses of the modern negro and we must bear this in mind when we take into our service these 'modern children of nature.'" By comparing servants to house slaves, Mary suggested that slaves were better off in their masters' homes than living on their own after emancipation. Clubwomen most commonly expressed this more vicious view of blacks in their frequent discussions of domestic servants. An article written by P. T. of Charleston, for example, described inadequate black servants in the South who stole from their employers as members of a "race of educated devils." Like all other white Southern pronouncements on what was best for blacks, he concluded, "We Southerners alone know the inherent race tendencies of the negro."[32]

It did not take much to push clubwomen from stereotypes of childlike blacks to a more virulent racism. In the *Keystone* article "Southern Life in American Fiction," Virginia Hughes attacked the depiction of blacks in *Uncle Tom's Cabin*. She questioned Harriet Beecher Stowe's characterization of blacks by asking, "Hence this determined character, heroic fortitude, unflagging industry, passionate love of offspring, high moral principles, and spotless religion. Are these negro traits? . . . Neither are they true of the Afro-American of to-day, still dirty, still stupid, still relapsing in to voodooism, still lazy and shiftless."[33] For white clubwomen and the UDC, ignoring the presence of blacks or explaining them away as loyal slaves usually succeeded in rendering them less threatening. Occasionally, however, they resorted to more vicious rhetoric. This happened rarely, though, because as is evident from their program of promoting "true" Southern history, white women understood that it was in their best interest to stress the South's ability to handle African Americans without interference from the North.

Clubwomen created a white Southern identity by not only excluding blacks but also explicitly promoting clubwomen's "Anglo-Saxon" identity. For example, Louisa began her article, "Woman's Work in the South," by referring to the racial make-up of the section: "The South, as no other region of this country, has been and still is the most pronounced inheritor of Anglo-Saxon characteristics, customs, and traditions."[34] The pride in Anglo-Saxon purity was especially evident in promoting work among the mountain whites. Southerners praised the Anglo-Saxon purity of the mountain whites, in comparison to the immigrants living in the North. The *Keystone* also printed many appeals to work for the mountain whites and reports from clubs on their progress in this area, including an account written by a mountain school teacher, Miss Maura Pinckney.[35] This emphasis on racial purity was undoubtedly particularly important to white Southerners, who were surrounded by the offspring of interracial unions dating back to the days of slavery. A significant part of the constant process of creating and privileging whiteness derived not only from contrasting black and white but also by explicitly defining whiteness through Anglo-Saxon heritage and "inherent" traits of the race. In the eyes of white clubwomen, Southern equaled white.

Even though white clubwomen in South Carolina rarely extended a hand, black clubwomen sought their cooperation. Other white women, especially those associated with the Episcopal Church, were more receptive than those in the SCFWC. In spite of, or more probably because of, the status of race relations in the region, Southern black women took the lead in the women's interracial movement in the 1920s. NACW leader Margaret Murray Washington believed that to forge cooperation black women needed to impress upon Southern white women that they, too, shared a Southern sense of place. As long as whites continued to think of the South as white, they could ignore the needs of blacks. Almost in anticipation of Sarah Boyle's reaction thirty years later, Margaret Washington told Southern white women at the meeting to establish a women's section of the Commission on Interracial Cooperation, "I might as well tell you at the beginning, that I feel that I belong to the South and I love it. . . . I have lived in the South all my life and have all the little things that A Southerner usually has."[36] If they were going to win recognition from white Southern women, then African Americans had no choice but to take the lead in the interracial movement.

Cooperation existed through individual efforts facilitated by clubwomen, churchwomen, and other organizations, and through the women's division of the Commission on Interracial Cooperation (CIC) and state and local CIC branches. The term "interracial cooperation" must be understood in the context of the Jim Crow South. It implied neither a movement for racial equality nor even cooperation to end racial discrimination. Rather, interracial cooperation often meant only that black and white women (or men) worked together for a common concern, such as temperance or public health. In its more "radical" form in the 1920s, interracial cooperation meant that black and white women worked together through the CIC to improve social and economic conditions for African Americans. Even in this stage, however, proponents worked within the parameters of segregation and white supremacy.

Before 1920, cooperation between black and white women in the South was relatively rare. Historians of North Carolina have found that the 1880s brought a "melting time" or the possibility for crossracial alliances of the "better classes" of whites and blacks around such issues as temperance. However, in the 1890s the threats of interracial political cooperation and black progress led a new generation of white men to disenfranchise black men and institute Jim Crow, and women's interracial cooperation ceased.[37] In North Carolina, the melting time was over by 1900; not until after 1910 were there signs of another possible thaw. Other attempts at formal cooperation beyond the temperance movement took place before World War I through missionary societies, especially those in the Methodist Church, and the YWCA, both of which provided some blacks and whites the experience of working together.[38]

Whether North Carolina's experience was common throughout the South is still unclear. Until the new constitution passed, North Carolinians had prided themselves on having peaceful race relations that did not necessitate the harsh measures taken by lower South states, such as Mississippi, ten years earlier.[39] In South Carolina black crowds also gathered in support of temperance and formed black branches of the WCTU. Despite such evidence of their support for temperance, as in other Southern states, whites scapegoated black voters when legislation failed. When former WCTU leaders took up woman suffrage, they argued that the greater number of educated white women in the state would aid in disenfranchising blacks.[40]

Despite this early collaboration in the temperance movement, white Southern women's clubs generally did not embrace cooperation.[41] Clubwomen, who originally focused more on literary study than community service, had less opportunity to establish a tradition of interracial work in the 1880s and 1890s, before the new wave of disfranchisement, segregation, and violence at the turn of the century.

In the 1920s, the CIC tried to fill the void. Following the death of Booker T. Washington, the Great Migration, the participation of blacks in World War I, and subsequent race riots nationwide, moderate white and black leaders in the South joined in an attempt to improve tense and violent race relations. When William Alexander, a Methodist, formed the CIC in 1919, it was originally composed of men only; some people hesitated to form an organization that included both white women and black men.[42]

Black clubwomen played the leading role in opening the CIC to both black and white women, especially those with experience in the YWCA and Methodist missions. Lugenia Burns Hope, who had been trying to start a black YWCA in Atlanta, invited white women Carrie Parks

Johnson and Sara Estell Haskin to the 1920 National Association of Colored Women convention. Following that convention, Johnson and Haskin met with a select group of black women at the home of Margaret Washington. Attendees included:[43] Marion Wilkinson, Charlotte Brown, Lugenia Hope, Mary Bethune, Janie Barrett, Jennie Moton, wife of Robert Moton and dean of women at Tuskegee Institute; Mary Crosthwait, registrar at Fisk University; Lucy Laney, founder of Haines Institute, Augusta, Georgia; and Mary Jackson McCrorey, president of the Baptist Division of Missions for Colored People and wife of the president of Johnson C. Smith College, Charlotte, North Carolina (all Southern black women).[44] Here, black women drafted a position paper on interracial cooperation and the needs of African Americans.

Following this meeting, the committee arranged a Women's Conference in Memphis on October 6–7, 1920, which resulted in the formation of the Committee on Women's Work of the CIC, jointly funded by the CIC and the Methodist Woman's Missionary Council. In Memphis, three black women, Margaret Washington, Elizabeth Ross Haynes, and Charlotte Hawkins Brown, addressed a group of about one hundred white women.[45] Charlotte Brown electrified her white audience with an impassioned address about racial oppression, black women's supposed immorality, and the need for white women to control men on lynching.[46] These white women, rather than representing federated white women's clubs, were drawn primarily from church groups and the YWCA. The meeting was intended to correct white women's ignorance of educated African American women. The black women were concerned that white women whose contact with blacks was limited to their domestic servants would never realize that African American women could be just as educated, mannered, and civilized as white women. Thus, a meeting between the "better classes" could unite black and white middle- and upper-class women on common ground; shared class and gender would overcome race difference.

Although white women proclaimed themselves enlightened by the meeting, there was much mistrust to overcome, especially by skeptical members of the NACW. At the 1926 NACW meeting in Oakland, California, for example, Marion Wilkinson explained the work of the CIC to the delegates. Although the NACW decided to endorse interracial work, their resolution suggests the unease with which both black and white women entered this new partnership. Black clubwomen proclaimed, "whereas it was with some misgiving that the Negro men and women met the challenge of the white South in an interracial conference, ... whereas this interracial commission has given sufficient evidence of success in this line to warrant confidence and cooperation, Be it resolved: that the NACW put itself on record as endorsing the work of the Inter-racial Commission of the South."[47] This statement is best described as cautiously enthusiastic. Their mistrust was magnified by white reluctance to acknowledge unjust conditions to blacks and black aversion to admit to shortcomings of African Americans to whites. Furthermore, blacks had two practical fears: the movement might be merely a camouflage designed to stop the exodus of blacks to the North, and white women's real goal was obtaining better domestic servants.[48]

As racially liberal as the white women involved were in comparison to the rest of white Southern society, they stopped far short of endorsing any motion that hinted at racial equality. In consequence, mistrust abounded. Carrie Parks Johnson read a weakened version of the black women's statement to the white women at the Memphis meeting. To a strong preface against lynching, she added the mitigating phrase, "deploring any act on the part of Negro men which excites the mob spirit." Furthermore, Johnson deleted both an unflinching preamble that demanded for black women "all the privileges and rights granted to American womanhood" and a following resolution regarding suffrage.

Incensed at her changes, black women in the committee wanted to publish their statement as originally written. Margaret Washington discouraged this and defended Johnson, "Let us stand shoulder to shoulder with the two white women and their followers. This Mrs. Johnson, in my mind, is a sincere Southern white woman ... we are expected to mark time." Lugenia Hope and Marion Wilkinson, among others, were outraged by Johnson and Washington. Negotiations dragged over several months. Johnson finally dropped her financial support for printing the pamphlet, and in June, the Southeastern Federation of Colored Women's Clubs adopted the statement as its platform and published it under the title, "Southern Negro Women and Race Cooperation." In printing the booklet, the Southeastern compromised: clubwomen omitted the preamble, but they included the demand for suffrage.[49]

The Southeastern clearly believed that interracial work was one way in which to reach its goal of race uplift, and to that end its members worked intimately with the CIC. Its council on interracial relations was appointed by and included the federation president. Mary McLeod Bethune believed that the Southeastern's role in the interracial movement was perhaps the prime justification for its existence; in her notes for talks on the Southeastern's relationship to the NACW, Bethune commended the group's efforts to pay for publicity of the interracial committee, ample reason to justify the organization.[50]

As a member of the Southern network of black club leaders, Marion Wilkinson, one of the black women who originated the women's CIC, helped bring the movement back to South Carolina. Five white South Carolina women, including four representatives of the Methodist Church and a Presbyterian who represented the Charleston YWCA, attended the October 1920 meeting.[51] White women organized the state women's division in 1922. Clelia McGowan, a founding member, chaired the women's committee and then the state CIC. Meanwhile, Marion Wilkinson organized a parallel black women's committee and was named vice chair of the state CIC. Together, McGowan and Wilkinson led the state CIC. Although McGowan held the higher office, the minutes clearly show that Wilkinson played a major role in the committee, often speaking and at times leading the meetings. Wilkinson was also on the board of directors of the national CIC. Although her husband Robert was not a member of the CIC, his statement in support of the movement was included in a pamphlet entitled, *The Opinion of Those Who Ought to Know: What Representative Negroes Say of the Interracial Movement.*[52]

Wilkinson's white counterpart in the CIC, Clelia Perroneau McGowan, was born January 30, 1865, daughter of William Raven Mathewes and Eliza Perroneau Mathewes.[53] Clelia married William C. McGowan of Abbeville, son of Confederate General and Judge Samuel McGowan, one of the state's most prominent citizens. A leading suffragist in Charleston, Clelia was not only appointed to the School Board of Education from 1919 to 1922 but also elected the first woman to the Charleston city council in 1923. McGowan was a member of the housing authority, the library board, the art commission, the South Carolina Society for Colonial Dames, the Huguenot Society, and the garden club.[54] A member of the UDC, she presided over the state division in 1898. She attended her first meeting of the CIC in Blue Ridge, North Carolina. Returning to South Carolina, she organized the Florence and Charleston chapters. She also traveled on behalf of the CIC and spoke in New York, New Jersey, Philadelphia, Baltimore, Washington, and Columbus, Ohio.

McGowan's transformation from UDC president to CIC chairman apparently came from both her record of civic service and her interest in African American welfare. She grew up on a large plantation where observers commented on the kind treatment those slaves received. A tribute to her in 1940 claimed that growing up "surrounded by Negroes who stayed on after 'freedom,' and 'Maum Venus' in the kitchen, and 'Daddy Dennis' in the mill guarded and guided her and her young brothers, teaching them manners, morals, and religion."[55] McGowan's relationship with blacks was marked by not only close contact but also paternalism on the part of her family. Despite her good intentions, some blacks found McGowan too patronizing. Mamie Fields recalled that McGowan "was one of our Charlestonian 'aristocrats'—from South of Broad Street—and dressed the part. Stately, she wore her elegant suits and dresses. She talked slowly and softly. 'Now we must be friends,' says Mrs. McGowan, 'and we must all work together in the community.'"[56] McGowan was unable to relinquish completely racial conceptions of African American inferiority, an attitude she herself undoubtedly had once promoted as the state UDC president.

Even so, McGowan's decision to undertake interracial work was extremely difficult. In the 1920s, few white women were willing to break with race conventions. She understood that many people, including some who were close to her, did not support her. Other white women interested in aiding blacks, like Abbie Holmes Christensen, the daughter of Massachusetts abolitionists who lived for decades in Beaufort, hesitated to speak their most radical views publicly. Christensen's biographer argues that her most defiant actions were personal: Christensen addressed black women as Mrs. and socialized with them in her home.[57] McGowan's efforts, which seem limited from the perspective of the early twenty-first century, must be understood in terms of their "radical" nature in the 1920s. McGowan spoke regularly at the SCFCWC annual meetings and publicly received much praise from African Americans for her efforts on behalf of race relations. The *Palmetto Leader* wrote that she was "one of the leading white women of Charleston both in public matters and church work, and has done more, perhaps, than any other single individual in South Carolina at the present time to bring about better relations between the races."[58]

Under McGowan, the state and local committees in South Carolina were interested in improving education and other opportunities for blacks. According to state CIC minutes throughout the 1920s, the committee worked to ensure black school representation at the county and state fairs; to extend public health aid, especially that which came through the Shepard-Towner bill for children; to secure justice in the lower courts;

to fight illiteracy and improve schools; to better conditions for rural farmers; and to aid black juvenile delinquents, especially through the Fairwold Home for Delinquent Girls. Other projects were local. Black clubwoman and CIC member Louise Fordham Holmes reported that she was getting black authors into the library in Florence.[59] The South Carolina women's committee was also recognized by *Southern Workman* for its strong antilynching statement, passed in 1923. The committee demanded protection for all women across race and boldly asserted, "There is no greater fallacy than that which holds up the shield of Southern womanhood in defense of the crime of lynching and burning of human beings, claiming that such acts are the outcome of Southern chivalry."[60] The resolution thus both acknowledged the virtue of black women and refused to accept the standard defense of lynching as necessary for white women's protection.

The *Palmetto Leader* believed that the CIC was an important medium for teaching whites about black experience. It remarked that Professor Benjamin Mays of State College had given an address on black authors at a CIC meeting, "which was surprising information to many white members present."[61] At the same meeting, Thomas Parker of Greenville, a wealthy white mill owner, admitted that he knew little about blacks—precisely what the CIC hoped to change.

Under Wilkinson's leadership, the SCFCWC actively supported the CIC. Among the federation's active forty-three-member interracial committee were some of the most prominent SCFCWC women: Marion Wilkinson, Etta Rowe, Celia Dial Saxon, Louise Holmes, and Belle Vincent, all of whom joined the CIC. As a sign of their support, the SCFCWC sent a $200 donation to the general CIC, which set an example for men in the community. In response, "The chairman stressed the point that the men had not aided the work of the committee financially, and suggested that the men's clubs might be induced to contribute if properly approached."[62] One reason for the SCFCWC's interest in the CIC was its hope to gain state support for the home for delinquent girls, a goal that underscored black women's limited but realistic hopes for the CIC: white members could help provide access for blacks to state funding. The CIC and its members unsuccessfully helped clubwomen lobby the legislature for funding. Locally, clubs from Charleston were also active in the CIC. As early as 1922 McGowan attended a Phyllis Wheatley Club meeting and addressed the members.[63] Presumably club members worked with the Charleston CIC chapter, which had been established under the auspices of the YWCA by McGowan and others after a post–World War I riot involved both white sailors and local blacks.[64]

Clubwoman Susie Dart Butler and McGowan also worked together to establish a public library system with white and black branches. Butler, a prominent Charlestonian and SCFCWC officer, was the daughter of Julia Pierre and Rev. John L. Dart, minister at Morris Street Baptist Church and owner and editor of the *Southern Reporter*. Rev. Dart held an extensive collection of books in his home, which he opened to the young men of his church. In the late 1920s, Butler and McGowan worked to transform his private collection into a public library branch open to blacks. Butler described the genesis of the library as follows:

> One cold night . . . a young high school girl, Lillian Patrick, attending Avery came to my home to inquire as to whether I had the poems of Shelley and Keats and their biographies. My father . . . had collected a large number of books for his library and I knew these books were among them. The girls went with me to his library. . . . The room was very cold, but the girl said she did not mind the cold. She would rather sit there and read because at her home a small cottage, there were her sister's young children playing and older folks talking, which made it hard for her to concentrate on her work. This picture was always in front of my eyes. I knew her situation and thought of many others like her. Where could we start the reading room?

In 1927 Butler opened a reading room for boys and girls by using her father's books and the print shop. The students at Avery gave a concert to raise money to repair the shop, and McGowan donated additional books. McGowan suggested that they pursue the Rosenwald Foundation, which was interested in funding libraries for blacks in the South. Butler conducted a survey of available books and space; after her library was open, she began to work with the Foundation and the County to match funds for a Charleston County public library system for blacks and whites. The Dart Hall branch for blacks, located in the former school building, opened July 31, 1931.[65]

Although McGowan reached out to women in the white federation, they showed far less support for the CIC than black clubwomen. The Woman's Auxiliary of the Episcopal Church supplied much leadership and support rather than white clubwomen, for whom interracial work was never a major focus.[66] For instance, when SCFWC President Bessie Drake was requested by McGowan to join the CIC, she accepted. However, in Drake's annual report she admitted that the federation had not been able to cooperate this year; she added, "we commend this work to the in-coming regime. It is a challenge to us of the South."[67] The following year the federation heard a letter from a Mr. Ford regarding the Better Homes movement in the "Negro Women's Federation of Clubs," and McGowan led an interracial meeting in 1926.[68] Despite these small signs of progress, McGowan had a difficult time recruiting federation leaders to her movement. She apparently had won the support of president Katherine Furman, who then resigned soon after. Although McGowan thought Furman's resignation a setback, McGowan resolved to approach the new president, Gertrude Magginis. Without the support of its leadership, the federation would not pursue such a controversial issue. A cross-listing of SCFWC officers throughout the 1920s with women noted as present at CIC meetings revealed only two women: Bessie Duncan, SCFWC chair of the arts committee from 1926 to 1929, and Bertha Munsell, chair of social and industrial conditions committee from 1919 to 1921.[69]

White clubwomen did support and lobby for the Fairwold Home for Delinquent Black Girls, although the Episcopal church and the CIC joined together to lead this effort. A committee led by Bishop Finlay and I. S. Leevy, a black merchant, included representatives from the SCFWC and other white women's organizations. Munsell, Nell Duncan Freeman, and Isabelle Cain, as chairs of the SCFWC's social and industrial conditions and public welfare committees, all endorsed Fairwold.[70]

Locally, clubs showed little commitment to the CIC. When McGowan invited the Perihelion Club to attend a meeting on interracial cooperation at the Chamber of Commerce, the club appointed a committee to attend and urged all members to do the same. Yet, despite their apparent willingness to attend McGowan's meeting, their minutes show them neither taking up any reform projects that aided the black community nor further indicating intentions of interracial cooperation.[71] The Amelia Pride Club also worked with black clubwomen when they voted to cooperate with other clubs in giving assistance to black clubwomen of Rock Hill, who were soon to entertain the South Carolina Federation of Colored Women's Clubs and wanted the white women to help them. A survey of minutes from fifteen clubs revealed only one other reference to interracial work (besides working against TB): the New Century Club had Mrs. Fisher show members handiwork done by black students at Booker T. Washington High School in Columbia, where Fisher was a trustee.[72]

Although they may have desired to keep interracial work silent and away from public view, federation, local clubs, and CIC documents still reveal little support from clubwomen for interracial work, especially in comparison to records of the Episcopal Woman's Auxiliary, which explicitly recorded its involvement. The striking contrast between churchwomen and clubwomen presents a reminder that, despite the obstacles, some level of interracial cooperation was possible if white women wanted to participate. Most women in the SCFWC apparently did not. This attitude is verified by black clubwomen, who claimed that the clubs always worked separately. No black woman interviewed recalled any cooperation between black and white women's clubs, except when white clubs in Orangeburg made arrangements with Wilkinson for black clubs to donate items to the poor house.[73] For white clubwomen in South Carolina, an emphasis on Southern identity prevented meaningful participation in the budding interracial movement. It would be difficult to work side by side with a member of a race one viewed as immoral and inferior at best. It was up to other women, primarily from church associations and the YWCA, to reach across the racial divide that clubwomen themselves had helped to strengthen.

One major barrier to progress was that black and white women were not bold enough to challenge segregation, and whites remained paternalistic.[74] The CIC meetings in Charleston were segregated by both race and gender. Blacks and whites sat on opposite sides of the room, and men and women met separately until 1931 to avoid having white women meet black men. Both black and white members went through elaborate lengths to maintain some level of separation even as they advocated cooperation. The Women's Committee was divided into white and black committees; however, these committees had identical subcommittees designed to work together. In addition, each race had six officers represented on the executive committee, "which meets in joint or separate sessions as needs may demand." Beyond the committee itself, support for the committee also had to be carefully organized. McGowan explained, "Because of the peculiarities of some people here," money donated to the CIC from the Charleston Community Chest had to be paid to her personally, and she would then turn it over to the CIC.[75] Like that coming from white clubwomen, such anonymous support, while helpful, was not enough to bring justice to blacks.

According to its critics, the committee was so ineffective that it could not even gain the approval of the Board of Education to allow both white and black students to enter an essay contest on "Negro Progress Since the Civil War."[76] For those critics, white willingness to discuss conditions for blacks in the state, while well-intentioned, was not enough to effect real change. Furthermore, Benjamin Mays feared that effective dialogue was not even taking place. He attended a meeting in 1925 as a guest of Marion Wilkinson. There he heard Jessie Daniel Ames, a white leader in the Association of Southern Women for the Prevention of Lynching, an offshoot of the CIC, who, he recalled, was considered liberal at the time. She said that the only way to advance the black child was to advance the white child two steps. Dissatisfied with her reasoning, he argued that even in the interracial meetings, blacks and whites did not converse.[77]

The attitudes of whites and blacks seemed most intractable. Rebecca Reid, a member of the state CIC, explained her frustration with locals in Sumter, South Carolina, to Jessie Ames in 1929. According to Reid, the way of thinking "is so subconsciously fixed, impregnated, deep-rooted, and is inculcated from babyhood." Lost Cause rhetoric helped solidify such a mind set. Reid seemed unsure of how to begin to make progress. "Discussion, except with a very few who catch a glimmer of light," she wrote, "is worse than useless. What the first step should be here, is a question that I have pondered deep in my heart. Please hurry on and lend a hand."[78]

The intransigence and racism of so many whites in the state made it difficult for blacks to know how hard to push: Would they achieve better results through a more accommodating stance, or were they required to be aggressive in their demands? In the Southern club movement, black women negotiated a middle ground, promoting industrial education at the same time they fought Jim Crow laws.[79] Yet, because Margaret Washington, Booker T. Washington's wife, and other more "conservative" women were leaders in the South, some conflict experienced in both the NACW and Southeastern was perhaps owing to tension between women who differed in their uplift strategies. Washington, like her husband, was careful in her work and avoided controversy. She wrote to Lugenia Hope, "We are moving along slowly. Somehow I feel we ought to go slow. Not long ago I was on the train coming South and heard an old Colored man say to another, "Brother if you want to go fer [sic] go slow.' I hope you agree with me that we ought to go slow or rather slowly."[80] One can almost hear the frustration with which Hope, a much more outspoken woman, read this letter.

Washington's caution came under fire when she was editing, printing, and paying for the *National Notes* at Tuskegee. Apparently some Northern women believed that she was also purging them of any discussion she (or her husband) considered too radical. Josephine Silone-Yates, a friend of Washington's from Missouri, queried Washington about why some women wanted a national magazine when the NACW could barely afford the *National Notes*. "Is it that they (?) think if the magazine is printed in the North," she asked, "there can be a wider discussion of some subjects that it might not be well to discuss at Tuskegee?" Yates, agreeing with Booker T. Washington's philosophy of racial uplift, argued that blacks needed to take advantage of opportunities rather than complain about discrimination.[81] Later, Ida B. Wells, an outspoken clubwoman from Chicago, proposed that the NACW elect an editor for the *National Notes* so that it would be published more regularly, but according to her, the proposal failed because no one was willing to find fault with Margaret Washington.[82]

Two years later, Yates clearly differentiated between a Northern and a Southern strategy. Noting black outcry against Thomas Dixon's book, *The Clansman*, Yates pondered with Washington whether to go "ranting and tearing around . . . or whether the quiet working, hammering away day after day wills a purpose in view . . . or whether both are needed." Yates declared herself to be a "quiet hammerer." She concluded that the South, like the West, requires "intensely practical workers," who cannot afford to spend their time quibbling over terms such as "Afro-American" versus "Negro" the way that women in the Northeast do.[83] Implicit in her conclusion is the understanding that by living in different circumstances, Northern and Southern women arrived at different solutions to race discrimination.

Charlotte Brown, a good friend of Washington's, was more complicated. Every inch a lady, Brown was concerned with appearances. She also depended on white benefactors for her school in Sedalia, causing Du Bois to complain once that Brown was too interested in her white heritage and her white friends, and that she "represent[ed] the white South."[84] However, Brown was well known for her impassioned address at the first women's interracial meeting in Memphis. Of the three speakers, she most brutally shared the experiences of black women's oppression with white women. When the printing of the resolutions was held up after the meetings, Brown disagreed with the conservative Margaret Washington.[85]

In Georgia, Lugenia Hope was outspoken, which her biographer attributes to her Northern background. Hope had already worked with white women like Jane Addams at Hull House, and as a result she was perhaps more frank. During the controversy over the statement written by the black clubwomen for the CIC, Hope wrote, "It is difficult for me to understand why my White sisters so strenuously object to this honest expression of Colored Women." Hope acknowledged that while she might be "over insistent," others were "too cautious."[86]

In South Carolina, the state federation can best be described as "moderate" in its approach to combating oppression and bettering race relations. Much of this was owing to Wilkinson's leadership. In Orangeburg, as the president of State College's wife, Wilkinson was well respected by whites. Her position and wealth protected her and some other families from feeling the effects of segregation to the same degree that most blacks in Orangeburg did. Her prominence extended to those who worked for her. Robert Evans recalled that if he walked into a store and asked to buy a suit on credit, he only had to say that he worked for Mother Wilkinson and he was able to purchase whatever he wanted.[87]

Even though she did not have to fight the same battles that ordinary black citizens faced daily, Wilkinson tried to do as much good as she could in her own way and was "still quite outspoken."[88] She was capable of being more aggressive in her rhetoric and actions. For example, she distributed copies of the December 27, 1925, issue of the *Crisis* report on education to the public schools and the superintendents so that whites "may see that the Negroes are fighting for full manhood rights."[89] This stance may have followed Wilkinson's relationships with Brown, McCrorey, and Hope, with whom Wilkinson was most intimate in the network of black clubwomen. She sided with them against Washington in favor of the stronger statement from black women at the CIC. "Like you," she wrote to Hope, "I cannot see where any self respecting, forward looking colored woman can object to one statement contained in our paper. There is nothing radical about it." Wilkinson asked who had objected to it, "for I do not wish to be unjust to anyone, but I feel this matter very keenly." Further, she informed Hope that she had decided to send out the uncensored statement to the white members of the state CIC, thereby "letting them know that it is the expression of the sentiments of the colored women of the South."[90] Her letter provides some evidence that Wilkinson and other blacks in the interracial movement, especially because of their wealth and elite status among blacks, must have resented the paternalism of whites. To hear even liberal white friends continue to stress that the races should remain separate and that blacks were "pathetically" grateful for white aid must have pained her. Rather than alienate those who were at least interested in the lives of blacks, however, Wilkinson and others tried to balance an appeal to white's paternalistic desire to aid blacks as well as to their sense of justice. Wilkinson understood that she had to be careful not to alienate those "sympathetic" to her cause. Wilkinson and the CIC had to walk a fine line; they demanded justice without asking directly for equality. The mixed record of the CIC hints at the intransigence of Southern whites when faced with the greater demands of the Civil Rights movement of the 1950s and 1960s.

Locally, black clubs also had to forge their own ways. Despite Marion Wilkinson's friendship with Margaret Washington, the state federation was barely six years old when Booker T. Washington died in 1915. By the 1920s the NAACP was growing in Charleston, Columbia, and other cities. Members of the state federation became involved in the Charleston NAACP's successful drive to gain black teachers in the black schools. Also in Charleston, the Phyllis Wheatley Club was composed of several members who belonged to the NAACP or came from families who did. This club openly supported Du Bois and the NAACP. The club sent birthday greetings to Du Bois and in 1930–1931 even received Du Bois as a guest at the birthday party of the club. Members also read a petition to collect money for the NAACP million-dollar antilynching campaign, to which "every member contributed one dollar to the cause," and supported improved railroad car conditions for blacks.[91] Other clubs in the federation and members, such as Lilian J. Rhodes, a superintendent at Good Samaritan Hospital, and Mrs. R. T. Brooks, who served on the executive committee of the Columbia branch, also supported Du Bois and the NAACP.[92]

African American clubwomen in the state tried to work within the CIC for better race relations. As a federation, the organization strongly condemned segregation and lynching. Ultimately, however, most of their projects concentrated on aiding those in the black community who were in need, especially girls, rather than on agitating for an end to discrimination. Aware of their "place" in South Carolina, black clubwomen moved cautiously. At the same time, white clubwomen persuaded themselves that they could best deal with the "Negro problem" by ignoring the presence of blacks in their community and denying the existence of black colleagues in the club movement. Under this approach, they were unable to bridge the parallel experiences of black and white clubwomen.

Despite this tactic, Southern black women took the lead in the interracial movement of the 1920s. In South Carolina, they approached the CIC with realistic expectations and achieved limited results. The success of black clubwomen's efforts at interracial work, therefore, is difficult to evaluate. They did not succeed at coalition-building with their counterparts in the white club movement, although they were more successful at reaching other church women through the CIC. In a racially conservative state like South Carolina, few blacks before World War II were willing to risk direct confrontation with whites. Even as black clubwomen differed over the best approach, they appreciated the spirit of the CIC and the willingness of those whites involved to hazard disapproval. At the same time, black clubwomen understood that they had to negotiate reasons, modify demands, and monitor rhetoric to retain white support. They took what they could from interracial cooperation and kept working to improve their condition in as many ways as they could; they valued self-reliance rather than white benevolence.

Black clubwomen's most significant claims to Southern identity came about because they did not believe the myth of the Lost Cause and because, as proponents of the interracial movement, they asserted their right to coexist with Southern whites. The inability of black and white clubwomen to work together on a sustained basis in the South caused difficulties when black and white Southern women joined national organizations.

1. Louisa Poppenheim

2. Louisa Poppenheim *(center)*, president of the South Carolina Federation of Women's Clubs and officer in the General Federation of Women's Clubs, in a 1949 pageant depicting the fiftieth anniversary of the founding of the Charleston City Federation of Women's Clubs. Courtesy of the General Federation of Women's Clubs—South Carolina, Special Collections, Winthrop University, Rock Hill, S.C.

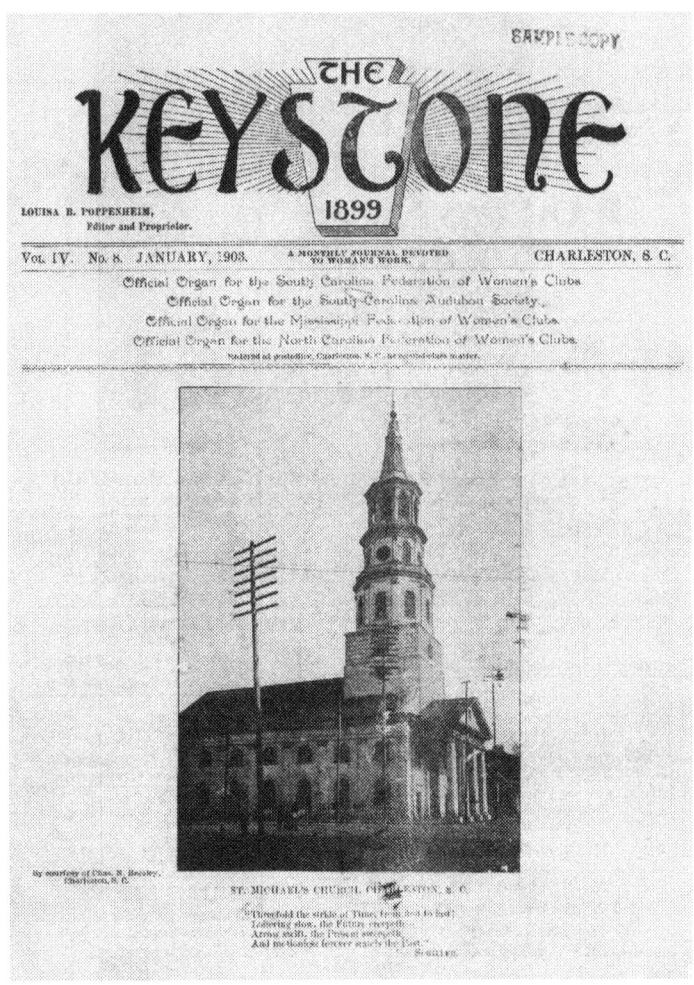

3. Mary and Louisa Poppenheim published the *Keystone* from 1899 until 1913, reaching thousands of clubwomen across the South. The *Keystone* included club news, editorials and articles on education, social reform, and Southern history and literature, as well as book reviews and recipes. Courtesy of the General Federation of Women's Clubs—South Carolina, Special Collections, Winthrop University, Rock Hill, S.C.

4. Leaders in the International Council of Women of the Darker Races: Marion Wilkinson *(front row, left)*, Mary McCleod Bethune *(front row, right)*, Jennie Moton *(back row, center)*, and Lugenia Burns Hope *(back row, right)*. Organized after World War I, the ICWDR's mission was to unite women of color around issues of racial justice and to promote African American history in schools. Courtesy of the Neighborhood Union Collection, box 14, folder 7, Atlanta University Center, Robert W. Woodruff Library, Atlanta.

5. The Marion Birnie Wilkinson Home for Girls, formerly known as Fairwold Home for Delinquent Girls, was one of the most important projects supported by the South Carolina Federation of Colored Women's Clubs in the 1920s. Marion Wilkinson visited the house on many occasions. Courtesy of the Johnette Edwards Papers, Special Collections, Winthrop University, Rock Hill, S.C.

6. Marion Birnie Wilkinson, the leading black clubwoman in the state, was president of the South Carolina Federation of Colored Women's Clubs and was active in the YWCA and the state Committee on Interracial Cooperation. She dedicated herself to uplifting African Americans, especially girls. Courtesy of the Johnette Edwards Papers, Special Collections, Winthrop University, Rock Hill, S.C.

Chapter 4

"Unity in Diversity"

South Carolina Clubwomen, the South, and the Nation

In 1927, a fellow South Carolina clubwoman accused Louisa Poppenheim, who had worked for so long to encourage Southern states to join the General Federation of Women's Clubs, of compromising herself and her state for the national body. Reluctant to challenge a General Federation stipulation that the member states support the national's policies, for a brief moment Louisa seemed willing to forgo the long-held South Carolina doctrine of states' rights. However, Lena Springs asked, "Do we, as South Carolinians, regardless of opinions and principles have to take orders from anyone?" Then Poppenheim remembered her heritage and quickly asserted, "I would be the last to take orders. We are South Carolinians. We will act as we please."[1]

Negotiating national concerns with local loyalties was fraught with tension for clubwomen in the South. For both black and white Southern clubwomen, the identity they worked so hard to solidify had implications for their relations with the rest of the nation. At the turn of the century they understood themselves to be members of the "Union" as well as the "Southern nation." Thus, their Southernness shaped their participation in the national women's clubs organizations: the General Federation of Women's Clubs (GFWC) for white women and the National Association of Colored Women (NACW) for black women. Despite the bonds women across the nation shared, sectional difference still marked their relationships. Yet, sectional identity did not override racial difference. Black and white Southern clubwomen each looked to Northern women of their own race, rather than to each other, for cooperation and inspiration.[2] More important, they judged themselves according to standards set by Northern women, who entered clubwork earlier and commanded greater resources.

The intensity of racial and economic oppression experienced in the South caused black Southern clubwomen to feel inferior in comparison to their Northern counterparts in the NACW, evident in an indepth study of the Southern and Southeastern Federations of Colored Women. For white Southern clubwomen, participation in the General Federation was part of their effort to rehabilitate a regional identity, necessary for the South to reconcile with the North on equal footing. Southerners understood that their presence at national meetings was another medium through which they could defend the region. Tension between white Southern women and the General Federation peaked during the controversy over admitting black women into the General, and friction lingered in Southern women's continued unwillingness to compromise state's rights. While Georgia and Kentucky were at the forefront of these episodes, the reaction of the South Carolina Federation of Women's Clubs illuminates just how deep the conflict ran. The experience of Southern clubwomen was subtly but significantly different from that of their Northern sisters.

DEFINING SOUTHERN IDENTITY FOR AFRICAN AMERICAN CLUBWOMEN

African Americans clearly rejected the Lost Cause; instead, they favored a history that focused on emancipation, American citizenship, and black pride. If white Southerners defined Southern identity around the Confederacy, did blacks in the region still consider themselves Southern? If they did not define their identity around the ideals of the Confederacy, how did they then define themselves as Southern? What did their Southern identity mean in the context of the national black women's clubs movement?

Black women in the South Carolina Federation of Colored Women's Clubs (SCFCWC) could wax rhapsodic about the South and South Carolina, just as white women did. They even claimed the symbol of the state, the Palmetto tree so often evoked by white clubwomen, in the state federation song, composed by Lizelia A. J. Moorer of Orangeburg. The song included the following chorus: "We are women of Palmetto, Loyal Women of Palmetto; By our labors in Palmetto, We are lifting as we climb." When Louise F. Holmes of Florence invited guests to the joint meetings of the State and Southeast Federations, her language used imagery common to the *Keystone*. For example, Holmes reminded her readers that "the palmetto and the pine beckons."[3] In 1920 Margaret Washington claimed Southern identity while speaking to white Southern women at the interracial meeting in Memphis. Such simple statements hid the subversive nature of their claims. For black women to emphasize their regional identity was to write themselves into the very history white Southerners had written them out of.

Yet, because they appealed to this imagery less often than white Southerners did, and because they criticized the region for its discrimination against blacks, the press sometimes accused African Americans of being anti-Southern. In response to one such accusation, the *Voice of the Negro* replied, "We are thoroughly and distinctly Southerners. By birth, by reading, by training, and by every tie of kinship we belong to this section. We love this great Southern country with all its golden glory. . . . We do love this land. It is revenge, murder, lynchings, lies, injustice we hate."[4] The *Voice of the Negro* claimed Southern identity for African Americans simply by virtue of having lived there for generations, building families and communities on the land. Blacks also belonged in the South because of the region's dependence on their labor in slavery and following the war. In one of several articles in the *Independent* by women on race relations, a black Southern woman wrote, "And when the Southerner says if we do not like the South, let us leave it, I answer him, we do like the South, it is our home. . . . The South, especially, is as much the black man's as the white man's; for every plantation, town and city shows the work of his hands."[5] Statements such as these indicate the depth of feeling that some blacks felt for their homeland.

Not all Southern blacks, however, embraced a specifically Southern identity. A descendant of charter members of the Sunlight club in Orangeburg recalled her mother and aunt; she argued that the isolation experienced in small towns in South Carolina prevented such a regional identity from forming. She believed that Sunlight club members instead focused their efforts on addressing local needs. According to her, such women defined themselves primarily as members of their local community and did not hear too much of what was going on in other towns of either the South or the nation.[6] Marion Wilkinson and her fellow leaders in the Southern black club movement strove to end this feeling of isolation. They tried to create communality in the region and with black women across the nation through both informal networks and the Southern and Southeast Federations of Colored Women's Clubs.

Wilkinson, part of this national network, became close friends with several of its members. This network included many wives of college presidents as well as heads of schools themselves. Because they shared common background, interests, and problems, these women supported each other and their work. They belonged to the same organizations, including the NACW, the YWCA, the Women's Commission on Interracial Cooperation (CIC), and the International Council of Women of the Darker Races (ICWDR).[7]

Wilkinson was primarily involved with the Southern network of reformers.[8] The most well known women included Lugenia Burns Hope, Mary McLeod Bethune, Charlotte Hawkins Brown, and Margaret Murray Washington. Other women in the Southern network included Mary Croswaithe, Jennie Moton, Mary McCrorey, Lucy Laney, and Janie Barrett. Also prominent among the Southern network were Nashville's Nettie Napier, president of the NACW and connected to Fisk University through her husband's membership on its board of trustees, and Maggie Lena Walker, founder of the St. Luke Penny Savings Bank of Richmond, Virginia.[9]

The only member of this group from South Carolina, Marion Wilkinson played a significant role in the network. She served as vice president of the International Council of Women of the Darker Races (ICWDR), which counted most leaders in the NACW among its members.[10] As the founder of the YWCA at South Carolina State College, Wilkinson was also involved in that national organization. She was a member of the committee convened by Lugenia Burns Hope to appeal to the national YWCA to gain greater control over black branches by allowing black women to oversee them in the South.[11] Finally, Wilkinson was one of seven in the black women's committee of the Commission on Interracial Cooperation (CIC). Because the white women's CIC had a seven-member committee, Charlotte Brown suggested that black women also have a seven-member committee, which consisted of Brown, Hope, Moton, Bethune, Washington, McCrorey, and Wilkinson.[12]

In the NACW, Wilkinson was vice president at large (1920–1922), parliamentarian (1914–1918), chair of the resolutions (1926–1928) and the domestic science (1912) departments, and a member of the advisory board (1928). She spoke several times at national meetings, offered the response to the welcoming address in 1922, and presided over several sessions. In her acceptance letter for the advisory board position, Wilkinson wrote, "I desire to express to you . . . my pleasure in serving as a member of the advisory board, in fact, the National is so much a part of my life, that I am willing to serve in whatever capacity they see fit to use me."[13] Her role could have been greater, but she withdrew from candidacy for chairmanship of the executive board in 1928, a move that Etta B. Rowe cited as proof of her humility. "So peculiarly sweet and delicate was her ambition," claimed Rowe, "that at a National Association meeting in Washington, when the crowd was yelling, 'make Marion Wilkinson President,' she declined with modesty in favor of Mary McLeod Bethune, giving as her reason that Mrs. Bethune had had far more struggles than she, lets [sic] honor her."[14]

Of the women in this network, Wilkinson was particularly close to Charlotte Hawkins Brown, Lugenia Burns Hope, Mary McLeod Bethune, and Mary Jackson McCrorey. Brown was frequently a guest at State College, and they sometimes traveled together. Wilkinson supported Brown in her work and congratulated her in a telegram after a speech, "We listened with interest. State College very proud of you. Feel that we are next to Sedalia in your affections."[15] Brown spoke at State College on numerous occasions, and asked Wilkinson, Bethune, and Nannie Burroughs to speak at the twenty-fifth anniversary of the Palmer School.[16] Marion also did not hesitate to ask Brown for her help. She asked Charlotte to place her daughter Lula for a year at Palmer, first writing that she wanted Lula to be under Brown's good influence to become a "full-fledged teacher," before more bluntly admitting that despite Lula's degrees from Oberlin and Columbia, she had no other job prospect because she was waiting to hear the results of the New York state teacher examinations. Following the death of her husband Robert, Marion thanked Brown for her love and support. "I can never make you know just what your friendship has mean[t] to me at all times," Wilkinson wrote, "but especially at the time of our sorrow when I so much needed you. Your thought, your love, your loyalty has strengthened and heartened me greatly, and made me feel as close to you as I would to a sister. Next year let us plan to see even more of each other. Come whenever you can. I want you to feel that in my home you have a place that is especially your own, and that the door is open wide at all times."[17] Friendships like that with Brown were meaningful because as a member of the same network, Brown understood completely Wilkinson's trials and triumphs working in women's associations.

Because of Wilkinson's relative isolation in Orangeburg, regular contact with friends in other states, especially those who lived in larger cities, sustained Wilkinson and provided her with inspiration to meet her own state's needs. She must have particularly appreciated the interaction with this network after moving to Orangeburg, which had a small black population and fewer black institutions than the larger elite population in Charleston.

Despite different personalities and approaches to race relations and the conflicts that these engendered, the network of Southern clubwomen was primarily one of mutual support and loyalty. In particular, the women associated with educational institutions all experienced constant stress over inadequate funding for their schools and colleges. Rather than competing with each other, they empathized and even financially supported one another. In 1920, Wilkinson wrote to Charlotte Hawkins Brown and updated her on the progress at State College. She indicated that they were having "building troubles." Despite having won an appropriation for building a new hospital, the college was unable to begin work on it because bricks and other building materials were in short supply. Despite the fact that each woman was fund raising for her own institution, each supported the other with token gifts. For example, Nannie Burroughs, founder of the National Training School for Women and Girls in Washington, D.C., and a leader in the Women's Auxiliary of the National Baptist Convention, and Mary McLeod Bethune both sent Brown money for the Palmer Institute.[18]

Because keeping clubs active and organized was difficult, especially given the rural nature of the South, Southern clubwomen counted on representatives from other states to encourage club participation. Prominent leaders had to look out for more states than their own. Margaret Washington warned Charlotte Brown to be alert in North Carolina. After a trip to Florida, she wrote, "I have just been down in Florida sounding the trumpet. You just have to keep after these to keep them at work. Do not let NC go to sleep."[19] Maintaining organization on so many levels—local, state, national and regional—proved nearly impossible. In 1920 Lugenia Hope wrote to Bethune to ask her to speak at a mass meeting planned to jumpstart the Atlanta city federation. "Our City Federation is not by any means thriving at this particular time," she worried. "I hope you will give this invitation your very careful consideration, as it will mean so much to us. Our work needs the very inspiration that you can give us." Bethune also lamented to Brown, "I am very much concerned now about our Southeastern meeting. . . . I feel this is a big job that we have to pull over, and that it is going to take concerted action and a consecration of motive to do it." Never one to give up, Bethune concluded, "I believe that working hand in hand, we will be able to do it, in a most efficient way."[20]

The NACW also recognized the need to foster Southern interest, especially in the early years of the Southern federation, before South Carolina and other states federated. NACW leaders visited the region to drum up interest in women's clubs. NACW president Victoria Earle Mathews and Elizabeth Carter made tours of the South in 1895 and 1912 respectively.²¹ In 1904, Josephine Yates asked Margaret Washington whether Southern states, including South Carolina, Tennessee, Arkansas, and Georgia, would start state federations. "Do you find workers from these states in the Southern Federation?" she asked. "Is there any way of arousing their interest?" She recommended to Margaret Washington that the national organizer, who was responsible for establishing new clubs, should be a Southern woman because other sections of the country were already well coordinated. Aware of the potential for distrust, she remarked that "a resident from the Southern section could do more satisfactorily than someone outside."²²

Furthermore, Wilkinson believed that it was crucial to expose clubwomen in South Carolina to these national leaders. Wilkinson brought leaders to the state, including Hallie Q. Brown, then president of the NACW, who spoke to a crowd of more than one thousand people in Orangeburg in 1923 on a tour that also included Georgia, Florida, South Carolina, Kentucky, and North Carolina. Brown reported on the contrasts in the South—the beautiful land and climate, and "vile" inhabitants, the great progress some had made, and the oppression that most African Americans still experienced. In response, she sounded the "clarion blast" to the women of the NACW to educate children there and thus begin to change conditions.²³

One of the best opportunities for South Carolina clubwomen to meet such prominent women was when the Sunlight Club and Orangeburg hosted a joint meeting of the State and Southeastern Federations. This meeting attracted Bethune, Hope, and Brown as well as host of South Carolina leaders to Orangeburg. One delegate said she would "never forget the masterful, intelligent, well-prepared women who came from all over the Southeast."²⁴ Delegates listened to speakers and socialized with guests. Wilkinson held a social at the president's home for delegates, members of the Summer School Faculty, and guests.²⁵ Wilkinson also brought in prominent black male speakers, including E. Franklin Frazier of the Atlanta School for Social Work and David Jones of the national CIC.²⁶ These speakers were influential. Mamie Fields credited a speech by Mary Church Terrell at the Mt. Zion A.M.E. Church in Charleston as inspiring Charleston clubwomen. She recalled, Terrell "brought the excitement to us.... The women hardly knew what to do when Mrs. Terrell got through speaking. We felt so stirred up, nobody wanted to wait till morning to pick up our burden again. Everywhere you might look, there was something to do."²⁷ Mary Bethune and Margaret Washington joined Terrell in South Carolina. When Terrell spoke to the Charleston Free

Kindergarten Association in 1912, she complimented them on their work and informed them about the accomplishments of other black women.[28]

Wilkinson and Bethune also encouraged clubwomen to travel when possible to the regional and national meetings of clubwomen. After the Sunlight club formed, representatives—among them, Wilkinson, Cora S. Boykin, Susie Butler, Lela Levy, L.A.J. Moorer, and Celia Saxon—attended their first national meeting in 1912, in Hampton, Virginia, and a group of delegates from South Carolina continued to represent the state at all NACW meetings.[29] Attending regional meetings provided clubwomen with role models. Mamie Fields responded to Bethune's invocation to "Go to the national meetings. . . . Meet the world. Know how people are in other places." According to Fields, Bethune instructed South Carolinians, some of whom came from rural areas, about behavior: "And, in case anybody didn't know how to do when they got to that part of 'the world,' she would go right ahead and give a lecture to everybody—for example, if the meal was going to be in many courses with many forks."[30] Because Bethune had been born in poverty herself and sent away to school at Scotia Seminary (where she encountered forks for the first time) Bethune understood how best to inspire other small town Southerners.[31] With the exception of Wilkinson, South Carolina women were never central figures in the national body, although they did hold minor offices, including the chairmanships of the illiteracy and the hospital departments.

Clearly these informal and formal national and especially regional networks helped draw Southern clubwomen out of isolation and into sustained contact with colleagues around the nation and the section. Because discrimination in the Jim Crow South was more severe than in the North, the regional networks were perhaps more influential. Southern clubwomen acknowledged their unique needs by organizing a regional federation of clubs affiliated with the larger NACW. In addition to her offices in the NACW and the State Federation, Wilkinson was also vice president and honorary president of the regional Southeastern Federation of Colored Women's Clubs (the Southeastern), founded in 1916.[32] The Southeastern revived the original Southern Federation of Colored Women (the Southern), which was organized in December of 1899 and dissipated sometime after 1905. A notice in the *National Notes* issued the call for a meeting in Montgomery, Alabama, on December 28–29, 1899, for Southern black women. Although no names were given, Margaret Washington, first president of the Southern, was probably the driving force behind it. The Southern was the first regional federation in the NACW, indicating that Southern women experienced stronger regional identity than other clubwomen.[33]

The first meeting was called with the following goals of regional cooperation: "First the object of this meeting is to bring together the Southern state organizers, so as to make in reality, what exists now only in name; well-rounded state organizations. Second in order to bring about a more perfect union in general among the Southern clubs. Third to arouse a closer acquaintance and more active sympathy among Southern women, with a view of extending the work on a broader base."[34] More than two hundred women from Alabama, Georgia, Tennessee, and Mississippi attended the conference. South Carolina clubwomen were not present at the original meeting, and their role in the Southern, if it echoed participation in the national organization, was probably minimal. The only clubs from the state listed in the *National Notes* before 1910, the Woman's League of Charleston and the Charleston Woman's Christian Temperance Union, had already been dropped from NACW club listings by then.

After the Montgomery meeting, the *National Notes* reported that Southern women believed that they were determined to meet the great and peculiar needs in the region. They were concerned primarily with morality and passed resolutions condemning excursions, alcohol, mob violence, and improper dressing. They promoted care for the sick and indigent, patronage of black businesses (especially those that employed women), and kindergartens.[35] At the Vicksburg meeting two years later, delegates again passed resolutions against "promiscuous" excursions and in support of temperance. Sessions focused on mothers, social purity, temperance, the influence of women teachers, the evils of excursions, and the unity of womanhood.[36]

By 1904, morality remained a focal point, although clubwomen shifted their emphasis to the home and family. Washington, underlining the Southern's work for mothers and children, cited industrial classes in sewing and cooking, day nurseries, kindergartens, reformatories, and an initiative to enlist the cooperation of teachers in reaching out to mothers to affect the home life. She also promoted a "home pledge," in which women promised to save money and buy a home within a specified number of years. Plans for the 1905 meeting, which never took place, featured the theme, "more homes (ownership) and better homes," with topics such as magazines in the home, keeping children from the street, and the mother's influence.[37]

The Southern Federation met annually, in Montgomery, Atlanta, Vicksburg, New Orleans, and Jacksonville, probably drawing most of its members from these lower South states.[38] It is not clear how many women joined the Southern. At the Vicksburg meeting, for example, only forty-nine delegates attended, although crowds of as many as one thousand were reported for open meetings.[39] The Little Rock meeting, scheduled for December 1905, was canceled because it came so soon after the NACW biennial in St. Louis, and evidence of the Southern disappears from the record after this date.[40] One reason for its demise may have been its struggle with organizational structure, as clubwomen debated whether clubs or individuals should join and whether the Southern and the Northeastern should join the NACW.[41] The Southern was open to any woman, even one without club affiliation. In 1905, Addie W. Hunton, then president, hoped that the need for the Southern would dissipate not when sectional differences ended, but when each state federation was well organized; Hunton hoped it would hark back to the original goals of the Southern.[42]

More than ten years later, Mary McLeod Bethune founded the Southeastern Federation with the call for a conference in Daytona, Florida, in 1916; she wanted to encourage more effective work to promote the welfare of the South and to increase interest and cooperation in the work of the NACW. North Carolina, South Carolina, Georgia, Florida, Mississippi, and Tennessee sent delegates. South Carolina, particularly well-represented, contributed two of the five speakers. Lilian Rhodes, of Sumter, and Marion Wilkinson spoke along with Charlotte Brown, Rebecca Stiles Taylor of Savannah and Edwina Thomas of State College, Georgia. Wilkinson was elected vice president-at-large under first president Bethune, who was originally from South Carolina.[43] Rebecca Taylor followed Bethune as president, from 1923 to 1927, when the Southeastern, like the Southern before it, became temporarily dormant until its revival in 1938 by Ora Brown Stokes and new president Bertha Johnson of Mississippi.[44]

The Southeastern had a fairly radical agenda for race uplift. In 1923, the Southeastern enumerated its most critical goals as follows: support of the Southeastern Inter-racial Committee, better educational facilities because of segregated schools, the end to Jim Crow cars and other forms of segregation, the end of the peonage system and reform in the Southern penal system, intensive voter registration of men and women, the privilege of serving on juries, the enforcement of the fourteenth amendment, the acquisition of justice in the courts and the end to lynching, and more access to military training.[45] The Southeastern's emphasis on the special problems blacks faced in the South is evident from this list. Of these goals, all but the last (and the general call for an end to discrimination in public places) applied primarily to the Southern states.

The intensity of oppression for African Americans in the region differentiated the Southeastern from the NACW. One daughter of a charter member of the Sunlight Club of Orangeburg believed that Southern women had to deal more with service to the needy than Northern women, because, although the problems were the same, the severity of the problems in the South was greater.[46] Addie Hunton also understood that Southern black women perceived themselves dramatically in the midst of the battlefield: "About them the air is surcharged with the smoke of battle. Around them they hear the threat-throbs and sighs of a people crying for light."[47] Moreover, she claimed that Southern women wanted NACW conventions to be held in the South, because, as one of the most successful weapons in defending black womanhood, they were most needed in the region where discrimination was greatest.[48] The pages of the *National Notes* and NACW records, as well as the papers of individuals, are replete with references to the belief that Southern blacks suffered the most from racial oppression and consequently needed the most help. Mary Bethune argued in a speech that the opportunity for service in the South was much greater than in the North because white Southerners were committed to "keeping the Negro in his place. That place, by all accepted teaching and belief, is and must be, for all time, an inferior one."[49] African American clubwomen knew that discrimination existed throughout the nation, but it was not unleashed with the same fury in the North as it was in the South.

Because of the nature of the conditions in the South, Southern black clubwomen understood that their role in uplifting the race was crucial. When Josephine T. Washington reported on the Southern Federation Meeting for *The Colored American Magazine*, she noticed that the most distinguishing feature of the federation was the seriousness of the delegates, as noted by a Northern woman. Washington explained, "The fault is not in ourselves, but in our stars—that we are weighted with care."[50]

Southern clubwomen did face challenges unique to them. For example, the Southeastern appealed to members to become active in the junior federation movement and establish junior, or girls' clubs, because in the South there were no Girl Scout troops for African American girls. Daisy Gordon Lowe, founder and president of the Girl Scouts, of Savannah, explained to Taylor that there were no black troops because Southerners would not allow both races in the same organization, although she denied her personal aversion to it, and because there were no trained leaders. Rather than tackling this discrimination head on, Taylor advocated instituting junior clubs; she reminded clubwomen that "a rose by another name is just as sweet." This example underscores how every move made by the Southeastern, although seemingly similar to those of clubwomen throughout the nation, had an urgency or a necessity not found elsewhere. Taylor explained, "Our National has touched the matter lightly because the situation is not as acute in all sections as it is in ours." She linked this movement to the movement for girls' reformatories, which the Southeastern supported.[51]

Owing to the severity of conditions in the South, however, Southern women needed the aid of Northern women, and Southerners knew it. They shared their needs with the national body through biennial conventions. Charlotte Brown gave a talk on the "Peculiar Mission of the Southern Negro" at the 1914 biennial. When the NACW convention met in Tuskegee in 1920, Southern women took the opportunity of meeting in the region to draw attention to their own situation. Talks on the South included "The Need of Community Centers in Southern Cities" and "Awakening of the Southern Woman to the Needs of Club Work." These addresses undoubtedly stressed both the great need in the section as well as the achievements of Southern clubwomen.[52]

Southern women, however, had to take care in how they presented themselves as unique at the NACW. To gain the much-needed aid that Northern women provided they carefully negotiated a relationship with Northern women, whereby they at once stressed both their similarities and their differences. Bethune wrote notes for a series of talks on "The Relations of Southeastern Federation to the National," in which she stressed that, despite the unique needs of Southern women (and consequent justification for the Southeastern Federation), the Southeastern's platform should conform to that of the National because *"we are one in spirit."*[53] Southern women then capitalized on their unique needs but common spirit, for example, in an appeal to Northern women to give to the NACW's education fund. They enumerated the differences in funding for black and white children in Southern states: South Carolina was cited as spending $5 for every black child and $60 for every white child. The Southern NACW members challenged Northern women, whose states "give so freely" to educate their own children, to give to the fund to aid Southern children.[54] Though all blacks walked a fine line between attention to the positive progress made and attention to the problems still existing, Southerners had to be even more careful. As the *National Negro Digest* special issue on education in South Carolina noted, they had to "overlook the ugly and bloody things (at least for the moment)" and instead honor those who were making a difference.[55] The editors presented their study of educational progress in South Carolina, a state admittedly near the bottom of the country in black literacy, as a corrective to more common tales of discrimination, violence, and the Klan. Southern clubwomen did the same; they carefully drew attention to their successes—and their continued needs.

Despite the efforts of leaders in the South to increase sectional participation in the NACW and Northern attempts to welcome them, antagonism still marked the relationship between Southern and Northern black clubwomen. The supposed inferiority of Southern women was most often at the root of this conflict. Southern white clubwomen also experienced tension and supposed inferiority in the General Federation of Women's Clubs. Both black and white women formed clubs and federations several years later than in the North. Common sentiments—such as, "In the South, where movements for reform work more slowly than at the North" —applied equally in an article about assessing black kindergartens or one detailing the efforts of white women.[56] In response, white Southern women emphasized pride in their section through a stronger embrace of the Lost Cause. Black women did not have this option.

The South hosted only one of the first twelve NACW conventions, in Nashville, in 1897, and produced few officers, with the notable exceptions of Washington and Bethune.[57] Southern black women undoubtedly were insulted by the low attendance at the Nashville meeting, blamed on yellow fever outbreak and the belief that Northern women stayed home rather than ride Jim Crow railroad cars into Nashville. When the 1920 meeting was held in Tuskegee, seventeen Pullman cars were arranged to bring delegates to Alabama without Jim Crow conditions. At that same meeting, Marion Wilkinson gave an address in which she described "the part the woman of the South had played in the development of the National Association."[58] Whether or not Wilkinson also addressed Southern women's unique needs as she outlined their contributions to the NACW has not been preserved.

Jim Crow laws were not the only things separating Southern and Northern clubwomen. Geraldine Zimmerman, a clubwoman from Orangeburg, contended that Northern women caused problems with their snobbery.

"Southern women did not think of themselves as different," she contended, "but Northern women did." Southern black women believed that Northern black women saw them and their work as inferior, she continued, "in lifestyle, finance, and maybe in education and social graces." This perceived snobbery infuriated Southern women who thought that they were equal and knew that they had decent homes despite the popular misconception in the North. According to her, "Southerners got real angry. They had to prove themselves to Northern women." She recalled that her mother resented the fact that Northerners saw themselves as missionaries.[59] Such a condescending attitude would have been particularly galling, especially when considering the elite status that these clubwomen held in their own communities.

Southern black women reacted differently to suggestions of their inferiority. Although even Margaret Washington recognized the gulf between sections, she tried to assuage their fear by reminding them of the aid Northern women had already given. She admitted, "Many women in the South . . . are inclined to mistrust the interests of their Northern club sisters." Rather than dwelling on the distrust, she reassured Southerners that "there are many whose efforts cannot be doubted for one moment, for from the very beginning of our career as organized club workers . . . certain Northern women have stood always bravely in the front . . . [and] have never tired of working to bring our cause before the country and to insist upon the recognition of other colored women less fortunate than themselves." Despite Washington's best intentions, surely some Southern middle-class clubwomen resented the reference to themselves as "the less fortunate."[60]

Because of their supposed inferiority, for some women Southern identity was "more like an apology" that could be used to either excuse or justify lack of achievement rather than to inspire women to achieve more. Zimmerman thought that Southern women offered their Southernness as an excuse because not only did they lack the amount of money that Northern women had at their disposal but they also faced far more hostile race relations; thus, struggling Southern black women could claim, "We can't do this because we're in the South."[61]

Other women responded with the opposite attitude: they were inspired to work harder, to try to catch up, and to prove their equality. Mamie Fields called on Southern women to actively support their region because the Northeast and Northwest were more progressive; Fields sought to inspire competition by citing examples of the women's prowess in club houses, day care, libraries, and so on.[62] Women in the Northeast did surpass the South in many programs; for instance, by 1927 a top priority in the Northeastern was building club houses, but in the South women were still focused on building girls' homes and reformatories.[63] Southerners had to do what they could within the confines of their section. Josephine T. Washington quoted a delegate at the Southern meeting, "I don't know much, but I do what I know." For Fields, national leaders from the region were crucial in enabling Southern black women to make progress because they understood their plight. Fields was inspired by Mary Bethune:

> At the same time, being a Southerner, Mrs. Bethune never talked through her hat at you, the way some people will who don't understand what's what. If she said do this or do that, you knew that you were listening to a lady who had stood up to the selfsame thousand fights, large and small, that made up our barriers in the South. So we understood each other. She didn't have to tell us what went into doing the things that she did. We didn't have to tell her what it was that would discourage you from day to day. "I know, but nevermind," that was her message for us, even before she spoke.[64]

Like Bethune and Fields, Rebecca Taylor constantly tried to motivate Southern clubwomen by writing fiery editorials for the *National Notes* and the *Southeastern Herald*. Her columns indicate that she was not ashamed of the acute nature of the difficulties facing Southern blacks; rather, she challenged Southern black women to work harder to confront those difficulties and simultaneously reminded Northerners of their duty to aid the South in its struggles. Without minimizing problems, Taylor's rhetoric worked to convince Southern clubwomen that problems could be surmounted, that the Southeastern could "wage a MIGHTY BATTLE until the WALLS OF SOUTHERN PREJUDICE come tumbling down. IT IS POSSIBLE."[65] Such a positive attitude was necessary because of the magnitude of oppression that they faced.

The experience of Southern black clubwomen was significantly different from that of Northern women. Southern identity for black women was not a matter of asserting pride, tradition, and honor to a past way of life, as it was to white women, but rather a complex tangle of positive and negative associations. Black women rejected the Lost Cause in favor of an emphasis on American citizenship and racial identity. Although on occasion they proudly claimed the South because of their history there, they also sometimes equated Southern with inferior. This perceived subordinate status caused tensions within the NACW and inspired the need for their own regional federation, which recognized their unique conditions.

WHITE SOUTH CAROLINA CLUBWOMEN AND THE GENERAL FEDERATION OF WOMEN'S CLUBS

White women, too, fought to prove themselves on the national level through their participation in the General Federation of Women's Clubs. Like black women, they at times felt inferior, and their records consistently assert their place in the national. Thus the story of white South Carolina clubwomen and their national federation, like that of black Southern clubwomen and the NACW, is at once a coexistence of national and regional identity in a sometimes uneasy, sometimes unequal, relationship.

The Lost Cause that white clubwomen celebrated along with the United Daughters of the Confederacy was as much about remaining a people apart as it was about reconciliation. Many proponents of the Lost Cause understood that the South could not be a separate political nation, and they sought to rejoin the Union—but on their own terms.[66] They believed that they had to honor Southern culture first, so that they would be reconciled on equal footing, rather than as inferiors. While participation in the Spanish American War and World War I allowed men to prove their loyalty to the United States without abandoning their heritage, so too women joined national organizations without sacrificing their unique identity.

The General Federation of Women's Clubs began to reach out to Southern women by the late 1890s. In 1895 the executive council held its meeting in Atlanta, and the third biennial was held in Louisville in 1897. Southern clubwomen hoped to showcase the progress that they had made at the meetings. Addresses such as "Southern Women in Organized Work" and "Advantages of Club Life for Southern Women" acknowledged achievements at the same time they stimulated the development of new clubs.[67] Just as African American clubwomen received inspiration from national organizers, the Atlanta meeting resulted in the formation of the Atlanta Women's Club and the Georgia Federation of Women's Clubs. Atlantan Rebecca Lowe's election to the presidency of the General was perceived as a great honor to Atlanta, to Georgia, and to the South as a whole. The Atlanta newspaper praised her own club, the Atlanta Women's Club, as the "the leading organization of Southern women" while Louisa Poppenheim proudly noted Lowe's position in the *Keystone*: "The president is a Southern woman, Mrs. Lowe, of Atlanta, and she has been commented upon by all, especially the men, as being the most wonderful presiding officer ever known."[68] Further, both Southern and Northern women explicitly acknowledged that the General Federation's motto, "unity in diversity," linked the two regions and stressed reconciliation and union.

Despite these good intentions, however, Southern clubwomen who belonged to the General Federation had a chip on their shoulder. They consistently had to defend themselves and their work to the national body. Southern clubs and state federations generally formed ten to twenty years after those in the North. As in other cases of perceived sectional problems, Louisa Poppenheim justified this delay because of their impoverished state following the war and the fact that the South was "hampered by a large, ignorant negro population."[69] The Poppenheims were quick to point out that the SCFWC overcame these setbacks. They realized that their successes—such as in building up the number of libraries in South Carolina—came about despite the conservative atmosphere in the state. "That this federation has proven itself active and progressive is apparent from the results of its work," the Poppenheims wrote. "That its members are conservative at times is but a proof of their knowledge of local conditions."[70] To prove their equality, the Poppenheims compared the South to the North. The *Keystone* editorials and reports on biennial conventions of the GFWC always proudly noted the activities of Southern women, for example, by naming each officer or presenter from their section at the biennials.[71]

The Poppenheims promoted Southern regional successes, rather than limiting themselves to South Carolina's achievements. The GFWC, as a national federation, promoted individual state pride through state badges, songs, and other marks of distinction. South Carolinians exhibited this pride, but they also focused on the region as a whole. Nothing Southern escaped the Poppenheims' attention. They even believed Southern accents should be a point of pride, exhorting Southerners to pass on "that gentleness of speech." Their loyalty to the region despite membership in the GFWC was unmistakable. On the seventh anniversary of the *Keystone*, the Poppenheims declared, "Our influence is pledged first for the South with its ideals, its principles, and its traditions; then for the highest and best in American life."[72] Clearly Southern identity came before national identity.

Clubwomen's need to assert that the Southern states were "keeping up" with the rest of the nation explains the process of reconciliation with the North, which the Confederate celebration eventually promoted. Before Southerners could rejoin the nation, they had to prove themselves on equal footing with the rest of the country. The Lost Cause, while focused on regional identity, was necessary before the region could embrace a nationalism beyond their region. Although members of the United Daughters of the Confederacy came from forty states, it was primarily a sectional organization. The clubwomen of South Carolina, as members of the GFWC, participated in a national organization more so than the United Daughters of the Confederacy ever could. To participate as equals, clubwomen had to promote pride in the South, in its history, character, and economic progress.

Therefore, they participated in the national federation explicitly as Southern women. Poppenheim reminded her readers that Southern women brought distinctive characteristics to the General Federation biennial, including their ideals of manhood and womanhood. In addition to their unique character, they also shared a common experience. At the 1908 biennial, presidents from South Carolina and Florida held a conference of Southern clubwomen on education and organization, a move that featured the commonality of their problems and solutions, which they were unable to discuss in the general meetings.[73]

Yet Southern clubwomen also realized that they had to participate in the GFWC to help Northerners understand conditions in the South. Despite the hostility lurking in the Lost Cause, clubwomen, perhaps more than the UDC, understood that GFWC membership was yet another vehicle through which to portray the South accurately to the nation.[74] Mary Poppenheim attempted to share Southern culture with the General as chairman of the literature department. She led the literature session at the 1908 biennial, where she planned for Olive Tilford Dargan, a Southern poet, and Thomas Nelson Page, the well-known Southern author, to speak.[75]

In a speech to the SCFWC, as a representative of the GFWC, Louisa Poppenheim explained to her audience, "The Southern Club woman is busy at home, but she has need of the General Federation, and the General Federation has need of her." She then described the exchange possible between Southern clubwomen and their Northern sisters. Although they shared club ideas, in the case of Southern women, these were "modified by Southern inheritance, Southern environment, and Southern home training." What did the Southern woman gain? "In return," Poppenheim argued, "she is receiving from other sections a broadening of her sympathies, and that inspiration which comes from the esprit de corps found in any organization devoted to high and noble ideas of living."[76] Through the *Keystone* the Poppenheims promoted the attendance of Southern women at the GFWC's Biennials. Reconciliation was possible: they participated in the national federation. Yet their participation was only possible within the context of a sectional identity. Such a negotiation of the South and the nation was evident, even in the UDC: following a convention held in the nation's capital, the Daughters proclaimed themselves to be both, "no less Confederate and far better Americans."[77]

South Carolina white clubwomen, like their black counterparts, therefore believed that their experiences (and, for white women, character) were substantively different from those of Northerners. Because of the seemingly unbridgeable racial divide, each race's relationship to the national body, rather than their relationship with each other, served as a point of reference for them. Southern women's relationship to women of the North produced in both black and white Southerners some sense of inferiority or defensiveness. This feeling is pervasive even though inherent bonds of friendship and interests among women linked them with other women across the nation. Many Northern white women shared the racist assumptions that guided Southern women, even as certainly some Southerners were undoubtedly more racially liberal than some Northerners. The support of Louisa Poppenheim, Marion Wilkinson, and other Southerners for the GFWC and the NACW shows that the tension did not keep Southerners out of the national body, but it did shape their experiences within it.

SEGREGATING THE GENERAL FEDERATION

The most significant problem for Southern white women in the GFWC was the prospect of racial integration of the national body. It ultimately remained segregated to appease Southern white women, but the debate and ensuing compromise exposed the dangers that Southern white women faced when they joined a national organization. Press coverage in clubwomen's own publications and in black and white newspapers reveals how clubwomen explicitly and implicitly supported segregation and hoped to deny black claims to equality. Most significant, the controversy shows how race was at the heart of white Southern women's self-understanding.

Between 1900 and 1902 the General Federation of Women's Clubs debated whether to admit black women. The dispute began over the seating of Josephine Ruffin, an African American from Massachusetts, at the 1900 Biennial. Ruffin traveled to Milwaukee as a delegate from the black Woman's Era Club, as well as to represent the predominately white New England Woman's Press Club and the Massachusetts state federation. General Federation President Rebecca Lowe, of Atlanta, admitted the

Woman's Era Club before she realized it was a "colored club." Lowe quickly had the board of directors delay formal recognition of the club by returning their dues and "laying upon the table" a decision on their admission. Ruffin was offered a compromise, that she represent the white Press club, but not the Woman's Era, which she refused on principle. The board of directors ultimately delayed a decision concerning the Woman's Era Club status until the following biennial to be held in Los Angeles in 1902.

In Milwaukee, Lowe and others in the federation used many different tactics to quash the controversy over Ruffin. While Southern delegates caucused and declared their intent to secede should Ruffin be admitted to the convention, the Massachusetts delegation met outside the hall to frame their demands that Ruffin be admitted. Ultimately neither group was allowed to speak on the convention floor. The General Federation's newspaper, called *The Club Woman*, reported that "the color question, about which so much has been said and written, was not allowed to come up on the floor for discussion, owing partially to Mrs. Lowe's tactful guidance and statesmanship, and partly to the efforts of the Massachusetts's delegation, who desired harmony and peace with all their hearts." *The Club Woman* understated the situation and admitted only the most minimal controversy: "Of course there was a lively interest in the case and much discussion of it outside the meetings, but fortunately it was not allowed to come up on the floor."[78]

In reality, Lowe's "tactful guidance and statesmanship" involved some deft maneuvering. The committee on credentials, which at previous biennials had identified each delegate by name, only reported the number of delegates, preventing Massachusetts clubwomen from protesting Ruffin's omission. Furthermore, they unexpectedly gave their report in the morning, instead of the afternoon, while the Massachusetts clubwomen were apparently not in the convention but meeting outside to write their protest. Southern delegates, who had threatened to secede from the General Federation if African Americans joined, saw nothing comic about these tactics; in fact, they considered them vital. Annie Johnson, president of the Georgia Federation, took issue with Northern newspaper reports that spoke of "the idle threats of the southern women." Southern women, she claimed, were neither making idle threats nor acting in the heat of the moment; instead, they were acting with "cool determination" and "conviction" and would stand firm in their decision to resign should a decision be made to admit black women. Furthermore, Johnson offered as proof of their seriousness the fact that "the two leading officers of the Georgia

Federation were never absent from a business meeting at the same time, in order if one was not present to protect the southern women at home whose interests they represented the other would be, and these two officers were women of northern birth."[79] These incidents reveal the lengths to which white clubwomen went to guard the doorway to the GFWC and bar African American women.

Following the contentious Milwaukee biennial, clubwomen across the nation continued to debate the issue for the next two years. Georgia and Massachusetts, the home states of Rebecca Lowe and Josephine Ruffin, were at the forefront of the controversy. Each desired that the federation make an explicit law concerning the color line: Georgia wanted to declare that only white clubs and white women could join the General, while Massachusetts wanted to ensure that the General Federation did not use race as a qualification for membership. Georgia proposed to safeguard against integration by no longer allowing state federations to join; instead, by retaining individual club memberships the national organization could specify that those clubs be composed of white members.[80] The state forwarded a notice to the board of directors that claimed Georgia would propose such an amendment to the constitution at the next biennial and declare that "clubs desiring to join the General Federation of Women's Clubs must be composed of white women and must show that no sectarian or political list is required for membership." Furthermore, Georgia requested that due to "the importance of this matter and that fact that upon the outcome of it will hinge the integrity of the Federation the Georgia delegates respectfully request that the Board will during the ensuing two years refrain from admitting any other colored club to membership, and that it will require the club of colored women now in the Federation to withdraw."[81] Massachusetts, however, proposed eliminating individual club memberships and having only state federations belong. In this scenario, black clubs could join a state federation and thus indirectly belong to the General. Ironically, Massachusetts took a position in favor of "states' rights"; thus, individual state federations could decide whether to allow or disallow black women to join, even as Southern states looked to the national to enforce segregation.[82]

In February 1902, three months before the Los Angeles biennial, representatives from Georgia and Massachusetts met in the parlor of the New York home of Caroline Granger, Georgia Federation of Women's Clubs president, to forge a compromise: clubs that were members of their state federations were eligible to membership in the General, but, to satisfy the Southern states, the membership committee and the Board of

Directors of the General retained the ultimate power to accept or reject clubs. Therefore, even if a state federation admitted a black club, that club would still have to be approved unanimously by the membership committee.[83] The compromise, which passed overwhelmingly, was widely recognized at the time as a victory for the Southern delegates by enabling de facto segregation to continue.[84]

Although one might think white Southern clubwomen would have triumphantly announced the South's victory, in at least one regional clubwomen's periodical there was little gloating. Virtually no discussion of the issue reached the Poppenheims' *Keystone*. Although the compromise was meant to mollify the section, the Poppenheims chose not to draw attention to the controversial matter. Southern clubwomen had several reasons for downplaying the episode. Mary Poppenheim believed that too much press coverage of the controversy drew attention away from the good accomplished by clubwomen. In a letter instructing Louisa on how to cover the biennial for the *Keystone*, she wrote Louisa that "the papers give small notices each day but the political situation is all they consider." She complained that the general press had "lost sight of the vast educational, philanthropic, civic and economic issues unsolved aside from the wonderful value of such a gathering in unifying the interest of the *homes* of *America*. . . . The idea for national unity is too fine to be lost and if the Federation splits make more of the value of these meetings as uniting the country." She concluded by admonishing Louisa, "It is a fine idea and you must use it in your report for the *Keystone*. The Club papers have a chance now for fine effects for the Daily press is not grasping the ethical value of the movement."[85] Mary thus argued that it was the responsibility of the *Keystone* and other papers published by the clubs themselves to draw attention away from race issues and toward the achievements of clubwomen. Sarah J. Hagan, writing for the *Atlanta Constitution*, also claimed that newspapers had tried to stir up sectionalism where there was none.[86] The Poppenheims clearly wanted to avoid articles like an editorial that ran in the *Norfolk Dispatch*, which blamed Ruffin for interrupting the proceedings in Milwaukee. "Mrs. Ruffin's determined but unsuccessful invasion erased the whole program, and reduced the session to an hysterical squabble over a thoroughly insignificant matter," the editorial complained.[87] Concern over press coverage was strong because the propriety of women's clubwork was still controversial. In the South, suffragists and clubwomen alike had to be careful not to jeopardize their work with accusations of racial integration.

Some Southerners may have also downplayed the conflict because the compromise itself, like laws passed by Southern state governments to disenfranchise black voters, did not explicitly mention race, and Southerners may have believed it better to carry out the color line quietly than to continue to draw attention to it. The New Century Club of Columbia, in its decision not to take action on the better servant movement, declared, "it was decided that at the time it was best to take as little notice of the negro as possible—less said soonest mended."[88] By refusing to acknowledge the situation, the white Southern clubwomen sought to make it disappear; but, more significant, their decision would not legitimize the very desire of black women to be included in the General Federation. When Ludie M. Coleman submitted South Carolina's report to *The Club Woman* in December of 1901, she focused primarily on the federation's achievements. Coleman, however, did address the race controversy: "The color question which has caused so much comment and which has agitated so many clubs north of us, has failed to arouse even a passing interest, with the real problem of how and where shall it all end, here in our midst; its proximity possibly making us apathetic as to what other sections may do. The disposition of our clubs appears to be to await developments feeling that we can safely trust the true hearted and wise women who projected the great sisterhood that united us in the cause of humanity." Coleman could afford to be disinterested because she knew that if the wise women of the General Federation did admit black women, South Carolina would withdraw. There was no need for debate in South Carolina; they knew their position quite well. Coleman explained, "It is our purpose to have a representation at the biennial that will vote 'agin it,' for we know that the time has not yet arrived, for assimilation such as would follow the admittance of colored clubs into the Federation. With another century of civilization between the Negro and barbarism such assimilation may be possible, but hardly probable in all parts of the United States."[89] Coleman's disaffected tone in this case seems to come from the sense that integration was impossible, so unimaginable, that there was no need for undue excitement. It simply could not happen.

For these reasons, there were no references to the race question at the Milwaukee Biennial in the *Keystone*. Between the Milwaukee and Los Angeles biennials, the only three references to color and the GFWC were a brief comment from the Laurens, South Carolina, Women's Club that they were interested in the question, a report from the Kentucky Federation, which stated that it would vote against black women joining, and a notice in an editorial that the Illinois Federation chose not to discuss the matter at its 1901 convention, which underscored the editors' belief in the wisdom of an imposed silence.

Following the Los Angeles Biennial where the compromise was approved, the Poppenheims were scarcely less reticent. B. S. Childs stated in the convention report, "We had anticipated some excitement when a lady from Missouri introduced a motion to admit the Negro Clubs in the Federation, but a very strong feeling of opposition was soon realized, without much argument, and the vote was cast strongly against."[90] Louisa Poppenheim was even briefer in her comments on the biennial in the *Keystone*. She simply wrote, "The color question was settled to the satisfaction of all." Furthermore, she smoothed over the situation by adding that, "The mixing of Southern and Northern delegates is breaking down sectional prejudices."[91]

More than thirty years later Poppenheim candidly revealed her role in the matter in a SCFWC history published in the *State*. "I was authorized to go as a delegate to the Milwaukee biennial of 1900," she wrote, "with the understanding that if any Negro Clubs were admitted to the General Federation, for South Carolina to withdraw at once." Poppenheim continued by explaining her state's reaction to the decision. She added, "This was a grave question at that time as a club with negro members had applied for membership. The Southern leaders at Milwaukee had many conferences on this vital subject, but, much to our joy and relief, the Negro clubwomen were not admitted, so South Carolina could remain in the Great General Federation. The question was settled for all time."[92] Despite this admission, at the time, Poppenheim publicly downplayed the "gravity" of the situation.

Locally, interest in the controversy must have been high, although few clubs left written statements concerning their views. The Amelia Pride Club recorded their reaction with a comment in their minutes, "We were glad that the Black woman was bounced at the Women's Fed."[93] Although the New Century Club of Columbia did not make any similar observations in its minutes on the Los Angeles Biennial, its members did not approve of interracial gatherings. In 1913 the secretary noted "a great deal of discussion" on a proposed Home-Keepers Association. The New Century Club went "on record as opposing a mass meeting before a conference with representative negroes."[94] Certainly they would not have approved of the presence of black women at the biennial.

Yet in comparison to the reluctance of the editors of the *Keystone* to discuss the issue, the local press had a field day. Black and white newspapers across the country reported extensively on the situation, including Columbia's *State*, which revealed, "The attitude of the board of directors toward the color question, though supposed to be strictly secret, has leaked out. They have decided not to take the color question from the table and if it comes before the convention it will be an independent motion." This decision forced Southern states to join forces behind such a motion. According to the report, "This attitude has induced Georgia to be more aggressive and this morning after the Southern states had caucused and decided to stand shoulder to shoulder in their determination not to countenance colored clubs, every delegate found in her mail box a big circular headed: suggestions from Georgia to the delegates."[95] After airing the situation, the *State* then published an article on the local Elks meeting, in which the Elks "gridironed" the SCFWC with a play mocking women's clubs. The satire included a Mr. William Elliot, Jr., who "made a great hit in presenting in negro dialect the claims of the negro women's clubs for recognition." Men laughed because they believed their wives would never socialize with black women in the club setting. They either were unaware of the possibilities for cooperation in reform projects or knew that their wives for the most part rejected this scenario as well. Elsewhere sectional newspapers supported the compromise and the position of Southern delegates. These papers did not hesitate to gloat over the Southern victory.[96] Because at the time newspapers and many white Southern men, in general, did not take clubwork seriously, the controversy did not seem to seriously threaten white supremacy; thus, newspapers could afford to publicize and even laugh about the unrealistic possibility. For women, however, the affair was much more grave.

In comparison, an article printed in the *State* reported by a clubwoman, A. L. Robertson, president of the Columbia Art League, reflected the attitude of the Poppenheims: "Even the question of admittance of colored clubs was disposed of by a good natured tilt and compromise between Massachusetts and Georgia, and left where it was before, and where it will not do us of the South any harm. The newspaper and sensationalists tried in vain to get up an undue excitement on the subject but every body was in too good a humor to enter into any bitter political discussions."[97] Like Poppenheim, Robertson emphasized the "friendly" nature of the discussions, rather than the Southern states' threat to withdraw from the General Federation.

The General Federation's publication, *The Club Woman*, did not fear discussion of the controversy but instead introduced a new column called the "Open Arena" for clubs to submit their views.[98] Southern clubs were united in their desire to keep the General Federation all white. The Alabama editor suggested that clubwomen everywhere read *Southern States of the American Union* and *The Civil History of the Confederacy* by Southerner J.L.M. Curry; the suggested reading provided a means to educate Northern delegates before they voted. Not all women were so subtle, however. Those at the front line, from Georgia, were especially vocal in defense of their "benevolent" views: not only did black women have their own organizations, but also Southern whites knew what was best for blacks. In an echo of a common argument, Caroline Granger claimed that blacks were loyal and capable of much good; however, blacks also wished to be separate as much as whites did. She and others noted the existence of the National Association of Colored Women as the appropriate organization for Ruffin. Granger concluded, "It would be too bad to ask the colored women to take a secondary place, as they would, in our clubs, and it would be a shame to take away from the colored federations the best and most cultured among their women." Granger's logic was based on the unquestionable assumption that black women would have to be "secondary," not equal. Further, she erroneously assumed that black women would want to leave the NACW once allowed into the GFWC.[99]

As proof of the fact that they had the best interests of African Americans at heart, Georgia reminded her Northern sisters that Southerners were "most active in the bettering of the condition of the race" by providing assistance with moral, religious, and educational training. Many white Georgia clubwomen did support kindergartens for black children, ironically, with the financial assistance of the Woman's Era among other Northern clubs.[100] Rebecca Lowe and Mrs. John K. Ottley, the Georgia Federation secretary, paid the expenses for Alice Carey, an African American woman from Georgia, to travel to Montgomery, Alabama, for the Southern Federation of Colored Women's Clubs meeting in 1900 to promote kindergartens for black children throughout the South. Carey, who became chair of the Southern's kindergarten committee, returned to Atlanta and started a kindergarten with funds from Lowe and Ottley among others. This was important to swaying the vote of many Northern clubwomen. According to a report by Louisville delegates, Ottley "turned the tide" when she spoke on social conditions in the region, including kindergartens for black children.[101] Echoing Mary's emphasis on the good achieved by women's clubs, the *Woman's Journal* pointed out that, while it deplored the prejudice shown by Southern clubs, Lowe had done much for black kindergartens, and Southern women's clubs had performed good in other areas and so should not be roundly condemned.

Yet in assisting with kindergartens, the white women donated funds and helped funnel aid from Northern clubwomen, but they themselves did not teach the children. Mrs. Frank P. Gale, general manager of the kindergarten league of Georgia, and Mrs. L. M. Gordon, who "pledged . . . to undertake the work of morally training the negro children of the South" both stated that they would not teach the children. According to a newspaper report, an unidentified supporter said, "The theory is beautiful and simply grand, but I would not be suited to the task of teaching the negro children. I would not teach them, for I do not believe I could permit myself to do so under any circumstances. It would be lowering myself."[102]

This points to the crucial reason that white Southerners provided against the admission of black clubs: it promoted social equality between the races. The biennial meeting of the GFWC included meals and social functions as well as business meetings, and white Southern women loudly protested the possibility of black women dining or socializing with them. Although Lowe aided black women in kindergarten work, she established clear limits to her relationships with them. Using a narrow definition of friendship at best, Rebecca Lowe noted that she had worked with black women to establish kindergartens for black children and claimed that they "are all good friends of mine. I associate with them in a business way, but, of course they would not think of sitting beside me at a reception or of standing with me on the platform at a convention." Her colleague, Annie Johnson, a transplanted Northerner, "emphatically" argued that, although Southern white women provided much assistance to blacks, "'social equality' is now and always will be impossible at the South."[103] White clubwomen saw membership in the same organization as entailing social intercourse that they were unwilling to share with black women because it threatened the lines dividing a superior from an inferior race.

For white Southerners the ultimate taboo of social equality was that it would lead to interracial sex and marriage. Atlantan Isma Dooly claimed that Southern women would not countenance social equality. In regard to the socials associated with the General Federation, Dooly asked, "Would the colored members, with their sons and daughters, be invited?" She concluded that if Northern clubwomen really understood what they were proposing they would realize they were ultimately supporting "a principle that would lead to an amalgamation of the races." Ottley also argued that those who advocated that black clubwomen join the General were "blind" to its consequences. According to Ottley, these included miscegenation, which, she reminded her readers, was illegal in Southern states. "To invite a man to come into your drawing-room," she said, "and to put his knees under your mahogany whom it would be a dishonor to have offer himself to your daughter in marriage is an anomalous kindness which is as cruel as it is unreasonable and dangerous." The danger came because dining together was a mark of social equality, which, she reasoned, would filter down to too close relations and eventually interracial marriage in the lower classes.[104]

Clubwomen like Dooly and Ottley raised the specter of interracial marriage when faced with the possibility of social equality. Although Ottley believed this would take place in the lower classes, not among clubwomen themselves, others went so far as to suggest that clubwomen might mistakenly marry across the color line. Along this line, several months before the Los Angeles biennial, *The Club Woman* printed—by request of an unidentified clubwoman—a story, "The Rushing in of Fools." In it, Mrs. Dare, a Northern clubwoman, shuns rumors that a Mrs. Darlymple has black ancestry and invites her to join her club. Eventually Mrs. Dare's daughter marries Mrs. Darlymple's son. When their child is born with black skin and hair, the young mother tragically dies of shock.[105] Clubwomen evidently saw clubs as an extension of the home, blurring lines of division between public and private. Catherine D. Schureman equated the club with equal, intimate relationships and therefore the need to keep it segregated. "Is there anything which brings women nearer together socially than the intellectual club?" she asked. "If Mrs. I. and Mrs. W. are on equal footing intellectually and socially, their children become very intimate and their grandchildren marry. Now, if Mrs. I. does not want Mrs. W.'s grandson to ask the hand of her granddaughter in marriage she must not encourage social equality."[106] The danger of interracial marriage in this story and the unequivocal statements by clubwomen reflect a common tactic at the time, and the atmosphere allowed Rebecca Felton to make her well-known comment that lynching was an appropriate punishment for black men who raped white women. Clubwomen undoubtedly feared that men would find women's clubs even more dangerous if they were integrated. Their stance also acted evidenced their own fear of how social equality would play out in their own homes.

Moreover, black clubwomen's membership would acknowledge their presence as middle- and upper-class ladies with similar interests and rights to improve their community in the South, the very civic-mindedness that Southern white women sought to deny. Ruffin's case was particularly difficult because she was a Northern-educated elite African American woman. Ruffin was the widow of George L. Ruffin, a Harvard Law

School graduate, judge, and member of the Massachusetts legislature and Boston City Council.[107] Although this credential made her acceptable to many Northerners, it made her all the more threatening to many Southerners. Rebecca Lowe complained, "It is the 'high-caste' negroes who bring about all the ill-feeling. The ordinary colored woman understands her position thoroughly."[108] By attempting to join the General Federation, black women indicated that they considered themselves to be at the same level with white clubwomen. This contrasts strongly with the image of African Americans that clubwomen preferred: loyal and happy slaves in the antebellum, and servants in the postbellum South. Indeed, these were the only ways in which blacks were consistently portrayed in the *Keystone*.

Many Northern and Western individuals, clubs, and federations took a stand against drawing the color line in the GFWC. Unfortunately, their decision to speak against segregation is overlooked because of the outcome. Some simply stressed peace and compromise, but others explicitly spoke against segregation. Many Massachusetts clubs withdrew or threatened to withdraw from the GFWC if black clubs were not allowed to join. The Medford Women's Club even sent its resolutions of withdrawal in protest over Ruffin's denial to the Associated Press in November 1900.[109] Such strong statements against segregation have been largely disregarded, rendered seemingly irrelevant by the decision to segregate.

Once the decision was made in Los Angeles, states ceased debate, and the report in *The Club Woman* on the Biennial meeting itself was similar to that in the *Keystone*. It simply noted that many communications had been received between the 1900 meeting and 1902 regarding the issue, that a resolution allowing colored women to participate in the GFWC through their membership in state federations failed, and that the compromise had passed. The GFWC seems to have returned to its earlier desire to avoid controversy and focus instead on its many program and achievements. That the GFWC shared the same concerns delineated by Mary is evident from a comment made by Local Biennial Board member Ella Enderlein, who claimed that "the week of intimate association finally aroused a spirit of democracy, of altruism, which seemed to sweep through the Federation, leaving no barrier of 'color line' or of any political or local issue, all of which will add greatly to the success of future work."[110] Moreover, members evidently decided that the General Federation motto, Unity in Diversity, applied to regional diversity and that their power as a national organization was in jeopardy. Southern states' threat to withdraw if black women were admitted was significant. In March 1901 the Massachusetts

Federation acknowledged that, although one-quarter of member clubs in the General were from Massachusetts, Southern clubs were equally vital because they gave the federation its national character.[111]

After the Los Angeles Biennial, the newly elected president of the General, Dimies T. S. Denison, declared, "The Civil War is past; the old wounds have been healed; the North and the South have been reunited, and we cannot afford to take any action that will lead to more bitter feeling.... We must not, and I feel that the delegates will not, do anything that threatens disruption of the Federation, of which we are all so proud." When race threatened to disrupt the unity of the national organization, Northern women did what was necessary to keep the organization unified. White Southern women were appeased at the expense of black women.[112]

In contrast to some white attempts to bury the race question, black women adamantly wanted to publicize it. They fought to disseminate the truth as they saw it about the incident at the Los Angeles Biennial. Ruffin took a particularly strong stand at the Milwaukee convention. According to Ruffin, a woman came to her and told her that she should only represent the white clubs, not the Woman's Era Club, for if she did Kentucky had threatened to withdraw from the General Federation. Ruffin refused and told her that she "had never yet sold or mortgaged my principles, and requested her to go back to her Southern women and say to them that they had not money enough to get me to betray my principles, or to insult my colored club." She then hired a lawyer to investigate whether she could be legally excluded from the convention. The Woman's Era Club notified the General when its dues were returned to it that they refused to waive their membership rights because they had paid dues and received a certificate of membership. But the Board responded that they were "labouring under a misapprehension as the club had never been admitted to membership in the General Federation."[113] By the time of the Los Angeles Biennial, Ruffin had tired of the controversy. She claimed that the Woman's Era club was satisfied with their membership in the Massachusetts Federation and did not need the General; she conceded that the fight was not on the part of her club to enter, but between Northern and Southern white women. When the compromise passed, Ruffin concluded that "northern women were simply outwitted."[114]

Although the National Association of Colored Women did not issue an official statement, its president, Josephine Silone Yates, wrote to *The Club Woman*. She declared that black clubwomen believed that basing membership on one's skin color was a "step backwards" and pointed out many other women's organizations that did not. The NACW *National Notes* also featured an article concerning the admission of black women into the General Federation. This journal chose to highlight a positive aspect of the situation: the support of one particular white club for black admission to the GFWC. The article profiled the white Freeport [Illinois] Women's Club, which endorsed the admission of black women by a vote of fifty-eight to fifteen.[115]

Other prominent black clubwomen spoke out more harshly. Writing for the *Colored American Magazine*, Pauline Hopkins detailed the convention debate and emphasized that more than "a few delegates from the midwest" discussed the matter. She bitterly denounced the compromise, which she noted passed despite Jane Addams's support for black clubs.[116] Hopkins concluded that the participation of Southern white women in national organizations provided an additional setting in which the nation's desire for sectional reconciliation overrode interest in the rights of blacks. Furthermore, she indicted Southern women for their responsibility in "society's deeds," in an apparent veiled reference to interracial sex. Hopkins declared that "the rapid life of society . . . is not suggestive of absolute purity, and the black is no worse than his environment . . ." and that white clubwomen in the South remained "intolerable toward the victims of her husband's and son's evil passions." Like Ida B. Wells and others, Hopkins wanted to reframe the references to interracial sex and expose the truth about white men who raped black women.

Another prominent clubwoman, Fannie Barrier Williams, argued that black women who knocked at the door of the General were not seeking social equality but inspiration for advancement possible from a group of progressive women. She pointedly insisted that black women did not take white women's messages of inferiority to heart: "She does not think herself inferior to those who insist that she is inferior." Further, she implied that if the General held itself back by prejudice then it hampered its ability to do good work for the nation.[117] Williams was so outraged by the incident that she included a lengthy description of the events and the statement by the Women's Era club in an article on black clubwomen she wrote for *Progress of a Race*, edited by J. W. Gibson. In it, she compared the outcry against integrating the GFWC to the slandering of abolitionists fifty years earlier, and she mocked whites who worried about interracial marriage. Ultimately Williams concluded that the "brighter side" of the controversy was the support of many Northern white women and the publicity generated for black clubwomen and the good they had achieved.[118] The outspoken Ida B. Wells was incensed by the "Rushing in of Fools" story printed by *The Club Woman*. In a letter to the Chicago *Tribune* she argued that there were many marriages in Chicago in which one member had one drop of black blood and they did not produce jet black babies—a reminder to whites of the interracial mixing that had been taking place in the nation for a long time.[119]

Some black clubwomen, however, declared their lack of interest in joining the General. S. Lillian Coleman, a clubwoman from Milwaukee and retired secretary of the NACW, declared that they did not want to affiliate with the General. Coleman argued that black women would receive no benefits because the white women in it were too prejudiced and would not work with black women for the benefit of the race.[120]

Few Southern black clubwomen made public statements about their feelings. Although she did not speak out publicly during the controversy, in 1896 Margaret Washington had privately denounced white Northern women who allowed themselves to be run by white Southerners. She wrote a friend, "I do not belong to the aggressive class but I believe if such women, as Miss Willard, Mrs. Henrotin[,] Mrs. Dickinson and others were to show a little less fear of their southern sisters, these conditions of which I speak would be altered." Washington believed that the role that Southern white women played in nurturing segregation was imperative. She discussed segregation on the railroads: "Another thing, the southern women keep up this thing. They are behind the men because their education is more limited—they have little to do except to nurse their prejudices. They do not object to the colored woman who is their servant but they especially object to colored people who are not thus located." Washington thus anticipated the arguments over social equality that the clubwomen from Georgia articulated.[121]

Black newspapers around the country also covered the controversial biennials; some expressed dismay at the segregation of the federation, and others pointed to the existence of the NACW as proof that black women were not interested in and did not need the General. In one of the harshest criticisms of the General, the Chicago *Broad-Ax* argued that the controversy boiled down to "whether women of color in the United States should remain free women or should be again reduced to the condition of human chattels." Furthermore, they intimated that if a color line was strictly enforced, then white women would be found to have black blood in them.[122] When white women played upon fears of interracial sex as the ultimate defense against social equality, some African Americans dared accuse white women with complicity in such incidents.

Despite their victory, the issue still deeply concerned white Southern women. Tension over the "race question" continued. Caroline Granger noted that some women refused to join clubs because of the controversy. The participation of Southern women, such as Louisa Poppenheim and Rebecca Lowe, in GFWC leadership was therefore crucial to ensuring segregation in the federation, and to reassuring the region that the General Federation respected their interests. Poppenheim drew upon her own experiences as an officer to remind Southerners that they were well-represented in GFWC leadership and therefore in its decision making. Poppenheim understood her responsibility as a conduit of sectional ideals to the General Federation. "As a Southern clubwoman," she continued, "you sent me out as your representative in the Councils of these club women of America and imposed in my care your principles and ideals. I have given to these councils these principles and ideas and now returning to you as their representative, I assure you that they have found a place and have received a recognition."[123] Such a statement undoubtedly referred to race as well as to other Southern mores. Poppenheim, Lowe, and other Southern officers in the General Federation served much as white registrars did when they put literacy and other voting tests into practice: as members of the membership committee and board of directors, they would continue de facto segregation despite the lack of an official color line in the General's constitution. As the only Southern member of the Membership committee, Poppenheim was especially crucial to maintaining an all-white membership.[124]

Poppenheim's allegiance to the General Federation was not unlimited. Her advocacy of the General Federation seems odd at first, when considering her dedication to states' rights and her sense of place. But she resolutely supported the General Federation for several reasons. On a personal level, her experiences socializing with Northern girls while attending Vassar College may have helped her to appreciate friendship and cooperation with women from across the nation. As a skilled organizer, she consistently showed great enthusiasm for the organization and cooperation that city, state, and national federations brought to women's clubs. Moreover, Poppenheim was undoubtedly proud of her leadership role in the GFWC, along with President Lowe and other Southern women, and did not want them to withdraw from the GFWC.

Because Poppenheim believed so strongly in the GFWC, she downplayed the race issue and instead promoted Southern women's participation in the General Federation. South Carolina had only joined the GFWC after strong debate following an appeal from Rebecca Lowe.[125] As Georgia had encouraged South Carolina to join, South Carolina then turned to her neighbors. Poppenheim fought the hesitation of several Southern states to join the General Federation, by traveling throughout the area and encouraging their participation. She emphasized the role of Southern women in the national body, the ideals it represented, and the benefits of membership. After Poppenheim helped convince North Carolina to join, the NCFWC commented in the *Keystone*, "Under the spell of the speech of this magnetic woman, the Federation was made to feel that the General Federation was not the vague far-off thing they have supposed; but was as nigh us even to the very doors, ready to extend a handclasp of help and sympathy." That sympathy was all the more apparent through meeting GFWC leaders, and Poppenheim helped bring officers to the South, where they often stayed at her house while visiting.[126]

Poppenheim went even further in her uncompromising support of the General Federation in 1907 when she was instrumental in a controversial election for GFWC President. She supported May Alden Ward from Massachusetts and wrote letters to women across the country soliciting support for Ward. Her solicitation drew mixed responses, but the responses from Southern women are revealing.[127] They were reluctant to support a woman from Massachusetts, the home of Josephine St. Pierre Ruffin and the historical center of abolition in America. Moreover, Ward was president of the Massachusetts Federation at the 1902 biennial and president of the Cantabrigia Club of Boston, which in 1901 sent out a letter to clubwomen across the nation protesting the exclusion of the Woman's Era Club from the GFWC.[128]

In May 1908, Florence Matthews of New Orleans wrote to Poppenheim and assured her that she was "very fond" of Ward, but Matthews cautioned that she would wait to confer with the other Southern delegates before making any commitments. She reminded Poppenheim that when the International Council of Women met in New Orleans and admitted African American delegates, "not one N. O. woman, with the exception of the negro Mrs. Williams, a teacher in the Colored University, went near the meeting"; Matthews indicated that if black women were allowed in the GFWC, New Orleans women would leave the organization. Despite her hesitations, Matthews concluded, "but if Mrs. Ward is a friend to the South instead of a Mass[.] abolitionist I see no reason why we cannot support her . . . and if I remember right Mass[.] stood by Ga[.] in the fight in Cal[.], it was Penn[.] and Ohio with part of Illinois for the negro."[129]

The controversy eventually convinced Ward not to run for president. She wrote Louisa Poppenheim of her decision after receiving notification that the Virginia Federation had decided that they would not join the

General Federation because they heard that a Massachusetts club had black members, who would be "entitled to the same rights and privileges" as any Virginia club members. In a letter informing Sarah Decker, president of the GFWC, of this decision, Alice J. Kyle, president of the Virginia Federation, threatened that if the new president came from Massachusetts, Southern clubs would be forced to withdraw from the General Federation and form their own regional organization. Although the Virginia Federation was somewhat vague in its report on its decision not to join in the *Keystone*, members explained their stand more fully in a resolution passed and printed in the Lynchburg News, which stated that the "line of social separation between the races must be kept absolutely without a break."[130] Apparently, the understanding behind the compromise was not enough to comfort Virginia white women, who were appalled at the Massachusetts Federation allowing black clubs within its state federation. The Virginia Federation refused to join the General until the bylaws were changed. A newspaper editorial compared clubwomen's heroic stand to their loyalty to the South during the Civil War.[131] Fearing Kyle's threat of the Southern states' withdrawal, Ward asked Poppenheim to use her influence in the region to prevent any resolutions or reference to race at the Boston Biennial later that year, which might tear the federation apart. "You have so much influence with all the Southern States," Ward wrote, "that I am very sure that you can prevent the offering of any inflammatory resolutions or any reference to the question of color."[132]

The issue did not go away. The St. Louis *Globe-Democrat* reported in 1916 that black women's clubs were again an issue. Southern delegates threatened to shift their support from a Laura Sneath of Ohio to Ione Cowles of California because of rumors asserting that Sneath planned to allow African American women's clubs into the federation. Both Sneath and Cowles were forced to issue statements denying interest in revisiting the issue of the color line.[133]

Even as white women hoped to ignore the presence of black women in their local communities and exclude them from their organizations, they were forced to confront issues of race constantly. Race underlay their decisions as they considered both pursuing a particular reform and joining a national body of women with views different from their own. Southern white women could not ignore African Americans even as they refused to help them. What they could do, and did do, was force Northern white women to choose between national reconciliation and the rights of blacks. Despite their "inferiority" in terms of programming, Southern women used the race question as a means of power to exert some control in the

General Federation. Just as white Northerners turned their backs when Southern lawmakers disenfranchised and segregated blacks in the South, the General Federation chose national unity among white women and closed its doors to black women who were too much like themselves. By barely acknowledging this turn of events in the *Keystone*, the Poppenheims tried to negate the possibility that they could have chosen otherwise.

Once racial segregation was established in the General Federation, Southern members continued to encounter difficulties concerning federal legislation and states' rights ideology. South Carolina, the first state to secede, strongly advanced the belief in the authority of the state. The Poppenheims' advocacy for states' rights as a philosophy pervades the *Keystone*, not only in direct reference to the Lost Cause. For example, the Poppenheims ran an editorial on "minority opinions," which told their readers to have the "faith, hope, courage and tenacity" to support a minority opinion if they believed in it, and to "stand true to our convictions knowing that 'minority' when founded upon truth and justice will in the end read 'success.'" Although this article did not mention states' rights or the Confederacy, it clearly evokes the Lost Cause.[134]

The states' rights argument also shaped Southern states' dealings with the General Federation, which endorsed various federal laws and constitutional amendments as part of its reform agenda. Just as Southern suffragists struggled over whether to back a federal amendment for woman suffrage, the SCFWC was uncomfortable with General Federation's series of resolutions calling for federal legislation in the late 1920s. One area of debate was over the proposed federal child labor amendment to the constitution, which the GFWC supported. The Southeastern Council of Federated Club Women, which was an intermediary between the Southern state federations and the General Federation, endorsed a minority report prepared by Lucy Worthington Blackman of Florida against the federal child labor amendment in 1925. She argued that the amendment was "contrary to the fundamental principles of the American government" and urged instead that individual state federations study child labor in home states and promote recreational and educational opportunities for children.[135]

During the 1926 GFWC Biennial held in Atlantic City, clubwomen debated whether to pass a resolution in support of the proposed child labor amendment. The Louisville, Kentucky, Women's Club delegates, speaking without the support of their state federation, argued that the bill jeopardized individual clubs in the General Federation because it forced them to acquiesce to the majority approval despite their own position against the bill. Such strong opposition surfaced because of a majority rights ruling passed at a GFWC Council meeting at West Baden in 1925: "When a resolution has been adopted at such meetings, either unanimously or by a majority, it should be regarded as the action of the organization. State Federations or individual clubs, opposed to the action taken, should not conduct a campaign in the name of the State or the Club, in opposition to that of the General Federation." Thus, if the GFWC resolution in favor of a federal child labor amendment passed, clubs or state federations that opposed it were forbidden to work against it.

According to the women from Louisville, this ruling destroyed their minority rights. They argued that the General Federation motto, "Unity In Diversity," had upheld states' rights before, noting the 1902 compromise, which they characterized as a states' rights issue. While the Kentucky Federation did not support the Louisville club, the Louisville *Courier-Journal* endorsed the Club's attempt to retain "democracy" at the General. In protest, the Club offered a resolution rescinding the majority rights ruling which lost. Furthermore, the resolution in support of the child labor amendment won, by a vote of 692 to 249.[136]

The manner in which South Carolina clubwomen reacted to this debate reveals the depth of their own beliefs in states' rights, and furthermore Louisa Poppenheim's attempts to retain a states' rights stance without jeopardizing her state's status within the General Federation. She and Maria Croft Jennings, state publicity chair, reported on the biennial in the club newspaper column. They informed local clubwomen that the child labor amendment resolution had passed, and "it was interesting to note that the plea was made for states' rights and there was not a division between North and South. Many New England states voted with the Southern states." Poppenheim claimed that the press had given "undue prominence" to the Louisville resolution. She emphasized that their own state had not supported them and called it "unfortunate" that they had circulated their resolution. Thus, despite her support of states' rights, Poppenheim emphasized unity at the GFWC and disapproved of the Louisville insurgents.[137]

The following year, at the SCFWC convention, Poppenheim's compromising stance became even clearer. Lena Springs, a South Carolina delegate and chair of the SCFWC committee on constitutional amendments, informed the body of the GFWC's ruling for majority rights. Springs proposed that the state federation adopt the following resolution: "The department of legislation, through its chairman and members, shall conduct the work of this department in accordance with the program submitted to and endorsed by the (state) federation convention," thus circumventing national endorsements and the majority rights ruling. One wonders if Springs knew that she was taking on Louisa Poppenheim, still a force in the federation after twenty-eight years, with her proposal.

In response, Poppenheim rose to ask, "What has that to do with the report of the committee on constitutional amendments." Springs replied that her resolution would affect their constitution because it specified how to conduct legislative work. She continued, "States' rights is the strongest claim South Carolina has made since its formation." Springs explained that in regards to the majority rights ruling, she had asked the meaning of the word "Should" and had been told that it meant "must," and that therefore the state federation resolution was needed to protect their rights. In addition, she argued that the Southeastern Council, in adopting the Florida report against the child labor amendment, had already gone against the majority rights ruling. Undaunted by Poppenheim's stature, Springs went for the jugular. "I do not deny for a moment," she said, "the right of the majority, but do we, as South Carolinians, regardless of opinions and principles have to take orders from anyone?" Caught between defending the integrity of the General Federation and states' rights, Poppenheim did not hesitate. As the opening of this chapter indicates, she immediately responded, "I would be the last to take orders. We are South Carolinians. We will act as we please. We will decide here what we will do."

Poppenheim, however, could not resist blaming Springs for having "put us in a box" by asking for clarification of the word "should"; Poppenheim implied that South Carolina could have more easily circumvented the ruling before its meaning was clarified. The tension between the two evidently extended to other officers in the federation. One can only imagine the explosive atmosphere when Poppenheim rose to challenge Springs. That fall, Springs wrote Louisa a strained letter, in which she complained that even though the executive committee had voted to allow her to represent South Carolina at the Southeastern Council, she had not received the invitation. She attributed this to "personal prejudice upon the part of any Federation officials" and asked to be represented on the program.[138] Despite their differences, Poppenheim, Springs, and the entire convention voted to adopt the resolution for the state federation to determine its own legislative program. States' rights still ruled in South Carolina.[139]

Poppenheim returned to the issue of states' rights when the General Federation resolved its support for a federal constitutional amendment to establish a uniform divorce and marriage law across the states. Poppenheim told delegates at the convention that South Carolina was "averse to any law that would allow divorce within our state." Black and white Republicans overturned South Carolina's ban on divorce during Reconstruction. In response, in 1895 when the state voted in a new constitution designed to disenfranchise blacks, they explicitly banned divorce. By 1926 South Carolina was the only state that did not permit divorce. Historian Janet Hudson argues that opposition to divorce "became a symbolic issue for many South Carolinians who fought to retain the state's unique stance against divorce in an attempt to bolster state pride, distance themselves from the abhorrent connotations of Reconstruction, and vicariously recapture a semblance of their state's antebellum glory."[140] South Carolina's unique stance thus remained a point of pride for clubwomen in the 1920s.

After a delegate from Indiana proclaimed herself in sympathy with the idea of states' rights, but in favor of uniform law in this instance, Lena Springs also spoke. She reiterated her state's position against federal laws. She then pointed out the that resolution called for members to be educated on the provision "preparatory to an active CONGRESSIONAL DRIVE at the strategic time." This, according to Springs, was impossible for South Carolina clubwomen to endorse because they could not go in front of their congressional delegation in favor of the amendment. Springs asked the convention to consider the "rights of the minority": "However, can the General Federation afford to go on binding the several states to resolutions which are directly contrary to the policies and principles of the citizens of those states?" Despite Springs and Poppenheim, however, the resolution was immediately voted upon and passed with only three dissenting votes from South Carolina.[141]

The following year at the state convention, Emma Eaton White, GFWC legal advisor, clarified the majority ruling. She contended that clubs did not have to support legislation endorsed by the General Federation but they should not work against such legislation, and she specifically told South Carolina clubwomen that they were not required to "stress" the marriage and divorce law supported by the GFWC.[142] These incidents reveal that participation in the GFWC was fraught with pitfalls for Southern clubwomen, who sought to protect their values as Southerners. In this case, they prioritized their belief in states' rights over their loyalty to the General Federation.

The implications of the Southern "inferiority complex" were many. White Southern women, and to a more limited degree, black Southern women, identified themselves as Southern. For black women, their regional identity was sometimes a badge of shame and a source of not only bitterness but also defeat in the face of the problems surrounding them. White privilege meant that white Southern clubwomen did not experience the same sense of defeat. They were, however, restricted in other ways. Even black clubwoman Mary Terrell recognized how the refusal of some Southern whites to join the General because of their desire for segregation ultimately only hurt whites.[143] They were reluctant to champion federal laws, despite their support of the bills' intent.

The parallel experiences of black and white South Carolina clubwomen were closer even than they realized. Both groups faced an additional dilemma—how to participate in their national organizations as Southern women. Bonds of sisterhood overrode most sectional differences, and women united to achieve similar purposes. Yet, the defeat in the Civil War for white women, life in the heart of segregation for black women, and the general poverty throughout the South that they both experienced, gave them a sense of inferiority to their sisters in the North. White South Carolina clubwomen used their participation in the General Federation to bring about reconciliation on their own terms, which meant standing up for states' rights sixty years after the Civil War. They could take pride in the honor they helped restore to the South through the Lost Cause. Black Southern clubwomen had no such well of pride. Instead, they had to celebrate their own progress made against the odds.

Inferiority was not only limiting. Greater needs could also translate into greater effort. For black and white clubwomen equally, the need to prove themselves could be a strong motivational force. Understanding themselves as different, as Southerners, sparked them to work to improve their region, so that they could transform shame into pride. White women were more easily able to call upon a proud past for motivation. Yet each was cognizant of their relationship to the rest of the nation; they compared themselves, their living conditions, and their abilities and limitations to that of their Northern sisters. Their reform successes—building libraries, lobbying for reformatories—and failures reflect their status as Southern women.

Chapter 5

Reluctant Reformers, Resistant Legislators

White Clubwomen and Social Reform

Emily Plume Evans, chairman of the subcommittee on industrial and social conditions of women and children in the South Carolina Federation of Women's Clubs, was deeply concerned with the plight of women and children workers in the state. How could she rouse her fellow clubwomen to the cause? Evans first wrote letters that requested clubwomen to survey the conditions locally. Most did not. Those that did conduct a survey found high numbers of underage children at work. Frustrated with the apparent apathy within the federation, Evans proclaimed her support for federal intervention, in the form of a federal child labor law. Such a radical suggestion, however, had to be carefully made. Evans couched hers in a language in which white South Carolina clubwomen were well conversed. She reminded them, "It was a Southern statesman who said, 'A patriot is one who loves the home he inhabits, the trees that give him shade and the hills that stand in his pathway.' Woman makes the home. Let us then see to it that every wage-earner receives that to which he is entitled and for which God created him."[1] With leaders such as Evans, who was deeply committed to passing child labor legislation, why did the federation fail to gain passage of such effective child labor laws? Why was Evans unable to garner stronger support from the membership? Where did the other federation leaders stand? What reception could those in favor of reform expect from mill workers, mill owners, legislators, and men generally? Could Southern pride and a desire to create prosperity in the New South motivate women to embrace this reform, or would it paralyze clubwomen into an unwillingness to critique the region?

Like women across the nation, white clubwomen in South Carolina moved naturally from self-education to social reform, most often justifying their new role as municipal housekeepers. But their efforts were also motivated by their focus on Southern identity. Pride in the Southern past gave white clubwomen additional incentive to embrace social reform; they wanted to build a New South from which they could reenter the nation on equal footing. Thus, the Lost Cause celebration inspired social reform.[2]

Yet clubwomen who strayed from memorial and historical work they shared with the UDC to more progressive social reform agendas jeopardized their moral authority. Furthermore, because of their focus on Southern pride, some overly defensive clubwomen had difficulty acknowledging serious problems, such as child labor. Literary clubs sometimes were adamant that they were not formed for the purpose of social welfare work. Clubwomen hesitated to criticize their husbands and fathers, the mill owners and leaders of the New South economy. Reluctant reformers, clubwomen were often their own worst enemy. But clubwomen's failures came from outside as well as from within the federation. White clubwomen who lobbied the legislature had to take care lest they be seen as stepping out of their place as women and attempting to take over male political authority. They found it difficult to rouse the support of male legislators, editors, and the public.

White clubwomen's reform agendas focused on educational reform and children's needs. Clubwomen built their own institutions—kindergartens and libraries—while pushing for state recognition and funding for many of their projects—albeit unsuccessfully. They worked within a region and a nation in the midst of change, with New South spokesmen calling for industry and progress in the South, while nationally progressive reformers tried to mitigate the problems industrialization and urbanization wrought.

Calls for an industrial New South challenged the established hierarchies in the South. Former planters struggled to hold onto economic and political power, as well as social position, some adapting well to the new economy while others resisted. The move to industrialization and a cash economy required investors for mills and merchants for goods and supplies.[3] Many mill owners in the South Carolina up-country were new merchants and industrialists, not members of the former planter elite.[4]

Middle- and upper-class clubwomen were concerned with rebuilding the South. As members of the social and economic elite, their own future depended upon a prosperous and stable South. Many were related to mill owners or merchants, whose business interests provided an example of the need for Southern economic progress. The Poppenheims reflect well these circumstances. Although he was the son of a planter, Mr. Poppenheim did not remain on his father's plantation after the war. Instead, he moved his family to Charleston and established a store that sold dry goods, guns, and agricultural implements. *Life Magazine* described him as "a planter who turned merchant, completely reversing Charleston's aristocratic tradition." He therefore illustrates the role of former planters who became businessmen, although in his case, he was only a twenty-six-year-old newly married man, who, because of the war, had not yet established himself on his own plantation. He did not invest in a cotton mill, the most visible sign of industrialization in the New South, but his investment in phosphates and fertilizer indicate that he supported the new economy. He bought stock in the Edisto phosphate company in Charleston in 1887 and at one time was president of the Royal Fertilizer Company.[5] His readiness to adapt a commercial economy in the New South reflected changes taking place across the state.

Mary and Louisa's interest in preserving Southern identity while their father stood in the vanguard of Charleston's commercial businessmen reveals insight into a significant question of Southern continuity: could Southern culture be preserved from Old South to New South, even as the current economic changes were bringing the region closer to the industrialized North? In other words, the work done by Mary, Louisa, and other clubwomen was cultural: they sought to preserve the Southern way of life, social mores, gender and race relations, and values of family and community. As members of the economic and social elite, they hoped to shape identity in the New South around traditional shared meanings and values. Therefore, against a backdrop of economic progress, these women were responsible for providing stability in a changing society. Because women made sure that the South did not lose its cultural traditions, men were free to invest in cotton mills and dedicate themselves to economic change. Louisa Poppenheim reminded clubwomen that their service was crucial to the state because "men are so engrossed with business cares that matters of social service to the community and the state are of necessity crowded out."[6]

Clubwomen were crucial to the success of the New South. Although they honored the Old South, their desire for prosperity and progress allowed them to support the industrialization their husbands and fathers sought.[7] When the inevitable problems associated with industrialization arose, women took care of them without blaming the men or the mills.

Because of their duty to children, to women, and to civic improvement, they worked to ameliorate the negative consequences change brought. Women reformers eased the difficult transition from farm to factory through education reforms that helped train the workforce needed in the New South, but the women did not criticize the segregated economic system that depressed wages.[8] In this sense, women simultaneously embraced and critiqued the New South.

Clubwomen in the early twentieth-century South faced a formidable task: through pride in the past the women sought to draw attention to present economic needs and build a New South. This ability to link the past systems with present economic needs separated clubwomen from the United Daughters of the Confederacy (UDC). In honoring the past, clubwomen in South Carolina also believed that the Confederacy left a legacy of glory, which compelled them to address current social and economic problems. The clubwomen interpreted this obligation as necessitating social reform work in education, health, and civic improvement. They hoped that these efforts would aid in creating an economically prosperous but culturally traditional community–that is, a New South. Louisa Poppenheim called for women to look to the glory of the past and the strength of their foremothers for inspiration. "As [Southern women] look out into the misty morning of the future," she wrote, "they receive fresh courage from the prestige of the past, for they believe that inspiration for the future can be secured through the contemplation of that past."[9] Unlike the UDC, however, which limited itself to memorializing the past and preserving it for the next generation, clubwomen were driven by that past to embrace present and future reform. They did not separate memory work from reform work—both sprang from the same source. Southern women used all the reasons offered by their Northern sisters to justify their work in the public sphere. Yet as Southern women, not only did they emphasize their maternal duty to better health and safety conditions for their children, but they also argued that their duty as daughters of the Confederacy was the improvement of the New South. Their use of Lost Cause discourse to inspire and to justify social reform was significant; the language was not merely a rhetorical device meant to assuage their opponents; rather, the clubwomen invoked the Lost Cause because they believed in it.[10]

Thus, despite their attention to the past, clubwomen knew they were needed in the New South. The editors of the *Keystone* looked ahead by submitting a statement that contradicted much of what the UDC stood for; "This present [year], the one we have with us now, and are living today, is the most important. The years that are passed have their records locked from us forever; we cannot alter them one jot or tittle." Clubwomen recognized that pride in history did not necessarily make them bound to tradition.[11]

Several leaders in the South Carolina federation attempted to rouse clubwomen in South Carolina by invoking their sense of place. Sarah Visanska, president from 1910 to 1912, was a leader in the Charleston Civic Club and the Charleston section of the National Council of Jewish Women.[12] One of the most prominent Jewish women in the federation, Visanska was born in Charleston, educated at the Charleston Female Seminary, and married to a merchant. Although childless herself, she was dedicated to child welfare. Her espousal of Southern identity indicates the pervasiveness of this ideology, for there is no evidence that she was even a member of the UDC. Yet, clearly she understood the importance of linking reform with tradition. In 1900, in an address entitled, "The American Woman of To-day," Visanska argued that the New South should be built upon the old South. She reminded clubwomen that, as one of the original thirteen colonies, South Carolina sounded "the bugle call of progress and reform" and that, despite the region's suffering during the war, "those clarion notes have been stilled but never quite forgotten." Visanska hoped for a return to that progress and reform in the New South, and she envisioned a role for women in it. She told clubwomen, "Once again the eyes of the nation are turning Southward. . . . We, daughters of the South, as well as our brothers, realize how crowded is the present hour with vast opportunities and grave responsibilities. Each one of us, whose heart throbs responsive to the cause of country and of womanhood, should proudly assume the task to improve the one, and faithfully discharge the other." After using references to the past to motivate clubwomen, Visanska issued an impassioned call for reform. She specifically spoke of the importance of women's clubs and stressed their new focus on community service. The centerpiece of her talk was the plight of working women, for whom she demanded equal pay for equal work.[13]

Visanska also spoke to clubwomen at the SCFWC convention about their role in the New South. After establishing that the economy needed women's aid, she called Southern women to respond according to the example set for them by their ancestors, "In the past, untrained and unprepared, our women rose magnificently to the duties imposed by calamitous war and untold privations. To-day we must answer the call of new conditions!" Visanska enumerated the problems facing women: mill children who needed education, guidance, nutrition, and cleanliness; growing cities that needed parks, playgrounds, free libraries, and better sanitation;

and working girls who needed a guarantee of safety and morality. Lest anyone question the intention of public-minded women, this work, she concluded, would be the work of "the loyal daughters of a beloved state."[14] In both of these addresses, Visanska drew upon the example of the past to inspire clubwomen to meet new needs in a New South. Because Visanska was not a member of the UDC, it is possible that she stressed the past because it made for persuasive language. Her colleagues, however, were fervent adherents to the Lost Cause.

Ida Lining, the original owner of the *Keystone* and a member of both the SCFWC and the UDC, was even more explicit in her espousal of women's role in creating a New South. Her article, "What the South Needs," praised a *News and Courier* editorial, "Let the South Alone." For Lining, the glories of the Southern tradition compelled Southerners to take their future into their own hands to make it worthy of the past. She based her argument on the idea that "interest to be real must be born within us and love of home must be there to give the right stimulus to patriotic effort"; this meant that Northerners did not have the "true" interest of the region at heart because they did not share the love of home inherent in the Southerner.

That love of home, combined with pride in the past, was enough to inspire action. Lining reminded Southerners that they were behind the country's most important advances. She named George Washington, Thomas Jefferson, John C. Calhoun, Robert E. Lee, and others as worthy leaders who should erase any shame that the South might feel after defeat. "Is our 'pride humbled'?" she asked. "Perish the thought, Southerners! We have nothing to be ashamed of. When 'our storm-cradled nation fell' and we furled our banner forever, it was with the applause of the whole world. Its tattered folds do not conceal dishonor." Southerners had risen above the hardships encountered and survived them. They achieved an honorable legacy: "When we take our education affairs in hand, we will overcome illiteracy. If we are 'let alone' we will settle the color question." Lining continued by emphasizing continuity with the past. "This is not a 'new South,'" she wrote, "It is the same old South under changed conditions. . . . The re-incarnated spirits of our heroes, both men and women . . . should stimulate us to prove it in the eyes of the world a 'just cause' and we are doing it." Lining finally concluded that in order to be "self-respecting Southerners," clubwomen needed to establish schools and libraries, aid the poor, and end illiteracy.[15] Such language and references to the Confederacy are reminiscent of speeches typical of the UDC, and Lining was a UDC officer. In this article, however, she addressed clubwomen in the *Keystone*, for it was clubwomen who were building schools and libraries, aiding the poor, and fighting illiteracy.

Maria Croft Jennings, a graduate of Columbia College, was SCFWC president in 1925–1926. Particularly active in regional clubwork, she was also a delegate to the Democratic national convention.[16] As chairman of the Southeast Council of the General Federation of Women's Clubs, she hoped to draw Southern women into the General Federation with references to their particular history and land. She described Southern women as strengthened by the war experience: "given patience by long suffering, made brave by the burdens of war, clinging to the ideals of those who fought and bled and died for us, awakened to the wonderful industrial possibilities of our section, her women furnish a combination of power and sentiment that fits them to take their place in National achievements." After enumerating all that Southerners had to be proud of—including their patriotism and chivalry—she then argued that the General Federation was a force in uniting women across the nation without regard to section. Jennings made a direct pitch linking reform to history; she argued that because of the "indomitable spirit" of Confederate women, which remained with them, "a new South will rise from the ashes of the old, resplendent with characteristics of both." She advocated preserving the music, art, forests, and natural scenery of the South, and she called on clubwomen to aid in the completion of the Confederate monument at Stone Mountain, which she considered critically important. Jennings exhorted Southern clubwomen, "Most of all, let us preserve the traditions of our Southland—our customs, our chivalry, our home-life." Finally, Jennings followed her references to hallowed regional traditions with attention to the social welfare issues evident in the postwar South. She suggested that Southern women work on economic and social conditions unique to their section, by focusing on rural women and children and illiteracy.[17]

This sense of place and of the past also pervaded reform movements throughout the Southern states. Many Southern women also expressed their calls for reform in rhetoric tied to the Southern past. For example, Mary Munford, president of the Richmond [Virginia] Educational Association, in a paper addressed to the Conference for Education in the South in 1909, focused on the devotion and duty of Southern women, evident now in their work on school improvement. She claimed that the devotion of women of the Confederacy, "having known sorrow and death, has had the mark of immortality stamped upon it. By her refusal to admit defeat, the Southern woman of the past was courageous and endured."

And now? For Munford, New South women inherited their mothers' fortitude. The Southern woman, she posited, "rich in this inheritance . . . trained to cherish reverently the memories of the past . . . has built monuments to her country's heroes that her children and her children's children might meet the tasks of to-day in the spirit of high adventure and devotion to duty characteristic of their forefathers." Confederate heroes exemplified perseverance and devotion to duty.

Having justified women's devotion to their work, Munford then turned to the substance of her talk: improving public education. This, she claimed, was the focus of Southern women because it had been advocated by none other than General Lee as the "point of departure in the reconstruction of our Southern life." After outlining the work of various states, Munford concluded that patriotism and service were united for Southern women, who "recognized, in the South, the people's splendid idealism, their native capacity for statesmanship, their power of persistent effort in the face of difficulty, and their willingness to die for the idea that possesses them."[18] Dedication, courage, fortitude, perseverance—all these characteristics marked the social welfare work of Southern women.

Southern clubwomen focused on the South's unique welfare needs. The Poppenheims often informed them of the programs already in place in the North and urged Southern women to copy them.[19] Clubwomen, however, did not advocate projects taken up in other states if they seemed inappropriate to the region. For example, B. S. Childs claimed that although working girls clubs were beneficial, there was no need for them in the South.[20] South Carolina clubwomen therefore sought to alleviate those problems particular to the New South. Unable to recapture the plantation economy, now gone forever, clubwomen saw that to make the South worthy of pride they would have to rekindle the prosperity of its living breathing citizens, not just build marble memorials to dead soldiers. In particular, they looked to aid children and improve education.

Like clubwomen throughout the nation, white clubwomen in South Carolina prioritized education reform. Although they worked alongside the UDC to ensure that schools exposed children to their Confederate history and culture, clubwomen went further. They recognized that access to adequate education was crucial to improving South Carolina's social and economic conditions, as well as to shaping its culture. They particularly focused on education for women, manual and domestic training, kindergartens, and libraries.

Public education was a most crucial need after the War because the South did not have a free public school system before Reconstruction, owing to rural isolation of white children and total neglect of education for the black population.[21] The school system in South Carolina was abysmal. School spending statistics reveal the lack of financial support for white schools and inadequate school facilities; black schools fared even worse. In 1900, the white school term was 88.4 days in South Carolina, compared to 177 days in the North Atlantic states; average daily expenditure per child was $0.05 cents per child, compared to $0.20 cents in Massachusetts; average annual expenditure $1.80 compared to $21.55 in Massachusetts; and average teacher salaries were $122.28, compared to $566.09 in Massachusetts. Moreover, illiteracy in South Carolina stood at 35.9 percent, second highest in the nation.[22]

As bad as things stood for whites, they only got worse for blacks. Per capital spending in 1894 for whites was $3.82, for blacks $1.58; by 1921 white schools received $11.97 per student, and black schools $1.23. South Carolina did not open a state supported high school for black students until 1906; by 1929, only three black public high schools issued state-accredited diplomas. Illiteracy rates reflected the inequitable institutional support. In South Carolina 13.6 percent of whites were illiterate compared to 52.8 percent of blacks in 1900.[23] Not wanting to draw attention to the inequities, Southern clubwomen were reluctant to accept Northern aid flowing into the region. Despite the lucrative sums of money available, they sometimes preferred to be left alone to control literature and history in the curriculum and to limit spending on black schools. The editors of the *Keystone* reprinted an article from the *New York Tribune* on education in the South, which advocated that the North stay out and let the South handle their own affairs, without fear because the "South means to do its education duty by the negro."[24] But white clubwomen did not do their "duty by the Negro"; rather, they supported the state's inequitable funding by improving schools and establishing kindergartens and libraries for white children only.

Through the process of examining applicants for the college scholarships they sponsored, clubwomen realized that a preponderance of unqualified girls indicated a lack of adequate elementary school training. They quickly turned their attention to primary schools. In addition to surveying teachers' qualifications and salaries, clubwomen focused on the school buildings. The chairman of the art department, Azalea Willis, proposed that clubwomen visit their schools and hang pictures by great artists on the wall. She also asked women to see that schools were painted or whitewashed as needed and to plant flowers and shrubs on school grounds.[25]

Clubwomen also argued that kindergartens were crucial to improving education. They worked to establish local kindergartens and to train kindergarten teachers through scholarships. Although part of the national kindergarten movement, South Carolina clubwomen also explicitly linked the need for kindergartens to the New South. Using images of urban centers teeming with immigrants and factories, more appropriate to cities in the Northeast than the South, Sarah Visanska perhaps hoped to inspire women to work to avoid the fear that the South might become like the North. She argued that the nineteenth century would be remembered for urbanization, which was accompanied by immigration and overcrowding problems. Poor children suffered the most. Rather than striving to alleviate the poverty of the family, Visanska directed the attention of clubwomen to the children and proposed that kindergartens were the solution. "The feeble cry of the children of the poor has been heard in the land, and fortunately, with the want has also come its relief—the free kindergarten," she contended. Visanska may have been naïve to think that kindergartens could cure poverty, but her answer was one that clubwomen could readily provide. Clubwomen should establish kindergartens to care for children, whose working mothers could do little more for them then feed them, she argued, "while the poor little hearts and minds are starved or become hardened by neglect, and of ill-treatment." After describing the kindergartens in Charleston, Visanska called for clubwomen to open kindergartens in their hometowns, especially for children in factory towns.[26]

While they agreed on the benefits of kindergartens, clubwomen disagreed on who was in need of those benefits. While they formed kindergartens in the mill districts of their towns and promoted kindergartens for poor children, clubwomen still believed them to be unnecessary for their own offspring. An article in the "Woman and Society" column of the *State* newspaper, which appears to have had the backing of the Columbia Kindergarten Association, defended kindergartens by stressing the needs of poor children. In an attempt to persuade the unconverted, the article accused kindergarten opponents of thinking only of children in "clean homes" and ignoring those brought up in squalor and without the moral influences imbued in kindergartens.[27] This view came under fire in the *Keystone*, in an excerpt from an article by Patty Hill of Louisville, Kentucky. Hill reprimanded clubwomen for believing kindergarten to be unnecessary for children of "intelligent" mothers and intended only for "poor" neglected children. Despite her opposition of "poor" and "intelligent," Hill emphasized that kindergarten provided a valuable educational benefit for all children and urged readers not to regard the school as a mere daycare needed only by mothers who could not adequately care for their children.[28] However, the Charleston Civic Club apparently did not take Hill's lesson to heart, for the club reported that they had hoped for more factory children in attendance at their playground, but it had attracted instead children who were "too respectable."[29]

Eventually clubwomen petitioned the legislature to fund local public kindergartens. In the 1920s the child welfare department chairwoman, Minnie MacFeat, reported that despite the efforts of the legislative committee, a new kindergarten bill was killed in committee and did not even come to a vote. Notwithstanding legislative setbacks, clubwomen succeeded at establishing kindergartens on the local level. In 1891 the Kelly Alumnae Kindergarten Association of Charleston, named after teacher Henrietta Aiken Kelly, founded a free kindergarten, which was "said to have been, 'the first free kindergarten South.' It was located in 'the mill village.'" Two years later, the South Carolina Kindergarten Association opened another Charleston kindergarten, which for many years operated in the basement of St. Philip's Episcopal Church.[30] White clubwomen were determined to establish kindergartens, with or without state funding.

Clubwomen also believed that libraries helped educate children as well as adults. Many member clubs first moved from literary study to community service by establishing a library. Clubwomen also collected and distributed traveling libraries to small towns throughout the state. Ludie Coleman, first president of the federation, was responsible for "launching" the federation's interest in traveling libraries and worked with railroad lines to donate free transportation for such collections through 1907. The dissemination of traveling libraries was crucial to reaching the small village and rural population that still predominated the state.

The library movement also moved clubwomen into political action. Louisa Poppenheim first planted the seed in an article in the *Keystone* extolling Wisconsin as a model and asking for a state library commission to run the public and traveling libraries. Both the considerable amount of time and effort that clubwomen devoted to libraries and the cost of the traveling libraries (once railroads decided to stop carrying the books free of charge) fueled this demand.[31] The federation legislative committee annually sponsored a bill for a library commission. In 1907, clubwomen argued that South Carolina needed to join the other twenty-five states that had already established library commissions. They passed a resolution calling for a state library commission to manage the more than seven thousand books collected by clubwomen, "with the understanding that the Federation will assist in carrying on its work." Their proposal featured a five-member commission, with three males, and two females who were to be recommended by the federation, thus guaranteeing their say in the future of the books they had collected. Mrs. L. T. Nichols, chair in 1907, realized that the clubwomen would want to "look after the interest of the work they have so much at heart." At the same time she assured the state that it would benefit as well: "By keeping in touch with the work they continue their assistance and donation of books."[32] Despite their continued attempts to gain a commission, annual reports on the bill recorded no success. In 1923, the federation decided to change tactics and ask for an appropriation for school libraries, which was quickly approved by the state legislature (the county and the school put up one third each of the cost of the library). Because the initial $5000 appropriation was spent so quickly, clubwomen continued to remind their legislators of its importance.[33] At the same time that the federation fought the state legislature for funding, local clubs were hard at work successfully establishing town libraries.

Although clubwomen successfully established libraries and kindergartens throughout the state, they were unable to garner support from legislators, especially before woman suffrage. The state refused to mandate universal public kindergartens; instead, the legislature specified that kindergartens be established according to "local conditions" and failed to pass a state library commission. South Carolina did not embrace school improvement to nearly the same degree as some other Southern states, such as North Carolina, led by Charles Aycock, the "education governor." This lack of support was in part owing to the compulsory education law debate, which overshadowed other attempts at school improvement and which in turn was dominated by a fear of enacting any laws that would improve black access to education. South Carolinians reacted strongly to intertwined fears of race and Northern intervention. For example, the Southern Education Board (SEB), led by New Yorker Charles C. Ogden, was never able to overcome suspicion of "foreign" aid, and therefore the board did not aid South Carolina as it did other states.[34]

Despite their lack of legislative success, clubwomen could boast about the local kindergartens they either staffed or funded and the libraries they built. They also obtained an illiteracy commission headed by SCFWC member Wil Lou Gray. Moreover, education in the state did improve. Clubwomen undoubtedly helped lower the state's illiteracy rate directly through Gray's commission and indirectly through encouraging literacy with new library access. The illiteracy rate decreased from 13.6 percent for whites over age ten in 1900 to 5.2 percent in 1930.[35] In addition, the state increased school spending from approximately $827,000 to $3.3 million between 1900 and 1915. Moreover, for white schools, the term increased from 105 to 133 days, the average teacher salary more than doubled, and expenditure per pupil in attendance rose from $6.51 to $23.76.[36] Although clubwomen cannot take sole credit for these changes, they pushed hard to draw attention to the need for education reform. For the most part they were better at founding their own institutions than lobbying for legislation for public funding or state institutions.

White South Carolina clubwomen had a hard time getting lawmakers to listen to them in other areas as well, which can be attributed to both their political (non-)status as women and the political climate in the state. Annual committee reports on resolutions and bills proposed by the SCFWC show that clubwomen presented bills to the legislature year after year without success. The SCFWC legislative committee endorsed a variety of resolutions—from calling for the formation of a juvenile court to the demand that a woman be placed on the State Board of Charities.[37]

Clubwomen, ever-mindful of the community's lack of support for women in politics, had to defend their interest in legislation as "womanly." Regarding reform work, the Poppenheims' reminded their readers that a woman's political involvement was but a natural extension of her maternal duties: "It will be noted that in every case woman's interest in legislation is aroused by her love and care for the interest of the child." As mothers, clubwomen were obligated to work for social reform. According to Mary and Louisa, "Woman has a large part to play in the creation of public opinion and organized womanhood has a larger part, and therefore a greater responsibility in bringing about a high moral tone in a community." Furthermore, they reasoned that once "the impulse to civic betterment" was understood to be the province of women, this "naturally leads to the interest in laws governing civic conditions, and Southern women's civic activities have led them to a deeper and more earnest consideration of the work of the General Assemblies."[38] These editorials were directed at both legislators and individual members and clubs in the federation.

Clubwomen who lobbied the legislature surely believed that male legislators who shared the same race and class would support them. As women, they took for granted that they knew best how to care for children, and they expected their recommendations on education and juvenile reformatories to be passed. Perhaps they assumed that their gentlemen protectors in the chivalric South would honor their wishes. But legislators saw it differently; they resisted the intrusion of women into politics, feared women's interference with the industrial economy, and did not share clubwomen's vision of an activist government.

Opponents commonly criticized clubwomen for backing too many unnecessary and expensive resolutions. When Judge Whaley spoke to the Current Literature Club of Columbia, not only did he advocate against women's jury duty, but he also "urged (to quote his own words) that they be 'slow, sane, careful and practical in suggesting legislation and not to give their backing to any bills that are not fundamental and needed all over the state.'" As Emily Evan noted in the case of child labor, women resented being told to limit their agenda, while men seemingly proposed an unlimited number of bills.[39]

To add to their difficulties, clubwomen often were unable to rally the support of local editors. Newspapers routinely criticized and mocked women's clubs, to the degree that Louisa Poppenheim commented on "the absence of adverse criticisms and flippant remarks" after a federation convention.[40] Early in 1903, the Charleston *News and Courier* was anxious for women to form a Civic Improvement Society to beautify the city. The paper recognized that women had "a reluctance . . . to interfere in those concerns which their early training taught them to regard as properly within the sphere of men, and under the supervision of certain committees of the city government." However, the paper claimed that women in other locations were successfully beautifying city streets and parks "without in the least invading the special province of the various committees appointed to attend to such matters by the City Council." If women acted "as auxiliaries to the various civic committees, rather than as independent workers," the editorial continued, the city could only benefit. Thus, although women were welcome to work for the city, they had to take care lest they interfere with the proper authorities—that is, males.

The paper apparently was unaware of the Civic Club, founded two years earlier. Undoubtedly the Poppenheims contacted the editor to correct this oversight because later that year the paper once again drew attention to the need for a women's Civic Club. This time the *News and Courier* acknowledged that a club was already in existence. However, the newspaper complained that the club had focused on aiding the children of factory workers and that its efforts in city beautification had faltered. Even if the club managed to get its petitions heard at the City Council, "that was generally the end of the matter, the ordinance being neglected and forgotten through lack of enforcement, and the trees left to die for want of proper care." The club had sponsored lectures by prominent men on city beautification and sanitation, but these were poorly attended. In the face of such ineffectiveness, the paper did not bother to warn women to tread carefully; instead, it called for more citizens to show interest in this important endeavor. Despite this limited support for women's limited work within Charleston, the *News and Courier* remained steadfastly against more substantial measures eventually advocated by clubwomen, such as raising taxes for education or regulating compulsory education.[41]

Clubwomen in Beaufort had the support of their local editors, but they struggled with a reluctant town council. The Civic League, an offshoot of the literary Clover Club, succeeded in publicizing their complaints about town sanitary conditions in the *Beaufort Gazette*, a paper edited by the sons and brothers of members Abbie Holmes Christensen and her daughter, Winnie. However, the public airing of their demands did not go far. A town warden patronizingly accused them of meddling without adequate information. He wrote, "We would . . . ask that they be slow to condemn for there are many circumstances and conditions existing of which they have little knowledge and I feel that we can assure them . . . in due time every particular practicable measure will be carried out." This brush-off must have rankled club members, but without suffrage they had little recourse.[42]

Although clubwomen chose their projects carefully, they often faced defeat, especially from a legislature unwilling to grant appropriations easily. Clubwomen wanted a more activist government than was in place. Nationally, progressive women reformers succeeded in transforming the role of government by forcing it to take over social welfare duties previously considered women's charity work. From 1900 to 1930, South Carolina had few governors who supported Progressive reforms.[43] Although Governors Duncan Heyward (1903–1907) and Martin Ansel (1907–1910) supported some degree of reform, they were unable to extract cooperation from the legislature. The state superintendent of schools, Oscar B. Martin, for example, could not increase school funding due to a recalcitrant legislature. Yet in 1907 the legislature appropriated $10,000 for a statue to John C. Calhoun in Washington, D.C., and consistently appropriated funds for Confederate reunions.[44] Clearly UDC women, focusing on memorial work, were on the right track.

The next governor, Coleman Blease (1910–1913), was adamantly opposed to reform. He resisted state government intervention in the lives of millworkers and argued against child labor legislation, compulsory education, and medical inspection in the schools. Blease, like his ally Ben Tillman (governor, 1890–1894, and senator, 1895–1918), used gendered and racial imagery to emphasize the independence of white males and thus reject an overbearing state. Blease vehemently opposed middle-class reformers, whom he characterized as "intellectuals," "fool theorists," and members of the "holier than thou crowd." While he accused male reformers of being unmanly and "nigger lovers," he also dismissed female reformers, whom he believed should have been home with their children rather than interfering with mills and advocating "drastic reforms." According to Blease and his supporters, when clubwomen reformers, interfering in the lives of white male millworkers, stripped them of their independence, it was a case of women exchanging "their dresses for our pants."[45] Such strongly gendered imagery reflects tension over changing gender roles. Male workers seemed to be losing patriarchal authority by leaving the independence of the fields for the mills; at the same time women were overstepping the boundaries of their sex by working for reform and woman suffrage.

Not until the election of Governor Richard Manning in 1914 did a reform advocate control the state. Manning pushed through an impressive reform agenda. He reorganized the state hospital for the mentally ill, created a State Board of Charities and Corrections, and obtained compulsory education and child labor laws. He doubled state appropriations for education.[46] The progressive atmosphere surrounding Manning's terms waned under his successors in the 1920s, especially as the agricultural economy began to deteriorate.[47] In light of the indifference and sometimes outright hostility of most South Carolina governors to reform, clubwomen made little progress advancing their welfare agenda.

To make matters worse, legislators frustrated clubwomen with an apparent lack of frankness. They sometimes assured clubwomen of their interest, but then they failed to pursue the bills once the legislature was in session. Southern manners probably prevented some legislators from saying no to women, who until 1920 were not even voting constituents. Hannah Coleman, president of the SCFWC from 1912 to 1914, reported that "a large number of the members of the General Assembly" sent endorsement letters for the medical inspection of the schools bill to the SCFWC legislative chair. Despite this apparent show of support, however, the legislators did not follow through. As Hannah Coleman described it, "The bill was in the hands of deeply interested men, and yet it was not introduced until the last days of the Legislature, and did not reach even a second reading in the House." Clubwomen, therefore, were hindered even more by this lack of action than by those who forthrightly refused to support them. Coleman concluded with the discouraging news that "the bill for Compulsory Education had scarcely better luck, and the work for the Legislative Committee next year, unless active work on these two measures is discontinued, will be over exactly the same expensive and discouraging ground."[48]

Tenacious clubwomen continued their work despite constant defeat. The Poppenheims reminded their readers that "when [a clubwoman] makes up her mind that a thing is good for her family, 'the state,' she keeps at it until it is accomplished." Despite the discouragement, clubwomen kept going over the same grounds annually. The benefit of such perseverance was not in the passing of bills, but rather in the growth of the political experience for women. Mary P. Gridley, legislative chair in 1924–1925, told her colleagues that although they made few real gains in passing legislation, "we are better organized. All women's organizations are working together and we are learning how to use our power. We are less hysterical; more definite in our efforts; and we know a great deal more about legislative procedure."[49]

Clubwomen made more radical demands of legislators than other women's associations, such as the UDC. This difference can be seen in a 1911 *Keystone* report on various state federations. After detailing the frustrations of clubwomen in North Carolina, who lost an increased appropriation for the library commission, the editors noted, "The UDC in North Carolina were most successful in their legislative efforts in 1911." Their bill for a Confederate women's home was passed, the North Carolina Room at the Confederate Museum appropriation was doubled, and a memorial to the women of the Confederacy approved for the state normal school. The fact that the Poppenheims contrasted the UDC's successful record to that of clubwomen underscores the difference between them.[50] Apparently legislators were more willing to celebrate the Lost Cause than to address social and economic problems in the New South. Moreover, the UDC was apparently perceived as less threatening than reforming clubwomen.

Editors, governors, and male legislators were not the only problem. South Carolina clubwomen themselves were reluctant reformers. Leaders of the legislative committee and other clubwomen who advocated social reform had to work nearly as hard to get individual clubs to support their agenda as they did the legislature and the general public. Although some women expressed interest in the cause but declared themselves too busy, others simply were uninterested in reform, and, even if they were interested, they limited themselves to working for libraries. Some clubs were primarily social, including the Castalian Club, of Rock Hill, which proclaimed that their single aim was "to have a good time."[51] A few literary clubs, such as the New Century Club of Columbia, were exceptional in their social welfare programs. As the interest in reform grew, the number of Civic Clubs expanded. These clubs, however, focused primarily on local rather than statewide reforms. A brief examination of several clubs from Columbia, Rock Hill, and Charleston, reveals the varying degrees of interest in reform found in member clubs in the federation and explains the difficulties SCFWC leaders sometimes experienced in rallying support for their work.

The Civic Club of Charleston was typical of the reform-driven clubs. Christie Poppenheim, Mary and Louisa's youngest sister, founded the club in 1900 with fifteen charter members. Clubwomen embraced a wide range of reforms under the umbrella of "civics," including city beautification, health, sanitation, and education improvement. Civic improvement meshed with local boosterism, as clubwomen worked not only to add beauty and improved sanitation but also to make cities more appealing for the commerce of the New South.[52] Despite its active agenda and success, the Charleston Civic Club concentrated on local improvements, rather than the state federation legislative agenda.

For its first project, the club rented a vacant lot on the southern side of Charlotte Street for the summer to establish a playground. The Civic Club supported it financially with money from club dues, and members supervised the children at play. The following summer, the club asked the city to use the school yards as play areas for the children, but were refused. Louisa Poppenheim complained, "The City would let horses and cows graze in the school yards, but the space was not available to the children for use as a playground." Owing to clubwomen's persistence, within ten years, the city opened the Mitchell Playground, the first municipal playground in the state. The Club continued its influence through the Municipal Playground Commission, made up of men and women who had to be Civic Club representatives. These were the first women on a Charleston municipal commission, which Louisa Poppenheim chaired in 1917.[53] The clubwomen's interest in children and education extended to the formation of a Home School Association, and after an investigation of school conditions, the women successfully lobbied the county legislative delegation for building and renovating Mitchell and Bennett Schools. This was the first time that Charleston women addressed the legislature.[54]

Like the Civic Club, the City Union, later known as the Charleston City Federation of Women's Clubs, was also extremely active in local reform. This federation of local women's clubs began in June of 1899 when

Louisa Poppenheim invited five clubs—the Century Club, the South Carolina Kindergarten Association, the Memminger Alumnae, the Charleston Female Seminary Alumnae, and the Psychology Club—to band together. One of the city federation's primary accomplishments was acquiring a female matron in the police station and the county jail. Before this measure was passed, officers routinely searched female prisoners, "a humiliating experience even for these derelicts." Members, fighting for such a position for three years, only encountered the response that "Ladies never come here." According to history written for the *South Carolina Clubwoman*, "the City Federation's quick retort was that they did not want a matron for *ladies*. *Ladies* can take care of themselves." Because officials were unresponsive, one member offered to pay the first month's salary for the matron. With no financial investment required, the city council finally acquiesced. Once established, however, the matron was so popular that the city eventually ended up paying for two matrons, to guarantee round-the-clock presence of a female officer.[55]

Although most literary clubs in the federation were not as active in reform as the Civic Club or the Charleston City Federation, the New Century Club of Columbia was considerably more involved than most other literary clubs. The New Century Club, organized in February 1901, was the oldest women's club in the city. According to a club history, Vivian Moore was unhappy that card parties were the only afternoon social parties available for women and decided to form a club.[56] The club almost immediately turned its attention to community service by forming a committee to look into street cleaning in Columbia. In addition, on January 2, 1902, the club passed resolutions commending the efforts of the King's Daughters to gain a child labor legislation bill, which they attempted to have published in the *State*.[57]

However, even the New Century Club, one of the most reformist-minded of the literary clubs, had boundaries. Selective in their interests, they were cautious about taking on new projects suggested by the federation. For example, they did not act on letters from Margaret McKissick asking for support for compulsory education or from the Civil Service Committee asking for clubs to look into charitable institutions in the state. Several months later, they donated money to the rural school improvement fund but responded by "laying upon the table" a letter concerning the state library commission.[58] As a club that included members of prominent families in the capital city, the New Century had access to legislators, but initially the group hesitated to take advantage of their proximity. By 1917, the club, more comfortable with the idea of lobbying the legislature, decided to take a more active stance on favoring a home for the feebleminded. Not only did they send a card to the daily papers stating their position, but also "each member of the club was appointed to attend the meetings of the legislature, if possible, when such a bill is discussed. A central committee to know when such a bill will come up was appointed. This committee will scan the calendar and keep in touch with the matter and notify the other members."[59] Despite this surge in reform activity, clubs like the New Century emphasized the literary and social aspects of their organization, and they deemphasized their reform work. Ignoring (or concealing) all of this activity, in a history of the club in the *Columbia Record*, the club described itself as "Strictly literary" and asserted that it had done "practical work or raised money," only once, during World War I.[60]

The New Century Club was much more active in reform than most of its sister literary clubs. More typical of the literary clubs was the Thursday Club of Columbia. Clubs like the Thursday Club, although interested in libraries and at times willing to donate money to worthy causes, primarily devoted themselves to their own literary edification. They were founded for social and educational purposes only. They did not participate in reform movements in the community, lobby legislators, or vigorously support the work done by the federation.

An offshoot of the New Century Club, the Thursday club was formed in 1910 for the purpose of study. Members were hesitant to discuss current events because "it seemed rather to be the opinion that present day happenings introduced might prove fatal to success in the object of the club."[61] The club did not engage in any outside projects until 1914 when it decided to donate money to the Columbia Associated Charities. Later, members reviewed their policy and denied a request from the South Carolina Children's Home Society for a monthly or annual contribution because the club's purpose and funds did not permit regular financial assistance in philanthropic work. The Club did not take up any projects of its own; one short-lived decision to visit convalescent homes was apparently thought better of, as it decided to ascertain whether such assistance was really needed.[62]

The SCFWC was hampered in its reform agenda by either the limited or nonexistent participation of literary clubs such as the Thursday club. Maintaining federation membership, let alone support for projects, was subject to the vagaries of clubs. The Thursday Club, like many others, was inconsistent in its membership in the state federation; at first the club refused to join, then dropped out, then was readmitted, and then reconsidered dropping out again. In what was standard procedure in many literary clubs, and certainly must have been frustrating for federation leaders, the Thursday Club heard letters asking for support of various projects and noted them as "received as information" or "laid upon the table." The Over the Teacups Club of Rock Hill did not send a delegate to the 1916 state federation meeting because it was "thought best to wait another year and not tax ourselves any more this year." Although this decision probably referred to collecting money to reimburse travel expenses of the delegate, the sentiment is clear. Finally, local clubs also exhibited a desire to control their own agenda without federation guidance. The Darlington Old Homestead Club voted twelve to one to "continu[e] to run its own independent course regardless of the federation standard." Notably, the club was primarily a literary club, with little participation in social reform.[63]

It was difficult enough for some clubs to muster sufficient support for their own meetings, let alone the federation. Sporadic attendance forced the Castalian Club and many others to institute mandatory attendance policies. The Castalian Club secretary noted a suggestion "that something be done concerning the great number of absences and the lack of interest taken in the club by the members." Reorganization and expelling nonattending members did not completely solve the problem; three years later the secretary bemoaned, "It is very hard to have an interesting lesson when most of the members seem to take so little interest in coming to the meetings."[64] These clubwomen were not likely to support the federation's ambitious reform agenda actively.

Members of the Social Survey Club of Columbia studied questions concerning women and child labor, but they seemed uninterested in or unwilling to act in their own communities. Organized by Bessie Schumpert and Mary Rucker to study sociology, the club studied topics including health, unemployment, the home, housing conditions, trade unions, child labor, and law and crime. As a study club, however, they did not establish schools, survey mills, or keep records of their political lobbying to the legislature until 1927.

This limitation meant that some literary clubs were at once "radical" in their choice of study and "conservative" in their unwillingness to go beyond study. These clubs introduced women to the issues and allowed them to gather facts on problems that individual members then took action on in a different forum—through a civic club, federation leadership, the YWCA, or other organizations. In this sense, the clubs were incubators for radical progressive reform. However, when many literary clubs held back from acting, their reluctance hampered the federation. These literary clubs had formed expressly for the purpose of study and self-improvement—not reform—and their members probably felt that there were other venues available for such projects. This pattern of limited support for reform in literary clubs was common. The Thursday Club of Laurens, for example, while more active than some, concentrated on study as a club, while individual members, including Wil Lou Gray, became involved in social welfare through other organizations or leadership in the federation.[65]

The lack of support for legislative resolutions came in part from clubwomen's fear of taking positions in the political arena. Clubs with more elite members may also have clung to traditional gender roles more tightly and eschewed lobbying the legislature. Others may have hesitated lest husbands or others disapprove of their action. For instance, the Castalian Club of Rock Hill, like many other clubs, originally supported the petition for a woman's building at University of South Carolina, which the State Federation endorsed. However, at the next meeting, it reconsidered their approval in light of an editorial from the Anderson newspaper against the building. The minutes report, "The club decided that it had acted previously endorsing the appropriation without sufficient information, and after further consideration, it was voted to go on record against the appropriation."[66] Whether clubwomen reconsidered the issue because of the data reported by the newspaper or whether they hesitated to support a contentious issue is not revealed in their minutes, although their susceptibility to public opinion is clearly indicated.

These women's literary clubs were closer in spirit to the UDC than to Progressive reform associations. The minutes of local clubs indicate that the driving forces inspiring social reform in women's clubs were the state federation as a body and certain leaders in particular. Only a limited number of specific clubs, mostly civic clubs or city unions and a few literary clubs, ever responded to the call. Many clubs declined to participate in this reform agenda, the more "radical" aspect of clubwomen's work, even though encouraged by leaders such as Louisa Poppenheim, Sarah Visanska, and Emily Evans.

There is no pattern to indicate why certain women and certain clubs responded to the reform movement more readily than others. Some may have been inspired by the rhetoric of the Poppenheims, who stressed their obligation to the South. Pearl Fant was also probably typical of many who drew zeal from religious faith. Writing about her prison reform work, Fant emotionally described the prisoners' tears and conversion as "some of the sweetest moments of my life."[67] Where clubwomen lived was also important. A survey of federation leadership shows that the up-country of South Carolina predominated. The up-country was the home of the mills and growing cities, while the low country, with the exception of Charleston, remained largely agricultural with a larger black population. Women living in the piedmont areas would have been more exposed to the problems that urbanization and industrialization caused. The leaders most aggressive in pursuing social reform, such as Louisa Poppenheim, Sarah Visanska, Bessie Duncan, Emily Evans, and Wil Lou Gray, were all from either the up-country or Charleston. Others, such as Martha Orr Patterson and Margaret McKissick, also from the up-country, worked hard for the reformatory and other efforts, but as wives of mill owners, they did not push for child labor legislation. Women in the piedmont had an additional advantage—the black population was not as large in their counties. This might have diffused concerns over the possibility of black beneficiaries to state welfare programs. Finally, some of those who pushed hardest for reform were ardent suffragists. Whether their desire for reform informed their decision to support woman suffrage, or vice versa, is not clear.

Clubwomen's difficulties in garnering support for reform from both outside and within the federation itself are perhaps most evident in their limited campaign against child labor. Despite its similar focus on the needs of children, child labor legislation was considerably more controversial than education reform. Clubwomen quickly found that the debate over child labor was linked to concerns regarding Northern intervention, the fortunes of leading men, resistance from millworkers, and ultimately the New South program of industrialization itself. They were stymied by their own hesitation to criticize the New South as well as by tenacious opposition from legislators and family. They therefore devised alternative solutions that focused on education instead of legislation.[68]

When Southerners began to espouse industrialization for a New South, they focused on the cotton mill. South Carolina was the third largest textile-producing state in the nation at the turn of the century.[69] Unfortunately, the state was also a leader in employing children in the cotton mills. As white families moved off the farm and into the mill village, children began to work the spindles and looms at alarmingly young ages. In Southern mill villages all members of the family were expected to work. In 1900 the state had more than eight thousand children working in the mills; the children represented 30 percent of the mill population.[70] They worked long hours for little pay.

When children in South Carolina went to work at the spindles, they did not go to school and were overwhelmingly more likely to be illiterate. Therefore, proponents of child labor laws also advocated compulsory education laws. School attendance was only 53.4 percent for seven- to twenty-year-olds in the state in 1910; that number reflects 61.9 percent of white children and 47.5 percent of black children.[71] Clearly, if education reforms were to be meaningful, a higher percentage of children needed to be in school rather than at work.

The child labor problem in the South began to attract national attention at the same time that clubwomen in South Carolina founded the state federation.[72] Clubwomen were cognizant of the issue from the beginning, evident from discussions that took place at some of the first state meetings. Yet they hesitated to seek legislation banning or regulating child labor and instead concentrated their effort on improving educational opportunities available to mill children. Sarah Visanska was one of the first federation leaders to discuss the mill problems. In "The City Woman in Club Life," she described serious problems peculiar to the New South: children and poor white families laboring in the cotton mills. Visanska refrained from blaming mill owners for poor working conditions. Rather she appealed to women, who formerly gave alms to the poor, now to train the needy through better education, kindergartens, and industrial education, to make "useful, happy citizens of tomorrow." Visanska did not want to halt the "progress" of industrialization in the South, but she did recognize its consequences. The New South industrialization creed could not create a prosperous South for all whites without women to aid those adversely affected by industrialization.[73] Clubwomen wrestled with how best to address these problems.

Their class status affected their struggle: as elite women, personal relationships with mill owners undoubtedly influenced many clubwomen. Margaret Smyth McKissick, president of the SCFWC from 1906 to 1907, was intimately tied to the mills through her father and husband. McKissick, born in Charleston, later lived in Greenwood. McKissick was a member of the UDC and president of her local women's club, as well as an officer in the National Civic Association. Her father, Captain Ellison Smyth, president of Pelzer Mills, was a leading mill owner in the state, and her husband, A. Foster McKissick, presided over several mills including Grendel Cotton Mills in Greenwood.[74] McKissick's relationship to Pelzer is critical because it was considered a model mill town, with substantial education and welfare programs for workers, notably atypical of most mills in the state.[75] In the eyes of the federation, however, this tie, rather than creating a conflict of interest, uniquely qualified her for work on the child labor committee. After McKissick reported that she had corresponded extensively with clubwomen throughout the nation about child labor, the *Keystone* editors glowingly noted that "she is so well fitted to give information in this direction." McKissick then joined the General Federation Committee on Industrial and Child Labor; the Poppenheims again approved heartily, "Mrs. McKissick is familiar with industrial conditions in the South, and no better selection could have been made to represent the South on this committee."[76]

McKissick's family ties to the industry, and her position of influence, reflect the position of other clubwomen like her, whose family and friends were mill owners and supervisors and who were reluctant to criticize the mill owners directly. James L. Orr, the father of SCFWC president Martha Patterson, was another prominent defender of mills. August Kohn, a journalist for the *News and Courier* who wrote a series of articles praising the mills, married Irene Kohn, a clubwoman and president of the UDC.[77] Kohn, a prolific supporter of the mills, focused on the relative improvement of mill life over rural life.[78] In 1901 he sided with mill owners against a proposed bill promoted by "outside agitators," and invoked the specter of Northern interference in Southern life. The newspaper contended that women, who were "unbusinesslike," and labor, who would naturally work against the owners, were hurting Southern industry, which needed to be protected until it caught up to industry in the North.[79] Irene McFadyen, who was sent by the American Federation of Labor (AFL) to the South to report on mill conditions, complained that she could not get clubwomen in South Carolina to support her because "the ladies who were assisting to get the bill through, feared me as a representative of organized labor."[80] To them, organized labor implied Northern influence and vice versa.

Clubwomen also supported the owners by their choice of speakers to state federation meetings. National Child Labor Association leaders, such as A. J. McKelway, spoke to other state federations. But the South Carolina Federation instead had Thomas Parker, president of the Monaghan Cotton Mills of Greenville and a spokesmen for mill owners, address their convention. He described the cotton mill towns and then asked "the womanhood and manhood of South Carolina to better the conditions of the people in the mills *where they own stock*."[81] By putting it this way, Parker effectively tied women's hands. How could they attack mill owners when the mills were the source of their bread and butter?

Rather than blame family and friends for the conditions of mill workers and the persistence of child labor, reformers therefore blamed parents for the shiftless behavior that forced children to work. For example, clubwoman Mary P. Screven described the procession of fathers bringing lunch buckets to their children. Lazy parents sending children to work while they drank or otherwise wasted their days made for good drama. This, however, would not be a rational economic decision, as children were paid substantially lower salaries than adults.[82] Dempie Anderson Adams echoed a common claim at the SCFWC convention in 1899 when she accused parents of making children work at factories. "It is not poverty," she argued, "but indifference which influences. Enough is spent for whiskey and tobacco to educate every child in America, and the bulk of this vast sum comes from people who claim to be too poor to pay for tuition." These stereotypes did little to aid those in need.[83]

Although South Carolina clubwomen never gave up advocating for libraries or other legislative solutions, which were ignored or ridiculed by men in the state, child labor reform was different. In this case, the economic prosperity and integrity of family and friends were at stake. Moreover, promoting a positive good missing from the South, such as a library, implied only that the region was slow in adopting such benefits. However, child labor reform involved criticizing a practice already in place and directly related to the economic development of the state and the New South. Clubwomen essentially followed the economic and social policies supported by their husbands; they hoped only to ameliorate poverty through training the workforce, not to tackle an economic system with depressed wages caused by segregation.[84]

In addition to this unwillingness to confront the men of their class, their reticence to criticize the South factored in their conservative approach to this problem.[85] Child labor reform, or lack thereof, was closely tied to the emphasis on pride in the South, which often was manifested as defensive behavior. Sometimes this defensive pride hindered the federation's progressive reform. After the National Educational Association had its annual convention in Charleston in 1900, an editorial in the *Keystone* congratulated South Carolina clubwomen by claiming that Southern teachers, "have shown themselves to be not in the slightest degree behind in educational progress; quite to the contrary."[86] Yet, the Southern states still lagged far behind the North in literacy rates, educational spending, and school facilities, and the South showed little sign of catching up.

Similarly, clubwomen also downplayed the child labor problem in Southern textile mills. They were reluctant to criticize cotton mills, the central feature of New South industrialization. Moreover, child labor reform was different because by the early twentieth century the press often presented child labor as a Southern problem. Articles in the national press detailed the horrors of child labor, often in somewhat sensationalistic language.[87] In the pages of the *Keystone*, however, in a reference to press concern with child labor, the Poppenheims chose instead to highlight an article of the opposite extreme. These editors were encouraged by an article in *Harper's Magazine*, which asserted that "the child laborer in the Southern cotton mill was often well provided for with night school, kindergarten, and opportunities for learning practical housekeeping and kindred trades." Mary Applewhite Bacon, comparing the cotton mill schools favorably to mountain cabins, implied that the cotton mill life was an improvement over previous conditions and concluded that "cotton mill life, as a whole, is by no means as dismal as it is often painted."[88] This picture did not square with most other articles.

The Poppenheims also commented on an article in *Charities* that discussed newspaper boys as a problem in large cities. Despite the many other references throughout *Charities* concerning the problem in the Southern mills, they praised *this* article for pointing out that child labor was not just a mill problem, but also a problem for large cities; in other words, it was a Northern problem, too.[89] However, lest anyone believe that they approved of the principle of child labor, they observed, "The ethical theory of child labor is so simple, the practical application of the theory so difficult!" Recognition of the problem did not easily translate into solutions.

This refusal to acknowledge the depth of the problem in the South resulted in emphasizing improved education in mill towns rather than lobbying for legislation banning child labor. When the topic first surfaced at the SCFWC annual meeting in 1900, both Sarah Visanska and Mary P. Gridley, a mill owner herself, spoke on the horrors of child labor without urging legislation outlawing it. Gridley instead proposed that factory towns needed to provide children alternative places rather than mills in which to spend time. Mary Poppenheim suggested playgrounds and free kindergartens. Local clubs responded eagerly to her recommendation as a sufficient solution to the problem.[90] The Over the Teacups club in Rock Hill was one of many clubs to build a library in the mill district in their town, and clubs supported kindergartens in mill districts in Anderson, Columbia, Charleston, Greenville, Greer, Laurens, Spartanburg, Pelzer, and Pacolet. The Castalian Club also had a visit from a mill worker who thanked them for the benefits she received at the Opportunity school, which they sponsored.[91] These efforts enabled clubwomen to feel that they were doing something about child labor without demanding that the legislature ban it.

In their work to improve educational facilities, clubwomen cooperated with mill owners. The Kelly Free Kindergarten Association, for example, opened a kindergarten at the Charleston Royal Bag Manufactory for the children of operatives. This venture was possible, given owner cooperation, and the Association reported that "the factory authorities supplied the house and were willing to give all necessary assistance to the Clubwomen in perfecting their plans. The authorities and the Club-women are working in harmony along all lines that will better the condition of the mill operators."[92] It is difficult to ascertain whether clubwomen really believed that a kindergarten was a better solution than a tough law; certainly they understood it was easier to affect.

A major problem with this approach to welfare was that supporters exaggerated mill philanthropy. According to historian David Carlton, "no mill spent as much as one percent of its capital a year on welfare work." School attendance was a big problem. Although Pelzer required children under age twelve to attend school, it also required those above age twelve to work in the mill. Furthermore, federal inspectors found that Pelzer generally ignored the attendance requirements, despite Smyth's claims of perfect attendance awards. Mill policies requiring one worker per room in the house overrode school attendance. Mill schools also suffered from shorter terms than public schools and a larger pupil-teacher ratio. Mill district schools had between 57 and 125 pupils for each teacher (Pelzer, the most widely praised mill in the state, had 84 students per teacher); the statewide average was 38, and towns and city schools averaged 45.5.[93] Clubwomen's decision to work with mill owners clearly was ineffectual.

Louisa Poppenheim approved of clubwomen's more conservative approach. In her annual report as state federation president in 1902, she noted she had heard addresses on child labor and manual training at the General Federation Biennial. Although she was an uncompromising supporter of clubwomen's legislative efforts in many areas, in this case, she uncharacteristically wrote, "I feel that we in South Carolina where the mill population is growing so rapidly, should occupy some time in considering these problems. By this I do not mean to interfere with legislation, but to acquaint ourselves with existing conditions in the mills and with the

[?] houses, and prepare ourselves to discuss the subject intelligently, and to lend a helping hand where assistance is needed."[94] Such a statement was in complete contrast to her zeal for legislation in other areas.

Poppenheim was not alone in cautioning clubwomen to exercise care in their legislative agenda. Lillian Milner Orr, president of the Alabama Federation of Women's Clubs in 1902, also advocated restraint. When her federation met for the express purpose of influencing the legislature for child labor legislation, she reminded her listeners "that by maintaining a body of conservative, level-headed women we accomplish our ends much more surely than by becoming agitators on any and all subjects, regardless of the surrounding conditions." Orr suggested that clubwomen influence their own husbands and fathers, "instead of calling the neighbors in to see how they have strayed from the right way."[95] Neither Orr nor Poppenheim was prepared to battle mill owners over child labor legislation. It was one thing to ask legislators to provide libraries and kindergartens, and another to accuse husbands of actually harming their workers: the sin of commission seemed harsher than the sin of omission.

Perhaps Louisa Poppenheim was also influenced by her participation in the conservative South Carolina Child Labor Committee (SCCLC), a branch of the NCLC. Poppenheim was one of a few women on the SCCLC, and she diligently reported meetings back to clubwomen through the *Keystone*.[96] Her report in December 1910 cryptically describes the SCCLC meeting. After noting the members who were present, she wrote, "Upon invitation a committee from the South Carolina Cotton Manufacturers met with the Child Labor Committee and discussed present conditions and possible future legislation in behalf of the children in mill villages.... *It is interesting to note* that South Carolina is the only State where the Child Labor Committee has conferences with the representatives of the mills." Louisa generally used this phrase to highlight a point of pride for the state or for women's clubs, but in this case her intention is ambiguous. Was she proud of this cooperation as well, or did she want to hint at the power of the owners? She then related that the committee did not decide on its legislative agenda until *after* the mill men left the meeting. They proposed legislation to amend the poverty exemption for child labor, to prohibit night labor for children under sixteen, and to require birth registration.[97] Poppenheim noted further that both the committee and the mill men were committed to compulsory education, although they did not propose a resolution on it that year. Mill owners typically used the lack of a compulsory education law to protest child labor laws, under the guise that children would have nowhere to go if not to work. Poppenheim then printed additional resolutions that had passed in which the committee appears to soften its demands for reform: "*that any reference to the raising of the age limit be stricken out of our child labor bill . . . that the South Carolina Child Labor Committee place itself on record as favoring a gradual rise of the age limit to fourteen years, as soon as in the opinion of the committee the conditions are favorable.*" She concluded her report by defending the SCCLC with the comment, "The policy of the Committee is conservative and humanitarian, and the members are working earnestly to better conditions among the poor children in South Carolina."[98] The committee was unable to shake the influence of the mill owners, who in 1911 convinced it to stop pursuing a fourteen-year-old age limit and instead eliminate the loopholes in the under-twelve limit.

According to Poppenheim, then, the committee, while cooperating with mill owners and retreating on demands for legislation, was doing its best to improve conditions. Even if she disagreed with its policies, she did not go on record to advocate more effective measures. She continued to urge South Carolina clubwomen to support the committee.[99] Clubwomen followed the tactics of the committee and worked with, not against, the mill owners.

Yet, despite their reticence to criticize the South and the mill owners, clubwomen wanted to ameliorate industrial working conditions. For example, the *Keystone* quoted Josiah Strong speaking on Women and Social Betterment. Strong maintained, "It looks as if women's clubs might take a leading part in the great work of industrial improvement and in establishing right relations between employers and employees. As wives they sympathize with the complexities of the former, and as women they sympathize with the hardships of the latter. With a hand upon each they may do much to reconcile both." Clubwomen also, while downplaying the problem, did at least acknowledge that there was work to be done; they did not simply praise the progress of mill workers in their transition from the farm to the mill.[100] Therefore, clubwomen tried to finesse a position of support for the New South while ameliorating its negative consequences through welfare and education programs; moreover, they sought not to blame New South leaders.

Despite clubwomen's interest in mill conditions, they did not make child labor reform a legislative priority. There is little evidence that they actively supported minimum age laws. In 1905, they reported that they had no need to work on the issue because South Carolina had already passed a law banning work for children under age twelve. Yet, this law had exceptions, was not enforced, and finally had to be replaced with a stronger minimum age law in 1909. Moreover, clubwomen reported to the General Federation that "we have done nothing at all, for our excellent law on the subject has now gone into effect." This attitude strongly contrasts with their more aggressive statements regarding other reforms. At the same time, it allowed South Carolina clubwomen to put a good face forward to the national federation. The defensive nature of this remark certainly was in response to an earlier request from the General Federation's social work committee that requested that the "backwards" states work "vigorously" for effective laws.[101]

Although South Carolina finally passed a minimum age labor law set at fourteen in 1917, clubwomen did not devote any attention to passage of the law in their reports. Clubwomen in South Carolina also did not support a federal law banning child labor because of the Southern states' traditional argument against federal regulations: states' rights. At the General Federation Biennial Meeting in 1926 Lena Springs, then president of the SCFWC and the wife of a mill owner, voted against the child labor resolution because her state favored self-determination and opposed federal intervention in the South.[102] In the state as a whole, child labor laws passed excruciatingly slowly.[103]

Convinced there was little work for them to do on child labor, clubwomen pushed instead for compulsory education laws. Perhaps they wanted to work indirectly to establish the conditions in which a strong and enforceable minimum age child labor law would be acceptable. Yet clubwomen called for a compulsory education law to aid "idle," not working, children. The *Federation Bulletin* reported in 1905, "Now if we can only succeed in having passed a compulsory education bill which will force the idle children into the schools, we shall have done all we possibly can."[104] Their compulsory education resolution, however, failed every year until 1915, and even through 1937 weak compulsory education laws allowed poverty exemptions.[105]

A main reason many South Carolinians resisted compulsory education was that race pervaded the debate. They feared that more black children than white mill children would take advantage of educational opportunities. In 1903 Governor Duncan Heyward told the General Assembly that "more negro children than whites are attending our public schools. Do our white people realize what this means for the future?" In fact, school attendance figures show that attendance by seven- to twenty-year-olds was consistently higher for white children than for black. In 1910, 61.9 percent of whites attended school, compared to 47.5 percent of blacks, and in 1920, 73.3 percent of whites and 64.1 percent of blacks attended.[106]

Opponents of child labor legislation, such as Governor Cole Blease, also sided with mill workers who resisted state intervention in their lives, especially male operatives who perceived the laws as threatening their control over their families.[107] Blease argued, "These people are our people; they are our kindred; they are our friends, and in my opinion they should be let alone, and allowed to manage their own children and allowed to manage their own affairs." Southern tradition distrusted government intervention, especially that which came at the state or federal level. Workers also distrusted reformers because elements of social control and the imposition of white middle-class culture infused the otherwise humanitarian efforts of reformers. While child labor law advocates aided the welfare of children, they also promoted state interference in family life, imposed middle-class conventions of childhood, and potentially robbed the family of income crucial to its economic survival.[108]

Clubwomen who pushed for mothers to raise children and keep their homes according to middle-class standards at times found their outreach programs rejected. In Spartanburg, a mill nursery organized by middle-class women failed because mill mothers believed that the nursery reflected negatively on their competence as mothers. Likewise the Civic Club's efforts to staff a playground that would teach factory children "good citizenship" also failed; they complained that they reached only "respectable" children instead. These difficulties came about because clubwomen saw themselves as needing to "rescue the unfortunate from a restless and idle existence." Such a patronizing attitude was undoubtedly evident to mill workers and others.[109]

As middle- and upper-class women, members of the SCFWC attempted to aid poor white rural and mill families because they viewed them as essential to the prosperity of the region as a whole. Furthermore, they focused on what they had in common, their whiteness, at the same time they refused to cross racial boundaries and aid blacks. Mary and Louisa Poppenheim's mother once warned them "poor white people are often more provoking than negroes and require great patience to manage them."[110] They were perhaps "more provoking" because their behavior required upper-class whites to recognize that skin color did not ensure attributes of "civilization," which they assumed that all Anglo Saxons shared.

Ironically, when mill owners claimed that children preferred to work in the mill rather than go to school, they often accurately represented the views of workers, or at least of their parents. Mill workers expressed their opinion through petitions against child labor and compulsory education laws and through their overwhelmingly support for Governor Coleman Blease.[111] Child labor defenders, however, who claimed that the children themselves preferred to work were less convincing. Former governor and Piedmont mill president James L. Orr, the father of SCFWC president Martha Orr Patterson, claimed that the hundreds of children in his mill preferred to work. He described their days as filled with play, "We have money now—we don't have to sit up all day and behave, we have more fun, and we can run about all over the mill when not at work."[112] The SCFWC did not directly challenge him.

Despite the resistance from mill workers and owners, antilegislation atmosphere in the state as a whole, and the conservative approach of the federation and leaders such as Poppenheim and McKissick to child labor reform, several exceptional SCFWC leaders were deeply committed to workers' needs. However, they were unable to make their concerns a priority within the federation. Visanska attempted to lead the federation toward more substantial support for working women and children and a more active social reform agenda. She implored working women and housewives to be supportive of each other, and she even went so far as to suggest that housewives be paid for their work in the home. In 1915 Sarah Visanska and her committee in the Department of Conservation recommended a legislative program both to abolish child labor and mandate compulsory education, maximum hours, and minimum wage laws. Visanska challenged the federation by asking, "Shall our men, women and children progress towards a higher citizenship or be allowed to deteriorate through adverse surroundings, unwise legislation and avarice? Forward or backward?"[113] Despite her strong words, the federation did not respond to her proposal. Perhaps this was because less than a dozen leaders in the federation can be identified as wage earners. Although the actual number may have been higher, given that many were married to businessmen and professionals, and that statewide only 15 percent of white married women worked at the time, the percentage of working women in the federation was undoubtedly small. The Poppenheims often repeated that they were not paid for their work on the *Keystone*.[114] Because so few white clubwomen worked for wages, they did not prioritize aid to working women, despite a growing number of female mill workers.

That same year, Emily Evans chaired the subcommittee on industrial and social conditions of women and children in South Carolina. One of the most liberal members of the federation, Evans was born in New York. She moved to South Carolina following her marriage to John Gary Evans, state governor from 1894 to 1897. In Spartanburg, Evans started the New Era Club, a woman suffrage club, and she served as vice president of the state Equal Suffrage League. Evans was deeply interested in education and illiteracy, as well as labor conditions. Despite her wealthy upbringing (her father was a millionaire) and perhaps owing to her Northern roots, Evans was particularly concerned with the fate of working women and hoped the right to vote would help protect them.[115] She reported that she had written to forty clubwomen and asked them to research the conditions of women and children in the mills, stores, and offices. However, she received reports from only eleven clubs, eight of which were from her home county, Spartanburg. Despite the low response, she compared their reports to that of the State Labor Commissioner and the national and state child labor committees and found the same results: a depressingly high number of children under age sixteen were working in the mills, and 91 percent of the mills were violating existing laws. Although Evans did report favorably about a Spartanburg County mill, which provided generous services to its employees, unlike the Poppenheims, Evans noted that the mill was exceptional, rather than praising it unduly.[116]

Two years later, Evans was still personally interested in the cause but fighting a lack of interest on the part of member clubs. She wrote to twenty-six clubs, those who were supposed to be most interested in industrial and social conditions, and, even from this self-selected group, she received responses from only three of them, an astonishingly low response rate. She requested that clubwomen and churches observe National Child Labor Day, January 24th. "I was away from home the month of January," she reported, "but fully expected that these days would be observed by the Federated Clubs in Spartanburg and was deeply disappointed on my return to find that they, as well as the churches had failed to do so." Disillusioned with the results, she only commented on the success of Charleston clubs in establishing a juvenile court.

Evans is notable because, unlike her colleagues in the federation, she praised welfare work in mill towns but refused to allow it as an acceptable alternative to legislation. She argued for "the necessity of not allowing any kind of welfare work to prevent us from recognizing the fact that it does not give to those people the thing that is fundamental to their proper growth, namely: time for self-development." Such time would need to be legislated through minimum age and maximum hours laws. Evans praised the new state minimum age limit recently passed at age fourteen and recommended that the federation work toward age sixteen. Unlike Lena Springs, Evans also endorsed the Keating-Owen federal child labor law, without a word about states' rights. Finally, she recommended that the federation work for the eight-hour law for men and women, a minimum wage for women, and compulsory education. She acknowledged that these were radical ideas in the South, but exhorted women to remember their duty to the "Brotherhood of Man." Evans couched her radical appeal in the language of religion and patriotism familiar to Southern clubwomen. Invoking a Southern statesman, she told them it was their patriotic duty as women to help wage-earners make a better home for themselves.[117] Evans seems to have caught on to the Southern rhetoric pervading the federation. Unlike most of her fellow clubwomen who lived and breathed their Southernness, the New York-born Evans may have couched her appeal in such language deliberately rather than genuinely.

The next year, Evans reported no material successes, but at least she noted an increase in interest. Shamed by her report, many clubs responded to her letters, especially regarding the availability of seats in stores for female clerks, a much less controversial issue. Although pleased that the national Keating-Owen bill passed, Evans was disappointed that South Carolina had failed to pass a statewide compulsory education law and complained that, in her opinion, "bills of far less importance received careful consideration." Moreover, she did not accept the general assembly's claim that it was unable to grant appropriations for a state Institution for the Feeble-Minded because of financial constraint. "We are unwilling to accept this excuse," she boldly stated, "when we witness the large appropriations made for less vital needs." Evans also subtly promoted woman suffrage by suggesting that although legislators asked the women's clubs to limit the bills they endorsed, 1,400 bills had been introduced to the General Assembly; she was left to conclude that the lack of representation of women resulted in their demands not being taken seriously despite their significance to the state.[118]

In addition to Visanska and Evans, Bessie Duncan, chair of the education committee, passionately argued for an enforceable compulsory education law. A graduate of Converse College, Duncan organized the Aiken County Suffrage League and ran her husband's newspaper while he was in public service. Concerned about both illiteracy (she petitioned the governor for an illiteracy commission of which she later became a member) and compulsory education, Duncan forthrightly reported to the federation that the local option compulsory education law was a failure because "there is nothing compulsory about it." Furthermore, Duncan circumvented the state superintendent of education and asked county superintendents for information regarding the bill because, as she claimed, the state office's information was "inaccurate and cannot be relied upon." Most significant, she found that African Americans in the counties contacted had not taken advantage of the compulsory education law. This discredited those politicians who had disapproved of the law because they argued that the number of black school children would increase. Duncan and Evans were delighted when a stricter compulsory education law was finally achieved in 1919. Once passed, however, proponents had to try to keep compulsory education on the legislative agenda because even this law was for only four months and unenforced by truant officers.[119]

After Evans's term, no social and industrial conditions committee chair, despite the continued interest in compulsory education, focused directly on mill conditions again until the late 1920s. When Isabelle Lindsay Cain, a member of the state interracial committee and a leader in the state Episcopal social welfare department, surveyed conditions in 1927–1928, she had only positive news to report. Despite her "liberal" stance on race and social welfare issues, Cain wrote that she was "happy to be able to report that so far as my investigations have gone, conditions are good, the mill owners of the state seeming to be keenly concerned in regard to welfare of the men and women in their employ."[120] Even she was uninspired by the weak child labor and compulsory education laws.

In comparison to South Carolina clubwomen's weak stance, clubwomen in other Southern states varied in their approach to child labor reform. Women in states not as dependent on the new mills as the Carolinas and Georgia faced less opposition. They also had less to be defensive about and risked less in criticizing the New South. In Mississippi, women's clubs focused on legislation from the beginning; the state federation president in 1902 painted a heart-wrenching portrait of children being forced to work for mills in "*this* state" and asked clubwomen to seek legislative solutions.[121] Some clubwomen were inspired to tackle the problem because of their pride in the South and desire to build a better New South. This is most evident in Rebecca Lowe's presidential address to the 1900 General Federation Biennial. Rather than following the tactic of Louisa Poppenheim or Margaret McKissick in defending Southern practices, Lowe, a clubwoman from Georgia, addressed them head on. She called for a more intense effort by Southern women to fight child labor. "In the South, . . . this must be the main point of attack," Lowe declared. "No club woman shall rest content while a single child is suffered to lean eleven hours a day over a spindle. . . . In the South, with its totally new industrial life, the evils of an unrestricted child's labor are upon us in tremendous force, with thousands of little children in our mills."[122] One wonders if Louisa Poppenheim cringed to hear the South's dirty laundry being aired at the General Federation meeting.

Despite a more concerted effort for child labor reform in some Southern states, many clubwomen in the South shared the hesitation shown by South Carolinians. In North Carolina, clubwomen also focused on alternative solutions to legislation, such as schools for mill children with offerings in sewing and home sciences for girls and agriculture and textile courses for boys.[123] Rebecca Lowe aside, many clubwomen in Georgia desired a voluntary agreement, like that advocated by Lillian Orr in Alabama. In both Georgia and Alabama, unions played a major role in initiating campaigns for child labor legislation, which were later joined by clubwomen, who often remained on the periphery. In Alabama, progress was slow, hindered by Orr and other clubwomen related to mill owners. According to historian Mary Martha Thomas, "Some of the prominent club leaders who were connected with leading manufacturers resented the constant criticisms of the cotton industry." Those who pushed for stricter laws had to work hard to keep the Alabama clubwomen interested in the cause.[124]

White clubwomen and other reformers could not muster a strong challenge to child labor, which remained a problem in South Carolina.[125] By 1919, more than three thousand children under age sixteen still worked for wages.[126] Moreover, the compulsory education laws passed in 1915 and 1919, while increasing school attendance, were weakened by the poverty exemption. School attendance increased from 1910 to 1920, from 61.9 to 73.3 percent for white children aged seven to twenty, but decreased slightly by 1930, to 71.3 percent, perhaps because of the weak agricultural economy of the 1920s. Weak laws and weak enforcement meant that, without a federal law, child labor would not cease. South Carolina and other Southern states, however, rejected several attempts to pass a federal amendment. The state finally passed a sixteen-year-old age limit in 1937 and a compulsory education law for children aged seven to sixteen, but even then they retained the poverty exemption.[127]

Southern clubwomen operated within the constraints of their society.

Married to mill owners, influenced by politicians, newspapers, the SCCLC, and to a lesser degree even the operatives themselves who opposed regulation, clubwomen in South Carolina waged a half-hearted campaign against child labor in their state. Although they were willing to stand up to opposition and support other legislation, notably various education reforms, child labor legislation was riskier, complicated by its association with economic prosperity.[128] The mills paved the road to the New South in the state, and the Poppenheims and their colleagues, focused as they were on building Southern identity and pride, were hesitant to find fault with that progress in their state, especially if it opened the door to criticism from Northerners.

Although some other clubwomen in the region were busier than they, South Carolina clubwomen understood their local conditions. Mary Poppenheim once wrote about the high number of free libraries in the state: "That this Federation has proven itself active and progressive is apparent from the results of its work; that its members are conservative at times is but a proof of their knowledge of local conditions." That conservatism was so deeply ingrained that the secretary of the New Century Club claimed a paper read on modern poetry was "sufficiently modern to quite astound the conservative New Centuryites."[129] Leaders committed to reform, such as Evans, were unable to overcome the conservative messages preached by others in the federation, and South Carolina clubwomen let child labor reform get away from them.

White clubwomen did what they could. They focused on the need for Southern clubwomen to rebuild a New South around an ideal of progress that necessitated reform work in education, kindergartens, libraries, and care for delinquent children. Despite the progress clubwomen made in these areas, their reluctance to criticize the mills and mill owners in the child labor reform campaign reveals just how conservative clubwomen could be. They encountered resistance from legislators and their intended beneficiaries alike. This uneven record, however, of participation and of achievement, when considered within the atmosphere surrounding women's reform in the South, contained more successes than failures. Looking back on the occasion of the twenty-fifth anniversary of the Charleston City Federation, Sarah Visanska evaluated women's clubs accordingly: "The founders of this organization gratefully realize, that, despite the disappointments, discouragement's, and deferred hopes, which came to them all as pioneers,—they really 'builded better than they knew.' . . . In City, State and Nation, the Federated Clubwoman has long been recognized as an uplifting force, a power in every 'Battle for the Right.'"[130] The SCFWC, despite defeat, despite discouragement, and despite lacking support from both outsiders and insiders, made a number of ladies of the club into social reformers.

White clubwomen were able to lobby the legislature, although primarily for whites only, and even then, with limited success. In the context of South Carolina politics in the early decades of the twentieth century, the legislative agenda of the SCFWC was in the vanguard of social reform. Their demands concerning education, health, civics, and industrial conditions were great, and we can only imagine the changes they would have wrought had they succeeded in fulfilling their ambitious agenda. Like other clubwomen throughout the South and the nation, clubwork enabled some women in South Carolina to begin to consider the social and economic conditions in their communities and drew some into a public and political fight for legislative relief. This was no small feat for women at the time. They had to continue to assure the public—and themselves—that they remained womenly women and that their interest in politics came from their maternal instincts. That they encountered a lack of support from both within and without—from those clubwomen who were more interested in literary self-improvement, from their own inability to self-critique in the case of child labor, and from legislators and family members who ridiculed or ignored their concerns—speaks to the magnitude of the successes they did achieve, rather than their failures. Certainly, for their fellow white citizens, they "builded better than they knew."

Black South Carolinians, however, received little aid from white clubs. For that, they had to rely on black women's clubs, who had even less success in the halls of the legislature.

Chapter 6

"Exalting the Cause of Virtue"

Black and White Clubwomen and Juvenile Reformatories

In December 1925, a fire started in the Fairwold Home for Delinquent Colored Girls, outside of Columbia, South Carolina. Although no one was hurt, the twenty or so girls housed there were left homeless. The home was the responsibility of the South Carolina Federation of Colored Women's Clubs (SCFCWC), which had raised money to purchase an old farmhouse in Fairwold to provide an alternative to prison for "wayward" black girls. The fire magnified the need for state support for the home: South Carolina had already built reformatories for white boys, white girls, and black boys, but not black girls. Although they were unsuccessful in fighting for state recognition (the state did not build a reformatory for black girls until 1949), through this campaign black clubwomen in South Carolina declared their citizenship and insisted that they be included in progressive reforms in the New South.

A comparative study of Fairwold and the state home for delinquent white boys shows how black and white clubwomen, although performing similar community services, drew motivation from different sources and worked toward different goals.[1] Regional influences were significant motivators in pushing women to embrace social reform during the Progressive era. The discourse surrounding Fairwold illustrates how black women worked within the limits of the state where they lived. They had to promote respectability and morality to fight devastating stereotypes of their race. Their early acts of community uplift planted seeds of political resistance reaped by the Civil Rights Movement.[2] White women believed that a reformatory for white boys furthered their work for a New South;

accordingly, they convinced the state to build a reformatory for delinquent white boys. Meanwhile, black women approached the legislature with a request to appropriate funds for a reformatory for black girls. That they were less successful than white women comes as no surprise.

Although white clubwomen in South Carolina struggled to get legislators to listen to them, with rare exception black women's clubs in the state did not even bother trying. They focused more effort on their own fundraising than legislative lobbying because blacks were generally excluded from state support and disenfranchised. Unable to create systematic changes in the black economic and social position, they still succeeded at raising large sums of money and ameliorating local conditions.

Black women's clubs had a strong orientation toward service. Because of their concern with race uplift, many black clubs are distinguishable from white clubs simply by their names. Some chose to name their clubs after nationally known African Americans, such as Marian Anderson, George Washington Carver, Marion Wilkinson, Mary McLeod Bethune, and Jane E. Hunter.[3] A great number of other clubs highlight their dedication to community service in their name: the Uplift Club, Busy Bee Club, Lend a Hand Club, Ever Ready Club, One More Effort Club, Sunlight Club, Over the Top Club, and the Helping Hand Club.[4] This attitude of service is eloquently stated in the South Carolina report to the NACW. The report used the example of snowflakes, which must bond together to force a snowdrift, and drops of dew, which unite to form a brook. Without such cooperation, the individual drops would either melt or evaporate. According to the article, "The simple act of being kind, and lending a helping hand to those who faint along the road, the recognition of our debt to humanity, prompts into being loftier impulses and finer feelings, losing ones self in the interest of others, some care for the poor, some thought of those we know less well and we had advanced a little."[5]

Like their white counterparts, black women's clubs were especially concerned with children and their education. African Americans emphasized education beginning in Reconstruction because they understood that it was crucial to race progress. Education was all the more evident when disenfranchisement was legally justified on the basis of illiteracy. Educators believed that individual progress was linked to progress of the race as a whole.[6] Education also proved that African Americans as a race had intellectual capacity. South Carolinian clubwomen undoubtedly knew that they could help refute Governor Coleman Blease's statement that "God Almighty never intended that [the black man] should be educated

... God made that man to be your servant ... a hewer of wood and a drawer of water.... When you attempt to break down the barrier of social equality by educating the Negro, bringing him into the professions and giving him the ballot, instead of making an educated Negro you are ruining a good plow hand and making a half-educated fool."[7]

The SCFCWC incorporated their prioritization of education into their constitution. Its first article of purpose was "to promote the education of colored women and to hold an educational convention annually." Thus, the annual meeting of the federation was envisioned as an opportunity for delegates to further their education."[8] Annual meetings hosted many speakers on the subject, including Asa Gordon, a history professor at State College, and Wil Lou Gray, a white clubwoman who pioneered adult literacy schools in South Carolina.[9] Black and white South Carolina clubwomen supported education at all levels—kindergarten, elementary, secondary, and college. Significantly, like their white counterparts, they especially stressed access to higher education for girls and women. For example, the federation created scholarships to send two female students to the School for Social Work in Atlanta and one to the University there. The Tanner Art Club gave scholarships to two young women to the state normal school and to Voorhees College in Denmark, South Carolina.[10]

For many black families, education for their daughters was critical because it allowed them to find jobs other than those as domestic servants in whites' homes. Education could therefore provide a measure of protection from the constant danger of sexual abuse that domestics confronted.[11] By promoting higher education, black clubwomen tried not only to fulfill their need for greater intellectual opportunity but also to ensure some level of physical safety and to prove the ability of their race. At the lower grades, through the federation, African American clubwomen raised money for rural schools, distributed leaflets on education to teachers, and gave prizes to local students.

Black women in South Carolina also supported kindergartens for black children, as part of the larger kindergarten movement. Georgian clubwoman Addie Hunton noted the accomplishments in Charleston in an article on the NACW for the *Colored American Magazine*. She argued, "In the South, the awakening of our women to the importance of maintaining these institutions for our little ones has been one of the most valuable efforts of the club movement. ... In South Carolina and Georgia the work has grown extensively. Atlanta has four splendid kindergartens and Charleston two."[12] The Alice D. Carey Kindergarten in Charleston was named for Alice Dugger Cary who opened the first free kindergarten for black children in Atlanta. This kindergarten received financial support from a fund established by Mary Church Terrell for kindergartens through the sales of her pamphlets.[13]

When Mamie Garvin Fields, Lem Lewis, and Viola Ford Turner founded the Modern Priscilla Club in Charleston in 1926, they claimed that the object of the Modern Priscillas was "to lift womanhood and young ladies to high levels of living and caring."[14] This club focused particularly on children, especially the needs of youth in recreation, education, and industrial opportunities. They provided scholarships, initiated a Better Behavior campaign in the schools, and assisted the nursery for black children in Charleston. They also volunteered at the Old Folks Home and donated money to both Fairwold and the Jenkins Orphanage in Charleston.[15]

Even those clubs that focused on literary self-improvement, such as the Book Lovers Club of Charleston, also performed community service by supporting neighborhood and youth activities such as the Jenkins Orphanage, the YWCA, and the high schools. The Phyllis Wheatley recorded their purpose in their constitution: "We, a company of Colored women of the city of Charleston, seeing the need of informing ourselves in literary work and also a great need of general community work among our people."[16] These clubs indicate the strong orientation to service and race uplift among black clubwomen. As elites, they undertook self-improvement through literary study; as African Americans, they worked to uplift the race; and as women, they concentrated on the needs of children, especially girls.

The Sunlight Club, organized in 1910 at Trinity Methodist Church in Orangeburg by Marion Wilkinson, extended its outreach to not only children but also poor blacks of all ages. Unlike some clubs in Charleston, which had significant literary interests, the original purpose of the club was simply to serve the community needs of poor people in Orangeburg. The club quickly donated sheets, sleepware, and food to patients at the poorhouse.[17] Sunlight Club members knew that there were people in their own community who lacked necessities, such as wood and coal in the winter. In 1928, the *Palmetto Leader* claimed that the Sunlight Club had "practically taken over the charity work of Orangeburg for colored people." They noted that less than fifty women in the club raised and spent more than $300 on the needy at Christmas.[18]

The club also paid particular attention to the needs of women, girls, and families. Because the Sunlight Club primarily focused on fund-raising and community service, when they had self-improvement programs at their monthly meetings, they were often of a more practical nature, as opposed to a literary or historical program. For example, they studied family finances, with talks on various topics: what a wife should know about her husband's business; systematic spending for the family; budget work; and insurance and local banking.[19] The Sunlight Club also aided an employment agency. Their program for 1930–1931 provides evidence of their growing interest in the home and women and girls. It included programs ranging from the ideals of modern homemaking, home decoration, chaperonage for girls, play spirit in the home, learning from their daughters, to budgets and women as purchasing agents.

Other clubs indicate that they did "uplift" or "charity" work, although it is difficult to know whether they focused on education and children or other issues. In Sumter, the One More Effort Club, originally a social club, took up charity work following the suggestion of Margaret Washington, who was in town for a speaking engagement. The One More Effort Club joined the federation in 1911 and was led by Anna Andrews, the first president and an avid participant in the NACW. Their sister club, the Progressive Club, was founded in 1924 by Victoria Spears for "uplift work" and support of Fairwold.[20]

The Tanner Art Club of Florence received an award from the federation for its fund-raising efforts from 1927 to 1929. Maggie O. Levy organized the club in 1910, when it was the first club in Florence. The club reported to the NACW that their most outstanding achievements were the aid given to three students in higher education and Christmas donations to the aged and orphan children. In addition, the club functioned as a traditional Ladies' Aid Society by giving charity to individual families when food, fuel, or money was needed. The club also instituted community meetings, in which girls, boys, and parents made ten-minute speeches, which undoubtedly built confidence and pride while addressing local issues. Finally, the Tanner Art Club devoted attention to art, mostly needlework. Because they sold their needlework, this effort doubled as fund-raising.[21]

The Tanner Art Club's efforts demonstrate the phenomenal fund-raising among black women's clubs. Given the political disenfranchisement of African American women and men, the unsuccessful drive for public support for Fairwold aside, black clubwomen focused more on raising funds themselves than on legislative appeals. Clubs went to great lengths of creativity and dedication to raise desperately needed money. The Phillis Wheatley Club formed a Play Committee, which took charge of the various plays, sketches, and pageants performed by members. In 1922, a performance of *Lady Windemere's Fan* netted a $48.00 profit after performances in Charleston and at State College.²² The women donated the money they raised to Fairwold, the YWCA and the YMCA, and to the Avery Institute, a private high school in Charleston, and they purchased books on black history. The Sunlight Club of Orangeburg also sponsored plays to benefit Fairwold, which received the bulk of South Carolina clubwomen's donations. Clubs also supported Voorhees College, including a $71.00 donation made jointly by thirty-four clubs.²³

The sums of money that clubwomen were able to collect only continued to grow. In 1926, five federated clubs in Charleston raised a combined total of nearly $1,700 while the Sunlight Club alone donated $1,350.²⁴ In fact, the fund-raising efforts of South Carolina clubwomen were noted in the *National Notes*. When South Carolina submitted its report in 1921, the state was noted as a leader in fund-raising, having collected $15,000 for rural schools, $3,000 for recreation for the soldiers, and $1,000 for a tuberculosis camp. Their ability to raise such funds came from their own wealth, which was considerably higher than the average black income in the state, from their dedication, and from their creativity. One club even planted a small field of cotton, realizing at least one bale that was then sold.²⁵

Despite the aid black clubwomen provided their communities, their class status sometimes caused them problems. Middle- and upper-class African American clubwomen clashed with the beneficiaries of their work on occasion. Clubwomen were removed to some degree from the experiences of those black families to whom they extended their aid. In comparison to white clubwomen, black clubwomen, with a higher number of wage earners in their midst, and with less wealth even though they were considered elite, were comparatively closer to their beneficiaries. This relative lack of distance enabled black reformers to concentrate more on universal services, such as in education or health, rather than means-tested benefits such as preferred by white clubwomen.²⁶

Yet, many black clubwomen had achieved enough distance to be "condescending." They hoped to instill a middle-class agenda of manners and morals as part of their strategy of gaining "respectability" for the race. Such a strategy was inherently flawed. In effect, clubwomen blamed the victim through their emphasis on changing the behavior of poor blacks to fight discrimination. Clubwomen's elite status therefore affected how they defined their agenda, according to their own experiences as well as what they perceived to be community needs.

Moreover, their understanding of race uplift was colored by their own hopes for acceptance if respectability could be achieved. Therefore, elite black clubwomen sometimes expressed the desire to be disassociated from the poor. Although white prejudice had sometimes distinguished among blacks by class, Jim Crow laws did not, and the few privileges that elite blacks enjoyed were in danger of being lost. In an often-quoted statement, NACW president Mary Church Terrell expounded on the duty of clubwomen to aid poor blacks. "They know that they cannot altogether escape the consequences of the acts of their most depraved sisters," she said. "They see that even if they were wicked enough to turn a deaf ear to the call of duty, both policy and self-preservation would demand that they go down among the lowly, the illiterate and even the vicious, to whom they are bound by ties of race and sex, and put forth every possible effort to reclaim them." Terrell and other clubwomen therefore made it quite clear that they were "allied, not united," and that despite the ties of race and sex which allied them, these women remained separated by "social and cultural distance."[27] The NACW motto, "Lifting as we climb," perfectly captured this paradox: even as clubwomen saw themselves as different from the masses, they understood that they had to uplift all members of the race for any member to overcome discrimination.

Terrell's statement was later quoted by South Carolina clubwoman Cora Gethers, who wrote a series of articles for the *Palmetto Leader* on the role of black women in the uplift of the race. Gethers argued that the NACW motto meant that educated clubwomen "should come in close contact with the masses of our women that they may be properly trained to grow their children in a healthy, moral atmosphere, and they will imbibe the salutatory influence and they will become a mighty power in the future solution of this great problem." She too lamented the fact that all African Americans were judged by the behavior of the "most illiterate and vicious characters." According to Gethers, it was their Christian duty to reach out to such a woman, and if she did not attend meetings, then clubwomen needed to go into her home and "lift her to her feet." Furthermore, she stressed that it was up to black women more so than black men to uplift the race because of their influence on the home.[28] Thus, the elitism of NACW leaders reached local South Carolinians, who, though not as wealthy as Terrell, still had higher status than those they wanted to reform.

Despite the potential for conflict, especially in Charleston where a strong elite tradition existed, reports from clubwomen and local newspapers indicate only appreciation for the work of the clubwomen. Recollections from a former resident at the Fairwold Home for Girls echo Marion

Wilkinson's positive image, as expressed by her colleagues.[29] In 1970, SCFCWC President Johnette Edwards challenged the federation at its annual meeting by imagining what questions the organization's founders might now ask: "Do you know where you are going, or more important perhaps, do you know where you want to go?" She pointed to the fact the convention was meeting in the Wade Hampton Hotel for the first time; this location, in itself, raised another set of questions: Would the founders congratulate them on that achievement? Or would they wonder if the members had become too accustomed to luxuries and out of touch with those around them. "Now that you are meeting here in the most comfortable of surroundings," Edwards queried her audience, "are you becoming the victims of pride and ambition and losing touch with, and disdaining responsibility for those, who in this most affluent society, lack the very necessities of life? If they ask, we must answer, and what will our answer be?"[30] This soul-searching speech indicates that the difficulties encountered by the federation, when as elite women they came together with the purpose of aiding those less fortunate them themselves, continued into the 1970s.

Notwithstanding the troubles elitism caused, however, class status also provided motivation for clubwomen: it engendered within them a sense of noblesse oblige and a desire to uplift the race.[31] Despite the privileged position of members of the Sunlight Club, African American women in South Carolina gathered around Marion Wilkinson with the goal of aiding "wayward" girls. For such elite clubwomen, there was little contradiction in the fact that membership in a woman's clubs was in and of itself a symbol of elite status, regardless of wealth, and the fact that the woman's club was also the vehicle through which they reached out to blacks in their community as they sought to uplift the race. Class status and a concern for respectability were especially evident in the federation's devotion to the Fairwold Home for Girls, founded by black women several years after the white federation convinced the legislature to establish a state-run reformatory for white boys. The contrasts between the campaigns for these two homes further illustrate the gulf between black and white clubwomen, who worked on similar goals for different reasons.

White clubwomen in South Carolina had their biggest legislative success in obtaining a state supported boys' reformatory, which they began to work for several years before black women opened the Fairwold Home for Girls. By the late nineteenth century concern for juvenile delinquents grew nationally as urbanization and immigration produced higher numbers of unsupervised wayward boys and girls in the cities. Illinois was the first state to establish a separate juvenile court to handle cases; that court stressed education and aid over punishment. Before 1890, Southern states lagged precipitously behind the North. That year, no Southern state, but almost every state outside the region, had established reform schools to provide an alternative to incarceration with adults for juveniles convicted of crime or otherwise in need of institutional care. This discrepancy occurred because antebellum white Southerners saw little need for such schools: no special provisions were enacted for black children, and a higher tolerance for the "exploits" of white children prevailed. Women's clubs and the Woman's Christian Temperance Union were integral to drawing attention to the problem in the South.[32]

Espousing New South ideology, white clubwomen in South Carolina worked diligently to aid white boys, whom they believed to be morally fit but simply needing another chance in life. The reformatory fit into their program of industrial education and improved opportunities for poor white children in the state. Although they usually focused on girls when it came to higher education, they saw boys as integral to the future of the economy. Clubwomen hoped to build Southern prosperity through "increas[ing] the number of efficient men and women citizens of their state."[33] The movement to build a reformatory therefore addressed issues of economic progress for the region and class tension.

The idea for a reformatory for delinquent boys apparently came when a representative from the Alabama school spoke at the South Carolina Federation annual meeting in 1903. Following her address, the SCFWC decided to establish a committee for a reformatory at the next convention.[34] Martha Orr Patterson, president of the SCFWC from 1902 to 1903, championed the reformatory. Patterson had experience with politics and with the boys from mill towns who were likely candidates for the reformatory. She was the daughter of a former governor, James L. Orr, and married a secretary of a cotton mill, William C. Patterson. Known for her quick wit, Patterson attended Greenville Female College and was a member of several women's clubs and the UDC. After she resigned, president Margaret Smyth McKissick, also married to a mill owner, took up the cause.[35]

From the beginning clubwomen turned to the legislature for aid. Although clubwomen were willing to volunteer at kindergartens and schools, they proposed that the state build and staff a reformatory in cooperation with the justice system. To galvanize the legislature, clubwomen decided that they must first establish public opinion in favor of a reformatory. The federation urged clubwomen to talk about the reformatory at home, in church, and through the newspapers. South Carolina women also immediately began raising funds; however, their contributions were insufficient without state support. In an editorial on reformatories, the Poppenheims noted that the North Carolina legislature had granted an appropriation for a reformatory without preliminary support; in South Carolina the reverse seemed true: the clubwomen had already established the need for the school, but they were still waiting for state support. The editorial stressed that the magnitude of funds required to build, staff, and support a reformatory likewise required a state appropriation, although clubwomen were committed to continuing their own fund-raising.[36]

Their persistence paid off, and, in March 1906, the *Keystone* triumphantly announced that the bill had been passed. Although the appropriation was small—only $4,500—Margaret McKissick assured clubwomen that it would grow in the future. The school was to be located in Florence, and Dr. J. L. Mann, superintendent of the school system there, assumed charge of the project. Speaking to clubwomen at the 1907 convention, he assured them that, given their aid, they would be successful at obtaining a larger appropriation with which to begin building. The other significant change made by legislators to the federation's proposed bill was the exclusion of women on the board of trustees, headed by Mann. That decision was later overturned, perhaps because legislators realized that having a representative from the federation would help guarantee that clubwomen continued to fund-raise for the school. McKissick was appointed a trustee the following year, a position from which she continued to advocate funding for the school. When the Poppenheims reported on the reformatory for the *Keystone*, Mann was not even mentioned.[37] In 1907 the reform school appropriation only grew slightly, to $5,000. This was insufficient to build and maintain the school, and the *Keystone* reported the school was "stalled" because of a lack of appropriations. Clubwomen decided to compile statistics on juvenile delinquents and send them to the legislators. This tactic appears to have succeeded, because in 1908 the legislature finally granted a more adequate $10,000 to the school.[38]

The additional funding made it possible for the school to open November 1, 1908, with fifteen boys in attendance. By the spring of 1909, attendance had already increased to twenty-four, and the editors reported that the legislature had granted a higher appropriation, "with no protest worth speaking of."[39] For its part, the federation decided to give $1,100 to establish a library at the reformatory and donate $125 for a memorial plaque to Martha Patterson to recognize her role in opening the reformatory.[40] However, because they failed to raise enough money to build a library building, they instead gave some of the interest on the money they had raised to the library committee to buy books for the reformatory. By 1921, now with well over $1,700 in the bank, the federation relinquished their hopes for a library and decided instead to equip the new infirmary. L. O. Patterson donated furnishings for a convalescence room in memory of his mother, and Margaret McKissick gave money to furnish the operating room. Clubwomen also continued to hound county legislative delegations to maintain full appropriations.[41]

South Carolina clubwomen worked first for white delinquent boys and only later expanded their agenda to include white girls and some support for black boys and girls. Mississippi was the first Southern state to establish an industrial school for white girls in 1907, but South Carolina clubwomen lagged behind and did not announce their interest in a school for girls until the 1913 meeting. At that time, the Civil Service Reform Committee asked clubs to obtain information on jail conditions for female inmates, which would be compiled and used to evaluate whether such a facility was necessary. Apparently, both clubwomen and legislators determined that it was necessary, and a bill was passed in 1919, aided by a federal appropriation given to protect World War I soldiers at Camp Jackson from wayward girls. However, they never devoted the same energy or effort to the girls' home and admitted that this home was not a direct result of their work. They may have been reluctant to deal with delinquent white girls who belied their notions of female propriety and threatened white women's presumption of virtue.[42]

As work on the boys' reformatory progressed, it underwent a series of name changes, an indication of how clubwomen perceived delinquency and New South progress. McKissick advocated the term "industrial school," which not only reflected the popularity of industrial education but also reduced the stigma attached to the word "reformatory." Rather than viewing the boys as delinquents, McKissick saw them as wayward boys, who, in her words, needed "formation" rather than "reformation." In North Carolina, clubwomen shared similar sentiments. Mrs. Hollowell called for an industrial school for wayward boys, "A reformatory is not needed; it would be objectionable and obnoxious. The boy is not responsible for the conditions in which he is born."[43] To facilitate these distinctions, the reformatory in South Carolina was run separately from the penal system, under its own board of trustees, the governor, the superintendent of education and the state attorney general.

The wording also was racially coded, as clubwomen initially did not extend such excuses to black boys, whose reformatory was run by the state penitentiary. For example, in 1911, the Poppenheims appealed to clubwomen to keep supporting the juvenile courts, to streamline the process by which white boys would be sent to the "Industrial School" in Florence and black boys to the "Reformatory" in Lexington. By 1918, the reformatory for black boys also left the penal system and was placed under the same control as the white boys reformatory, "making it an educational institution as well as reformatory." White clubwomen did not work to affect this change, however.[44]

These name changes reflect the beliefs of Southern clubwomen in the natural potential of white children. Clubwomen believed in the inherent ability of white children, despite their circumstances, which often included poverty, illiteracy, and inadequate parental supervision. The movement for a reformatory dovetailed neatly with work on libraries, kindergartens, industrial training, and educational reform, each of which was intended to aid white children left behind or negatively affected by changes in the New South. Clubwomen believed that as men in South Carolina built mills and otherwise promoted economic prosperity in the New South, they as women could support those efforts through reform directed at the children of those who did not appear to be sharing in that prosperity. At the same time, these institutions helped train and reform white laborers needed in an industrializing South. These beliefs are evident in the clubwomen's concern with both general industrial education and the rhetoric of the New South.

As an industrial school, the reformatory underscored white clubwomen's interest in industrial education. Many white Southern reformers believed industrial education was necessary for white children to become skilled laborers in the newly industrial South, as well as useful, in combination with liberal arts, as training for all white children in neatness, character, and other worthy traits. This was especially true for girls, who learned to be better homemakers. Early on, however, the federation focused on scholarships for girls' higher education. Realizing this discrepancy, Christie Poppenheim, Louisa's youngest sister, contended that clubs needed to turn their attention away from higher education and toward manual training, which she believed to be the primary need in the South.[45]

Louisa Poppenheim also advocated industrial education. She argued that one problem of the New South was the overabundance of professionals and the lack of well-trained laborers. "We have too many professional men and women to-day," she claimed, "too many theorists and not enough laborers and artisans. A mechanic can always earn a living while a professor may starve although speaking seven languages. We need more men and women who can work with their hands, more who know how to work, and we should provide this training and then see to it that it is made use of."[46] In 1904, the federation went on record advocating manual training in the schools. Clubwomen quickly espoused domestic science for girls, especially after Poppenheim informed them that the Illinois federation had established a domestic science department, and she hoped that South Carolina clubwomen could likewise encourage domestic science, or cooking and sewing classes, in the schools.[47] Ironically, Poppenheim herself had received a college degree from Vassar, then the most prestigious women's college in the country, a far cry from the industrial education she proposed for fellow South Carolinians.

As with kindergartens, the debate over industrial education forced middle- and upper-class clubwomen to consider just who they wanted to aid—their own children or the children of the poor, especially the growing number of mill families in the upcountry. For example, following the 1904 convention, the *Keystone* printed the comments of a reader signed only as "Angus" of Newberry. In this letter, the writer praised clubwomen for the work being done with scholarships but questioned their focus on higher education. "Would it not be well," Angus asked, "to begin at the bottom and build up to a higher plane the poor white children of our state? An industrial department should be a feature of all public schools, especially in mill districts, where girls should be taught the useful handiwork of sewing, proper preparation of food and hygiene of their homes."[48] The SCFWC hoped to do both. Ultimately, clubwomen for the most part saw themselves offering a dual aid package: a scholarship program to aid their own children, and an industrial educational program in the public schools, mill districts, and the industrial home for boys designed to aid worthy but needy white youth.

Industrial education for white children prepared them to have clean and well-kept homes and provided basic skills necessary for factory labor, but it did not train them for opportunities beyond the mills. Ironically, clubwomen translated Booker T. Washington's program of industrial education for black children into a similar program for white children, who, because they were white, could not be ignored but could nevertheless not be expected to transcend class distinctions. Rather, they were "saved" by the opportunity to leave the farm for the mill villages; likewise, they provided the labor necessary for an industrial New South. Their opportunities remained restricted however. Elvira Moffitt, a North Carolina clubwoman, wanted to educate children for industrial progress. "We do not want education to go so far," she reasoned, "as to make men discontented with their lot or fill their minds with vain ambition—we need industrial progress—this makes a country rich.... We need intelligent labor and how can we have it unless we send our children to school."[49] Her statement underscores white clubwomen's complicity in retaining stringent class divisions in the South. White reformers' racial affinity with poor white children had its limits. Reformers could at once perceive industrial education as a positive good and therefore something that should be taught to poor whites; at the same time these upper-class reformers could praise Booker T. Washington for asserting that blacks needed industrial, rather than liberal arts education, to keep blacks "in their place," in subservient labor jobs.[50]

White clubwomen were probably more successful in building a state reformatory than winning state support for libraries or kindergartens because the increased number of white children in mill towns motivated legislators to deal with delinquents. By training these boys the state was actually training labor for the New South. The reformatory proved one of their most easily won legislative battles, especially in comparison to black women's inability to win over the legislature twenty years later.

On February 7, 1920, Marion Wilkinson wrote to her friend, Charlotte Hawkins Brown, "We are very hopeful of having a Bill passed taking over our Girls' Reformatory. Pray that the hearts of the legislators will be touched and this blessing will come to those who need every enlightening influence."[51] The state did not respond as Wilkinson had hoped, and South Carolina refused to take over the girls' home started by the SCFCWC. However, the home survived because clubwomen believed passionately in both the need for an "enlightening influence" on the individual girls concerned and the benefit of racial progress in general. That is, as part of their strategy of emphasizing the home, morality, and virtue to uplift the race, they sought to protect the most vulnerable class in South Carolina: young, black girls.[52]

Although black clubwomen did not succeed in their quest for African Americans' share in New South progressive reforms by obtaining an official state reformatory, the story of the Fairwold Home for Girls remains significant. It underscores the racism in the Southern Progressive reform movement and subsequent difficulties encountered in the interracial movement of the 1920s. Furthermore, it illustrates how black clubwomen, cognizant of the reality of their place in the South, created their own private institutions, while simultaneously seeking state support. Their demands for state funding reveal their belief in their citizenship and highlight their rights denied by the state.

The federation played a crucial role in joining clubwomen across the state in the common goal of providing aid to girls at the Fairwold Home. From 1917 to 1989 the SCFCWC spent significant amounts of time and money on this home for delinquent, then underprivileged, and finally, abused African American girls. Fairwold was such an important project for the federation that many clubs later formed explicitly to aid the home. Some clubwomen even attributed the origins of the Sunlight Club of Orangeburg and the state federation itself to Fairwold, although both were founded several years before World War I, generally recognized as the impetus for the home.[53]

During World War I, the government stationed military troops in Columbia. The presence of soldiers resulted in an increased number of arrests of young, especially homeless, black girls for prostitution and other crimes. At least one thousand black women were incarcerated in the state at the time.[54] To aid those girls who, according to black clubwomen, had fallen victim to the dangers posed by the military presence, the federation decided to open a home for delinquent girls. Notably, clubwomen did not blame girls for their transgressions; rather, they attributed the girls' moral collapse to the presence of soldiers around those most sexually vulnerable. The federal government had appropriated $80,000 for a home for delinquent girls, an effort to protect the men stationed at Camp Jackson. The state used this entire sum to fund a home for white girls; black women therefore were left to their own devices to protect black girls.[55]

The decision to aid black girls was critically different from white women's interest in reformatories. White women's interest in a boys' reformatory grew out of their focus on creating progress in the New South through educating poor whites and "wayward" boys. For black women, however, the need for a reformatory was related not to progress but to morality. Because whites blamed the supposed lack of morality among African Americans on a lack of virtue in black women, clubwomen focused on black girls, most vulnerable to charges of immorality. Thus, the SCFCWC adopted Fairwold as part of its mission. They never took up support for the black boys' home.

Members of the SCFCWC raised money to purchase an old farmhouse located near the Railroad station of Fairwold (ten miles outside of Columbia). Originally named the Fairwold Home for Delinquent Girls, young black homeless girls found guilty of misdemeanor crimes were sent to the home instead of to jail. The home consisted of two wood frame buildings on thirty acres of land. Problems occurred after the fire in 1925 when the home ran out of space and girls sentenced to the reformatory could not be placed there. A more significant difficulty surfaced in a separate case later that same year: two girls sentenced to the reformatory were instead resentenced to the penitentiary because the Fairwold home was not officially a state "reformatory"; this was a slap in the black women's faces, given the state's refusal to build an official reformatory.[56]

The SCFCWC was the primary source of economic support for the Home, although the girls also picked cotton and peas. As funding became increasingly difficult, clubwomen turned to the legislature for money. They decried the fact that the state supported homes for black and white boys, and white girls, but not black girls. According to Marion Wilkinson's correspondence, the fight for state assistance began as early as 1920, but was unsuccessful. Lacking political power, clubwomen realized that they needed help from whites. In one of the few instances of cooperation in the first decades of their coexistence, black clubwomen turned to prominent whites, including white clubwomen, for aid.[57] Although several white clubwomen participated in the biracial committee they formed, the most outspoken support from the white community came from the Episcopal Church and the state Interracial Committee (CIC).

In 1922, Mrs. R. T. Brooks, a black woman, reported to the Women's Section of the state CIC on "The Delinquent Negro Girl." She asked the women there to extend aid to the feeble-minded and delinquent without regard to race and begged the members to recognize that "there should not be a different yardstick for different peoples." She then described Fairwold to the committee and asked for their support. The committee, upon "discovering" these facts hitherto unknown to them, agreed to work to pass a bill for the General Assembly to take over the home. They presented their resolution to both the entire state CIC and the state Women's Legislative Council, which coordinated efforts among women's organizations; both groups endorsed it. The Department of Christian Social Service of the Upper South Carolina Diocese of the Episcopal Church also took up the cause that year. The state CIC agreed to send the legislature a committee of five: Episcopal Bishop Kirkman G. Finlay, Mrs. Cornell, president of Episcopal Woman's Auxiliary, Dr. W. T. Derieux, Mrs. Andrew Bramlett, and T. B. Lanham. Their lobbying efforts were unsuccessful.[58]

In 1924 and 1925, led by Bishop Finlay and I. S. Leevy, a black merchant from Columbia and a trustee of Fairwold, a larger committee approached the legislature; for both years the delegation secured a $2,000 appropriation, but no official recognition for a state reformatory followed. The committee was composed of representatives of white women's organizations, religious denominations (black and white), and prominent white men. In 1925, the committee included white members such as Clelia P. McGowan, chairman of the Interracial Committee; Maria Croft Jennings, president of the SCFWC; Isabelle Cain, trustee of Fairwold and president of the Episcopal Women's Auxiliary; and black members, Robert Wilkinson, and SCFCWC officers Celia D. Saxon, Lilian J. Rhodes, and Belle Vincent.[59] Many committee members, in addition to McGowan, were members of the Interracial Committee.

The white women's club federation added the colored girls' reformatory to their legislative agenda, although it never received even a fraction of the degree of support the federation had shown earlier for a home for white boys. In 1921–1922, Bertha Munsell, chair of the Social and Industrial Conditions Department, recommended that the federation aid Fairwold, which she reported as being "immaculately clean" and which taught the girls how to wash, iron, sew, and do garden work.[60] This report meshed with white women's desires that African American girls be trained to be better domestic servants. Later reports, however, gave less attention to the work already being done at Fairwold by black clubwomen. Chair of the Public Welfare committee, Nell Duncan Freeman, recommended that the legislature fill the need by establishing a state school for delinquent Negro girls because the current school (Fairwold) could not continue "under present management." One wonders if the federation members all realized that black clubwomen were in fact managing the school. Three years later, Isabelle Cain, a CIC member who was also chair of the federation's Social and Industrial Conditions Department, reported that per request by Clelia McGowan she had served on the CIC and had cooperated with the legislative committee to ask the legislature to establish a state industrial school for Negro girls. Even she did not mention their black counterparts in the SCFCWC. White women therefore broached the subject not as an example of cooperation with their black colleagues, which would have implied an equality they were not ready to admit, but simply as a worthy project to endorse. However, when Wilkinson spoke to the CIC about Fairwold, she was careful to draw attention to the black clubwomen's role by telling white committee members "gratefully of the loyal women of the South Carolina Federation of Colored Women's Clubs who had founded and made possible the opportunities it had thus far afforded."[61]

Although white women did support Fairwold, their limited role and lack of acknowledgment of black clubwomen underscores the dangers that interracial work posed in the early twentieth-century South. White women may have intentionally downplayed their work in their published documents. Whatever support white clubwomen gave, they did so with little publicity, fanfare, or public record. However, the interviews from black women and the minutes of a sample of white clubs reinforce the impression that the federation as a whole, and most individual white clubs and members, gave little more than token support.[62] White federation leadership did not embrace Fairwold as a significant item on their agenda. Moreover, white women were particularly hesitant to acknowledge black clubwomen as their equals or counterparts.

Following the decision to approach the state legislature for funding of a state reformatory, Etta Rowe, then corresponding secretary of the SCFCWC and later successor to Marion Wilkinson as president, wrote a stirring appeal for aid. Her letter was printed in the white clubs' *Federation Bulletin* and in the NACW's *National Notes*. Rowe began by praising the proliferation of rescue homes for girls, then asked, "Where are the Rescue Homes for Colored Girls?" She asserted that the SCFCWC had established Fairwold, whose object was to introduce girls "to a life of Christian cleanliness, industry, and uplift. To this end the South Carolina Federation of Colored Women has been working for the support of this school with a courage born of that deep love which one good woman has for the priceless clean life of another."[63]

Rowe described the home as a place where girls were taught "how to make an honest living by their own efforts." At Fairwold they learned practical skills including cutting wood, picking cotton, planting vegetables, as well as needlework. According to Rowe, the "delinquent, destitute, neglected and straying" girls were taught skills and values such as cleanliness and industry. Rather than asking for funds or for direct aid in lobbying the legislature to take over the home, Rowe concluded her press release with an appeal for divine intervention. She wrote, "Let us pray that God will touch the hearts of the executives, that they will lend a listening ear to this appeal of the Race—this heart cry of the colored women of South Carolina and give us a Home for Delinquent Colored Girls."

Rowe's letter reveals that black clubwomen understood that training girls to lead productive lives based upon domestic science skills appealed to both black women, who emphasized home life in their campaign for race uplift, and white women, who approved of such training, especially for girls likely to become domestic servants. Perhaps because it was intended for such wide circulation, Rowe did not explicitly stress race uplift or protecting black womanhood, which she did in later appeals sent to the black community. Rowe also accented the positive work accomplished by the federation without emphasizing the perils facing black girls, a comment that might have drawn further criticism of black women's supposed lack of virtue.

In December 1925, a fire destroyed the home, which was insured only for $1,000, a small part of its value.[64] The seventeen girls living there were temporarily transferred to St. Mary's Episcopal Mission in Columbia through Bishop Finlay's efforts. Because the home had been serving as the unofficial reformatory for black girls, the federation returned to the legislature for additional funding. James C. Dozier, executive secretary of the state board of public welfare, supported their request, although he reasoned that a reformatory was necessary because, "this class of Negro girls is a menace to her community and to the state at large."[65] As Rowe might have feared, Dozier played upon the already present stereotypes of the immoral black women.

Although the *Palmetto Leader* originally reported that Katherine Furman, then president of the white SCFWC, would make the appeal to the legislature, on February 6, 1926, a committee composed of many of the same members from the 1925 appeal, including Bishop Finlay, Isabelle Cain, Superintendent of Fairwold Ethel Martin, and I. S. Leevy, approached the legislature.[66] Meanwhile local black clubs had a spring drive to collect and raise money, in which they inaugurated a $12,000 campaign.[67]

African Americans hoped to appeal to the state for funding by arguing that white girls, as well as black and white boys, had state-supported reformatories, and black girls deserved no less. Clubwomen hoped "to educate the people so that they will realize that the responsibility for the care of these girls rightly belongs to the Commonwealth and not to the Negro women." The *Palmetto Leader* wrote a stinging editorial, demanding, "Why have you neglected [colored girls]? Do you not think it more important to care for such girls [as opposed to boys]? Can not your Christian duty point the way? Are you contented to put the dollar against humanity? Do you take the position that colored girls of that kind are not worth caring for?"[68] The state assembly was apparently not sufficiently impressed with the argument, nor with the stature of those who lobbied on behalf of the home. In response, African Americans quickly berated the assembly for its unwillingness to provide a reformatory for black girls; the criticism was again led by the editor of the *Palmetto Leader*, who concluded that whites "don't give a darn about colored girls."

The legislature finally approved an appropriation, which Governor Richards then vetoed. It was illegal, he argued, to make a donation to a private institution; not only did he neglect the fact that there was no public institution of its kind, but he also deligitimized the mission of Fairwold.[69] The state legislature, therefore, while refusing to build a state-supported reformatory for black girls, funded the Fairwold home for only two years, or for a total of $4,000, after granting $80,000 to a home for white girls.[70]

This lack of support from the state echoed other state services for blacks, such as education. For example, by 1915, blacks were 61 percent of the population, but they received only 11 percent of school funding. In the case of reformatories, black girls perhaps were not perceived as worthy of state assistance because whites were unable to see black girls as virtuous and therefore needing protection. The reform school for black girls was not funded until 1949.[71] The state's decisions to ignore the demands of African American citizens were made at the same time that the legislature granted money to the United Daughters of the Confederacy for Confederate memorials and other projects.[72]

Despite the paucity of support from the state, black clubwomen received a substantial amount of aid from the white-dominated Episcopal church. This was undoubtedly owing to Wilkinson, a devout Episcopalian, and the "unflagging interest" of white Episcopalians including Bishop Finlay, Isabelle Cain, and Clelia McGowan, all of whom were involved with the state CIC. Clubwomen secured the means to rebuild after the fire through the efforts of Bishop Finlay and Cain. At this time, the Episcopal church donated six acres of land in Cayce, just west of Columbia. The home itself, a three-story brick building, was paid for by the SCFCWC at a cost of $12,000. The new home had room for forty-five girls. Although the federation continued to provide almost the entire operating budget, the state interracial committee, faculty at State College, and others made small donations. Through Marion Wilkinson's influence, architectural students at State College also donated their services and purchased materials at cost.[73]

Keeping the home open grew more difficult without state aid when the Great Depression made donations scarce. In 1930, Wilkinson wrote to McGowan that her only hope was for more substantial state funding. "Something must be done," she wrote, "for in the present financial depression it is a struggle to keep the doors of the home open. The women haven't the money themselves and we haven't the heart to campaign with the zeal of past years. We know the situation too well to approach any but our salaried people." Wilkinson found solace from the loyalty of Cain and McGowan, but confessed, "Sometimes, I feel very discouraged, and then I take up the task with renewed faith."[74]

Fairwold's financial situation grew desperate enough that the SCFCWC actually changed the mission of the home to obtain funding from the Duke Foundation. In 1932, clubwomen decided that the program should serve orphaned and economically underprivileged girls rather than wayward girls or the "morally delinquent." They did not give up their concern for delinquents; they merely succumbed to practical constraints. When the federation originally appealed to the Duke Foundation for funds, they were rejected because the Foundation did not give to delinquent homes. However, it did give to orphanages. In response, clubwomen changed the focus of the home, and the Duke Foundation began donating an annual stipend. According to the *National Negro Digest*, "the federation still feels, however, the keen need for an institution for young female law offenders and other types of social misfits, but the maintenance of such an institution is too immense for them." Even with the Duke donation, clubwomen still paid for the bulk of the operating budget. This adaptation indicates the extreme measures that black clubwomen had to take to keep the home running because, despite repeated appeals to the legislature, the state provided no support. African American clubwomen took matters into their own hands to provide social welfare services when the state refused, and they correspondingly adapted their mission to acquire funding from a private foundation.[75]

Clubwomen had wanted the state to establish an "official" home to ensure that children could not be sent to jail, as the rulings had permitted in 1926. At the same time, however, clubwomen wanted to remain in control of the reformatory. When the Southeastern Federation of Colored Women's Clubs proposed that establishing homes should be a priority for all member states, President Rebecca Stiles Taylor cautioned, "It is hoped that these homes will be taken over by our State governments but that Negro women and men shall be placed in control." Her statement indicates that they had to weigh the risk of losing control to gain state appropriations. Likewise, when black clubwomen in Alabama gained state recognition of the boys' reformatory that they had started, they celebrated because they had been "recognized, endorsed and adopted by the state."[76] Control over institutions was essential because black women knew that the state and the justice system had abused rather than protected African Americans in the past. Rather than appealing directly to the state, clubwomen first created needed institutions and then sought state funding without which they risked eventual closure of the institution.[77] Clubwomen's strategy of institution-building reveals one method that black clubwomen utilized during a time in which white aid often was not forthcoming. While they sought to claim recognition from the state, they continued to work independently, with full appreciation of their lacking political power.

Because clubwomen themselves were its major supporters, the Fairwold Home was often the central topic at federation meetings. For example, in Spring 1927, following the withdrawal of the appropriation, clubwomen raised $4,000 in cash, including $1,144.31 from the Wilkinson's Sunlight Club. To continue the fund drive, Mary Earle, daughter of Thomas Miller, who had been the president of State College prior to Robert Wilkinson, agreed to travel the state on behalf of Fairwold. In 1928, the federation sponsored a Fairwold Day and asked churches across the state to speak about the home and solicit donations; in addition, one entire session of the 1929 annual meeting of the federation was devoted to Fairwold.[78]

Clubwomen throughout the state regularly raised funds through two annual events, the Wilkinson Tea in February and the Harvest Festival in October. The Wilkinson tea was held near Robert Wilkinson's birthday (February 18) in honor of his support for the home. In October, clubwomen brought truckloads of clothing and canned goods to the Home for a festival, at which the girls entertained their guests by reciting poems. Clubwomen also devised unique methods of fund-raising, such as the Christmas Tree in June, in which a tree was "planted" during the annual meeting, and clubwomen were asked to "decorate" the tree with dollar bills and coins. This event was stunningly successful. In 1925 Fairwold gained $235 in just twelve minutes.[79]

In addition to these two sources of income and goods, the federation continuously called upon clubs and individuals to donate money, clothes, and food. The SCFCWC organized clubs to donate staple groceries, including rice, bacon, grits, syrup, sugar, salmon, and dried fruit, and purchased a milk cow and a poultry plant for the home.[80] The Phyllis Wheatley Club sent a barrel of clothing to Fairwold in 1922, Christmas gifts annually, and in 1926–1927, donated $75 to the Fairwold building fund. Wilkinson solicited clubs to contribute; once she even extracted a $500-pledge from the Charleston clubs.[81] Individuals who could afford more substantial contributions made donations; in 1925 Marion Wilkinson and Anna Dickerson, a black clubwoman from Aiken, each donated $100. Finally, Mrs. Bradley, a SCFCWC member, left more than $2,500 to Fairwold in her will in 1925.[82] CIC members Clelia McGowan and Mrs. Samuel Stoney of Charleston also donated $100 each to the home during the 1928 fund drive.[83]

Clubwomen did not stop at shouldering much of the financial burden of Fairwold. They were also integrally involved in the programming and tried to ensure that the girls received good training, care, and affection. In 1940, the home had thirty-five girls under the supervision of Mamie Felder. The *National Negro Digest* claimed that the girls "live a normal and a happy life. They are not stigmatized as orphaned or underprivileged. All of them go to school." They were taught sewing, handicraft, cooking, housecleaning, laundering, poultry-raising, gardening, and dairying. In 1930, the federation made plans to establish a small poultry plant and purchase a milk cow, expressly to make Fairwold self-sufficient, although simultaneously teaching the girls how to make their own families self-sufficient. They were also exposed to "culture" through poetry or music programs during the evenings or talks on various subjects from the housemother. They attended church and Sunday school (Episcopal or Baptist) and the local elementary or high school in Columbia. Despite their own needy status, they brought "some form of cheer to the sick or the aged of the community."[84] When girls left the home, they were placed in families with a local clubwoman in charge of providing additional assistance and "mothering."

From this description it is evident that black clubwomen in South Carolina promoted industrial education for girls as part of the strategy of "respectability" to end racial oppression and to make blacks "worthy" of sharing in the New South prosperity. White women believed that the industrial education offered by their reformatory would aid white boys in becoming the skilled laborers necessary for an industrial economy to thrive in the New South. Black clubwomen in the SCFCWC had a different agenda. They hoped that by teaching advanced agricultural techniques and other skills such an education would aid blacks in their fight to share in the prosperity promised in the New South. Furthermore, they believed that by teaching these skills they could erase negative stereotypes of blacks and increase respectability.[85]

This approach dovetailed with rural school improvement that the federation had earlier embraced. Clubwomen worked to extend the school terms and, like white women, to emphasize manual or industrial training because they believed it to be more integral to the lives of rural children. They advocated teaching cooking, sewing, personal cleanliness, and housekeeping along with a general education. The basis of their agenda was to adapt the schools to meet the needs of rural children. Clubwomen believed that this approach would enable a teacher to "work with and not for the people in the rural districts," and by fulfilling the real needs of the community, a teacher ultimately could render "the people more happy and contented."[86] Such an emphasis on rural life was common in the South, and advocated frequently by Booker T. Washington.

In South Carolina, the industrial emphasis reflected the interests of Marion Wilkinson, whose husband, Robert, was president of South Carolina State College, a school that serviced agricultural workers and teachers predominantly. When Robert assumed the presidency of State College in 1911, the legislature granted the institution only a $5,000 state appropriation for 592 students, and the school did not award any degrees above the high school level.[87] Governor Coleman Blease vetoed an appropriation for a central heating plant for State College; he explained, "I see absolutely no use, sense or reason in taxing the white people of this state to pay for a heating plant for negroes to get up and dress by."[88] Despite these conditions, Robert was able to increase funding for the school.[89] He attempted to balance academic and industrial training.[90] As a member of the Conference of Negro Land-Grant College Presidents, he praised the increase in interest in industrial education while noting that it did not hurt colleges which focused more on classical education. Furthermore, Wilkinson argued that the Land Grant Colleges themselves "are being rapidly equipped and operated so as to give as much 'Liberal Education' as possible along with vocational training and specialized teaching. Culture and refinement are not being overlooked."[91] Robert also personally donated money to a fund drive for Claflin College, specifically to show his support for liberal arts education.[92]

Like her husband, as the president of the SCFCWC, Marion also stressed teaching practical skills along with exposing children to the arts. The Wilkinsons' approach to education reveals a practical, if somewhat limited, agenda: African Americans in South Carolina were largely excluded from mill jobs or skilled labor positions; therefore the Wilkinsons stressed those subjects that would give practical training in the most likely areas of employment, agriculture, and domestic service. At the same time, through art, literature, and other cultural events, they hoped to expose blacks to "the finer things" in life and to encourage achievement. Moreover, they hoped that such training would uplift the race through negating inferior stereotypes.

Significantly, because of the centrality of schools to black uplift, Marion and Robert's educational philosophies influenced black progress in the state. State College's mission as an agricultural college could have resulted in the SCFCWC exclusively promoting industrial education. However, because of Robert's fierce intellectualism and interest in the arts, he ensured that State College provided more than an agricultural education. Likewise, Marion did the same with the federation's reform agenda. The SCFCWC provided cultural programs at the Fairwold Home for Girls, even as it taught practical housekeeping skills. The Wilkinsons therefore demonstrate that black approaches to education cannot be neatly divided into those who favored industrial education and those who preferred classical education. Black clubwomen in South Carolina took inspiration from both approaches to best serve their community.

Marion Wilkinson's influence over the home was significant. She visited it often and brought the girls to State College for visits (in tribute to her devotion, the home was renamed the Marion Birnie Wilkinson Home for Underprivileged Orphans in 1931). A typical visit consisted of Wilkinson and other supporters such as James and Isabelle Cain, bringing food and cheer. Etta Rowe, in a tribute to Wilkinson after her death, contended that, "in her way of thinking and acting, she felt that the environment of the neglected girl should be as rich and as full as possible."[93]

Her focus on a girls' home reflected in part Marion Wilkinson's intense interest in the needs of youth—particularly girls. Her role in building and sustaining Fairwold exemplified her ideas about uplifting the race through protecting the morality of its women and her belief in the need to work simultaneously for her sex and her race. In addition to her integral role at Fairwold, Marion's devotion to girls and youth can be seen in several other projects she led, most notably the YWCA. Wilkinson founded the YWCA at State College, which featured the first YWCA building on an African American college campus.

The two clubs most intimately involved with Fairwold were the Sunlight Club, because of Wilkinson, and the Culture Club of Columbia, because of its proximity to the home. An editorial about their work in the *Palmetto Leader* commented that the Culture Club raised substantial sums of money "in order that the girls committed to that school might enjoy some of the blessings that otherwise are denied to them."[94]

The attention from Wilkinson and other clubwomen to the girls at

Fairwold suggests that the women may have been cognizant of the charges of elitism they faced. When elite clubwomen focused on the need for poor black women and girls to change their behavior, to become more moral, they shifted the blame for discrimination to black women themselves and away from white oppression. This point is clearly illustrated in whites' ability to ignore the demands for Fairwold support.[95] Yet, the care manifested here also suggests that clubwomen tried to avoid stigmatizing the girls even though they expected adherence to certain middle-class standards of moral behavior. Clubwomen in South Carolina maintained an attitude of respect for black girls by referring to the inhabitants of Fairwold as "underprivileged" rather than as "delinquent," before the home actually became an orphanage rather than a reformatory.[96] In addition, asking the girls to aid others would have chipped away at the class barriers between themselves and clubwomen. Because they were expected to reciprocate with visits to the sick and elderly, they were no longer just the beneficiaries of the largess of elite clubwomen; the girls became givers as well as takers. Additionally, the virtues and skills emphasized by clubwomen at the home may have been the same ones that the girls and their families were seeking, rather than merely having them imposed upon them.[97]

Clubwomen ensured that the girls who lived at Fairwold did their own part to increase public awareness of the success of the home. For example, the girls traveled to various cities and sang at churches, schools, and clubs. They also had booths at the state fairs (white and black) where they received prizes for their handiwork, including dairy products, bread and cake making, canning and preserving, and various types of sewing.[98]

Other Southern states also recognized the need for girls' homes, especially working through the Southeastern Federation of Colored Women's Clubs. The Southeastern justified its initiative on behalf of homes for black girls because "the Negro woman holds the key position to all future progress of the race." They prioritized the legislative drive for such homes across the Southern states above other social welfare projects. Black women claimed that in the home the race would be elevated and that delinquent girls were thus severely disadvantaged: without a state-sponsored home, the young women were either roaming the streets or incarcerated with hardened criminals and thus without the uplifting influence of a good home.[99]

South Carolina was one of the earlier states to become involved, followed in the 1920s by several other states, including Mississippi and Florida.[100] North Carolina followed the lead of South Carolina, and some evidence suggests that clubwomen there were directly influenced by Wilkinson and her federation or by Janie Porter Barrett and the Virginia home.[101] Under the North Carolina Federation of Colored Women's Clubs, a home was established at Efland, and a state subsidy secured in 1927. Although Etta Rowe claimed that the Virginia home was also modeled after Fairwold, Janie Porter Barrett was raising funds for it as early as 1909, and the Virginia home opened in 1915 before Fairwold. Barrett had some measure of success in gaining interracial support for the home. She appealed successfully to not only white clubwomen and the state for funding but also the Russell Sage Foundation. Black clubwomen raised more than $5,000 to open the original building, and then with such demonstrable success in hand they approached the legislature. The Virginia General Assembly responded more quickly and more generously than in South Carolina. They immediately appropriated $3,000 in 1915, and by 1918 the sum had increased to $20,000. The state then took over the institution, leaving Barrett as superintendent.[102]

The SCFCWC's intense dedication to the reformatory went far beyond rescuing the twenty or thirty girls who lived at Fairwold in any given year. Rather, Fairwold embodied the strategy of racial uplift espoused by clubwomen in South Carolina and the nation. The federation's theme song, written by Lizelia A. J. Moorer, a member of the Sunshine Club, expressed these primary interests:

> In the fight for integration we will conquer though we die;
> We'll exalt the cause of virtue till the vice away shall die.
> Making the home the type of heaven, causing wrong to fear and fly—
> We're lifting as we climb.
> Education is our watchword, bidding ignorance adieu;
> In the civic life we labor for the beautiful and true;
> So the gloom of night we're chasing while the dawning comes anew,
> We're lifting as we climb.[103]

"Lifting as We Climb" was the motto both of the NACW and the SCFCWC. Because clubwomen were generally members of the social and economic elite class in their community, and because they were aware that this elite status could and did cause tensions within the organization, they hoped to uplift the race by sharing their education and progress. More significant, however, was the philosophy of racial uplift through improving the home and achieving "respectability"—the philosophy embedded in this motto. After boldly proclaiming that clubwomen would fight for integration, Moorer emphasized attaining virtue and improving the home in her lyrics. She also named education and civic improvement as two specific areas of reform that had common appeal to both black and white clubwomen across the nation.

Clubwomen emphasized morality, manners, and respectability because they hoped these would decrease the oppression of a race thought to be undeserving of respect. They believed that rescuing delinquent girls and guiding them to an upright homelife could lessen the stigma of immorality attached to black women. Mary McLeod Bethune, a NACW leader originally from South Carolina and a friend of Wilkinson's, espoused a philosophy of education for black girls; she shows how the protection and education of girls was inextricably linked to the progress of the race. She stressed the need for girls to learn "good citizenship in the home." Bethune believed that by teaching a young black girl morals, cleanliness, and other facets of making a good home, she learned how to raise her family, and, in a home presided over by a good mother, family members could become better citizens.[104] Thus, the home made the citizen, and good citizens in turn could make the race better.

Clubwomen across the nation believed that African Americans needed to adopt certain values that would make them appear to whites to be "respectable." Evelyn Higginbotham contends that the Women's Convention of the Black Baptist church worked to achieve "middle-class" manners: sexual purity, hard work, frugality, temperance, punctuality, neatness, and piety.[105] She argues that this practice was at once conservative and radical; African Americans, although they worked to adopt the norms of the dominant society, were at the same time able to "transcend oppression" by demanding group respect.[106] In other words, by claiming these values and the respect that they commanded, African Americans wrested them from the monopolistic grip of the white middle class. At the same time, white reformers were able to define themselves as "white" in relation to the cultural values that they attempted to impose upon poor whites, but not on blacks. Thus, their identity as whites would be threatened if blacks were able to realize the same middle-class cultural norms that whites had appropriated.[107]

In the press explicit statements made by whites who claimed that black women possessed an utter lack of virtue drove Josephine St. Pierre Ruffin to call the NACW together in 1895, but these slanderous accusations continued into the early twentieth century.[108] Several of the most notorious statements came from a series of articles in the *Independent*, written by Northern and Southern white and black women, in which white women wrote, "Much has been said about the morals of the negro race. Their lack of morals would be a larger subject. . . . I, for instance, have never come in contact with but one negro woman whom I believed to be chaste"; and "I sometimes read of virtuous negro women, hear of them, but the idea is absolutely inconceivable to me. I do not deny that they exist, but after living in a section all my life that teems with negroes I cannot imagine such a creature as a virtuous black woman."[109] Black clubwomen tried to eliminate any evidence of immorality in the community through projects such as the girls' reformatory; in addition, they vehemently protested these statements in the press.

To defend themselves in both the white and black press, black women utilized three main strategies. First, they claimed that most black women were not immoral and contended that many whites misjudged the race based upon their interaction with their domestic servants or lower-class blacks who were not representative of the race. This strategy, of course, speaks to the elite status of leading clubwomen. Second, black women outlined the underlying factors leading to the immorality of those few black women, beginning with their experience in slavery, during which they were not allowed to maintain proper families or a good homelife. Black women blamed others: white men for their corruption of vulnerable black women and girls, white women for their acquiescence in their husbands' and sons' behavior, and black men for their lack of respect and protection of black women. The lack of protection and respect for black women struck a powerful note in the South, an area noted for and proud of its chivalry and protection of white women. Black women also asserted that poverty was a factor in the inability to sustain families and homes; they cited, for example, live-in domestic servants who were unable to be home supervising their own children. Finally, clubwomen emphasized the progress that they were making by showcasing the achievements of the NACW and local clubs in advocating better homes, education, reformatories for delinquent girls, and day nurseries and kindergartens, all of which aided in promoting respectability.[110] The public relations campaign around the activities of the NACW and the Southeastern Federation focused on the home, and particularly on black girls; the black clubwomen hoped that by encouraging high moral standards, and thus improving the home, they could prevent any further aspersion on themselves and their race.

Black women who embraced this strategy of uplift sought to protect young girls in particular. The sexual morality of the race was in the hands of its women, and therefore clubwomen desired to teach girls morality and to protect those who might have been easy prey to men, both black and white, or to crime.[111] In fighting for state support, black clubwomen subtly turned upside down the prevailing image of the promiscuous black woman and predatory black man. They stated, "The virtues of white girls are assailed by men of their own race; the virtues of the colored girls are assailed by men of both races." Thus, they drew attention to white (as well as black) assaults on black women, who were vulnerable to attack not because of an inherent lack of morality, but because of poverty and neglect. In a sense, they had to prove that they, too, along with white women, could be victims. At the same time, they asserted that white women were attacked by white men, not black.[112]

Although the problem was national in scope, this sexual vulnerability was intensified in the South, where white men, growing up in a culture where the white master had domain over and access to all female slaves as his possessions to use at will, continued to assault black women sexually long after slavery ended. Such attacks were intended to enforce white supremacy through intimidation and violence against blacks. For example, in 1871, the wife of a black Republican in Columbia reported that she was beaten and raped by members of the Ku Klux Klan because her husband voted Republican.[113] Furthermore, assumptions about black women's immorality and lasciviousness made them easy targets of rape by white men. Sexual vulnerability was a factor that contributed to the migration of black women out of the South. Once in the North however, migrant girls remained vulnerable unless they gained secure employment and housing immediately, a concern that led to the establishment of homes and other services for them in the North. This topic was visited and revisited at NACW conventions and in the *National Notes*. Southerners were asked to be sure that migrants made proper arrangements before leaving.[114] Thus, both Southerners and Northerners had to cooperate to solve the problem.

Because of the lack of respect for black girls particularly evident in the South, this strategy of race uplift had a more profound meaning south of the Mason-Dixon line. Whites believed that white women held the monopoly on purity and that the lynching of black men was justified in the name of protecting white womanhood. Black Southern women who promoted respectability for themselves therefore undermined white justification for oppression. Middle-class respectable black clubwomen confounded white supremacists by their manners. Moreover, their privileged economic status belied the rationale for segregation based on the presumed degraded status of blacks.

As part of their emphasis on respectability, Southern black women resented being denied the attributes usually accorded a white woman in the South. They, too, in some ways wanted to be treated as "ladies," a status granted only to white women. Charlotte Brown, for example, intensely desired the courtesies so infrequently extended to blacks. As a school principal, Brown complained about that white men never addressed black women as "Mrs." whether they were cooks or school principals. Brown understood that this was one small but significant way in which whites maintained white supremacy. The *Palmetto Leader* picked up on this aspect of the work done by Fairwold and its supporters and praised clubwomen because, "Being women, they realize that Negro womanhood should be given attention, even though their state does not think it worthwhile."[115] The editors accorded the respect due black women, respect that whites refused to give. To gain respect, black women focused on creating positive images of black women through both clubwork and church work. Although this was clearly a limited strategy in terms of attacking white supremacy, the focus on respectability was safer than direct confrontation.

South Carolina clubwomen's embrace of this strategy of race uplift is evident even before they adopted Fairwold as the central program of the state federation and most member clubs. Black women in South Carolina were already addressing the need for protection and virtue through their annual meetings. At the 1911 convention topics included, "Child Study as a Preparation for Moral Uplift," "What Steps to Elevate Our Young People," "How to Safeguard Our Girls," and "The Mother, Daughter, and Social Purity." The federation also discussed the attitude of the church toward problem girls. Members applauded E. Franklin Frazier, director of the Atlanta School for Social Work, and a guest speaker, who suggested that these girls needed serious social investigation and that "go-to-church-get-religion" was not enough to aid them.[116] They followed his talk with a discussion of the need for churches to respond to the needs of these girls and underscored the depth of their desire to confront the problem. Locally, in addition to supporting Fairwold, clubs also worked to meet the needs of girls in their own cities through more generally acceptable playgrounds and recreation.

South Carolinian clubwomen participated in these issues on the national level as well, and they may have been introduced to the need for such work at NACW meetings. In addition to Wilkinson's service as chair of the Domestic Science Department, Mrs. A. P. Dunbar of Columbia was scheduled to speak to the NACW at the 1912 convention on the moral problems of adolescents. Anna Andrews of Sumter and Celia Saxon of Columbia were also members of the NACW resolution committee, which resolved, among other things, that clubs pay more attention to neglected and ailing children.[117]

Three years after Etta Rowe's public appeal, the federation, turning to the black ministers of the state, asked for support in raising funds. In this appeal, the federation continued to stress the useful education given the girls, but they also explicitly appealed for the protection of colored womanhood. They urged that the ministers and citizens of the state help "the delinquent and unprotected girls . . . become useful citizens, heads of homes, and dignified members of the race . . . [and] raise the standard of womanhood."[118]

Underlying this request is the understanding that the progress of the race as a whole depended in part upon the "citizenship," "dignity," and "standard" of its women. Following author Alice Walker, historian Elsa Barkley Brown has termed this philosophy "womanism." She argues that black women did not experience race and gender oppression separately but simultaneously, and they therefore devised strategies of uplifting the race which simultaneously uplifted women. Black women understood that until they received respect, the race could not; they also understood that their economic progress and community leadership was essential to race progress.[119] Saving girls was therefore essential to the "fight for integration" expressed in the federation song.

In examining Southern black clubwomen, some historians have found that the urgent need for race uplift in the segregated South precluded an interest in feminism and forced clubwomen there to focus exclusively on race work.[120] However, the struggle of South Carolina women over the fate of Fairwold indicated that they could not prioritize the struggle for racial equality over sexual equality despite the comparatively worse discrimination they faced in the region; rather, the two struggles were inextricably linked. The Southern experience only magnified the intersection of sex and gender. Their sense of place invested them with a more profound embrace of the twin strategies of womanism and respectability.

In the articles she wrote for the *Palmetto Leader*, clubwoman Cora Gethers focused on woman's role in forming the home and therefore character. "I believe that it is only through the homes," she wrote, "that a people can become really good and truly great." She focused on the good that providing a moral, healthy, and refined atmosphere in the home provided for the family, and therefore the race, especially as that atmosphere was judged by others. According to Gethers, if black women could improve the homes and the moral standards of the masses, "Ethiopia's sons and daughters led by pious women will be elevated among the enlightened races of the world."[121] The Fairwold Home was one piece of the overall strategy of promoting respectability for the good of the race.

South Carolina black women were perhaps exceptionally concerned with morality and young girls because of the state's political leaders. Ben Tillman, governor and senator of South Carolina, was one of the most virulent spokesman for the lack of black women's virtue. In an article later written up in the *Crisis*, Tillman asserted that most black women were without virtue and argued against raising the age of consent from fourteen to sixteen because, he reasoned, black girls would seduce white boys and then white boys would be punished.[122] Tillman was later succeeded by Governor Coleman Blease, who expressed similar sentiments; Blease argued that "the negro race has absolutely no standard of morality. . . . They are, in that separate class by themselves, as marital infidelity seems to be their favorite pastime."[123] Their words and actions encouraged an attitude in South Carolina that left black girls unprotected and in which the legislature could get away with establishing industrial schools for all children, except black girls.

Black women in South Carolina took on many of the same social reform projects as white women, such as establishing a reformatory. However, as evidenced in the case of Fairwold, many of these projects had special meaning for black women: not only was there precious little other aid available to the community, but also these clubwomen desperately hoped to prove their respectability through improving the community's morality and behavior. African American clubwomen in the South therefore faced significant challenges to their social welfare reform agenda. Excluded from their programs and unaided, for the most part, by white clubwomen, black clubwomen had to carry a significant burden. They fought to force the state to acknowledge their needs by demanding a state reformatory for black girls. Denied by the state, they ultimately gained the aid of the Duke Foundation by adapting the home to Duke's requirements. Between this adaptation in the early 1930s and the building of a state reformatory in 1949 delinquent black girls in the state had no other option but incarceration. The home housed up to thirty girls at a time;

thus, the home met the needs of only a small percentage of needy girls in the state. In this way, clubwomen were perhaps more successful at aiding the needy in their own communities than through the home for delinquent girls.

The story of Fairwold, however, is not only a story of failure and adaptation. Despite their lack of success, through this effort black women confronted the assumptions of black inferiority undergirding Jim Crow laws. While asking for state support for the reformatory did not overtly challenge segregation, black women did assert their presence and try to claim a legitimate place for themselves in South Carolina and the New South. Because they refused to believe that black girls were unworthy of attention, they persisted, continuing to support the home. Through their efforts for Fairwold, clubwomen demanded respect for African American women in particular. Although they did not break the barrier of segregation, they resisted its message of inferiority and invisibility. They promoted care for black girls as necessary for the progress of the race as a whole through a strategy of race uplift that emphasized virtue and the home. Promoting respectability was more than a method of improving black living conditions or defending against accusations of immorality. It was imperative to their ability to contend with the triple burden of being African American, female, and Southern. Through their experience of living in the South, both black and white clubwomen were motivated to build youth reformatories. While a sense of place drew white women to white boys—the future of the New South as they saw it, black women focused on black girls—the future of their race.

Conclusion

"This Wonderful Dream Nation!":
Contesting Confederate Culture

On June 3, 1907, a gloriously sunny day, more than one hundred thousand Southerners gathered for the unveiling of the Jefferson Davis monument in Richmond, Virginia. Between speeches, bands played, and Confederate veterans reminisced. The Poppenheims glowingly described the day in the *Keystone*. The monument symbolized the honor and bravery of soldiers and the Southern people during the war. The crowd that had gathered about the monument was even more significant. "This wonderful dream nation!" they exclaimed. "Each year at the bugle call of the Confederacy, it assembles for a few brief hours to do honor to a noble past and a glorious army, and then silently melts away to live only in the hearts and by the firesides of a true and faithful people." For a few hours, the imagined community of the Southern nation became real.[1] Through literary and historical work, through relations with Northern clubwomen, and through social reform work white clubwomen worked to define that dream nation while black clubwomen asserted a place for themselves in it.

Almost one hundred years later, Southerners were still defining the dream nation. In 1995, a black teenager in Guthrie, Kentucky, shot and killed a white man named Michael Westerman who flew a Confederate flag on the back of his pickup truck. Westerman's family and friends claimed that he flew the flag to either represent his Southern heritage and generally rebellious personality or more simply to display colors that matched his truck. Yet, most Southerners, Westerman's family and friends among them, also knew that the flag sent a message to blacks, a recognizable symbol condoning slavery, and these white Southerners admitted that they realized the flag's apparent meaning angered African Americans. Shortly after the murder, the town of Guthrie became embroiled in a debate over the high school mascot—a Confederate rebel. Discourse clearly centered on race: whites took a stand to defend the flag against their perception of blacks elevated at the expense of whites. The Confederate flag and the mascot seemed connected less with Southern history than with contemporary racial animosity, which, according to many local citizens, had been buried for years.

Moreover, women, including Westerman's aunt, who had given him the flag, were at the center of the controversy. As one observer wrote, "It struck me that the media attention lavished on 'angry white males' neglected the considerable depth of female rage on display here, and at other gatherings in Todd County."[2] Today, angry white males are generally blamed for the resentment toward affirmative action and the surge in hate groups and antigovernment militia movements, yet the situation in Guthrie points to angry white women as well.

Just two years earlier, in 1993, the United Daughters of the Confederacy (UDC) had applied to Congress for a renewal of the patent on their insignia, a privilege rarely given to organizations. Senator Carol Moseley-Braun, an African American from Illinois, argued that Congress should not honor a Confederate symbol with recognition through a UDC patent because it represented the Confederacy and its defense of slavery. Her emotional plea brought forth a heated debate in the Senate; Moseley-Braun invoked the memory of her slave ancestors, and white Southern legislators also appealed to their own history, to their grandmothers who were members of the UDC. Ultimately, the Senate voted against renewal.

These incidents are only two examples in contemporary debates raging over Confederate history, Southern identity, and race, and the meaning of these to the South and the nation. South Carolina again was at the forefront, with a contentious debate over whether to remove the Confederate flag that flew over the state capital building in Columbia. A compromise —moving the flag off the building but relocating it on the grounds—did little to appease either side. The flag was not raised until the hundredth anniversary commemoration of the Civil War in 1962, an anniversary that coincided with the burgeoning Civil Rights movement. This timing belies claims that the flag represented Southern culture apart from white supremacy, that it did not represent a white defense of segregation and defiance in the face of threats to that culture. The state's Council of Conservative Citizens not only led a rally defending the Confederate flag, but, for example, these conservatives also included stories in their publications that detailed "a government-aided conspiracy to create a black-ruled 'Republic of Africa' in the South; [and] the rape and murder of a white woman by 'Malcolm X Followers.'" Such articles explicitly demonstrate the link in the minds of supporters between the need to defend the Confederate flag and white supremacy.³

This struggle over Confederate culture in the contemporary South forces us to ask fundamental questions about race and region in the twenty-first century, more than a century after the UDC and other groups organized to protect their ideas about Southern identity. The celebration of Confederate culture is so pernicious because it distorts the history of slaves and their ancestors. It equates "Southern" with "Confederate" and claims to represent "our history"; yet it simultaneously negates not only the contributions but also the existence of blacks. Moreover, understanding the Southern struggle is crucial to larger questions surrounding national identity and race. Just like Southerners, all United States citizens must decide who makes up the nation and whose history must be remembered.

Louisa Poppenheim, Marion Wilkinson, and the thousands of women in the white and black state federations of women's clubs deserve attention for more than what they achieved in the early twentieth century. Their work provides much needed insight and background into the issues informing our current crisis. The nation can learn much from the early twentieth-century attempts of white clubwomen to create a white Southern identity through Confederate culture and the concurrent struggle of black clubwomen to resist that version of Southern identity and to claim their own place. Black and white clubwomen in South Carolina worked to shape a New South according to their community's needs. Their work as clubwomen and as social reformers cannot be considered apart from their sense of place and their negotiation of Southern identity, nor can we understand the making of culture without studying the contributions of women and the politics of gender.

Led by Louisa Poppenheim, white clubwomen in the South Carolina Federation of Women's Clubs focused on Southern identity to an extraordinary degree; Southernness pervaded both their literary self-improvement and their social reform agendas. In this respect, they had more in common with the United Daughters of the Confederacy than with their Northern counterparts in the General Federation of Women's Clubs. Such a focus on Southern identity shaped why and how they conducted their work as clubwomen. Their desire to build pride in the Southern Confederacy gave them a distinctive purpose as they set about rebuilding the postwar South and inventing their "wonderful dream nation."

The life of Louisa Poppenheim reveals much about the motivations and experiences of club leadership. Like most clubwomen, Louisa was well educated, wealthy, and a Confederate daughter. Unlike many, her particular experience was also shaped by the time she spent at Vassar College in New York; furthermore, Louisa never married. Yet Louisa personified the Southern clubwoman most in her pride in the South and desire not only to better it but also to put its best foot forward. She did so in part with her sister Mary through their promotion of the South and the Southern woman in their monthly journal, the *Keystone*. Through their leadership in the club movement and the United Daughters of the Confederacy, and their journal, which served both constituencies, Louisa and Mary also dramatically illustrate the emphasis of Southern identity that clubwomen shared with the UDC.

For white Southern clubwomen, the past and the future, the old South and the New, were integrally linked. They could not work for progress in the New South until they had rehabilitated the old South through the Lost Cause; likewise, the Lost Cause was meaningless without prosperity in the New South. Southern Progressivism was indeed, as historian Dewey Grantham called it, a "reconciliation of progress and tradition." Such reconciliation was perhaps best achieved by women who were able to emphasize cultural continuity during a time of economic change. Because their embrace of Southern tradition and values was never in question, they were able to promote the industrialization espoused by their husbands even as they worked to ameliorate the negative effects it wrought. White clubwomen avoided criticism of either the mills or the mill owners at the same time they attempted to aid mill workers. White women, although expanding their public role, were careful not to tread on the patriarchy, which used notions of women's need for protection to underscore the need for segregation and maintain the status quo.

Moreover, white clubwomen's focus on Southern identity had profound implications for race relations in the early twentieth-century South. Not only did they ignore the needs of blacks as they extended reform benefits to whites only, but, by founding their social reform agenda in the past as they promoted Southern pride, both white clubwomen and Daughters embraced a Lost Cause that justified and strengthened segregation. Thus their social reform was linked to the Lost Cause, which was in turn rooted in the racial ideology of white supremacy. Through their monuments and their reformatories, they built a culture of segregation and helped define the New South around white supremacy.

This aspect of their work remains hidden unless one views it through the eyes of African American clubwomen and their families in the South. Blacks have always recognized and understood the profound racial implications of the Lost Cause even as many white Southerners today continue to deny them under the guise of celebrating Southern culture and other specious claims.

African American clubwomen in South Carolina attempted to resist that culture in many ways, from teaching black history to lobbying for a state reformatory for black girls. They rejected Lost Cause history and instead promoted American history and black literature. Simultaneously, through their social reform agenda they also demanded that their needs be met and that they be granted respect and recognition as legitimate citizens in the New South. Despite their initial failures black clubwomen helped lay the foundation for what would become the Civil Rights movement.

Furthermore, black Southern clubwomen felt compelled to work toward "respectability," which was inherently restrictive in its emphasis on middle-class manners. Such a strategy was perhaps even more necessary in the South than the rest of the nation, where assumptions about black women's supposed immorality juxtaposed with white women's purity allowed violence against black men and women. At the same time, clubwomen's elite status also provided motivation for their reform, as they lived the NACW motto, "Lifting as we climb." Moreover, South Carolina clubwomen recognized the need to fight against race and sex oppression simultaneously; this recognition was evident in their campaign for a reformatory for young girls. Through their focus on respectability and the morality of the black woman, black clubwomen created a role for themselves in race uplift that could not be fulfilled by black men.

Marion Wilkinson led the battle for respect and respectability in the South Carolina Federation of Colored Women's Clubs. Like other elite black clubwomen and teachers, Marion found inspiration in her own privilege to work to uplift others less fortunate than herself; her action was imperative, not only because by her inaction would she be dragged down with them but also because she believed it was incumbent upon her to share what she had with others. Her place in the national network of clubwomen, educators, and college president's wives reveals her dedication to racial uplift. In addition, her ability to work with whites through the interracial movement reveals both her hopes for the end of oppression as well as her realistic understanding of the actuality of Southern life.

Within these constraints, black clubwomen challenged the Lost Cause and rooted black claims to the South. Region, therefore, was important to black clubwomen in the South as well as to white women. Although they experienced shame and inferiority in relation to their Northern sisters, black women had to claim their place in the South when they dealt with white women in the interracial movement. They had to believe that they had helped build the South and that they belonged there. They had to exert their rights as Southern citizens to fight the degree of oppression experienced in the South and to claim state support for their social reform agenda.

The response of black clubwomen and the agenda that they created in South Carolina echo the insights of early twentieth-century black leaders and historians such as W.E.B. Du Bois. They knew that the Lost Cause was centrally about race and that perhaps their strongest weapon in the fight against white supremacy was their own sense of place and legitimate demands for recognition as Southern citizens. Rather than exploring when and why segregation statutes were made into law, this study sharpens our ability to see how these laws were transformed into a culture that seemed timeless and natural, through the everyday and seemingly inconsequential work of women who built statues, promoted histories, and aided only poor white children.

South Carolina, the first state to secede from the Union, was, and perhaps still is, uniquely focused on Confederate identity. After the war, parts of South Carolina led the region in cotton manufacturing; meanwhile, Charleston, with its emphasis on tradition and elite planters, was left behind. Therefore, the state offers comparison within its borders that mirrors the development of the entire region. Cities like Charleston and New Orleans stressed tradition, while Atlanta and Spartanburg, Rock Hill and Columbia all grew with the railroad and the mills. Because clubwomen across the state exhibited a similar concern with Southern identity, this book suggests that further study across the region may yield similar results. After all, the "wonderful dream nation," which the Poppenheims imagined, far exceeded the scope of South Carolina; their nation necessarily united all white Southerners and excluded all African American Southerners.

Notes

CHAPTER 1. SOUTHERN LADIES, NEW WOMEN

1. *Keystone*, May 1910, 3.
2. On Southern white clubwomen, see Anne Scott, *The Southern Lady*; Marsha Wedell, *Elite Women*; Elizabeth Hayes Turner, *Women, Culture, and Community*; Anastasia Sims, *The Power of Femininity*; and Mary Martha Thomas, *The New Woman*. On the women's club movement nationally, see Karen Blair, *The Clubwoman as Feminist*; and Anne Ruggles Gere, *Intimate Practices*. On Southern black clubwomen, see Dorothy Salem, *To Better Our World*; Jacqueline Anne Rouse, *Lugenia Burns Hope*; on black clubwomen generally, see Deborah Gray White, "The Cost of Club Work," 247–69; Anne Scott, "Most Invisible of All"; Stephanie Shaw, "Black Club Women"; Anne Meis Knupfer, "'Toward a Tenderer Humanity'"; and Tullia Hamilton, "The History of the National Association of Colored Women." For a comparative study, see Glenda Gilmore, *Gender and Jim Crow*.
3. Gaines Foster, *Ghosts of the Confederacy*, 178–79. For women and the Lost Cause, see Karen Cox, *Dixie's Daughters*; Antoinette Van Zelm, "Virginia Women as Public Citizens," 71–88; Sarah H. Case, "The Historical Ideology," 599–628; and W. Fitzhugh Brundage, "White Women and the Politics of Historical Memory."
4. In 1913, for example, the *Keystone* claimed to reach more than 28,000 women in the state federations of women's clubs in South Carolina, North Carolina, Mississippi, Florida and Virginia and the state divisions of the UDC in South Carolina, Virginia, and North Carolina. *Keystone*, June 1913, 1.
5. Cox argues that Confederate culture was racist, see *Dixie's Daughters*, 1–2, 6.
6. For a study of Tampa, Florida, which found that Latin, Anglo, and African American women experienced a kaleidoscope of shifting identities, see Nancy A. Hewitt, *Southern Discomfort*, 10–11. There immigration led to shifting identities not found in South Carolina.
7. Knupfer, "'Toward a Tenderer Humanity,'" 23.
8. Brundage, "White Women and the Politics of Historical Memory"; Cox, *Dixie's Daughters*, 32–33; and Case, "The Historical Ideology," 601.
9. For Texas, see Turner, *Women, Culture and Community*; McArthur, *Creating the New Woman*; and Enstam, *Women and the Creation*. For North Carolina, see

Gilmore, *Gender and Jim Crow*; and Sims, *The Power of Femininity*. On South Carolina women, for the antebellum period, see Weiner, *Mistresses and Slaves*. For Reconstruction, see Schwalm, *A Hard Fight for We*.

10. Gaston, *The New South Creed*, remains the best interpretation of the New South spokesmen.

11. Scott, *Natural Allies*, 74, 79–80.

12. In South Carolina in 1910 there were 13,059 white female cotton mill operatives, and by 1930, 24,506; similarly the number of teachers rose from 3,711 to 8,880. *Thirteenth Census of the United States Taken in the Year 1910*, vol. 4, Population, 1910, Occupational Statistics, table 7, 516; and *Fifteenth Census of the United States: 1930, Population*, vol. 4, Occupations, by State, table 11, 1483.

13. Scott, *The Southern Lady* and *Natural Allies*. See also Wedell, *Elite Women and the Reform Impulse*; Wheeler, *New Women in the New South*; Thomas, *The New Woman in Alabama*; Turner, *Women, Culture and Community*; McArthur, *Creating the New Woman*; Enstam, *Women and the Creation of Urban Life*; Sims, *The Power of Femininity*; and Goldfield, *Still Fighting the Civil War*, chapters 4–6.

14. Thomas, *New Woman of Alabama*, 42. In 1888, the South Carolina Methodist Women's Missionary Society held the first public meeting in the state to be presided over by a woman in 1880. One of the earliest women's clubs was the Ladies Literary Club of Spartanburg, founded 1884, to build a library for the town. Scott, *The Southern Lady*, 140–41, 152–53.

15. Louisa B. Poppenheim, "The History of the South Carolina Federation of Women's Clubs" in *South Carolina Federation of Women's Clubs, 1921–1922* (yearbook), ed. Mrs. John Drake, South Carolina Federation of Women's Clubs Papers (hereafter referred to as SCFWC Papers), box 6, folder 21, Special Collections, Dacus Library, Winthrop University, Rock Hill, S.C. (hereafter cited as Winthrop), 21, 23–24; and Le Coq, "A Women's Clubs Legacy," quotation, 67. The clubs were: Abbeville Literary Club; Century Club, Charleston, Palmetto Club, Sin Nombre Club, and Up-to-date Club, Chester; Thursday Club, Thursday Afternoon Club, and West End Club, Greenville; the Wednesday Club, Laurens; Altruruan Club, Pelham; Amelia Pride Club and Palmetto Circle, Rock Hill; Once-a-Week Club, Seneca; Ladies' Literary Association and Over the Teacups Clubs, Spartanburg; Paul Hayne Circle, Walhalla; and Every Tuesday Club, Union. Ludie Merriam Coleman attended the Leland School and married Matthew T. Coleman, a manufacturer/planter/merchandiser. They had three sons. She was president of the Once-A-Week-Club in Seneca, a regent of her local DAR chapter, and later a member of the Century Club in Charleston when she and her husband began dividing their time between Seneca and Charleston. *Keystone*, January 1904, 10–11.

16. June 1899, *Keystone*, 1. The five officers were President Ludie Coleman, Seneca; Vice President Mrs. J. Sumpter Means, Spartanburg; Recording Secretary Louisa Poppenheim; Corresponding Secretary Miss Mary Hemphill, Abbeville; Treasurer Miss E. J. Roach; and Auditor Mary Gridley, Greenville. Of twenty-six

standing committee members listed, seven were from Greenville, four from Chester, three from Union, two each from Charleston, Laurens, Walhalla, and Seneca, and one each from Abbeville, Columbia, Pelham, and Spartanburg.

17. Poppenheim, "The History of the SCFWC," 21; *Keystone*, October 1899, 8, and March 1909, 3. In 1912, when clubs were asked to identify their special interest, the answers were divided: 32—literary, 26—civics, 18—education, 7—library, 5—music, and 7—difficult to classify. *Keystone*, May 1912, 4.

18. Poppenheim, "The History of the SCFWC," 24, and *South Carolina Federation of Women's Clubs, 1928–1929* (yearbook), ed. Mrs. Ralph Ramseur, SCFWC Papers, box 9, folder 28, Winthrop.

19. Poppenheim, *A History of the United Daughters of the Confederacy*, 1–11, 21. In comparison, the North Carolina Federation of Women's Clubs had 2,882 members and the North Carolina UDC 4,300; the Virginia Federation of Women's Clubs had 1,800 members and the Virginia UDC 8,516. *Keystone*, June 1913, 1.

20. Salem, *To Better Our World*, 7–12.

21. This federation may have had some sort of initial gathering in Charleston. In an article for the *National Association Notes*, Pauline Miller claims that the federation was founded on May 27, 1907, at the Centenary M. E. Church in Charleston, with herself as the first president. See *National Notes*, November 1911, 5. However, all other federation documents state that the founding occurred at the Columbia meeting. See *National Notes*, April–May 1917, 9. (The *National Association Notes*, after 1923 called the *National Notes*, was the official publication of the National Association of Women's Clubs); *Minutes of the National Association of Colored Women*, 1908, *Records of the National Association of Colored Women's Clubs, 1895–1992*, part 1, ed. Lillian Serece Williams, microfilm (hereafter referred to as Records of the NACW), reel 1, pp. 7, 18; *Minutes of the National Association of Colored Women*, 1912, Records of the NACW, reel 1, p. 47; and *Minutes of the National Association of Colored Women*, 1914, Records of the NACW, reel 1, p. 28. A photo is in the *Fortieth Anniversary Booklet*, 2.

22. Marion Wilkinson to "My dear friend," South Carolina Federation of Colored Women's Clubs (SCFCWC), March 29, 1949. Mamie E. G. Fields Collection (hereafter referred to as Fields Collection), Federated Clubs Scrapbook (1949–86), Avery Research Center for African American History and Culture, College of Charleston, South Carolina (hereafter referred to as Avery).

23. Albertha Murray, "NACW Speech," 1962, Albertha Murray Papers, folder 6, Avery.

24. Louisa was also corresponding secretary of the General Federation as well as a member of its board of directors and an honorary vice president, a member of the Society of Pioneers of the General Federation, an honorary member of the Society of American Women in London and the Society of American Women in Vienna, and a member of several coed organizations, such as the Carolina Arts Association and the South Carolina Child Labor Committee. Information on Mary's and Louisa's various activities and offices can be found throughout the

Keystone, as well as in Leonard, ed. *Woman's Who's Who*; Logan, *The Part Taken by Women*, 384–85; *Charleston News and Courier*, May 1, 1921; Mary and Louisa Poppenheim, Biographical Records Questionnaires, 1930, 1938, 1947, Vassar Alumni Office, Vassar College, Poughkeepsie, N.Y. (hereafter referred to as Vassar); Johnson, *Southern Women at Vassar*; Johnson, "How Would I Live Without Loulie?"; and Johnson, "This Wonderful Dream Nation!"

25. *Keystone*, June 1899, 3. The editors explained that the *Keystone* was named for the "topmost stone of the arch," which "bind[s] it strongly together, neither dependent nor independent, but necessary to give it strength. The name defines the position of the Journal to woman's work." September 1899, 3.

26. Ibid., June 1913, 1. This number is somewhat inflated owing to the overlapping membership of some North Carolina, South Carolina, and Virginia women in their state federation and UDC Division. Many clubs circulated and incorporated the *Keystone* into their meetings, which allowed it to reach a substantial proportion of the membership who did not personally subscribe.

27. Ibid., July 1904, 3. For a description of the collating, see clipping, *Charleston News and Courier*, February 15, 1931, SCFWC Papers, box 31, folder 114, Winthrop.

28. "History of the Century Club," typescript, March 31, 1975, Century Club Papers, South Carolina Historical Society, Charleston. (hereafter referred to as SCHS).

29. Johnson, *Southern Women at Vassar*, 2–4.

30. Other studies of clubs and the UDC have found officers and members to be predominately middle to upper class. See, for example, Blair, *The Clubwoman as Feminist*, 1–5; Foster, *Ghosts of the Confederacy*, 107; Roth, *Matronage*, 89; and Thomas, *The New Woman*, 67.

31. Mrs. Emert S. Rice, "A History of the New Century Club," pamphlet, 1981, USC. A sample of significant leaders in both associations, as well as club members in Rock Hill, Columbia, and Charleston, yielded information concerning the following professions of 179 husbands: 45 businessmen (including insurance salesmen, bankers, bookkeepers, real estate agents, salesmen, editors/publishers); 28 merchants (including retail and wholesale and small-business owners); 26 teachers and professors; 20 physicians and scientists; 13 mill owners, bookkeepers, and secretaries; 11 public servants (including governors and commissioners); 10 attorneys and judges; 7 railroad company engineers and officers; 6 ministers/pastors; 5 architects/engineers; 4 planters/farmers; and 4 law enforcement officials. I have not been able to find any substantial differences between clubwomen and UDC members, except to note that UDC profiles often indicate that members were daughters of planters, even though their husbands were not. This information primarily comes from the Columbia, Rock Hill, and Charleston city directories; Utsey, ed., *Who's Who in South Carolina*; and biographical sketches in the *Keystone*.

32. Selma Lyttleton, *Keystone*, August 1900, 11.

33. I have identified "leaders" as women who held office in the federation for at

least four years. Educational status comes from biographical sketches in the *Keystone*. Roth found similar results in her study of Atlanta clubwomen and the UDC, Roth, *Matronage*, 92.

34. McClintock was born in Newberry, where her father was a planter and Scotch Presbyterian minister. *Keystone*, July 1904, 11. Burney was born in Yorkville but grew up in Columbia, where her father, Samuel W. Melton, was a lawyer and judge. Her husband, William B. Burney, was a professor of chemistry at the University of South Carolina. Burney was an officer of the SCFWC, UDC, DAR, and organized the city federation of women's clubs in Columbia. Utsey, ed., *Who's Who in South Carolina*, 71, and Collier, *Biographies of Representative Women*, vol. 3, 179–80.

35. For more on the Poppenheim sisters' Vassar experience, see Johnson, *Southern Women at Vassar*.

36. Ibid., 38, 42.

37. "Report Made by Perihelion Club Delegates to the Club on the Third State Convention of SCFWC at Charleston on April 21, 1900," typescript, Perihelion Papers, box 1, folder 1, Winthrop, 5.

38. Nina Honer, "Some Defects in Secondary Schools for Southern Girls," Converse College, *Keystone*, February 1901, 4–5.

39. *Keystone*, September 1900, 4–5.

40. Johnson, "This Wonderful Dream Nation!" 21; and *South Carolina Clubwoman*, January 6, 1950, 11, 22.

41. J.H.B. to Louisa Poppenheim, n.d., SCFWC Papers, Winthrop.

42. According to the 1910 U.S. Census, Wilkinson was thirty-seven years old, although according to the 1920 census she was forty-five years old. Gordon, *Sketches of Negro Life*, 140, 179–80; and Powers, *Black Charlestonians*, 246–47.

43. Biographer A. B. Caldwell described him as "a careful business man [who] has accumulated considerable property." Caldwell, *History of the American Negro*, 293–95. *Palmetto Leader*, October 9, 1926, 1; Drago, *Initiative, Paternalism, and Race Relations*, 102–3; *Who's Who in Colored America*, 1927; *Who's Who of the Colored Race*, 1915, reprint 1976, vol. 1; and *Dictionary of American Biography*, 229–30.

44. *Fortieth Anniversary Booklet*, 7.

45. Mays, *Born to Rebel*, 41.

46. *Thirteenth Census of the United States Taken in the Year 1910*, vol. 4, Population, 1910, Occupational Statistics, table 7, 516; and Tindall, *South Carolina Negroes*, 124, 141.

47. Founding members are listed according to their husbands' occupations: Mattie E. Stewart, Hazel Tatnall Pierce, Rosa Harris, Lillian Pinckney, and Alethia Lewis: professors at State College; Etta Butler Rowe (taught at Claflin and South Carolina State): doctor; Sadie Fordham Smith and Anna Belle Jenkins: brick masons; Mrs. Collin Embley: carpenter; Etta Simmon: cook at the Orangeburg Hotel; Bessie Sulton and Daisy Sulton: sawmill owners; Alice Kennerly: grocery store owner; Sallie Daniels: tailor; L. A. Moorer (a librarian at Claflin) and Antonia

Bowmen: attorneys; Alma McPherson: mail carrier; and Irene Brown: Methodist minister. Information comes from Drago, *Initiative, Paternalism, and Race Relations*; city directories; interviews; and Mack, *Parlor Ladies and Ebony Drudges*, chapters 1–3, esp. 108.

48. Powers, *Black Charlestonians*, 36–37. In 1850, Charleston had the fourth largest free black population in the South, with 3,441, smaller only than that of New Orleans, Baltimore, and Washington, D.C.

49. Jeannette Cox, "A History—by administrations of the Phyllis Wheatley Literary and Social Club," 1936, manuscript, Phyllis Wheatley Club Collection, Avery, box 1, folder 2.

50. Of thirty-three names mentioned as charter members or new members in the minutes between 1916 and 1930, I have positively identified seventeen members. Of these, fourteen clearly belonged to the elite class, and I presume that an additional four members also belonged to that network. Drago, *Initiative, Paternalism, and Race Relations*, 96, 149, 172–73.

51. Drago, *Initiative, Paternalism, and Race Relations*, 182–83, 191–92.

52. Fields, *Lemon Swamp*, 198. The others were Mamie Rodolph, the second wife of Herman Rodolph, Jr., whose first wife, Olive, was a member of the Phyllis Wheatley, and Ida Green, whose husband, the Reverend Nathaniel Green, was a pastor at Centenary Church and who organized the City Federation in 1916. *Fortieth Anniversary Booklet*, 56.

53. Biographical information on SCFCWC members comes from various sources including *National Notes* and city directories. For Clyde and Saxon, see Simms, *Profiles of African American Females*, 10, 111–12.

54. Drago, *Initiative, Paternalism, and Race Relations*, 95.

55. Ibid., 97–103.

56. Gordon, *Sketches of Negro Life*, 179–80; and Clark, *Echo in My Soul*, 28. Clark was born in 1898 and educated at Avery. She taught in South Carolina public schools but was fired owing to her connection to the NAACP. She attended the Highlander Folk School in Tennessee, with many others who were active in the Civil Rights movement, and opened citizenship schools in South Carolina. Simms, *Profiles of African-American Females*, 19–20. See also Shaw, *What a Woman Ought to Be*, chapter 3.

57. Rouse, *Lugenia Burns Hope*, chapter 4; and Thomas, *The New Woman in Alabama*, 72–82.

58. Saxon graduated from South Carolina State Normal School and married Prof. T. A. Saxon in 1890. Majors, *Noted Negro Women*, 111–12.

59. Reid, "'A Career to Build.'"

60. Hall, "The Mind That Burns," 328–49, and *Revolt Against Chivalry*, 194; and Wheeler, *New Women in the New South*, 18.

61. Scott, *Natural Allies*, 81. See also Sims, *The Power of Femininity*, and Wheeler, *New Women in the New South*, 3–9, 73–78.

62. *Keystone*, August 1902, 3; April 1904, 3; March 1905, 3; and May 1910, 3;

and Minutes, July 7, 1903, Amelia Pride Club Papers, Winthrop; on the Thursday Club, see *The Southern Clubwoman* (Jacksonville, Florida), March 1929, 7, 14.

63. *Keystone*, October 1905, 3; June 1899, 6; Sims, *The Power of Feminity*, 157–60; and Scott, *Natural Allies*, 81. Giselle Roberts argues that teenage girls or "belles" also found strength in their sacrifice, elitism, honor, and sense of self, which served them after the war. Roberts, *The Confederate Belle*, 179–80. Drew Faust and Laura Edwards have argued that women's support for the Confederacy in reality waned, with negative consequences for the Confederate cause. Faust, *Mothers of Invention*, chapter 11; and Edwards, *Scarlett Doesn't Live Here Anymore*, 79–99.

64. Thomas, "The Ideology," 125; and Leloudis, "School Reform in the New South," 905–9.

65. Whites, *The Civil War as a Crisis*, 14.

66. Brundage, "White Women and the Politics of Historical Memory," 119.

67. "Report Made by Perihelion Club Delegates to the Club on the Third State Convention of SCFWC at Charleston on April 21, 1900," typescript, Perihelion Papers, box 1, folder 1, Winthrop, 1, 9.

68. Grover Cleveland, "Woman's Mission and Woman's Clubs," *Ladies' Home Journal*, May 1905, 22; and *Keystone*, March 1905, 12–13.

69. *Keystone*, May 1908, 3; June 1905, 3; May 1903, 3.

70. Mrs. Wilbur K. Sligh, "President's Annual Report," SCFWC yearbook, 1905–1906, 9, Winthrop.

71. "Report Made by Perihelion Club Delegates to the Club on the Third State Convention." Perihelion Papers, Winthrop. The phrase is from Turner, "'White-Gloved Ladies' and 'New Women,'" 129–56.

72. Wheeler, *New Women of the New South*, 3, 100–27. On South Carolina and suffrage, see Bland, "Fighting the Odds," 32; Hornsby, *South Carolina Women*, 7–9; and Taylor, "South Carolina and the Enfranchisement of Women," 115–26.

73. *Keystone*, June 1900, 5; Baker, "The Domestication of Politics," 620–47; and McArthur, *Creating the New Woman*, 9.

74. *Keystone*, March 1900, 9–10; April 1900, 3.

75. *The Southern Clubwoman* (Jacksonville, Florida), March 1929, 7, 14.

76. Mrs. William A. Boyd, "The Thursday Club: A Sketchy Review," April 1964; and Minutes, December 4, 18, 1913; January 8, 1914; February 5, 1914; and February 19, 1914, Thursday Club Papers, USC. See also Minutes, December 13, 1914, Thursday Club Papers, USC, and Minutes, December 1914, April 28, 1919, New Century Club Papers, USC.

77. Minutes, December 9, 1914; January 20, 1915; and November 2, 1921, Wednesday Club Papers, Laurens County Public Library, Laurens, S.C.

78. Hannah Hemphill Coleman was born in 1872 in Abbeville and educated in the local schools. She married in 1892 and had four children. *Keystone*, October 1912, 4; Utsey, ed., *Who's Who in South Carolina*, 103; and McCandless, "Anita Pollitzer," 1–10.

79. Cora Gethers, "The Part the Negro Woman Is to Play," *Palmetto Leader*,

June 12, 19, and 26, 1926, 4. Gethers was quoting from various articles in Culp, *Twentieth Century Negro Literature*.

80. Gordon, "Black and White Visions of Welfare," 568–69. In this study of black and white women reformers, Gordon found that 85 percent of the black reformers were married. At the same time, despite their elite class status (the vast majority came from prominent families and married professional men), 88 percent worked for wages. Gordon links this biographical information to black women's concerns with the needs of working women—their interest in building day-care centers—and speculates that had black women been more influential in the creation of the welfare system, they would have provided for working women rather than using the ideal of a stay-at-home mother. In another survey, Tullia Hamilton found that 85 of 108 leaders in the NACW were married and 73 percent worked outside the home. Hamilton, "The History of the National Association of Colored Women," chapter 2.

81. Biographical information comes primarily from Robinson, interview, October 12, 1995; and the *City Directory*, 1920–21, Orangeburg, S.C.

82. *Fifteenth Census of the United States: 1930, Population*, vol. 6, Families, table 14, 1195.

83. Gordon, "Black and White Visions of Welfare," 568–69; constitution, SCFCWC, private collection, Robinson; *Fortieth Anniversary Book*, 38; Sunlight Club Year's Program, 1930–31; and *Southern Indicator*, February 12, 1921, 2.

84. White, "The Cost of Club Work," 252–57.

85. *Palmetto Leader*, February 4, 1928, 6.

86. Terborg-Penn, *African American Women in the Struggle*, 44–45. On Southern black suffragists, see Hine and Farnham, "Black Women's Culture of Resistance," 204–19. Rosalyn Terborg-Penn claims that "discrimination against Afro-American women reformers was the rule rather than the exception within the woman's rights movement." "Discrimination Against Afro-American Women," 17–27, (quotation, 17).

87. Mack, *Parlor Ladies*, 109–10.

88. Aptheker, *A Documentary History of the Negro People*, 305–9.

CHAPTER 2. "AS INTENSELY SOUTHERN AS I AM": BLACK AND WHITE CLUBWOMEN, THE UNITED DAUGHTERS OF THE CONFEDERACY, AND SOUTHERN IDENTITY

1. Mary Bouknight Poppenheim, "Personal Experiences," 254–61. Interestingly enough, when the editor, Matthew Page Andrews, excerpted Mary Elinor Poppenheim's remembrances, he did not include her cries against the Union army. In fact, he noted, "Parts of Mary Elinor Poppenheim's diary are here and later omitted for the reason that the sufferings and privations are too harrowing for present publication and because the conditions described may too easily be misinterpreted as an indictment of the Federal forces" (255).

2. On history, memory, and nationalism, see Kammen, *Mystic Chords of Memory*; and Lowenthal, *The Past Is a Foreign Country*.

3. Brundage, "White Women and the Politics of Historical Memory," 122–31; and Brundage, "Introduction," 3–4.

4. Hobsbawm, ed., *The Invention of Tradition*.

5. Hobsbawm, "Introduction," in *The Invention of Tradition*, 2. Although the Daughters did not claim that their rituals, such as Memorial Day celebrations, had occurred during the past, their need to link with the past is the same as that described by Hobsbawm.

6. Although the industrialization promoted by the New South creed did not come close to overtaking agriculture as the primary occupation in the South, Paul Gaston's exploration of the rhetoric of the New South spokesmen indicates that they created a larger sense of change than real conditions merited. See Gaston, *The New South Creed*, 189.

7. Cell, *The Highest Stage of White Supremacy*, 131–67; and Woodward, *The Strange Career of Jim Crow*.

8. Powers, *Black Charlestonians*, 78–79, 103; Avary, *Dixie After the War*, 395–401; and Lumpkin, *The Making of a Southerner*, 133–34. Gilmore argues that interracial class cooperation in social reform (prohibition) in the 1880s collapsed when whites feared that black Republicans could assume too much political power. Gilmore, *Gender and Jim Crow*.

9. Joel Williamson argues that radical segregationists scapegoated blacks for their own inability to fulfill their expected roles as breadwinners due to worsening economic conditions. His interpretation, however, does not fully examine how gender roles for men and women were changing. Williamson does not address women's increased public activity, which may have also spurred men's need to assert control (over blacks rather than white women). Williamson, *Crucible of Race*. Bryant Simon finds similar problems in "The Appeal of Cole Blease," 57–86.

10. Van Zelm, "Virginia Women as Public Citizens," 71–72. Varon, *We Mean to Be Counted*, argues that white women in the Old South were much more politically active than previously recognized.

11. Brundage, "White Women and the Politics of Historical Memory," 122–31; and Brundage, "Introduction," 3–4.

12. Cox, *Dixie's Daughters*, 32–33.

13. *Keystone*, July 1902, 13. See also Cox, *Dixie's Daughters*, chapter 7.

14. David Thelen calls for historians to study the use of memory in history in, "Memory and American History," 1117–29. See also Lindgren, *Preserving the Old Dominion;* Brundage, "White Women and the Politics of Historical Memory"; and Hall, "'You Must Remember This,'" 439–65.

15. David W. Blight argues that the drive for reunion of the nation overwhelmed the memory of the war as emancipatory for slaves, and the Southern, Lost Cause version of history prevailed. Blight, *Race and Reunion*.

16. On segregation in South Carolina, see Hemmingway, "Beneath the Yolk of Bondage," 53–60. On race, ideology, and segregation, see Barbara J. Fields, "Ideology and Race in American History," 155–62; Hale, *Making Whiteness*; and Williamson, *The Crucible of Race*.

17. Holt, "Marking," 16. Holt also argued (p. 7), "It is at this level . . . that race is reproduced via the marking of the racial Other and that racist ideas and practices are naturalized, made self-evident, and thus seemingly beyond audible challenge."

18. Blee, "Women in the 1920s Ku Klux Klan," 71, and *Women of the Klan*; MacLean, *Behind the Mask of Chivalry*; and Koonz, *Mothers in the Fatherland*. In the case of the Klan, Nancy MacLean argues that by their participation, women justified the Klan as upholding family values, thus winning public sanction for it.

19. Shaw, *What a Woman Ought to Be*, xi–xii, 5. For an emphasis on the positive actions of the African American community during the nadir of race relations, see also Hewitt, *Southern Discomfort*, 57.

20. An early interpretation of the Lost Cause by historian Rollin Osterweis followed up on Du Bois's insight and argued that the Lost Cause was centrally about race. Writing in the early 1970s, Osterweis seems to have been seeking to understand the recalcitrance of the Southern states during desegregation and finding an explanation in the Lost Cause. Osterweis, *The Myth of the Lost Cause*. Recent historians of the Lost Cause, however, have not emphasized the integral relationship between the Lost Cause, segregation, and race relations. See, for example, for the Lost Cause as a civil religion, Wilson, *Baptized in Blood*; for the Confederate Celebration, see Foster, *Ghosts of the Confederacy*. An interpretation by Fred Bailey analyzes the role of class in the significant and successful efforts of the UCV, the Sons of Confederate Veterans (SCV), and the UDC to control the history being taught to Southern school children. Bailey, "Free Speech and the 'Lost Cause,'" 452–77, and Bailey, "The Textbooks of the 'Lost Cause.'" An exception is Karen L. Cox, who acknowledges the racist ideology of the UDC in *Dixie's Daughters*, 160–62. On blacks and historical memory, see Blight, "W.E.B. Du Bois and the Struggle," in *History and Memory*, edited by Fabre, 45–71.

21. Van Zelm found that black and white women's participation in commemorations varied slightly before the 1890s, as white women raised and controlled funds more and black women appeared more visibly on the program. The latter changed once the UDC was organized. Van Zelm, "Virginia Women as Public Citizens," 72–83.

22. For example, Mary chaired the literature department of the General Federation of Women's Clubs and Louisa was on the credentials committee of the South Carolina UDC. See *Keystone*, November 1906, 3; December 1905, 14.

23. *South Carolina Federation Bulletin*, March 1927, 9.

24. Information compiled from the *Keystone* and minutes of both the SCFWC and South Carolina UDC.

25. The *Keystone* also gives many examples of this overlap in other Southern states, including, for example, Mrs. Cone Johnson, Texas Federation of Women's Clubs president and state UDC president. See *Keystone*, December 1905, 7. In a study of Atlanta women, Darlene Roth found that in the 1890s, 31 of 60 Atlanta Women's Club members also belonged to the UDC; this number decreased in the 1930s to 21 of 106. Approximately 70 percent of women in clubs, the UDC, the

DAR and the Society of Colonial Daughters was born in Georgia. Roth, *Matronage*, 90, 94–96. Although Mary Martha Thomas did not examine UDC membership in her study of Alabama clubwomen, she did find that 18 of 20 state federation presidents before 1920 were born in the South. Thomas, *New Woman in Alabama*, 67.

26. *Keystone*, June 1911, 11. Mrs. Joseph White to Mary Poppenheim, January 24, 1906, Poppenheim Papers, Duke. Mrs. Randolph is probably Janet Henderson Weaver Randolph, founder and longtime president of the Virginia UDC. My appreciation to Sandra Treadway for identifying Randolph. Nationally, the UDC adopted the *Confederate Veteran* as its official organ.

27. *Keystone*, April 1911, 4; Minutes, February 11, 1920, Wednesday Club Papers, Laurens County Library, Laurens, S.C. (hereafter referred to as Laurens); July 22, 1898, Amelia Pride Club Papers, Winthrop; and December 9, 1925, Current Literature Club Papers, USC.

28. Minutes, March 30, 1921, Wednesday Club Papers, Laurens.

29. *Keystone*, August 1899, 10. Such melodramatic rhetoric runs throughout club and UDC documents, and, although the tone was typical for the time, their words do capture the intensity with which some clubwomen approached their history.

30. Examples of references to Southern identity that follow in the text are representative from those found throughout the *Keystone*, as well as in the minutes and papers of the following clubs. From the city of Rock Hill: Perihelion Club Papers, Amelia Pride Club Papers, Castalian Club Papers, Outlook Club Papers, Keystone Club Papers, and Over the Teacups Club Papers (Archives and Special Collections, Dacus Library, Winthrop University, Rock Hill, South Carolina); from Chester: Palmetto Club Papers (Winthrop); from Darlington: Over the Teacups Club Papers and Old Homestead Club Papers (Darlington County Historical Commission, Darling, South Carolina); from Laurens: Wednesday Club Papers; from Columbia: Current Literature Club Papers, New Century Club Papers, Social Survey Club Papers, Thursday Club Papers (Manuscripts, South Caroliniana Library, University of South Carolina, Columbia, South Carolina) and Columbia Chapter, National Council of Jewish Women (American Jewish Archives, Hebrew Union College, Cincinnati, Ohio; hereafter referred to as AJA); and from Charleston: Century Club Papers, Civic Club Papers, Charleston City Federation Papers (South Carolina Historical Society, Charleston, South Carolina) and Charleston Chapter, National Council of Jewish Women (AJA).

31. Minutes, May 13, 1902; May 27, 1902; January 14, 1907; and "A Diary from Dixie," typescript, n.d., Over the Teacups Club Papers, Darlington. See also Minutes, 1901, vol. 1, folder 1, box 1, Castalian Club Papers, Winthrop.

32. Minutes, March 22, 1898, p. 68; April 6, 1898, p. 69; May 13, 1898, p. 71; July 22, 1898, p. 76, vol. 1, folder 2, box 1, Amelia Pride Club Papers, Winthrop. See also December, 1926, p. 51, vol. 4, folder 4, box 1, and April, 1923, vol. 3, folder 3, box 1.

33. Minutes, January 23, 1902, p. 29, folder 1, box 1; April, 1903, p. 63, folder 1, box 1; May 20, 1920, p. 18, folder 3, box 1; and Yearbooks, 1899 and 1900, folder 9, box 3, Perihelion Club Papers, Winthrop. The minutes do not specify if this was Margaret (Mrs. George) Williams or Corain (Mrs. Oscar) Williams.

34. Minutes, December 12, 1922, New Century Club Papers, USC.

35. *State*, September 9, 1917.

36. Mary Bouknight Poppenheim, "Bethany Hospital," 67–68. For women's roles during the war, see Scott, *Natural Allies*; Faust, *Mothers of Invention*; and Rable, *Civil Wars*.

37. Mary Bouknight Poppenheim to Louisa and Mary, April 30 and May 4, 1886, in Johnson, *Southern Women at Vassar*, 115–17.

38. *Keystone*, January 1903, 5.

39. Collier, *Biographies of Representative Women*, vol. 3, 179–80; "Holds Office in General U.D.C." Clipping, n.d., SCFWC, Winthrop; and *Keystone*, June 1904, 9.

40. *Keystone*, July 1904, 4; May 1908, 6.

41. Ibid., March 1911, 14–15; November 1900, 9–10; September 1904, 8–9; December 1900, 11.

42. Plum, *The Magnificent Enterprise*, 36. Salmon was also known for her efforts to relax social regulations and encourage student self-government, and was a suffragist. See Lynn D. Gordon, *Gender and Higher Education*, 130–33.

43. *Keystone*, November 1906, 8; October 1900, 3.

44. Ibid., June 1900, 5; March 1902, 5; September 1902, 5; and Cox, *Dixie's Daughters*, 111.

45. *Keystone*, January 1902, 3. These reviews dominate the book review pages of the *Keystone*. For a few of the many examples, see *Keystone*, February 1900, 13; March 1900, 13; May 1902, 12; April 1904, 11.

46. Ibid., January 1902, 3.

47. Ibid., February 1906, 8–9.

48. Minutes, August 12, 1896, Amelia Pride Club Papers, Winthrop.

49. See, for example, Minutes, January 11, 1922, p. 4, vol. 1; February 22, 1922, p. 55, vol. 1; January 23, 1924, p. 16, vol. 2; January 11, 1928, January 23, 1928, p. 118, vol. 2; May 25, 1921, p. 31, vol. 1 (on Page), Current Literature Club Papers, USC. After a reading of Thomas Nelson Page's "Mars Chan" by a member, February 22, 1922, p. 55, vol. 1, the secretary noted that "needless to say, there were few dry eyes in the room when she finished the beautiful story of Ole Virginia."

50. Clipping, May 3, 1903, Minutes, April 4, 1903, Old Homestead Club Papers, Darlington. See also Minutes, September 27, 1921; December 1921, January 17, February 22, October 17, December 22, 1922, and January 23, March 23, 1923, folder 3, box 1, Outlook Club Papers.

51. *Keystone*, April 1907, 12. Most members of the SCFWC were born in the South rather than transplanted Northerners.

52. Ibid., January 1901, 6–7; April 1901, 7; September 1901, 6–7.

53. Minutes, November 13, 1928, Outlook Club Papers, USC.

54. Bartlett, *Remembering*, 205, quoted in Brundage, "No Deed but Memory,"

5. See also Blight, *Race and Reunion*, especially chapter 8; and Cox, *Dixie's Daughters*, chapter 6.

55. *Keystone*, May 1901, 12. See "Faithfulness of Slaves," n.d., clipping in scrapbook, United Daughters of the Confederacy Relic Room and Museum, Columbia, S.C. The *Keystone* covered the death of a faithful slave, Charlotte Stewart of Fort Mill, S.C., who was buried with her former master's family. *Keystone*, November 1900, 7.

56. *Keystone*, February 1901, 6–7. On Coleman, see *Keystone*, January 1904, 10–11.

57. Charleston *News and Courier*, February 5, 1920; Minutes, November 27, 1906, Over the Teacups Club Papers, Darlington; Minutes, February 29, 1908, and November 27, 1927, Old Homestead Club Papers, Darlington.

58. See, for example, Mrs. Wullburn, "Education Institutions in South Carolina," typescript, n.d. (c. 1936–1938), Century Club of Charleston Papers, Charleston Library Society, Charleston, S.C.

59. *Keystone*, May 1902, 12; March 1905, 14.

60. Minutes, February 3, 1914, Amelia Pride Club Papers, Winthrop. The Amelia Pride Club also noted in its minutes that the Clansman "could not be acted in Columbia this season," a remark written over something that has been erased. Minutes, October 1, 1906, Amelia Pride Club Papers. This appears to be Jennie (Mrs. William C.) Hutchison, although it may have been Kate (Mrs. Davis) Hutchison.

61. Minutes, March 13 and 27, 1906; November 11, 1923, New Century Club Papers, USC.

62. *Keystone*, August 1904, 5; and Minutes, December 20, 1906, Over the Teacups Club Papers, Darlington.

63. *Keystone*, July 1900, 11; March 1902, 12; March 1900, 13.

64. Ibid., May 1903, 4. Favorites included histories by Mrs. Susan Pendleton Lee and Dr. William Jones.

65. Kate Hutcheson Morrissette, "Traveling Libraries in Alabama," *Sewanee Review*, October 1898, 345–48 (quotation, 347).

66. Minutes, December 18, 1930, Perihelion Club Papers, Winthrop.

67. *Confederate Veteran*, June 1916, 277.

68. *Keystone*, August/September 1905, 12.

69. *Keystone*, October 1900, 11; January 1905, 10–11.

70. Wotten taught at Madame Togno's school in Charleston and then Barhamville from 1854 to approximately 1863. MBW, "Some of Charleston's Most Noted Schools, Past and Present," *Keystone*, May 1900, 11. "MBW" may be Martha B. Washington, a member of the Charleston UDC chapter.

71. Minutes, January 15, 1915, Amelia Pride Club Papers, Winthrop; Minutes, January 1928, Perihelion Club Papers, Winthrop; Minutes, May 10, 1921, New Century Club Papers, USC; Minutes, May 13, 1901, book 2, Century Club Papers, SCHS.

72. Minutes, February 25, 1919, Amelia Pride Club Papers, Winthrop.

73. *Yearbook of the South Carolina Division, United Daughters of the Confederacy, 1931–1932,* 9.

74. *Keystone,* December 1903, 9.

75. Minutes, May 21, 1896; August 12, 1896; March 20, 1901; June 1901; September 18, 1906; April 30, 1907; May 24, 1909, Amelia Pride Club Papers, Winthrop. For the UDC and monument building, see Cox, *Dixie's Daughters.* For more on the monuments themselves, see Emerson, *Historic Southern Monuments,* and Widener, *Confederate Monuments.*

76. Historian Jimmie Franklin calls for more research into how African American Southerners were able to retain a strong African American identity and a Southern sense of place simultaneously. Franklin, "Black Southerners, Shared Experience, and Place," 3–18. See also Fabre, "African-American Commemorative Celebrations," for the tradition of African American commemorations and memory, in which Fabre argues that the nineteenth century concern with inventing tradition and celebrating the past was very future-oriented; and Davis, "Expanding the Limits," for an argument that African American authors who claim Southern identity are subverting or countering the presumption of Southern as white. See Knupfer, "'Toward a Tenderer Humanity,'" chapter 6, for African American women's literary clubs.

77. Blight, "'For Something Beyond the Battlefield,'" 1156–78, (quotation, 1159).

78. Blight, "Du Bois," 52–53.

79. *Palmetto Leader,* December 12, 1925, 4; November 12, 1927, 4. "My Maryland" was a popular musical based on the play by Clyde Fitch, who in turn based his story on a supposedly historic incident captured in *In War Time and Other Poems* by John Greenleaf Whittier. The 1899 play involves a young Southern woman who falls in love with a Union officer during the Civil War despite the disapproval of her friends and family. After he is killed in battle, she defiantly raises the Union flag from her balcony, and she is shot by a Confederate soldier who has gone crazy due to unrequited love for her.

80. Susie King Taylor, *Reminiscences of My Life,* 65–66.

81. "Constitution," n.d., South Carolina Federation of Colored Women's Clubs, private collection, Robinson.

82. Minutes, January 14, 1907, Over the Teacups Club Papers, Darlington; *Palmetto Leader,* April 17, 1926, 8; Minutes, May 25, 1921, Current Literature Club Papers, USC; Minutes, 1922–1923, folder 1, box 1, Phyllis Wheatley Club Collection, Avery; Minutes, August 12, 1896, Amelia Pride Club Papers, Winthrop; and "A History of the Club Movement Among the Colored Women of the USA," typescript, 1902, 49–51, Rosalyn Saunders Papers, Avery.

83. Jeannette Cox, "A History—by administration—of the Phyllis Wheatley Literary and Social Club," 1936, manuscript, folder 2, box 1; and Minutes, 1922–1923, 1926–1927, and 1931–1932, folder 1, box 1, Phyllis Wheatley Club Collection, Avery.

84. Brawley, *The Negro in Literature and Art.*

85. *Palmetto Leader*, May 26, 1928, 5; Julia Peterkin, *Black April*; and *Contemporary Literary Criticism*, ed. Jean C. Stine (Detroit, 1985), 301–12.

86. *Palmetto Leader*, August 8, October 18, 1930.

87. Ibid., April 17, 1926, 8; and "Year's Program, Sunlight Club, 1930–31," pamphlet, private collection, Robinson.

88. *Palmetto Leader*, May 2, 1925, 1; June 25, 1927, 1; and Minutes, Annual Meeting, SCFCWC, private collection, Robinson.

89. "A History of the Club Movement Among the Colored Women of the USA," 1902, folder 2, box 1, pp. 49–51, Rosalyn Saunders, Avery; and Mary Church Terrell, "The Centenary of the Birth of Harriet Beecher Stowe," typescript, ca. 1911, Container 29, Mary Church Terrell Papers (Manuscript Division, Library of Congress, Washington, D.C., microfilm) reel 21 (hereafter referred to as MCT-LOC).

90. *Palmetto Leader*, January 31, 1925, 4; January 3, 1931, 4. Wilkinson supported black newspapers as much as possible.

91. Cox, "History—by administration," Phyllis Wheatley Club Collection, Avery.

92. Fields, *Lemon Swamp*, 55–57. For examples of Emancipation Day celebrations, see Rev. E. A. Adams's Emancipation address to the Lincoln Memorial Association at Benedict College, in the *Palmetto Leader*, January 10, 1925, 1, 8, 11.

93. See The *State*, January 24, 1919, 3; January 25, 1919, 4; January 26, 1919, 9; May 18, 1919, 1.

94. Ibid., February 22, 1919, 10.

95. *Palmetto Leader*, May 5, 1928, 4.

96. Fields, *Lemon Swamp*, 45, 127. "Lala's" was Fields's cousin's school, formally called Miss Anna Eliza Izzard's School, which she ran from her home. There Fields learned to be proud of her ancestors' accomplishments during slavery. Benjamin Mays, a South Carolina State College graduate, friend of Marion Wilkinson, and president of Morehouse College from 1940 to 1967, stated in his memoir that he could not bring himself to sing the song "Dixie" because he associated it with a prosegregation viewpoint, but he could easily sing the national anthem. Mays, *Born to Rebel*, 275.

97. Simms, *The History of South Carolina*, 212–13. The Klan, however, is portrayed in a positive light.

98. Bethune, "Clarifying our Vision," 12.

99. Clark, *Echo in My Soul*, 18–19. See also Gere, *Intimate Practices*, 83–85.

100. Drago, *Initiative, Paternalism, and Race Relations*, 172.

101. Ibid., 175.

102. Clark, *Echo in My Soul*, 60–61.

103. *State*, February 6, 1919, 11.

104. Drago, *Initiative, Paternalism, and Race Relations*, 113; Fields, *Lemon Swamp*, 101–2; and Cox, "History—by Administration," Phyllis Wheatley Club Collection, Avery.

105. Minutes, 1931–1931, folder 1, box 1, Phyllis Wheatley Club Collection, Avery; *Fortieth Anniversary Booklet*, 11; and *Palmetto Leader*, January 30, 1926, 8.

106. Minutes, 1928–1929, Phyllis Wheatley Club Collection, Avery; and *Palmetto Leader*, January 30, 1926, 8.

107. See entries for each woman in *Black Women in America*.

108. For officers, see "Officers," n.d., typescript, folder 238, MCT-Howard; and letterhead, Addie W. Dickerson to "Dear Member," October 31, 1938, Records of the NACW, reel 9. Although primary documents do exist in several archival collections, few historians have studied this group. See, for example, Rouse, *Lugenia Burns Hope*, and Hoytt, "International Council," 54–55.

109. Marion Wilkinson to Margaret Washington, n.d., folder 240, MCT-Howard.

110. "International Council of Women of the Darker Races of the World," typescript, n.d., Container 20, MCT-LOC, reel 14.

111. Margaret Washington to Lugenia Burns Hope, September 15, 1922, MCT-Howard, folder 240.

112. The *Southern Workman* was a journal published through the Hampton Institute, Hampton, Virginia, though edited by whites.

113. "Genie" (Lugenia) Hope to Margaret Washington, September 21, 1922, MCT-Howard, folder 239; and Janie Porter Barrett to Margaret Washington, October 9, 1922, MCT-Howard, folder 239.

114. Minutes, Annual meeting, Women's General Committee, Commission on Interracial Cooperation, April 7–8, 1926, Commission of Interracial Cooperation Papers (hereafter referred to as CIC), reel 44, series 6:191.

115. "A Compilation of Topics and Speakers, September 8, 1913 to September 11, 1988," typescript, Chautauqua Circle, box 8, Scrapbook, Atlanta University Center, Robert W. Woodruff Library, Archives Department, Atlanta. See also the Utopian Literary Club Papers, Auburn Avenue Research Library on African-American Culture and History, Atlanta-Fulton Public Library System.

116. *Palmetto Leader*, January 24, 1925, 3.

117. Lumpkin, *Making of a Southerner*, 127–28; and Hall, "You Must Remember This."

118. Glassberg, "Public History," 7–23.

CHAPTER 3. "LESS SAID SOONEST MENDED": THE PARALLEL LIVES OF BLACK AND WHITE CLUBWOMEN

1. Boyle, *The Desegregated Heart*, 104.

2. On woman suffrage and race, see Wheeler, *New Women of the New South*; on the changes in the Lost Cause after World War I, see Cox, *Dixie's Daughters*.

3. Cox, *Dixie's Daughters*, 6.

4. Gay, "The Tangled Skein of Romanticism," 59; and Weiner, *Mistresses and Slaves*, 231–32. Elizabeth Turner points out that whites resented the newly freed slaves and thus took the attitude of withholding benefits in favor of allowing the

federal government to see to their needs. Turner, *Women, Culture and Community*, 124.

5. For Progressivism and segregation, see Woodward, *Origins of the New South*, chapter 14.

6. *Charleston News and Courier*, May 16, 1918.

7. Lillie Neely, "The History of the Castalian Club," n.d. (ca. 1939), Castalian Club Papers, Winthrop, box 1, folder 1. According to Monica Tetzlaff, the Clover Club in Beaufort succeeded in creating a library for whites only even with Carnegie funding. Tetzlaff, *Cultivating a New South*, 194–96.

8. Irene Ashby, "Child-Labor in Southern Cotton Mills," *World's Work*, October 1901, 1290–95.

9. Harlan, *Separate and Unequal*, 170. Wheeler also argues that suffragists from the deep South tended to be more vocal in their racism then those from the upper South; see her *New Women of the New South*, 100–34.

10. Elna Green, *Southern Strategies*, 57–77.

11. Cell, *The Highest Stage of White Supremacy*, 14.

12. Minutes, January 26, 1915; December 1918; and April 26, 1926, New Century Club Papers, USC. See also, for example, Mr. John Bennett's address on the "grotesque" and "lurid" black legends to the Charleston City Federation, *Keystone*, March 1908, 4–5.

13. Charleston *News and Courier*, November 14, 1926.

14. *Keystone*, January 1905, 14; February 1905, 13. See also an article by Mrs. J. J. Fretwell, of Anderson, S.C., printed in the *New York Sun* and the Charleston *News and Courier*, in which she argued that blacks were better off in the South, where whites know them and their needs. Charleston *News and Courier*, March 1, 1903, 9.

15. Minutes, January 25, 1916, and February 24, 1920, New Century Club Papers, USC; Minutes, February 17, 1916, Thursday Club Papers, USC; Minutes, May 6, 1901, Century Club Papers, SCHS; and "Yearbook, 1909–1910," Century Club Papers, Charleston Library Society, Charleston, S.C. See also Gere, *Intimate Practices*, 164–65.

16. *Minutes of the South Carolina Federation of Women's Clubs Annual Convention*, 1907, SCFWC Papers, Winthrop, box 2, folder 8.

17. *Tenth Biennial Convention, The General Federation of Women's Clubs*, 426.

18. *Keystone*, March 1903, 3. South Carolinian males would have had to pay $1.64 in comparison to only $0.74 per male in Massachusetts in order for both states to evenly contribute per child. See also Harlan, *Separate and Unequal*, 32.

19. Paternalistic whites also emphasized their responsibility to guide others. At an Amelia Pride Club discussion of the poem, "White Man's Burden," the secretary reported that some members "take it as a picture of the responsibility which belongs to the cultured races to labor, even thanklessly, for the uncultured." Minutes, March 21, 1899, Amelia Pride Club Papers, Winthrop.

20. *Keystone*, March 1900, 13.

21. Minutes, March 22, 1909, Amelia Pride Club Papers, Winthrop.

22. *The General Federation of Women's Clubs, Tenth Biennial Convention*, 1910, 426.

23. Charleston *News and Courier*, June 16, 1904. The Over the Teacups Club echoed this view of black intelligence in a report on Eliza Pinckney in which the author noted that she "even undert[ook] to develop the dense brains of her little black vassals." Minutes, February 5, 1901, Over the Teacups Papers, Darlington.

24. *Keystone*, June 1903, 9; and Cooley, *Homes of the Freed*, 4.

25. *South Carolina Federation of Women's Clubs, 1918–1919* (yearbook), SCFWC Papers, box 6, folder 20, Winthrop, 39–40.

26. Charleston *Evening Post*, July 1, 1920. Mary Fredrickson argues that in the example of the Methodist church, black women worked on projects, leading white women to action, while allowing whites to believe that they had gotten there on their own. Fredrickson, "Each One Is Dependent," 307–17.

27. *Keystone*, March 1909, 3; March 1912, 3. In Atlanta, a kindergarten for blacks, and in Tampa, a playground for blacks, were also justified with white self-interest. See Alice N. Parker, "The Kindergarten in the South," in *The South in the Building of the Nation*, X (Richmond, 1909), 384; and Hewitt, *Southern Discomfort*, 191–95.

28. Minutes, March 25, 1919, Over the Teacups Club Papers, Winthrop. On cooperation over TB, see Judson, "Building the New South City," chapter 2.

29. "Club Report of Activities," typescript, Amelia Pride Club Papers, Winthrop, box 1, folder 1. The Poppenheims also advocated housing reform in the South, "where so many servants live in their own homes, and where so much laundry work is done in the negro yard. The condition of houses of our servants means much for the health of the entire family." *Keystone*, May 1912, 9. Elizabeth Enstam found that Dallas clubwomen also self-servingly agreed to serve on the board of a school that trained African American girls for domestic work in one of their only moments of crossracial work. Enstam, *Women and the Creation of Urban Life*, 152.

30. Charleston *News and Courier*, January 25, 1907.

31. Mrs. John Drake, ed., *South Carolina Federation of Women's Clubs, 1920–21* (yearbook), SCFWC Papers, box 6, folder 21, Winthrop, 60; and Mrs. W. D. Maginnis, *South Carolina Federation of Women's Clubs, 1926–27* (yearbook), SCFWC Papers, box 8, folder 25, Winthrop, 88.

32. *Keystone*, May 1905, 12; May 1903, 6–7; March 1903, 4.

33. Ibid., February 1906, 9.

34. Louisa Poppenheim, "Woman's Work in the South," 622. This rhetoric of Anglo-Saxonism was common at the time.

35. See, for example, *Keystone*, June 1910, 6–7; June 1903, 8.

36. Mrs. Booker T. Washington, address, Women's Interracial Conference, Memphis, Tenn., October 7, 1920, typescript, Jessie Daniel Ames Papers, Duke, 53; and Hewitt, *Southern Discomfort*, 147, 248.

37. Gilmore, *Gender and Jim Crow*, 45–59. Leslie Dunlap found a similar cooperation in the Georgia WCTU, which ended by 1900 and then resurrected in the

late 1910s. "'On Doubtful Soil and Hopeful Ground': The Political Sources of Women's Interracial Ventures in the Woman's Christian Temperance Union, 1885–1925," paper presented at the Eleventh Berkshire Conference on the History of Women, 1999. For the coalition between several black and white women in Nashville in 1919, see Goodstein, "A Rare Alliance," 219–46. Goodstein argues that this rare and temporary alliance came about in Nashville because of the particular circumstances surrounding the race and certain individuals who were willing to forge such a partnership. It was not duplicated elsewhere in the state or after 1919.

38. For the history of YWCA and Methodist church interactions, see Jacquelyn Hall, *Revolt Against Chivalry*, 66–87.

39. Greenwood, *Bittersweet Legacy*, 113.

40. Woman's Christian Temperance Union, South Carolina Division, Records, USC. This history refers to various newspaper articles citing evidence of both Frances Willard and Mrs. Sallie Chapin of South Carolina speaking to "colored crowds."

41. Most historians of Southern clubwomen argue that black and white women worked separately. Thomas, *The New Woman In Alabama*, 7–8; Judson, "Building the New South City," 67–68; McArthur, *Creating the New Woman*, 88; Enstam, *Women and the Creation of Urban Life*, 102–3, 109, 124, 152; Hewitt, *Southern Discomfort*, 13, 40–41, 84, 167–70, 186, 199, 269; and Turner, *Women, Culture and Community*, 259–60. Neverdon-Morton cites a CIC document that admitted the CIC was not "popular with the rank and file of [white] club women in the South in 1920. Many women were indifferent while others were openly antagonistic." See Neverdon-Morton, *Afro-American Women of the South*, 230. In Georgia, white clubwomen rejected even the discussion of interracial cooperation as "unwise." Mrs. Hays (president of Georgia Federation of Women's Clubs) to Ida Fitzpatrick, CIC, reel 20, series 2:7. One exception was a joint movement for a police matron for black and white inmates led by the white Nineteenth-Century Club in Memphis, which, however, occurred early, in 1897. Marsha Wedell does not indicate that such cooperation continued. Wedell, *Elite Women and the Reform Impulse*, 91–94.

42. Hall, *Revolt Against Chivalry*, 62–64.

43. The *Southern Workman* described the two white women as "representing 250,000 Southern white women of the Methodist Episcopal Church." *Southern Workman*, September 1920, 392. The black women, however, represented various denominations. Bethune was AME Church; Wilkinson, Protestant Episcopal; Hope, Baptist; Crosthwait, Congregational; McCrorey, Presbyterian; and Washington represented women's clubs and Brown the YWCA. Minutes, Women's Committee, CIC, October 20–21, 1922, CIC, reel 20, series 2:20.

44. See entries for each woman in *Black Women in America*, edited by Hine.

45. Jennie Moton attended but did not speak, perhaps because some black women did not want her representing them. Lugenia Hope wrote to Marion

Wilkinson, "Mrs. Moton is (weak, very weak), well she is invited as company for Mrs. Washington, not to speak, however. I consider that more dangerous since she will talk with every person who will talk with her. Of course you know that she is too compromising in her attitude on race relationship. " Rouse, *Lugenia Burns Hope*, 151.

46. Ibid., 111.

47. *Minutes of the National Association of Colored Women*, 1926, Records of the NACW, reel 1, 40, 51–52.

48. See, for example, Jessie Daniel Ames to Mary Frayser, March 18, 1941; and "Report of Findings Committee, Annual Meeting, CIC, April 8–10, 1926, CIC Papers, reel 44, series 6:191.

49. Hall, *Revolt Against Chivalry*, 96–97, and Gilmore, *Gender and Jim Crow*, 201–2.

50. [Mary Bethune], "The relation of the Southeastern Federation to the National," n.d., manuscript, Records of the NACW, reel 6.

51. "Southern Women and Race Co-Operation," Records of the NACW, reel 6, 3–4, 12.

52. Will Alexander to "Dear Friend," May 5, 1936, Nannie Helen Burroughs Papers, container 6, Collections of the Manuscript Division, Library of Congress, Washington, D.C. Wilkinson led two special sessions, for example, one on negro schools and another on social welfare. Minutes, November 18, 1926, March 31, 1928, South Carolina State Interracial Committee, CIC Papers, reel 53, series 7:191. Jessie Daniel Ames paid tribute to their leadership by telling McGowan that "there would be no permanent outcome if we proceeded . . . without you and Mrs. Wilkinson." Jessie Daniel Ames to C. P. McGowan, May 16, 1931, CIC Papers, reel 53, series 7:192. On Robert's involvement, see McGowan's suggestion of him as a black speaker, in McGowan to Mr. Herbert, May 26, 1931, reel 53, series 7:192, and *The Opinion of Those Who Ought to Know*, pamphlet, n.d., reel 29, series 5:13, CIC Papers.

53. Charleston *News and Courier* (obituary), n.d., (ca. 1956).

54. Ibid.

55. Jeannie Heywood Haskell, "A Tribute Is Due," *The Southern Frontier*, April 1940, reel 30, series 5:30, CIC Papers.

56. Fields, *Lemon Swamp*, 192. Furthermore, the CIC was also hampered by the overly conciliatory attitude of some blacks involved. Fields contended that certain African Americans in Charleston who worked for whites essentially spied on the CIC meetings and reported back to whites; see pp. 108–9.

57. Tetzlaff, *Cultivating a New South*, 161.

58. *Palmetto Leader*, March 19, 1927, 1; May 17, 1930, 1.

59. See Minutes, South Carolina Inter-racial Committee, passim, and K. G. Finlay to Will Alexander, February 2, 1935, file 192–93, CIC Papers.

60. *Southern Workman*, February 1923, 56.

61. *Palmetto Leader*, November 28, 1925, 4.
62. Minutes, South Carolina Inter-racial Committee, November 19, 1925, CIC, file 192.
63. Johnson, "This Wonderful Dream Nation!"
64. Ibid., 143–44, 150.
65. See also Albertha Murray, "Tribute to Susan Dart Butler," n.d., Albertha Murray Papers, Avery.
66. On the role of Episcopal women, see Johnson, "The Shape of the Movement to Come."
67. Mrs. L. H. Jennings, ed., *South Carolina Federation of Women's Clubs, 1924–1925* (yearbook), SCFWC Papers, box 7, folder 23, Winthrop, 35.
68. Mrs. W. D. Melton, ed., *South Carolina Federation of Women's Clubs, 1925–1926* (yearbook), SCFWC Papers, box 8, folder 24, Winthrop, 142.
69. Minutes, South Carolina Inter-racial Committee, CIC.
70. Bessie Rogers Drake grew up in Bennettsville before living in Columbia. She won several awards when a student at Winthrop College. She was an officer in the DAR, UDC, and her local women's clubs as well as the state federation. Katherine Furman was from Sumter. Mrs. Willis D. Magginis was president of the Castalian Club in Rock Hill and an officer in the AAUW. Bessie Duncan, a graduate of Converse College, was most active in education and fine arts in the federation. She was also an ardent suffragist and helped organize the Aiken County Suffrage League. She occasionally ran her husband's newspaper, the *Aiken Standard*. Nell Duncan Freeman graduated from Winthrop College, taught school, and was president of the South Carolina School Improvement Association. *South Carolina Federation Bulletin*, March, 1927, 6–8.
71. Minutes, November 1924 and following, Perihelion Club Papers, box 1, folder 3, Winthrop.
72. Minutes, May 22, 1928, Amelia Pride Club Papers, Winthrop. Minutes, January 9, 1923, New Century Club Papers, USC. The only club in the *Keystone* to mention work with blacks was from Daytona, Florida. There the Palmetto Club had two kindergartens for black children. See *Keystone*, April 1903, 7
73. Zimmerman, interview, October 9, 1995.
74. Hall, *Revolt Against Chivalry*, 104–5.
75. See minutes, Woman's Section, South Carolina Committee on Race Relations, November 28, 1922, reel 53, series 7:197, and Clelia P. McGowan to Miss Jessie [King], n.d. (circa 1930), reel 53, series 7:192, CIC Papers.
76. Drago, *Initiative, Paternalism, and Race Relations*, 143.
77. Mays, *Born to Rebel*, 102–3.
78. Rebecca Reid to Jessie Daniel Ames, December 15, 1929, reel 53, series 7:192, CIC Papers.
79. Giddings, *When and Where I Enter*, 101–8. On the different ideologies of black clubwomen, see also White, *Too Heavy a Load*, 44–53, 83–86.

80. Mrs. Margaret Washington to Mrs. Lugenia Burns Hope, September 15, 1922, MCT-Howard (the letter is a copy from the Lugenia Burns Hope Papers, Atlanta).

81. Josephine Yates to Margaret Washington, May 9, and May 16, 1904, Records of the NACW, reel 5. Yates also wrote, "Undoubtedly the conservative tone adopted by this paper, and the determination of the National Organization from its incipiency, diligently to 'saw wood,' and this find no time for controversy, has had much to do in dignifying its aims and in increasing its scope and influence." "National Association of Colored Women," *Voice of the Negro*, July 1904, 285. Yates was the second president of the NACW, from 1901 to 1906. Born in New York, she taught in Rhode Island and the Lincoln Institute in Missouri before her marriage. Hine, *Black Women in America*, 1297–98.

82. Wells, *Crusade for Justice*, 328–29. In an interview, Alfreda Duster described the differences between her mother, Ida B. Wells and Mary Church Terrell by noting that Terrell "stayed in the South. My mother came to the North, and their careers were so different because of this difference in environment and location." She went on to explain that Wells believed that Terrell and Bethune and the NACW were not doing enough and could and should have done more. Alfreda Duster, interview, in *The Black Woman Oral History Project*, vol. 3, edited by Ruth Edmonds Hill (Westport, Conn.: Meckler, 1991), 146–50.

83. Josephine Yates to Margaret Washington, February 19, 1906, Records of the NACW, reel 6.

84. Gilmore, *Gender and Jim Crow*, 179–80; and Hall, *Revolt Against Chivalry*, 329, n.73. See letters between the two, Charlotte Eugenia Hawkins Brown Papers, Schlesinger Library, Radcliffe College, Cambridge, Mass. (hereafter referred to as CHB), microfilm, folders 36, 39.

85. Mrs. M. L. Crosthwait to Charlotte Brown, July 15, 1921, CHB, folder 44.

86. Lugenia Hope to Mrs. Archibald Davis, March 1, 1921, Neighborhood Union Papers, Atlanta University, box 10, folder 38.

87. Evans, interview, June 6, 1996.

88. Zimmerman, interview, October 9, 1995.

89. Asa H. Gordon, *Sketches of Negro Life and History*, 217–18.

90. Marion Wilkinson to Aunt Genie (Lugenia Burns Hope), May 28, 1921, Neighborhood Union Papers, box 10, folder 39.

91. Minutes, 1917; 1930–31; and October 1922, Phyllis Wheatley Club Papers, folder 1, Avery; and Drago, 150.

92. Salem, *To Better Our World*, 171.

CHAPTER 4. "UNITY IN DIVERSITY": SOUTH CAROLINA CLUBWOMEN, THE SOUTH AND THE NATION

1. *State*, April 6, 1927, 1, 5.

2. Similarly struck by the racial gap between black and white women, Nancy Hewitt argues that Anglo women in Tampa cooperated more with Anglo men than with Latin or African American women. Hewitt, *Southern Discomfort*, 116.

3. State Federation Song, private collection, Robinson; and *Palmetto Leader*, May 2, 1925, 1.
4. *Voice of the Negro*, October 1906, 396–97.
5. Amanda Smith Jemand, "A Southern Woman's Appeal for Justice," *Independent*, February 21, 1904, 438.
6. Robinson, interview, October 12, 1995.
7. For more on the importance of this network, see Rouse, *Lugenia Burns Hope*, 55; Linda Gordon, "Black and White Visions of Welfare," 564–68; and Hine, "'We Specialize in the Wholly Impossible,'" 83.
8. Rouse, *Lugenia Burns Hope*, 55.
9. Ibid. For biographical information, see entries for each woman in *Black Women in America*, edited by Hine. Jacquelyn Hall identifies a similar network of women who were involved in the beginnings of the CIC. See Hall, *Revolt Against Chivalry*, 80–81, 286, n.66. Anne Scott also identifies black colleges as important loci of club and other reform work; see Scott, "Most Invisible of All," 15.
10. Hoytt, "International Council of Women," 54–55.
11. Rouse, *Lugenia Burns Hope*, 100–101.
12. Ibid., 152.
13. Marion Wilkinson to Sallie W. Stewart, president of the NACW, October 17, 1928, Records of the NACW, reel 8. See also *Minutes of the National Association of Colored Women*, 1922, Records of the NACW, reel 1, pp. 12, 27; ibid., 1920, Records of the NACW, reel 1, p. 36; ibid., 1916, Records of the NACW, reel 1, p. 46; ibid., 1912, Records of the NACW, reel 1, p. 60; ibid., 1928, Records of the NACW, reel 1, p. 10.
14. *Book of Gold*, 8.
15. Brown gave a talk on the "Wings Over Jordan" radio program on NBC radio. Marion Birnie Wilkinson to Charlotte Hawkins Brown, telegram, n.d. (ca. March 12, 1940), CHB, reel 3, folder 48.
16. Charlotte Brown to Mary Bethune, April 7, 1927, Records of the NACW, reel 6.
17. Marion Birnie Wilkinson to Charlotte Hawkins Brown, July 30, 1932, CHB, reel 3, folder 45.
18. Nannie Burroughs to Charlotte Hawkins Brown, December 16, 1920, CHB, reel 2, folder 41, and Mary McLeod Bethune to Charlotte Hawkins Brown, December 16, 1920, CHB, reel 2, folder 41. For more on Burroughs, see Brooks, "Religion, Politics, and Gender," 7–22.
19. Minutes, June 29, 1917, 88–89, Chautauqua Circle Collection, Atlanta University; and Margaret Washington to Charlotte Brown, February 16, 1915, CHB, folder 35.
20. Lugenia Hope to Mary Bethune, September 12, 1920, Neighborhood Union Papers, box 2, folder 34; Minutes, March 1924, 44–45, Chautauqua Circle, Atlanta University; and Mary Bethune to Charlotte Brown, January 8, 1921, CHB, folder 42.
21. *National Notes*, January 1912; and "A History of the Club Movement among

the colored women of the United States of America, as contained in the minutes of the conventions, held in Boston, July 29, 30, 31, 1895, and of the National Federation of Afro-American Women held in Washington, D.C., July 20, 21, 22, 1896," Records of the NACW, reel 1.

22. Josephine Yates to Margaret Washington, January 8, 1904, Records of the NACW, reel 5; February 19, 1906, Records of the NACW, reel 6. February 28, 1906, Records of the NACW, reel 6. Josephine Silone Yates was the second president of the NACW, from 1901 to 1906. She was born in 1859 in Mattitcuck, New York, to a well-respected family. She was the first black person to be certified to teach in Rhode Island. Although offered the position of lady principal at Tuskegee by Booker T. Washington, she declined, and after her marriage to W. W. Yates, a high school principal, moved to Kansas City. See her biography in *Black Women in America*, 1297.

23. *National Notes*, April 1923, 4; May, 1923, 1. Brown was on a tour of the South and also visited Sumter, Darlington, Florence, Columbia, Spartanburg, and Greenville, before leaving for North Carolina. For Mary McCleod Bethune's visit, see *Palmetto Leader*, April 23, 1927.

24. Minutes, 1924–1925, Phyllis Wheatley Club Papers, Avery; and *Palmetto Leader*, May 2, 1925, 1.

25. *Palmetto Leader*, May 2, June 27, July 4, 1925. Washington was supposed to attend but died shortly before the meeting took place.

26. *Palmetto Leader*, June 12, 1926, 1.

27. Fields, *Lemon Swamp*, 189–91.

28. *National Notes*, February 1912.

29. *Minutes of the National Association of Colored Women, 1912*, Records of the NACW, reel 1, p. 30. Officers included Celia Dial Saxon, chair of illiteracy, and Lilian J. Rhodes, chair of hospital committee. Celia Dial Saxon to Mary McLeod Bethune, September 22, 1926, Records of the NACW, reel 6; and Lilian J. Rhodes to Mary McLeod Bethune, October 22 [1926], Records of the NACW, reel 6.

30. Fields, *Lemon Swamp*, 236–37.

31. Bodine, *South Carolina Women*, 61.

32. *National Notes*, June 1923.

33. Wanda Hendricks argues that Midwestern regional identity, owing to the industrial economy, influx of African American migrants, and large number of states with woman suffrage before 1920, also shaped Illinois clubwomen, in *Gender, Race, and Politics in the Midwest*, xi, 82–83.

34. *National Notes*, December 1899.

35. Ibid., February 1900, 1.

36. Ibid., February 1902, 1.

37. Ibid., July, 1904; and Addie W. Hunton, "The Southern Federation of Colored Women," *Voice of the Negro*, December 1905, 852.

38. *National Notes*, July 1904.

39. Ibid., February 1902, 1.

40. The St. Louis meeting was held in 1904.

41. Ursula Wade to Margaret Washington, November 17, 1903, and Josephine Yates to Margaret Washington, December 13, 1903, Records of the NACW, reel 5.

42. Excerpt of letter from Mrs. A. W. Hunton, in Carrie Clifford, "National Association of Colored Women," *Alexander's Magazine*, June 15, 1905, 10.

43. "Press Release," February 27, 1920, included in letter from Mary Bethune to Charlotte Brown, CHB, microfilm, folder 41. This press release lists the date as 1916; other sources list it as beginning 1919. See, for example, *National Notes*, June 1923, 1. The minutes from the 1916 NACW convention indicate that plans were underway for a council to meet the needs of the Southern states. *Minutes of the National Association of Colored Women*, 1916, Records of the NACW. Therefore, it appears that although the Federation may not have become a formal body until 1919, work on such a group began earlier. Member states included Virginia, North Carolina, South Carolina, Georgia, Florida, Alabama, Mississippi, Tennessee, Arkansas, Oklahoma, Louisiana, and Texas. Marion Wilkinson was also on several committees, including the education and Memphis Meeting committees.

44. *National Notes*, June 1923, 1. Ora Brown Stokes of Virginia succeeded Taylor, although she only served for a few months. According to historian Glenda Gilmore, the Southeastern was officially inactive between 1927 and 1940, perhaps due to the Great Depression. According to Gilmore, in 1940 at Tuskegee, Brown, Taylor, and others revived the association and restored biennial meetings in 1946. Glenda Gilmore, "Southeastern Association of Colored Women's Clubs," in *Black Women in America*, 1089. Rebecca Stiles Taylor (1880–1970) was born in Savannah, Ga. She was a teacher and reformer as well as president of the Southeastern and executive secretary of the NACW (under Bethune as president). For a time she was principal of the Mayesville Educational and Industrial Institute in Mayesville, S.C., where she may have had contact with Wilkinson. A close friend of Bethune, she was recruited by her to teach at Bethune-Cookman and participate in the Southeastern. She continued to serve the reorganized Southeastern, the NACW, and the National Council of Negro Women (founded by Bethune) throughout her life. In addition to her role in women's clubs in Georgia, the region, and the nation, she also edited the *Savannah Journal*, a weekly newspaper, and helped organize a local colored citizens' council. See her biography in Smith, ed., *Notable Black American Women*, Book 2, 631–35.

45. *National Notes*, June 1923, 1.

46. Zimmerman, interview, October 9, 1995.

47. Addie W. Hunton, "The Southern Federation of Colored Women," *Voice of the Negro*, December 1905, 852.

48. Addie W. Hunton, "The Detroit Convention of the National Association of Colored Women," *Voice of the Negro*, July 1906, 589.

49. Mary McLeod Bethune, "Union and Harmony are the Cause of the Order

of the world and the life of nations," typescript, Mary McLeod Bethune Papers, Amistad Research Center, New Orleans, Louisiana, microfilm, folder 17.

50. Josephine T. Washington, "Impressions of a Southern Federation," *Colored American Magazine*, November 1904, 679–80.

51. *Southeastern Herald*, April 1926, Records of the NACW, reel 24, p. 13.

52. *Minutes of the National Association of Colored Women*, 1920, Records of the NACW, reel 1, pp. 7, 22.

53. (Mary Bethune), "The Relations of Southeastern Federation to the National," handwritten manuscript, n.d., Records of the NACW, reel 6.

54. *Southeastern Herald*, March 1926, Records of the NACW, reel 24, p. 14.

55. *National Negro Digest*, 1944, 2.

56. Addie W. Hunton, "Kindergarten Work in the South," *Alexander's Magazine*, July 1906, 29. See also White, *Too Heavy a Load*, 83–84.

57. "Extracts from the Historical Records of the 1895–1896 Conventions of the Colored Women in America," Rosalyn Saunders African American Periodical Collection of Articles and Pamphlets, folder 1, Avery. Early officers from South Carolina included Mrs. Helen Crum of Charleston, vice president, National Association of Afro-American Women, and Mrs. Jennie Chase Williams of Abbeville, a sixth vice president of the NACW.

58. *National Association Notes*, April 1899; and *The Competitor*, vol. 2, no. 2, August–September 1920, 142.

59. Zimmerman, interview, October 9, 1995.

60. For example, under president Elizabeth Carter, "the women of the North and South were cemented as never before. We all came to feel that our cause was not sectional, but one big, strong fight of an undivided citizenship. " Carter took special interest in the needs of Southern migrants to the North. Washington, "Club Work Among Negro Women," 186, 189.

61. Zimmerman, interview, October 9, 1995.

62. "History of the NACW," manuscript, Fields Collection, Avery.

63. *National Notes*, January 1927.

64. Josephine T. Washington, "Impressions of a Southern Federation," *Colored American Magazine*, November 1905, 678; and Fields, *Lemon Swamp*, 236.

65. *Southeastern Herald*, May 1926, Records of the NACW, reel 24, 13.

66. For the process of reconciliation, see Cox, *Dixie's Daughters*, chapter 8; Wilson, *Baptized in Blood*, chapter 8; and Foster, *Ghosts of the Confederacy*, 6, 63–66, 154–57.

67. Croly, *The History of the Woman's Club Movement*, 157–63. Judith McArthur argues that the GFWC was much more successful at attracting Southern women than the WCTU, in part because of this leadership and in part because the GFWC avoided political questions like suffrage, which the WCTU endorsed early on. By the mid-1910s, when the GFWC began to embrace more liberal causes such as suffrage, Southern clubs were more ready to respond positively. At that point, the GFWC's policy of requiring local clubs to replicate the national agenda forced

Southern clubs to address issues they ordinarily might not have. McArthur, *Creating the New Woman*, 15–21. Yet in some cases, the WCTU did unite Northern and Southern women. Monica Tetzlaff found that Northern migrants to Beaufort, South Carolina, had little social interaction with whites living there already until Northern and Southern women together created the local WCTU chapter. Tetzlaff, *Cultivating the New South*, 103–5.

68. "Civic Circle Entertains," clipping, [1895], Atlanta Women's Clubs, Scrapbook, vol. 1, 1895; and *Keystone*, June 1902, 6.

69. Louisa Poppenheim, "The Southern Woman in Club Life," address to the Louisiana Federation of Women's Clubs, Lafayette, Louisiana, March 25–26, 1909, SCFWC Papers, box 19, folder 65, Winthrop.

70. *Keystone*, May 1905, 3.

71. See, for example, *Keystone*, July 1900, 5. Louisa mentioned four sessions; two featured speakers from Atlanta, and one featured Mary Poppenheim. Mary spoke at the press session, Mrs. Ottley spoke on "Industrial Problems in the South," and Mrs. E. G. McCabe on "Education in the South." See also November 1904, 8; November 1906; June 1910, 3; March 1906, 10; April 1906, 3, an editorial that urged Southern women to attend the biennial and listed the Southern members of GFWC committees.

72. *Keystone*, May, 1905, 3; June 1906, 3.

73. Ibid., May 1910, 3; October 1908, 4.

74. David Glassberg argues that historical pageants used the past as a uniting force to encompass both a local and a national loyalty. Glassberg quotes Frederick Koch, the maker of Carolina folk plays, who said, "The only way we can be truly national is by being loyally local." Glassberg, *American Historical Pageantry*, 251. See also Kammen, *Mystic Chords of Memory*.

75. *Keystone*, June 1908, 11.

76. Louisa Poppenheim, "Address to the SCFWC as a representative of the GFWC," May 17, 1905, SCFWC Papers, box 2, folder 7, Winthrop.

77. *Keystone*, December 1912, 3.

78. *The Club Woman*, July 1900, 132.

79. Ibid., March 1901, 181–83.

80. The question of local clubs or state federations belonging to the General was already under consideration. The convention was debating "reorganization" to alleviate difficulties encountered when a large city club, such as in Chicago or New York, rivaled its state federation delegation in numbers of delegates and power in the General.

81. Board of Directors, Minutes, bound volume, June 4, 1900, 254–55. General Federation of Women's Clubs, Washington, D.C. This communication was laid upon the table.

82. *The Club Woman*, April 1902, 250

83. New York *Times*, February 2, 1902, 24–26; February 5, 3. Article 2, section 2 specified: "From a State where a club is a member of the State Federation, it

would also be eligible to the General Federation if recommended to its executive board by the executive board of the State Federation; the power of admission to remain as given in article 2 of the bylaws, as follows." This article allowed each state to determine whether black clubs would be welcome in their state federation. Section 3 specified, "The President shall refer all applications for membership to the Committee on membership appointed by the Board of Directors for its action upon the same. The action of the Committee on Membership shall be in writing, and a unanimous vote of the committee shall be required to elect. In case the committee fails to agree, the application shall be referred to the whole board, the written vote of two-thirds of which shall be necessary to elect to membership. " Blair, *The Clubwoman as Feminist*, 108–10.

84. New York *Times*, May 7, 1902, 9, and May 6, 1902, 2–3. The Chicago *Broad-Ax*, a black newspaper, complained that the compromise was really a "complete surrender" by Northern clubs. May 10, 1902, 1.

85. Mary to Louisa Poppenheim, n.d. (ca. 1902), in Johnson, *Southern Women at Vassar*, 220–22.

86. Atlanta *Constitution*, May 6, 1902, 5.

87. Norfolk *Dispatch*, June 19, 1900.

88. Minutes, February 11, 1919, New Century Club Papers, USC.

89. *The Club Woman*, December 1901, 84.

90. *Keystone*, November 1900, 8; March 1901, 3; August 1901, 3.

91. Ibid., June 1902, 7.

92. *State*, December 14, 1938.

93. Minutes, n.d., Amelia Pride Club Papers, Winthrop, box 1, folder 2, p. 4, and "History," typescript, Amelia Pride Club Papers, Winthrop, box 1, folder 1.

94. Minutes, New Century Club Papers, March 1913, book 2, USC, 139.

95. *State*, May 3, 1902.

96. Louisville *Evening Post*, June 6, 1901. Not surprisingly, Georgia newspapers enthusiastically championed Rebecca Lowe and the Georgia delegation. The *Sunny South* from Atlanta blamed Massachusetts for clamoring for rights for blacks who were not even interested in them and stated the threatened breakup of the General "might be feasible and salutary." Reporting on Lowe's decision in 1900 to run for reelection, the Augusta *Chronicle* wrote, "The story of the alteration of her determination is the story of a plucky southern woman's victory against sectional influences brought to bear to defeat her; how the great state of Massachusetts was outgeneraled by Georgia in the women's convention." *Sunny South*, April 12, 1902; Augusta *Chronicle*, June 13, 1900.

97. *State*, May 22, 1902, 8.

98. *The Club Woman*, March 1901, 180.

99. Ibid., December, July, September 1901, 175; and Granger, New York *Times*, February 5, 1902, 3.

100. Atlanta *Constitution*, June 2, 1901.

101. Louisville *Courier-Journal*, June 17, 1900, 5; and clipping, no title, Atlanta

Woman's Club Papers, Atlanta History Center, Atlanta, Georgia, scrapbook, vol. 2. African Americans acknowledged Lowe's support for kindergartens, too. See Josephine Silone Yates, "Kindergartens and Mothers' Clubs As Related to the Work of the National Association of Colored Women," *The Colored American Magazine*, vol. 8, June 1905, 310.

102. *The Club Woman*, March 1901, 183; New York *Tribune*, June 10, June 21, 1900; and "Don't Want to Teach Negroes," clipping, (n.p., May 24, no year), Hampton University Peabody Newspaper Clipping File, Hampton, Va.

103. Lowe's comments appeared in the *New York Sun* and were reprinted in the *New York Age*, June 12, 1900. *The Club Woman*, March 1901, 183.

104. Isma Dooly, New York *Telegram*, May 29, reprinted in the Atlanta *Constitution*, June 2, 1901 New York *World*, April 6, 1902; and New York *World*, April 6, 1902 (Ottley quotation). North Carolina Sorosis club perhaps best expressed it: "Let an individual negro achieve all the eminence possible among his own race, we honor and applaud him for it; but when it comes to a question of sitting socially at or table and our hearth, and marrying with our sons and daughters, our every instinct recoils, and the idea is also naturally impossible to the truly intelligent of their own race." *The Club Woman*, May 1901, 50.

105. *The Club Woman*, February 1902, 184–85, and March 1902, 1, offer an explanation of the reason it was printed.

106. Ibid., March, 1902, 218.

107. *Washington Bee*, May 3, 1902, 1.

108. Gatewood, *Aristocrats of Color*, 240.

109. *The Club Woman*, December 1900, 1; January 1901, 125–28.

110. Ibid., September 1902, 13.

111. Ibid., March 1901, 180–81. In a gesture undoubtedly meant to further improve relations between the regions, the Massachusetts Federation in 1903 donated one thousand dollars to the Georgia Federation for its educational programs. The money was used to support the Massachusetts-Georgia Model School for industrial education, and Massachusetts continued to make contributions for several years. The school represented aid from the most organized state to a relative newcomer, as well as the triumph of sisterhood over animosity between the regions. Year Book, Georgia Federation of Women's Clubs, 1906–1907, 15, and 1908–1909, 103, Georgia Department of Archives and History, Atlanta, Georgia; *The Federation Bulletin*, January 1907, 156–57.

112. *Colored American Magazine*, August 1902, 275. For the triumph of white supremacy and sectional reconciliation in the nation as a whole, see Blight, *Race and Reunion*. Dimies T. S. Denison was Mrs. Charles Denison.

113. Wisconsin *Weekly Advocate*, June 7, 1900, 5; Indianapolis *Freeman*, June 23, 1900, 2; and Board of Directors Minutes, vol. 1, November 9, 1900, 270–71, 279, GFWC.

114. New York *Times*, April 2, 1902, 1–3; and Cleveland *Gazette*, June 16, 1902, 2.

115. *National Notes*, February 1901.

116. Pauline E. Hopkins, "Famous Women of the Negro Race: Club Life Among Colored Women," *The Colored American Magazine* 5 (August 1902): 273–77.

117. New York *Age*, April 10, 1902. Williams herself had been at the center of debate in the 1890s when she was invited to join the all-white Chicago Woman's Club. Corinna A. Bucholz, "The Ruffin Incident and Other Integration Battles in Women's Clubs, 1890–1902," master's thesis, Sarah Lawrence College, 2000, chapter 2.

118. Fannie Barrier Williams, "Club Movement Among Negro Women," 216–28 (quotation, 225).

119. Wells, *Crusade for Justice*, 270–71.

120. "Color Question in Wisconsin," clipping, (n.p., n.d.), Hampton University Peabody Newspaper Clipping File, Hampton, Va.. Mrs. A. L. Davis and Mrs. Agnes Moody also argued that "great bulk of colored women" were not interested in joining the General. New York *Age*, November 27, 1901.

121. Louis R. Harlan, ed., *The Booker T. Washington Papers*, vol. 4 (Urbana: University of Illinois Press, 1975), 237–38. Frances Willard was president of the WCTU, Mary Dickinson president of the National Council of Women, and Ellen Henrotin, president of the GFWC.

122. Chicago *Broad-Ax*, May 17, 1902, 1. The Wisconsin *Weekly Advocate* editor declared that as a black man he believed that blacks did not want to insert themselves where they were not welcome, and that black women had their own federation for women's clubs. June 7, 1900, 1, 4. Lowe referred to his article as evidence for her own point of view.

123. Louisa Poppenheim, "Address to the SCFWC as a representative of the GFWC," May 17, 1905, SCFWC Papers, box 2, folder 7, Winthrop.

124. *Keystone*, December 1902, 3.

125. Ibid., July 1899, 2.

126. Ibid., June 1906, 7. See for example, ibid., April 1907, 4, for Mrs. Sarah Platt Decker's visit, and June 1911, 4, for Mrs. Eva Moore's visit. Both were presidents of the GFWC.

127. See various letters throughout 1907–1908 in the SCFWC Papers, Winthrop. Louisa knew Ward because both were on the press committee of the GFWC in 1906, *The General Federation of Women's Clubs, Eighth Biennial Convention, May 30 to June 7, 1906, St. Paul, Minn.: Official Report*, 358–59.

128. Atlanta *Constitution*, June 2, 1901.

129. Florence Matthews to Louisa Poppenheim, May 23, 1908, Poppenheim Papers, Duke University, Durham, N.C.

130. Mrs. May Alden Ward to Louisa Poppenheim, June 1, 1908, Winthrop. Ward enclosed a copy of the letter that Alice Kyle wrote to Mrs. Decker on May 21, 1908.

131. Northington, *A History of the Virginia Federation of Women's Clubs*, 249–51.

132. Mrs. May Alden Ward to Louisa Poppenheim, June 1, 1908, Winthrop, and copy enclosed, Alice Kyle to Mrs. Decker, May 21, 1908.

133. May 31, 1916. Clipping. Laura Sneath was Mrs. Samuel B. Sneath and Ione Cowles was Mrs. Josiah Cowles. The General Federation did not make any attempt to integrate until the mid 1950s, when the presidents of the GFWC and the NACW began a relationship that resulted in the NACW joining the GFWC (though remaining a separate organization as well). Bucholz, "The Ruffin Incident," conclusion.

134. *Keystone*, June 1908, 16–17.

135. Mrs. W. D. Maginnis, ed., *South Carolina Federation of Women's Clubs, Year Book, 1926–1927*, SCFWC Papers, box 8, folder 25, Winthrop, 60–61. Lucy Blackman was Mrs. William F. Blackman.

136. According to the newspapers, the debate surrounding the issue was tense, and Mrs. Sherman, GFWC president, broke her gavel trying to gain attention. Mrs. Martin, from Louisville, asked, "Shall we, or not, deny liberty to the individual club?" Pamphlet (title page missing), resolutions proposed by Louisville Women's Club, 1926, SCFWC Papers, Winthrop; clipping, Louisville *Courier-Journal*, May 22, 1926, 6, SCFWC Papers, Winthrop; clipping, Philadelphia *Public Ledger*, May 30, 1926, SCFWC Papers, Winthrop; and clipping, Atlantic City *Gazette*, June 2, 1926, SCFWC Papers, Winthrop.

137. Charleston *Sunday News*, July 4, 1926.

138. Lena Springs to Louisa Poppenheim, October 13, 1926, SCFWC Papers, Winthrop.

139. *State*, April 6, 1927, 1, 5.

140. Hudson, "From Constitution to Constitution," 77.

141. *The General Federation of Women's Clubs, Biennial Convention, May 22 to June 5, 1926, Atlantic City, N. J.: Official Report*, 360–61.

142. Mrs. W. D. Maginnis, ed., *South Carolina Federation of Women's Clubs, 1927–1928* (yearbook), SCFWC Papers, box 8, folder 26, Winthrop, 124–25. Emma Eaton White was Mrs. Edward Franklin White.

143. Mary Church Terrell, "A Plea for the White South," *Nineteenth Century*, vol. 60, July 1906, 78.

CHAPTER 5. RELUCTANT REFORMERS, RESISTANT LEGISLATORS: WHITE CLUBWOMEN AND SOCIAL REFORM

1. *The South Carolina Federation of Women's Clubs, 1916–1917* (yearbook), SCFWC Papers, box 5, folder 19, Winthrop, 59–61.

2. Rebecca Montgomery found that white women in Georgia also were inspired by the Lost Cause to work for social reform. Montgomery, "Lost Cause Mythology," 174–98.

3. C. Vann Woodward argued that leaders of the New South movement for industrialization were new men; that is, they were not the former planters. Woodward, however, does point out the divided mind of the new South, in which the Old South was still important to many. See Woodward, *Origins of the New South*, chapter 6.

4. Carlton, *Mill and Town in South Carolina*, 46–53. Bypassed by the railroads, Charleston was especially slow to adapt to the programs of the New South, and Charleston elites continued to stress manners, family, the past. See Doyle, *New Men, New Cities, New South*, xii, 8–9, 57–60, 112–58, 226–45.

5. *Life*, April 14, 1947, 70; and *National Cyclopedia of American Biography*, ed. 1920, vol. 17, 183.

6. Scott, *Natural Allies*, 3; and Louisa Poppenheim, "Address to the SCFWC as a representative of the GFWC," May 17, 1905, SCFWC Papers, box 2, folder 7, Winthrop.

7. Interest in the New South as a topic can be seen, for example, in the Castalian Club's study of "the New South," and "Henry Grady and the New South," Minutes, November 1924, Castalian Club Papers, Winthrop.

8. Grantham, *Southern Progressivism*, 410–21. Wedell found that women did criticize New South spokesmen for their commercialism. For example, the Nineteenth-Century club members claimed that men were too concerned with money. Wedell attributes this to a woman's consciousness or culture. Wedell, *Elite Women*, 87. Sarah Case found that UDC national leader Mildred Rutherford also supported a new economy while defending the culture of the Old South. Case, "The Historical Ideology," 619–22.

9. Louisa Poppenheim, "Woman's Work in the South," 637.

10. For the "maternalist" justification argument, see Scott, *Natural Allies*, 144. Montgomery found that Georgia women also believed deeply in the rhetoric. Montgomery, "Lost Cause Mythology," 198.

11. *Keystone*, January 1910, 3. Michael Kammen suggests that "outside the South a preoccupation with progress and innovation (c. 1876–1939) caused history to be treated with respect as an educational discipline but tradition per se to be regarded somewhat warily as a potential impediment to progress." Kammen, *Mystic Chords*, 383.

12. Sarah Bentschner Visanska was born in Charleston in 1870. Her father, David Bentschner, came from Germany with his parents as a boy and her mother was a native of Copenhagen, Denmark. She graduated from Charleston Female Seminary in 1889, and in 1895 she married J. M. Visanska, a merchant who was born in Richmond but lived in Charleston all his life. Visanska was president of the Kelly Kindergarten Association; vice president of the South Carolina Kindergarten Association; president of the Civic Club; member of the Council of Jewish Women, Charleston, the Arts and Crafts Club, Carolina Art Association, the board of administration of the Charleston Exposition, and various benevolent organizations; president of the Charleston City Federation from 1908 to 1911; president of the SCFWC from 1910 to 1912 and chair of the SCFWC Civic Department; recording secretary of the Hebrew Ladies Benevolent Society; treasurer of the Sarah Gray Home for Girls. According to *Woman's Who's Who of America*, edited by Leonard, Visanska supported woman suffrage but restricted suffrage for both sexes. The Poppenheims also wrote about her, "Having had no children, Mrs.

Visanska has spent the leisure hours of her life in looking after the welfare of the little unfortunates in her community. Her interest may always be enlisted in behalf of Civic Betterment and the education and elevation of the children of the poor— 'the citizens of tomorrow.'" *Keystone*, February 1904, 11–12.

13. Sarah Visanska, "The American Woman of To-day," *Keystone*, March 1900, 9–10.

14. *Keystone*, June 1903, 4.

15. Ibid., February 2, 1904, 9.

16. *South Carolina Federation Bulletin*, March 1927, 8.

17. Ibid., October 1925, 10.

18. *Southern Workman*, May 1909, 265–69.

19. *Keystone*, February 1900, 4; September 1900, 3.

20. Ibid., June 1902, 7.

21. For example, in South Carolina, there was approximately only one elementary school per forty square miles before the war. Harlan, *Separate and Unequal*, 4–5.

22. Ibid., 9–11. South Carolina was generally comparable to other Southern states, particularly, North Carolina. For example, annual expenditure per child in North Carolina was $1.65. The North Carolina illiteracy rate of 35.9 percent compared to 10.7 percent for the national average.

23. In the nation, native white illiteracy stood at 4.6 percent, foreign white at 12.9 percent, and colored (including black, Chinese, Japanese, and Indian) at 44.5 percent. *Census Reports, vol. 2; Twelfth Census of the United States, Taken in the Year 19000, Population*, part 2, table 54, p. cv; Francis B. Simkins, "Race Legislation in South Carolina Since 1865," 179–71; and Everett, "Race Relations in South Carolina," 65–66.

24. *Keystone*, December 1902, 6.

25. Ibid., March 1902, 4.

26. Ibid., June 1899, 8.

27. *State*, February 22, 1902, 1.

28. *Keystone*, July 1899, 9.

29. Ibid., August 1900, 4; October 1900, 6; January 1901, 5.

30. Carrie T. Pollitzer, "The Free Kindergarten Association of Charleston," *South Carolina Clubwoman*, January 1950, 6, 24–25, SCFWC Papers, Winthrop.

31. *Keystone*, October 1902, 3; and Poppenheim, "The History of the SCFWC," 30.

32. *Keystone*, June 1907, 5; November 1907, 5. Mrs. L. T. Nichols is identified only as "Miss Bowen" in the entry on her husband in *Men of Mark*, vol. 3.

33. The *Keystone* and the yearbooks indicate that clubwomen asked annually through 1926 for such a commission, but they were unsuccessful. The sticking point appeared to be gaining an appropriation. See, for example, *Keystone*, April 1909, 3; April 1911, 3; and SCFWC yearbooks, 1914–1915, 1916–1917, 1924–1925, 1925–1926, 1927–1928.

34. Harlan, *Separate and Unequal*, 180–81, 188, 191–92.

35. *Fifteenth Census of the United States: 1930, Population*, vol. 3, part 2, table 7, 780. This compares with the national average for whites, which dropped from 10.7 percent to 4.3 percent, *Fifteenth Census of the United States: 1930, Population*, vol. 3, part 1, table 24, 18.

36. Harlan, *Separate and Unequal*, 205, 208.

37. *Keystone*, January 1909, 4; May 1910, 4.

38. Ibid., January 1912, 3; April 1911, 3.

39. Minutes, December 8, 1920, Current Literature Club Papers, USC.

40. *Keystone*, May 1900, 3. For the degrading stereotypes promoted in most of the press not controlled by women, see Gere, *Intimate Practices*, chapter 7.

41. Charleston *News and Courier*, January 25, 1903, 4; November 22, 1903, 4; and Harlan, *Separate and Unequal*, 180–87.

42. Tetzlaff, *Cultivating a New South*, 195.

43. This overview of politics comes from Grantham, *Southern Progressivism*, 54–60; Wallace, *South Carolina*, 614–92; and Harlan, *Separate and Unequal*, 180–87.

44. *Journal of the House of Representatives of the General Assembly of the State of South Carolina*, 1907, 554, 570.

45. Quoted in Simon, *A Fabric of Defeat*, 27–28.

46. Wallace, *South Carolina*, 666–68; and Carlton, *Mill and Town in South Carolina*, 258.

47. Wallace, *The History of South Carolina*, vol. 3, 461–77.

48. *The South Carolina Federation of Women's Clubs, 1913–1914* (yearbook), SCFWC Papers, box 5, folder 19, Winthrop, 12–13.

49. *Keystone*, January 1910, 3 (Poppenheim quotation); and Mrs. L. H. Jennings, ed., *The South Carolina Federation of Women's Clubs, 1924–1925* (yearbook), SCFWC Papers, box 7, folder 23, Winthrop, 97.

50. *Keystone*, April 1911, 3, 11.

51. Charleston *News and Courier*, November 30, 1902, 10.

52. Mrs. A. O. Granger, "The Effect of Club Work in the South," *The Annals of the American Academy of Political and Social Science* 28 (September 1906): 252.

53. Charleston *News and Courier*, June 20, 1952.

54. Yearbook, 1922 and 1932, Civic Club Papers, box 488 folder 1, SCHS.

55. Mrs. J. W. D. Zerbst, "The Charleston City Federation of Women's Clubs: Another Inspiring Story of Club Work Over the Years," *South Carolina Clubwoman*, January 1950, 13. See also Odem, *Delinquent Daughters*, 110–15.

56. Minutes, February 4, 11, April 24, and October 17, 1901, New Century Club Papers, USC.

57. Minutes, November 21, 1901, New Century Club Papers, USC. The minutes indicate that the interest in child labor was short-lived.

58. Minutes, January 22, 1907. Nor did they support medical inspection, January 9, 1912, or domestic science, December 31, 1912, New Century Club Papers, USC.

59. Minutes, January 26, 1909; January 9, 1917; May 13, 1919; May 23, 1922; November 28, 1922; and March 22, 1927, New Century Club Papers, USC. Their interest in women and child workers continued, although they took no recorded action between 1902 and 1914. That December, they heard a paper on Women and Children before the law in South Carolina by Mrs. Gibbes, which they decided to try and publish in the *State*, "in the most conspicuous part of the paper." Minutes, December 14 and 28, 1915, New Century Club Papers, USC.

60. Columbia *Record*, April 24, 1927, clipping attached to minutes, April 26, 1927, New Century Club Papers, USC.

61. Minutes, October 6, 1910, Thursday Club Papers, USC; and Mrs. William A. Boyd, "The Thursday Club: A Sketchy Review," clipping and history, Thursday Club Papers, USC.

62. Minutes, October 22, 1914; February 6 and 20, 1919, Thursday Club Papers, USC.

63. Minutes, March 17, 1912; January 16, 1919; October 20, 1921; January 12, 1922; October 4, 1923, Thursday Club Papers, USC; Minutes, 1916, Over the Teacups Club Papers, Winthrop; and Minutes, February 1928, Old Homestead Club Papers, Darlington.

64. Minutes, September 7, 1903; April 5, 1906, Castalian Club Papers, Winthrop.

65. Elizabeth Turner found similar results in Galveston, Texas. Turner, *Women, Culture and Community*, 154–63.

66. Minutes, December 1920, Castalian Club Papers, Winthrop.

67. *Keystone*, June 1908, 3. Fant to Louisa Poppenheim, June 30, 1913, SCFWC Papers, Winthrop.

68. For more on the child labor movement, see Carlton, *Mill and Town in South Carolina*, and Davidson, *Child Labor Legislation*. Black clubwomen were not interested in child labor legislation, especially because they were not allowed to work in most mills. *National Notes*, May/June 1915, 17–18. For Southern women and labor reform, see Storrs, "Gender and Sectionalism in New Deal Politics," 218–37.

69. Carlton, *Mill and Town in South Carolina*, 7, 133–34. The number of mills in the state grew to exceed 140 by 1907, the number of spindles in those mills doubled between 1900 and 1905, and the number of workers grew to more than 37,000 in 1905.

70. Davidson, *Child Labor Legislation*, 12–13.

71. In 1907, 50 percent of mill workers under age fourteen were illiterate, while statewide only 14.8 percent of white children, ages ten to fourteen, were illiterate. Harlan, *Separate and Unequal*, 188. For school attendance, see *Fifteenth Census of the United States: 1930, Population*, vol. 3, part 2, table 6, 779.

72. According to Davidson, *Gunton's* magazine was the first journal to devote attention to the mill problem in the South in the 1890s. Davidson, *Child Labor Legislation*, 2.

73. *Keystone*, March 1905, 12–13.

74. Charleston *News and Courier*, December 4, 1907. Margaret Smyth McKissick was born in Charleston in 1870; she attended private school in Charleston and the Edgeworth School in Baltimore. She married A. Foster McKissick in 1891 and had one son, Ellison Smyth McKissick. A Presbyterian, McKissick was also chair of the Industrial School and the Forestry and Civics Committees of the SCFWC; president of the Public Library Association; on the Executive Board of Women's Welfare department of the National Civic Association; president of the Catuchee Club, Greenwood; member of the DAR and the UDC; and vice chair of the GFWC Industrial and Child Labor committee. See *Woman's Who's Who*, and Logan, *The Part Taken by Women*, 595. Ellison A. Smyth was the grandson of Charleston merchant James Adger. He joined the family business and, after the failure of the firm's banking branch, moved to the South Carolina Piedmont to make his fortune in the textile industry. In 1907, Pelzer was the second largest mill corporation in South Carolina, with 130,000 spindles. Carlton, *Mill and Town in South Carolina*, 44–45.

75. Leonora Beck Ellis, "A Model Factory Town," *Forum*, September 1901, 60–65. The schools were open ten months, but, to accommodate working children, had night schools and special afternoon sessions for them. See also Carlton, *Mill and Town in South Carolina*, 92–102.

76. *Keystone*, June 1905, 4, November 1906, 4, April 1907, 9. Meanwhile, the General Federation in 1910 took part in congressional hearings on a "uniform legislation" or federal child labor bill. The General Federation report printed in the *Keystone* reminded clubwomen that the bill "does not interfere with those states' rights of which we sometimes are so much afraid." See *Keystone*, May 1910, 9. The NCLC, initiated by Edgar Murphy a clergyman from Alabama, although dominated by Northern members, did have Southern members, including Senator Ben Tillman from South Carolina. However, the NCLC was viewed by many in the South as under Northern influence. When they switched tactics to support a federal bill, they lost almost all support from the South. See Davidson, *Child Labor Legislation*, chap. 7.

77. Hennig, *August Kohn*, 44–48, 118–21. Other clubwomen intimately tied to the mills were married to or daughters of the following mill men: R. T. Fewell, president, Arcade Cotton Mills, Rock Hill; A. B. Calvert, president of Drayton Mills, Spartanburg; C. E. Graham, president of Camperdown Mills, Greenville; R. E. Ligon, Anderson Cotton Mills, Anderson; W. J. Roddey, president of Victoria Cotton Mills, Rock Hill; W. E. Lucas, president of Watts Mills, Laurens; LeRoy Springs, president of Eureka Cotton Mills, Chester, and Lancaster Mills, Lancaster; and G. A. Guignard, president of Southern Aseptic Laboratory, Columbia. In addition, clubwoman Mary P. Gridley was herself the president of Batesville Mill, a position she assumed after the death of her husband and father. See miscellaneous club papers for women, and August Kohn, "The Cotton Mills of South

Carolina," *Charleston News and Courier*, December 4, 1907, for listing of mill presidents.

78. Davidson, *Child Labor Legislation*, 91–92; and August Kohn, "Child Labor in the South," in *The South in the Building of the Nation*, 582–97.

79. Davidson, *Child Labor Legislation*, 56–57, 96.

80. For McFayden see, Davidson, *Child Labor Legislation*, 92–96. *Charities*, March 1, 1902, 192.

81. *Keystone*, June 1908, 4. Emphasis mine.

82. Carlton, *Mill and Town in South Carolina*, 172–74, 195–96.

83. *Keystone*, October 1899, 5; and Simon, *A Fabric of Defeat*, 24–25.

84. Leloudis, "School Reform in the New South," 906.

85. W. P. Few, "Some Educational Needs of the South," *South Atlantic Quarterly* 3 (July 1904): 201–11, criticized the "almost selfish local patriotism that praises exorbitantly the things of one's own community, State, or section of country," which hindered the ability to judge the needs of the community.

86. *Keystone*, August 1900, 3.

87. For examples of negative articles on child labor, see Irene M. Ashby, "Child-Labor in Southern Cotton Mills," *World's Work*, October 1901, 1290–95, and other articles throughout *Annals* and *World's Work*.

88. *Keystone*, December 1903, 3. In the national press Leonora Beck Ellis was another author who downplayed the problem. For example, in 1901, she had already declared that the "worst is clearly over," in "Child Labor Legislation in the South," *Gunton's Magazine*, July 1901, 53; she also wrote the article praising Pelzer as the model factory town of the South, Ellis, "A Model Factory Town," *Forum*, September 1901, 60–65. For other positive views of the mills, see Thomas Parker, "The South Carolina Cotton Mill—A Manufacturer's View," *South Atlantic Quarterly* 8 (October 1909): 328–37; "The South Carolina Cotton Mill Village—A Manufacturer's View," *South Atlantic Quarterly* 9 (October 1910): 349–57; and William P. Few, "The Constructive Philanthropy of a Southern Cotton Mill," *South Atlantic Quarterly* 8 (January 1909): 82–90.

89. *Keystone*, February 1903, 3. In fact, *Charities* also printed an article in which A. J. McKelway, assistant secretary of the National Child Labor Committee, criticized Miss Gertrude Beeks's article in the National Civic Association Review for presenting a false and positive impression of child labor in the mills. *Charities*, November 10, 1906, 271–73.

90. *Keystone*, May 1900, 5; January 1903, 4.

91. Ibid., May 1905, 5; June 1905, 7; and Mrs. Lilian Neely, "The History of the Castalian Literary Club," n.d., Castalian Club Papers, Winthrop, box 1, folder 1.

92. *Keystone*, January 1903, 4.

93. Carlton, *Mill and Town in South Carolina*, 94–108.

94. Louisa Poppenheim, "President's report," Annual Report, 1902, SCFWC Papers, Winthrop, box 2, folder 7.

95. *Manufacturer's Record*, September 4, 1902, 110.

96. The SCCLC was organized in 1905 but disbanded in 1907 for lack of effective action. The secretary decided to split from the committee and broach a compromise with the mill owners. It was reorganized in 1909 with Boone, a representative of the NCLC as secretary. See Davidson, *Child Labor Legislation*, 181–89. Other committee members included N. G. Gonzales, editor of the State; W. E. Gonzales; Bishops Ellison Capers and W. A. Guerry of the Episcopal Church; H. N. Snyder, president of Wofford College; W. Wallace; Joseph A McCollough; Charles A. Weltner, a Lutheran pastor; Miss Sophie Carroll and Mrs. Robert Gibbes, both of the SCFWC; A. T. Jamison; Dr. George B. Cromer, husband of Mrs. Marie Cromer, a SCFWC officer; J. E. MacDonald; and Knox Livingston. See also Carlton, *Mill and Town in South Carolina*, 193.

97. The poverty exemption said that children under twelve (or whatever age was currently designated as the minimum age for work) would be allowed to work if their parents depended upon their financial contribution, a situation usually owing to a disabled parent or widowed mother.

98. *Keystone*, January 1911, 9; emphasis mine in both quotations.

99. *Keystone*, October 1911, 7; and *Survey*, October 21, 1911, 1024. The committee never endorsed an age-fourteen limit. Davidson, *Child Labor Legislation*, 189.

100. *Keystone*, August 1910, 11.

101. Caroline Granger, "The Social Work of the General Federation," *Federation Bulletin*, March 1906, 280.

102. *The General Federation of Women's Clubs Eighteenth Biennial Convention, May 22 to June 5, 1926, Atlantic City, N. J.: Official Report*, 209–10. After rejecting the resolution, clubwomen in South Carolina advocated state work on child labor laws and compulsory education. See *South Carolina Federation Bulletin*, May 1926, 4.

103. Davidson, *Child Labor Legislation*, 97–101, 140–45, 187, 191.

104. *Federation Bulletin*, October 1905, 14–15.

105. *Keystone*, December 1908, 4. See, for example, the failure of compulsory education in 1911, *Keystone*, April 1911, 3. The first compulsory education law, passed in 1915, was a local option law, followed in 1919 with a universal law, and the 1937 law, which set the age at sixteen; all these bills, however, had poverty exemptions. Davidson, *Child Labor Legislation*, 191–94.

106. Quoted in Everett, "Race Relations in South Carolina," 31; and *Fifteenth Census of the United States: 1930, Population*, vol. 3, part 2, table 6, 779.

107. Simon, "The Appeal of Cole Blease of South Carolina," 57–86. Simon contends that Blease appealed to workers' sense of white patriarchy and deep need to be in control of their own households.

108. Carlton, *Mill and Town in South Carolina*, 181–82, 233–34 (quotation); and Scott, *Natural Allies*, 4, 182.

109. Carlton, *Mill and Town in South Carolina*, 209; and *Keystone*, October 1900, 6. Obviously it is difficult to glean the response of mill workers through the papers

of clubwomen. According to a report from South Henderson, N.C., of a school for mill children, the people were "most appreciative and thankful for a little ray of sunshine in their cramped and narrow lives." *Keystone*, February 1909, 6. "Rescue the unfortunate" quotation, "Report Made by Perihelion Club Delegates to the Club on the Third State Convention . . ." Perihelion Papers, Winthrop.

110. Mary Elinor Poppenheim to Mary and Louisa, February 23, 1888, in Johnson, *Southern Women at Vassar*, 195.

111. Carlton, *Mill and Town in South Carolina*, 202–35. Blease received more than 70 percent of the vote from many mill districts, including in Spartanburg and Union counties.

112. Carlton, *Mill and Town in South Carolina*, 177.

113. *The South Carolina Federation of Women's Clubs, 1914–1915* (yearbook), SCFWC Papers, box 5, folder 19, Winthrop, 28–29.

114. Louisa Poppenheim, "A Message from the Second President of the Federation and one who also served faithfully as its publicity chairman," *The South Carolina Federation Bulletin*, April 1926, 1.

115. Joyce Elhassani, "Emily Plume Evans," in *The Lives They Lived*, 60–64.

116. *The South Carolina Federation of Women's Clubs, 1914–1915* (yearbook), 30–32.

117. *The South Carolina Federation of Women's Clubs, 1916–1917* (yearbook), SCFWC Papers, box 5, folder 19, Winthrop, 59–61; and Elhassani, "Evans," 63. For more on the need to overcome opposition to federal law, see Storrs, "Gender and Sectionalism," 229–37.

118. *The South Carolina Federation of Women's Clubs, 1917–1918* (yearbook), SCFWC Papers, box 6, folder 20, Winthrop, 38–41.

119. *The South Carolina Federation of Women's Clubs, 1916–1917* (yearbook), 35–36; *The South Carolina Federation of Women's Clubs, 1918–1919* (yearbook), SCFWC Papers, box 6, folder 20, Winthrop, 59; and *South Carolina Federation Bulletin*, March, 1927, 7. For example, the 1920–1921 education report asked for a full school term instead of just four months. *The South Carolina Federation of Women's Clubs 1920–1921* (yearbook) SCFWC Papers, box 6, folder 21, Winthrop, 47.

120. *The South Carolina Federation of Women's Clubs, 1927–1928* (yearbook), 75–76.

121. *Keystone*, June 1902, 11; December 1903, 11; May 1906, 5; January 1908, 5; June 1908, 5. Judith McArthur also found Texas women working against child labor. She argues that despite their strong Southern identity, they sided with national women's organizations rather than New South industrialists. McArthur, *Creating the New Woman*, 143–44.

122. *The General Federation of Women's Clubs Fifth Biennial Convention, June 1900, Milwaukee, Wisc.: Official Proceedings*, 46.

123. For North Carolina, see Davidson, *Child Labor Legislation*, chapters 6 and 8; and *Keystone*, December 1905, 5.

124. Thomas, *The New Woman of Alabama*, 92–117, (quotation, 108); and Davidson, *Child Labor Legislation*, 23–26, 51.

125. In 1910, 3,623 ten- to thirteen-year-olds worked in the cotton mills, and

4,914 fourteen- to fifteen-year-olds, or a total of 8,537 workers under age sixteen; that represents an increased number from the 1900 total of 8,049. (A report issued by the South Carolina Department of Agriculture, Commerce and Industries in 1909 found 5,019 children under age fourteen, which is even higher than the census figures.) Defenders of the mills argued that this increase was slight in comparison to the general growth of cotton mill operatives, which more than doubled. In other words, the percentage of cotton mill workers who were children decreased. *Thirteenth Census of the United States Taken in the Year 1910*, vol. 4, Population, 1910, Occupational Statistics, table 7, 516; *Fourteenth Census of the United States Taken in the Year 1920*, vol. 4, Population, 1920, Occupations, table 1, 1014; South Carolina Department report cited in Thomas F. Parker, "The South Carolina Cotton Mill—A Manufacturer's View," in *South Atlantic Quarterly* 8 (October 1909): 328–37 (this article defended child labor); and August Kohn, "Child Labor in the South," 582–97.

126. Davidson, *Child Labor Legislation*, 273.

127. Ibid., 193.

128. Even the Marion Chapter of the UDC saw prosperity in the mills; the group noted in their minutes, "A brighter day has dawned for us, prosperity surrounds us . . . The busy whir of the loom and spindle is heard all over the land. The South has risen Phoenix like from the ashes of her defeat." Minutes, Marion Chapter, United Daughters of the Confederacy, October 21, 1903, book 1, USC, 17.

129. *Keystone*, May, 1905, 3; and Minutes, New Century Club, April 12, 1921, USC.

130. Visanska, "A Quarter Century of Federation Life," 27.

CHAPTER 6. "EXALTING THE CAUSE OF VIRTUE": BLACK AND WHITE CLUBWOMEN AND JUVENILE REFORMATORIES

1. White, *Too Heavy a Load*, 39–40, Knupfer, "Toward a Tender Humanity," 23.

2. Some historians of the Civil Rights Movement argue that rather than looking to the 1950s or 1960s for a starting point, we need to consider the longer trajectory of a movement for civil rights. See, for example, de Jong, *A Different Day*.

3. With the exception of the Book Lovers Club and the Phyllis Wheatley Club of Charleston, the minutes of individual black women's clubs from South Carolina are not available. Information on clubs was gleaned from various sources including SCFCWC records and the *Palmetto Leader*. Jane Edna Hunter, originally from South Carolina, founded the Phyllis Wheatley Association and Home in Cleveland, Ohio, for young, especially migrant, black women in the city. See Hunter's autobiography, *A Nickel and a Prayer*.

4. *Fortieth Anniversary Booklet*, 3.

5. *National Notes*, April–May 1917, 9.

6. Neverdon-Morton, *Afro-American Women of the South*, 6.

7. Quoted in the *Crisis*, March 1913, 216–17.

8. Constitution of the South Carolina Federation of Colored Women's Clubs, n.d., private collection, Robinson.

9. *Palmetto Leader*, June 26, 1926, 8; June 11, 1927, 1; June 25, 1927, 1; May 2, 1925, 1.

10. The two kindergarten associations were the Alice Cary Kindergarten Association and the Free Kindergarten Association, both in Charleston. *National Notes*, April–May, 1917, 9–10, and January–March 1921, 9; *Palmetto Leader*, May 2, 1925, 1; Sunlight Club Year's Program, 1930–1931, private collection, Robinson; *Fortieth Anniversary Booklet*, 38; and *National Notes*, July 1928, 17; November 1925, 8.

11. Shaw, *What a Woman Ought to Be*, 14–15, 23–25.

12. Addie W. Hunton, "The National Association of Colored Women: Its Real Significance," *The Colored American Magazine*, 14, July 1908, 421.

13. Josephine Silone Yates, "Kindergartens and Mothers' Clubs As Related to the Work of the National Association of Colored Women," *The Colored American Magazine*, 8, June 1905, 310.

14. "Founders of the Modern Priscilla Club, 1926–1982" typescript, Federated Clubs Scrapbook, Fields Collection, Avery.

15. *Fortieth Anniversary Booklet*, 38.

16. Minutes, Book Lovers Club Papers, Avery; and Constitution, Phyllis Wheatley Club Papers, Avery, folder 1.

17. Zimmerman, interview, October 9, 1995; "Sunlight Club," *Fortieth Anniversary Booklet*, 11; and Robinson, interview, October 12, 1995.

18. *Palmetto Leader*, February 4, 1928, 6.

19. "Family Financial Program and Study Outline for South Carolina's Federated Clubs," n.d., pamphlet, private collection, Robinson.

20. *Palmetto Leader*, March 24, 1928, 1. Other early federated clubs included Helping Hand Club, of Hartsville, founded in 1921; the Marion Birnie Wilkinson Club, of Chester, organized in 1928 by Mrs. Etta Stanback; the Golden Rule Club of Spartanburg; the Darlington Social Hearts Club; and the Star Social Club of Anderson. *Fortieth Anniversary Booklet*, 32; *Book of Gold*, 36, 40, and passim; *Minutes of the National Association of Colored Women*, 1908, Records of the NACW, reel 1, pp. 39, 42; *Minutes of the National Association of Colored Women*, 1912, Records of the NACW, reel 1, p. 49; and *Minutes of the National Association of Colored Women*, 1922, Records of the NACW, reel 1, p. 55. The *Palmetto Leader* reported the activities of the following clubs, whether they belonged to the federation is unknown: the Silver Leaf Club of Spartanburg; the Booker T. Washington Literary and Social Club of Georgetown, founded 1916; the Will Do Club, and the Sunshine Club, both of Greenville. The federation grew rapidly in the 1920s: in 1922, it had 2,500 members in 90 clubs; in 1924, 135 clubs; and in 1926, 170 clubs and 2,500 members. This was the most clubs reported in any state, and a large number of members considering the population of South Carolina (for example, in comparison, a much larger state with a substantial urban population such as Illinois had 3,000 mem-

bers). *Minutes of the National Association of Colored Women*, 1922, Records of the NACW, reel 1, p. 36; *Minutes of the National Association of Colored Women*, 1924, Records of the NACW, reel 1, p. 34.

21. *Book of Gold*, 33; and *National Notes*, November 1925, 5.

22. Minutes, 1921–1922, Phyllis Wheatley Club Papers, Avery, folder 1.

23. They sponsored *The Quest of Happiness* at State College. *Palmetto Leader*, April 3, 1926. Mrs. (J. E.) Linnie Blanton, (List of Clubs), ca. 1930, private papers, Robinson.

24. *Palmetto Leader*, June 26, 1926, 1.

25. *National Notes*, December 1926, 8.

26. Linda Gordon, "Black and White Visions of Welfare," 578. Nancy Hewitt also found that class distinctions in the African American community in Tampa were blurred owing to the fact that neighborhoods were racially segregated. Poor and wealthy black women lived as neighbors. Hewitt, *Southern Discomfort*, 135–36.

27. White, "The Cost of Club Work," 259–61,(quotation, 260). See also Gatewood, *Aristocrats of Color*, 185–96, 348; and Gaines, *Uplifting the Race*, 1–17.

28. Mrs. Cora Gethers, "The Part of the Negro Woman in the Solution of the Race Problem," in three parts, *Palmetto Leader*, June 12, 19, 26, 1926, 4.

29. Vennie Deas-Moore, "Lifting as They Climb," unpublished paper in the author's possession, 15–17.

30. Johnette Edwards, "The past two years . . . ," (ca. 1970), handwritten speech, Johnette Edwards Papers, box 1, folder 6, Winthrop.

31. Gatewood, *Aristocrats of Color*, 348; Knupfer, "'Toward a Tenderer Humanity,'" 58–75, who argues that women's clubs had a twin emphasis on social uplift and social status.

32. Mennel, *Thorns and Thistles*, 32, 49, 74–77, 130–34.

33. *Keystone*, October 1911, 3.

34. Ibid., May 1903, 4. In Alabama, clubwomen began working for a boys' reformatory in 1899 and had a charter approved almost immediately. Thomas, *The New Woman of Alabama*, 49–53.

35. Martha Orr Patterson was born at her grandfather's plantation in Abbeville, S.C. She was the daughter of South Carolina governor James L. Orr and married William C. Patterson of Philadelphia. They moved to Greenville, where he became secretary of a cotton mill. Patterson had one son, a lawyer. In addition to her role as state president of the SCFWC, Patterson was also a member of the Thursday club, the Greenville Female College Alumnae, Greenville Kindergarten Association, vice president of the Greenville City Federation of Clubs, and vice president of the SCUDC. *Keystone*, January 1904, 11.

36. Ibid., October 1907, 3.

37. Ibid., March 1906, 4; February 1907, 4; and Charleston *News and Courier*, May 10, 1907, 6.

38. *Keystone*, April 1907, 3; October 1907, 3; December 1907, 3; March 1908, 3.

39. Ibid., April 1909, 4.
40. Ibid., October 1904, 4; June 1906, 4–5.
41. Ibid., May 1912, 4; May, 1913, 5; *South Carolina Federation of Women's Clubs, 1912–1913* (yearbook), SCFWC Papers, box 5, folder 19, Winthrop, 52; *South Carolina Federation of Women's Clubs, 1919–1920* (yearbook), SCFWC Papers, box 6, folder 20, Winthrop, 63–64, 68–69; and *South Carolina Federation of Women's Clubs, 1921–1922* (yearbook), 32; and *South Carolina Federation of Women's Clubs, 1924–1925* (yearbook), 101, 106–10.
42. *Keystone*, June 1907, 6; May 1913, 4; *The South Carolina Federation of Women's Clubs 1913* (yearbook), SCFWC Papers, box 5, folder 19, Winthrop, 13; and *South Carolina Federation of Women's Clubs, 1918–1919* (yearbook), SCFWC Papers, box 6, folder 20, Winthrop, 59. A historical pageant tracing the SCFWC claimed that home for girls was "not due to the efforts of the Federation, but the Federation first aroused the interest of the clubwomen of South Carolina to the need of such an institution." *Time Marches On* (pageant pamphlet, n.p., 1939), 11.
43. *Keystone*, January 1906, 3; March 1906, 7.
44. Ibid., October 1911, 3; *South Carolina Federation of Women's Clubs, 1918–1919* (yearbook), 15; and *Acts and Resolutions of South Carolina*, 1906, 134–35.
45. *Keystone*, June 1902, 4.
46. Ibid., August 1904, 5.
47. Ibid., July 1904, 4.
48. Ibid., July 1904, 10.
49. Sims, "Feminism and Femininity," 111.
50. Book review of Booker T. Washington's *Future of the American Negro*, in *Keystone*, March 1900, 13.
51. Marion Wilkinson to Charlotte Hawkins Brown, February 7, 1920, CHB, microfilm, reel 2, folder 41.
52. On African American women and homes for juveniles, working girls, and the elderly, see Knupfer, "'Toward a Tenderer Humanity,'" chapter 4.
53. Casselberry, interview, March 1, 1996. See also Etta Rowe's statement in Asa H. Gordon, *Sketches of Negro Life and History*, 182.
54. Charleston *News and Courier*, May 16, 1918. For both Progressive era reformers' and the military's interest in preventing prostitution and sexually transmitted diseases on and near military camps during World War I, see Odem, *Delinquent Daughters*, 121–24; and Judson, "Building the New South City," chapter 3.
55. "Fairwold Home for Neglected Colored Girls, Columbia, South Carolina," n.d., typescript attached to Abigail Curlee to Mrs. S. W. Henry, December 9, 1930, CIC Papers, reel 18, series 1:367; and Burts, *Richard Irvine Manning*, 189–90.
56. *Palmetto Leader*, July 31, 1926, 4. The amount of money raised was reported as $30,000. If this is correct, it was well above the $12,000 later used to build a more modern brick building. For the second case, see *Palmetto Leader*, September 25, 1926, 4.

57. Judith McArthur found that one of the first instances of cooperation between the Texas black and white state federations of women's clubs also came in the 1920s over a reformatory for delinquent black girls. *Creating the New Woman*, 148.

58. Minutes, Women's Section, South Carolina CIC, November 28, 1922, CIC, reel 53, series 7:197; and Minutes, SC CIC, November 29, 1922, CIC Papers, reel 53, series 7:191.

59. *Palmetto Leader*, February 7, 1925, 1. In addition to those mentioned, the Committee consisted of the following white members: Miss L. C. Chappell, president of the State Council of Farm Women; Mrs. Christopher Fitzsimmons, League of Women Voters; Major J. C. Dozier, secretary, Welfare Board; and black members: Rev. D. H. Sims, president of Allen University; Professor T. L. Duckett, Benedict College; Rev. E. A. Adams, pastor, Bethel A. M. E. Church; Rev. H. M. Moore, pastor Second Calvary Baptist Church; Mr. W. H. Harvey, president, Victory Savings Bank, and state manager of the North Carolina Mutual Life Insurance Company; Rev. N. H. Smith, pastor, Wesley M. E. Church; Rev. J. R. Pearson, Charleston. Bishop Finlay noted in his Bishop's Journal that on February 2, 1925, he had "headed a delegation from various organizations to present the claims of the Industrial School for Delinquent Colored Girls before the Ways and Means Committee of the legislature." *Journal of the Fourth Annual Convention of the Protestant Episcopal Church in the Diocese of Upper South Carolina* (Columbia: R. L. Bryan, 1926), 53.

60. Mrs. John Drake, *South Carolina Federation of Women's Clubs, 1921–1922* (yearbook), SCFWC Papers, box 6, folder 21, Winthrop, 70.

61. For more on Rowe's letter, see Etta B. Rowe, "The Fairwold Industrial School for Colored Girls," printed in *Federation Bulletin*, November 1925, 5–6. See also Mrs. W. D. Melton, *South Carolina Federation of Women's Clubs, 1925–1926* (yearbook), SCFWC Papers, box 8, folder 24, Winthrop, 102; Mrs. Ralph Ramseur, *South Carolina Federation of Women's Clubs, 1921–1922* (yearbook), SCFWC Papers, box 8, folder 27, Winthrop, 75; and Minutes, Committee of Women's Work, SC CIC, November 28, 1924, CIC Papers, reel 53, series 7:197, p. 3.

62. One of the few white clubs to mention Fairwold in its minutes was the Current Literature Club of Columbia, who heard from G. Croft Williams, secretary of Public Welfare. He spoke on juvenile delinquency and advocated that the state take over Fairwold. Minutes, January 5, 1921, Current Literature Club Papers, USC.

63. Etta B. Rowe, "The Fairwold Industrial School for Colored Girls," printed in *Federation Bulletin*, November 1925, 5–6; and *National Notes*, March 1926, 11–12. The latter was published after the fire, and Rowe added a note to the effect that, if the state did not respond, then clubwomen would proceed with a fund-raising campaign.

64. Information on the fire and subsequent battle for funding comes from the

Palmetto Leader, 1924–1930; Zimmerman, interview, October 9, 1995, Orangeburg, S.C.; Mrs. Lavonia Atkinson, interview by the author, February 29, 1996, Columbia, S.C.; "Training Schools for Neglected Negro Girls," typescript, December 10, 1931, CIC Papers, reel 18, series 1:367; and Rowe, "Fairwold Industrial School."

65. *Palmetto Leader*, December 19, 1925, 1.

66. Ibid., February 6, 1926, 1.

67. Ibid., February 27, 1926, 4; June 12, 1926, 1; June 26, 1926, 1.

68. "Training Schools for Neglected Negro Girls," typescript, December 10, 1931, CIC Papers, reel 18, series 1:367; and *Palmetto Leader*, January 15, 1927, 4.

69. *Palmetto Leader*, March 12, 1927, 4; April 30, 1927, 4.

70. Although the *Book of Gold* says the appropriation was not withdrawn until 1929, the "excuse being that no Negro girl was worth saving," other sources seem to agree that it was withdrawn in 1926. See, for example, *National Notes*, July 1928, 17.

71. Harlan, *Separate and Unequal*, 11–15; and Wallace, *South Carolina: A Short History*, 668.

72. In Tampa, the city council gave a meager $50 to an African American hospital at the same time it granted $500 to a Confederate memorial. Hewitt, *Southern Discomfort*, 172.

73. This information on the Home comes from the following, unless otherwise indicated: *National Negro Digest*, 1940, 28–29; and "Training Schools for Neglected Negro Girls," typescript, December 10, 1931, CIC Papers, reel 18, series 1:367. The $12,000 came from the following sources: $1,000—insurance; $2,500—bequest left by Mrs. Bradley; $6,700—women's clubs; and the remaining in various donations including the interracial committee. Although many documents claim that the Bishop donated the land, I have been unable to find any official documentation in the diocesan *Journals of the Annual Convention*; a history of the diocese does mention it in passing. Albert Sidney Thomas, *A Historical Account of the Protestant Episcopal Church in South Carolina, 1820–1957* (Columbia: R. L. Bryan, 1957), 472; likewise, Bishop Finlay himself mentions the land in his column, "The Piedmont Churchman," March 1930, 1.

74. Marion Wilkinson to Mrs. McGowan, October 2, 1930, CIC Papers, reel 18, series 1:367.

75. Here, again, it appears that white Episcopalian women helped the Federation. According to the Upper South Carolina Diocese Woman's Auxiliary Yearbook of 1934, "one district chairman assisted in getting help from the Duke Foundation for a negro orphanage." Winthrop, box 5, folder 22, p. 12.

76. *Southeastern Herald*, February 1926, Records of the NACW, reel 24, p. 14; Thomas, *The New Woman In Alabama*, 82. The state provided funding at a rate of $7.00 per black boy, while it funded a reformatory for white boys with $12.50 per boy.

77. Shaw, *What a Woman Ought to Be*, 173.

78. *Palmetto Leader*, June 11, 1927, 1; June 25, 1927, 1; March 10, 1928, 1; and *Annual Meeting of the South Carolina Federation of Colored Women's Clubs*, 1929.

79. Zimmerman, interview, October 9, 1995; and *National Notes*, November 1925, 5.

80. *Palmetto Leader*, May 17, 1930, 1; and "SCFCWC Club Apportionment's of Staple Groceries for the Wilkinson Home for Orphans, 1933," private collection, Mrs. Robinson.

81. Minutes, Phyllis Wheatley Club Papers, Avery; and *Palmetto Leader*, February 13, 1926, 6.

82. *Palmetto Leader*, May 5, 1925; and *Southeastern Herald*, February 1926, Records of the NACW, reel 24, p. 1.

83. *Palmetto Leader*, February 11, 1928, 1.

84. *National Negro Digest*, 29. The home, which continued to function until the early 1980s, turned its attention to abused girls in the 1970s. In December 1989 the home burned to the ground, and the SCFCWC, which still owns the land, has not yet made plans to rebuild, but according to Mrs. Zimmerman, the club is trying to sell the land.

85. *National Notes*, April/May 1917, 7.

86. Ibid., 9.

87. *Dictionary of American Biography*, 229–30. His predecessor, President Thomas E. Miller, was forced to resign after the election of Coleman Blease as governor of South Carolina. Miller was a black Republican who was outspoken against white Democrats at the 1895 state constitutional convention, which disenfranchised most blacks in the state. Unhappy with Miller, Blease threatened to cut funding for State College, which left Miller with no choice but to resign.

88. Everett, "Race Relations in South Carolina," 92.

89. Ibid., 151.

90. *Dictionary of American Biography*, 229–30.

91. Robert Shaw Wilkinson, "Address to the Secretary of the Interior on behalf of the Conference of the Presidents of the Negro Land Grant Colleges," *Palmetto Leader*, May 15, 1926, 1. Robert was the author of *History of the Negro Land Grant Colleges*, Washington, D.C., U.S. Bureau of Education, 1926, and a member of the general advisory committee Land Grant College Survey, according to *Who Was Who in America*, ed. 1943, vol. 1, 1343.

92. *Palmetto Leader*, May 19, 1928, 2.

93. *Fortieth Anniversary Booklet*, 9; and *Palmetto Leader*, September 18, 1926, 8.

94. Etta Rowe, "Tribute to Mother Wilkinson on her death," Fields Collection, Avery; and *Palmetto Leader*, October 4, 1930.

95. White, "The Cost of Club Work," 259.

96. "Fairwold Home for Neglected Colored Girls, Columbia, South Carolina," n.d., typescript attached to Abigail Curlee to Mrs. S. W. Henry, December 9, 1930, CIC Papers, reel 18, series 1:367.

97. This was the case in the working-class families who sent their daughters to Nannie Helen Burrough's National Training School in Washington, D.C. Wolcott, "Bible, Bath, and Broom," 88–110.

98. *Palmetto Leader*, January 9, 1925, 1; May 5, 1925; December 26, 1925, 4.

99. "Training Schools for Neglected Negro Girls," typescript, December 10, 1931, CIC Papers, reel 18, series 1:367. In 1930, Abigail Curlee of the CIC wrote to black clubwomen and white CIC women throughout the South and asked them for information concerning the movement for a home in their state so that legislatures would know it was a "South-wide movement." She particularly asked black women why they prioritized this effort. The results of her survey are in the "Training Schools" typescript. For her letters, see Abigail Curlee [to various], September 24, September 30, 1930, CIC Papers, reel 18, series 1:367.

100. *Southeastern Herald*, April 1926, Records of the NACW, reel 24, p. 14; and "Training Schools for Neglected Negro Girls," typescript, December 10, 1931, CIC Papers, reel 18, series 1:367. In Mississippi, the effort was started late because a home was being established for boys in the late 1920s. Tennessee provided a state-run home in 1922. There was no progress reported by Akansas, Louisiana, Kentucky, or Oklahoma in the 1931 report.

101. Brown to the editor, *North Carolina Awake*, April 19, 1921, CHB, reel 3, folder 43.

102. Etta Rowe, *Book of Gold*, 8; Salem, *To Better Our World*, 110–11; and Neverdon-Morton, *Afro-American Women of the South*, 115–16, 137–38.

103. Lizelia A. J. Moorer, "South Carolina Federation Song," in Marion Birnie Wilkinson Home scrapbook, Mamie E. G. Fields Collection, Avery.

104. Bethune, "A Philosophy of Education for Negro Girls," n.d. typescript, Mary McLeod Bethune Papers, Amistad Center, folder 13.

105. Higginbotham, *Righteous Discontent*, 95–96. On respectability, see also Wolcott, *Remaking Respectability*; and Hendricks, *Gender, Race and Politics in the Midwest*, 19. In the case of African American clubwomen, Deborah White argues that gender and racial solidarity did not always overcome class differences, and some clubwomen resented being classed according to race with poor black women. White, "The Cost of Club Work," 259–61.

106. Higginbotham, *Righteous Discontent*, 96–97. See also Giddings, *When and Where I Enter*, and Hine, "'We Specialize in the Wholly Impossible,'" 70–93.

107. Similarly, Toni Morrison argues that white identity in American fiction, including characteristics such as individualism, authority, and autonomy, is expressed through difference from Africans or African Americans; that is, white identity is not possible without an oppositional black identity. Morrison, *Playing in the Dark*, 44–51.

108. Missouri editor John Jacks wrote a "scandalous" letter regarding black women to Florence Balgarnie, a British suffragist who sponsored Ida B. Wells's trip to England. Balgarnie forwarded the letter to Ruffin. Hamilton, "The National Council of Colored Women, 1896–1920," 14.

109. Quotations come from "The Negro Problem: How It Appeals to a Southern White Woman," *Independent*, September 18, 1902, 2226; and "Experiences of the Race Problem: By a Southern White Woman," *Independent*, March 17, 1904, 593.

110. This information is taken from the following articles (all but Terrell and Ruffin were Southern women): Mary Terrell, "The Club Work of Colored Women," *Southern Workman*, August 1901, 435–38; Josephine St. P. Ruffin, Address, National Conference of Colored Women, July 29, 1895 (quoted in Elizabeth Davis, *Lifting As They Climb*, 17–19; Addie Hunton, "Negro Womanhood Defended," *Voice of the Negro*, July 1904, 280–82; Cora Gethers, "The Part of the Negro Woman in the Solution of the Race Problem," parts 1–3, *Palmetto Leader*, June 12, 19, and 26, 1926, 4; Sarah Pettey, "What Role is the Educated Negro Woman to play in the Uplifting of her Race?" in *Twentieth Century Negro Literature*, edited by Culp, 182–87; the series of articles by Southern and Northern black and white women in the *Independent*, September 8, 1902, 2221–28; January 30, 1904, 266–74; February 21, 1904, 438–40; March 17, 1904, 587–99; January 15, 1912, 197–200; and articles throughout the *National Notes*.

111. Guy-Sheftall, *Daughters of Sorrow*, 55–57, 62–73.

112. "Training Schools for Neglected Negro Girls," typescript, December 10, 1931, CIC Papers, reel 18, series 1:367

113. Lerner, ed., *Black Women in White America*, 183–85.

114. *National Notes*, March 1899; and Hine, "Rape and the Inner Lives," 292.

115. Lerner, ed., *Black Women in White America*, 130; and *Palmetto Leader*, June 9, 1928, 6.

116. A. W. Hunton, "Women's Clubs: State Conventions," *Crisis*, September 1911, 211; and *Palmetto Leader*, June 26, 1926, 1.

117. *Minutes of the National Association of Colored Women*, 1912, Records of the NACW, reel 1, pp. 9, 42. Although Dunbar was in the schedule, the minutes do not indicate that she actually spoke, see p. 38.

118. *Palmetto Leader*, March 3, 1928, 1.

119. Brown, "Womanist Consciousness, " 610–33; and White, *Too Heavy a Load*, 24, 35–39.

120. Jacqueline Rouse argues that Lugenia Burns Hope was a "race person" and focuses on the urgency of the fight against segregation rather than the struggle against sexism; see *Lugenia Burns Hope*, 9, 131. Cynthia Neverdon-Morton also emphasizes races work in "The Black Woman's Struggle for Equality in the South, 1895–1925," in *The Afro-American Woman*.

121. *Palmetto Leader*, June 12, 19, 26, 1926, 4.

122. "Senator Tillman to the Editor of the Maryland Suffrage News," *Crisis*, January 1915, 141.

123. Quoted in Simon, "The Appeal of Cole Blease," 82–83.

CONCLUSION. "THIS WONDERFUL DREAM NATION!": CONTESTING CONFEDERATE CULTURE

1. *Keystone*, June 1907, 3. For nationalism as the imagined community, see Anderson, *Imagined Communities*.

2. Tony Horwitz, "A Death for Dixie," *The New Yorker*, March 18, 1996, 70. The school mascot remained.

3. Tony Horwitz, "Rebel Voices: The Face of Extremism Wears Many Guises —Most of Them Ordinary," *Wall Street Journal*, April 28, 1995, 1.

Bibliography

MANUSCRIPT COLLECTIONS

American Jewish Archives, Hebrew Union College, Cincinnati, Ohio
    Happy Workers Club of Charleston Papers
    National Council of Jewish Women, Charleston Chapter
    National Council of Jewish Women, Columbia Chapter
Archives and Special Collections, Winthrop University, Rock Hill, S.C.
    Amelia Pride Book Club Papers
    Castalian Literary Club Papers
    Johnette Green Edwards Papers
    Keystone Club Papers
    Outlook Club Papers
    Over the Teacups Club Papers
    Palmetto Literary Club Papers
    Perihelion Club Papers
    South Carolina Federation of Women's Clubs Papers
Avery Research Center for African American History and Culture, Charleston, S.C.
    Albertha J. Murray Collection
    Book Lovers Club Collection
    Mamie Garvin Fields Collection
    Phyllis Wheatley Literary and Social Club Collection
    Rosalyn Saunders Periodical Collection
Caroliniana Library Archives, University of South Carolina, Columbia, S.C.
    Charleston Ladies Benevolent Society Papers
    Current Literature Club Papers
    Mary Bouknight Papers
    Mary McLeod Bethune Papers
    New Century Club Papers
    Poppenheim Family Papers
    United Daughters of the Confederacy, Black Oak, Marion City, and James Island Chapter Papers

Charleston Public Library, Charleston, S.C.
  Vertical Files Collection
Darlington County Historical Society, Darlington, S.C.
  Our Homestead Club Papers
  Over the Teacups Club Papers
Laurens County Library, Laurens, S.C.
  Wednesday Club Papers
Moorland-Spingarn Research Center, Howard University, Washington, D.C.
  Mary Church Terrell Papers
Perkins Library, Special Collections, Duke University, Durham, N.C.
  Mary and Louisa Poppenheim Papers
  United Daughters of the Confederacy Papers
General Federation of Women's Clubs, Archives, Washington, D.C.
  General Federation of Women's Clubs Papers
  South Carolina Historical Society, Charleston, S.C.
  Anita Pollitzer Papers
  Century Club Papers
  Charleston City Federation of Women's Clubs Papers
  Charleston Female Seminary, Alumnae Association file
  Civic Club Papers
  Confederate Home and College file
  Poppenheim Family Papers

MICROFILM COLLECTIONS

Charlotte Eugenia Hawkins Brown Papers, Arthur Schlesinger Library, Radcliffe College, Cambridge, Mass.
Commission of Interracial Cooperation Papers, Atlanta University, Atlanta, series 7
Records of the National Association of Colored Women's Clubs, 1895–1992, part 1, edited by Lillian Serece Williams, Bethesda, Md., University Publications of America

ORAL INTERVIEWS WITH THE AUTHOR

Mrs. Lavonia Atkinson, Columbia, S.C., February 29, 1996
Miss Charlie May Campbell, Spartanburg, S.C., March 2, 1996
Mrs. Emma Casselberry, Orangeburg, S.C., March 1, 1996
Mr. Robert Evans, Orangeburg, S.C., June 6, 1996
Dr. Barbara Jenkins, Orangeburg, S.C., August 24, 1994
Mrs. Louise Robinson, Orangeburg, S.C., October 12, 1995
Mrs. Geraldine Zimmerman, Orangeburg, S.C., October 9, 1995, and by telephone, May 30, 1996

PUBLISHED BOOKS, ARTICLES, AND THESES

Anderson, Benedict. *Imagined Communities: Reflections on the Origin and Spread of Nationalism.* New York: Verso, 1991.
Anderson, James D. *The Education of Blacks in the South, 1860–1935.* Chapel Hill: University of North Carolina Press, 1988.
Aptheker, Herbert, ed. *A Documentary History of the Negro People of the United States, 1910–1932.* Secaucus, N.J.: Citadel Press, 1973.
Avary, Myrta Lockett. *Dixie after the War: An Exposition of the Social Conditions Existing in the South, during the Twelve Years Succeeding the Fall of Richmond.* New York: Doubleday, Page, 1906. Reprint, New York: Negro University Press, 1969.
Bailey, Fred Arthur. "Free Speech and the 'Lost Cause' in Texas: A Study of Social Control in the New South," *Southwestern Historical Quarterly* 97 (January 1994): 452–77.
——— . "The Textbooks of the 'Lost Cause': Censorship and the Creation of Southern State Histories," *Georgia Historical Quarterly* 75 (Fall 1991): 507–33.
Baker, Paula. "The Domestication of Politics: Women and American Political Society, 1780–1920." *American Historical Review* 89 (June 1984): 620–47.
Berkeley, Kathleen C. "'Colored Ladies Also Contributed': Black Women's Activities from Benevolence to Social Welfare, 1866–1896." In *The Web of Southern Social Relations: Women, Family, and Education,* edited by Walter Fraser. Athens: University of Georgia Press, 1985, 181–203.
——— . "Elizabeth Avery Meriwether, 'An Advocate for Her Sex': Feminism and Conservatism in the Post–Civil War South." *Tennessee Historical Quarterly* 43 (1984): 390–407.
Bilanchone, Linda Powers, ed. *The Lives They Lived: A Look at Women in the History of Spartanburg.* Spartanburg: South Carolina Commission for the Humanities, 1981.
Blair, Karen. *The Clubwoman as Feminist: True Womanhood Redefined, 1868–1914.* New York: Holmes and Meier, 1980.
Bland, Sidney R. "Fighting the Odds: Militant Suffragists in South Carolina." *South Carolina Historical Magazine* 82 (1981): 32–43.
——— . "Mad Women of the Cause: The NWP in the South." *Furman Studies* 26 (1980): 82–91.
Blee, Kathleen M. "Women in the 1920s Ku Klux Klan Movement." *Feminist Studies* 17 (Spring 1991): 57–77.
——— . *Women of the Klan: Racism and Gender in the 1920s.* Berkeley: University of California Press, 1991.
Blight, David W. "'For Something beyond the Battlefield': Frederick Douglass and the Struggle for the Memory of the Civil War." *Journal of American History* 75 (March 1989): 1156–78.

———. *Race and Reunion: The Civil War in American Memory*. Cambridge, Mass.: Harvard University Press, 2001.

———. "W.E.B. Du Bois and the Struggle for American Historical Memory." In *History and Memory in African-American Culture*, edited by Genevieve Fabre. New York: Oxford University Press, 1994, 45–71.

———. "'What Will Peace among the Whites Bring?': Reunion and Race in Struggle over the Memory of the Civil War, 1875–1913." Conference, "Recasting African American Intellectual History," Bellagio, Italy, May 24–28, 1993.

Bodine, Idella. *South Carolina Women*. Orangeburg, S.C.: Sandlapper Publishing, 1078.

Bodnar, John. *Remaking America: Public Memory, Commemoration, and Patriotism in the 20th Century*. Princeton, N.J.: Princeton University Press, 1992.

The Book of Gold: Fiftieth Anniversary, South Carolina Federation of Colored Women's Clubs, 1909–1959. 1959.

Brooks, Elizabeth. "Religion, Politics, and Gender: The Leadership of Nannie Helen Burroughs." *Journal of Religious Thought* 44 (Winter/Spring 1988): 7–22.

Brown, Elsa Barkley. "Womanist Consciousness: Maggie Lena Walker and the Independent Order of Saint Luke." *Signs* 14 (1989): 610–33.

Brundage, W. Fitzhugh. "No Deed but Memory." In *Where These Memories Grow: History, Memory, and Southern Identity*, edited by W. Fitzhugh Brundage. Chapel Hill: University of North Carolina Press, 2000, 1–28.

———. "White Women and the Politics of Historical Memory in the New South, 1880–1920." In *Jumpin' Jim Crow: Southern Politics from Civil War to Civil Rights*, edited by Jane Dailey, Glenda Elizabeth Gilmore, and Bryant Simon. Princeton, N.J.: Princeton University Press, 2000, 115–39.

Buck, Paul. *The Road to Reunion, 1865–1900*. Boston: Little, Brown, 1937.

Burton, Orville Vernon. *In My Father's House Are Many Mansions: Family and Community in Edgefield, South Carolina*. Chapel Hill: University of North Carolina Press, 1985.

Burts, Robert Milton. *Richard Irvine Manning and the Progressive Movement in South Carolina*. Columbia: University of South Carolina Press, 1974.

Caldwell, Arthur Bunyan. *History of the American Negro, South Carolina Edition*. Atlanta: A. B. Caldwell, 1919.

Carlton, David. *Mill and Town in South Carolina, 1880–1920*. Baton Rouge: Louisiana State University Press, 1982.

Case, Sarah H. "The Historical Ideology of Mildred Lewis Rutherford: A Confederate Historian's New South Creed." *Journal of Southern History* 68 (August 2002): 599–628.

Cash, Wilbur. *The Mind of the South*. New York: Knopf, 1941.

Cell, John W. *The Highest Stage of White Supremacy: The Origins of Segregation in South Africa and the American South*. Cambridge, England: Cambridge University Press, 1982.

Clark, Septima Poinsette. *Echo in My Soul*. New York: E. P. Dutton, 1962.

Clinton, Catherine. *The Plantation Mistress: Woman's World in the Old South.* New York: Pantheon Books, 1982.
Cohen, William. *At Freedom's Edge: Black Mobility and the Southern White Quest for Racial Control, 1861–1951.* Baton Rouge: Louisiana State University Press, 1991.
Collier, Margaret (Mrs. Bryan Wells Collier). *Biographies of Representative Women of the South.* College Park [?], Ga.: Published by the author, 1920.
Conklin, Viola A. *American Political History to the Death of Lincoln.* New York: Henry Holt, 1901.
Connelly, Thomas L., and Barbara L. Bellows. *God and General Longstreet: The Lost Cause and the Southern Mind.* Baton Rouge: Louisiana State University Press, 1982.
Cooley, Rossa B. *Homes of the Freed.* New York: New Republic, 1926. Reprint, New York: Negro University Press, 1970.
Cox, Karen L. *Dixie's Daughters: The United Daughters of the Confederacy and the Preservation of Confederate Culture.* Gainesville: University Press of Florida, 2003.
Croly, Jennie June. *The History of the Woman's Club Movement in America.* New York: Henry Allen, 1897.
Culp, Daniel Wallace. *Twentieth-Century Negro Literature.* Naperville, Ill.: J. L. Nichols, 1902. Reprint, New York: Arno Press, 1969.
Daniel, F. E. *Recollections of a Rebel Surgeon, and Other Sketches: Or, in the Doctor's Sappy Days.* Chicago: Clinic Publishing, 1901.
Datel, Robin. "Southern Regionalism and Historic Preservation in Charleston, South Carolina, 1920–1940." *Journal of the History of Geography* 16 (April 1990): 197–215.
Davidson, Elizabeth. *Child Labor Legislation in the Southern Textile States.* Chapel Hill: University of North Carolina Press, 1939.
Davies, Wallace. *Patriotism on Parade: The Story of Veterans' and Hereditary Organizations in America, 1783–1900.* Cambridge, Mass.: Harvard University Press, 1955.
Davis, Stephen. "Empty Eyes, Marble Hand: The Confederate Monument and the South." *Journal of Popular Culture* 16 (Winter 1982): 2–21.
Davis, Thadious M. "Expanding the Limits: The Intersection of Race and Region." *Southern Literary Journal* 20 (Spring 1988): 3–11.
de Jong, Greta. *A Different Day: African American Struggles for Justice in Rural Louisiana, 1900–1970.* Chapel Hill: University of North Carolina Press, 2002.
Dean, Pamela. "Learning to Be New Women: Campus Culture at the North Carolina Normal and Industrial College." *North Carolina Historical Review* 68 (1991): 286–306.
Desan, Suzanne. "Crowds, Community and Ritual in the Work of E. P. Thompson and Natalie Davis." In *The New Cultural History*, edited by Lynn Hunt. Berkeley: University of California Press, 1989, 47–71.

Dickson, Lynda F. "Toward a Broader Angle of Vision in Uncovering Women's History: Black Women's Clubs Revisited." Reprinted in *Black Women in United States History*, edited by Darlene Clark Hine. Brooklyn, N.Y.: Carlson, 1990.

Dictionary of American Biography. New York: Scribner's, 1963.

Doyle, Don. *New Men, New Cities, New South: Atlanta, Nashville, Charleston, Mobile, 1860–1910*. Chapel Hill: University of North Carolina Press, 1990.

Drago, Edmund L. *Initiative, Paternalism, and Race Relations: Charleston's Avery Normal Institute*. Athens: University of Georgia Press, 1990.

Du Bois, W.E.B. *Efforts for Social Betterment among Negro Americans*. Atlanta University Publications, no. 14, Atlanta: Atlanta University Press, 1909.

Edwards, Laura. *Scarlett Doesn't Live Here Anymore: Southern Women in the Civil War Era*. Urbana: University of Illinois Press, 2000.

Eggleston, George Cary. *A Carolina Cavalier: A Romance of the American Revolution*. Boston: Lothrop, 1901.

Emerson, Bettie A. C. *Historic Southern Monuments: Representative Memorials of the Heroic Dead of the Southern Confederacy*. New York: Neale, 1911.

Enstam, Elizabeth York. *Women and the Creation of Urban Life, Dallas, Texas, 1843–1920*. College Station: Texas A&M University Press, 1998.

Escott, Paul D. "The Special Place of History." In *The South for New Southerners*, edited by Paul D. Escott. Chapel Hill: University of North Carolina Press, 1991.

Everett, Robert Burke. "Race Relations in South Carolina, 1900–1932." Ph.D. diss., University of Georgia, 1969.

Fabre, Genevieve. "African-American Commemorative Celebrations in the Nineteenth Century." In *History and Memory in African-American Culture*, edited by Genevieve Fabre. New York: Oxford University Press, 1994, 72–91.

Faust, Drew Gilpin. *Mothers of Invention: Women of the Slaveholding South in the American Civil War*. Chapel Hill: University of North Carolina Press, 1996.

Fields, Barbara J. "Ideology and Race in American History." In *Region, Race and Reconstruction: Essays in Honor of C. Vann Woodward*, edited by J. Morgan Kousser. New York: Oxford University Press, 1982.

Fields, Karen. "What One Cannot Remember Mistakenly." In *History and Memory in African-American Culture*, edited by Genevieve Fabre. New York: Oxford University Press, 1994, 150–63.

Fields, Mamie Garvin. *Lemon Swamp and Other Places: A Carolina Memoir*. New York: The Free Press, 1983.

Fifteenth Census of the United States: 1930, Population, vol. 3, part 2. Washington, D.C.: Government Printing Office, 1932.

Fifteenth Census of the United States: 1930, Population, vol. 4, Occupations, by State. Washington, D.C.: Government Printing Office, 1933.

Flanagan, Maureen. "Gender and Urban Political Reform: The City Club and the Woman's City Club of Chicago in the Progressive Era." *American Historical Review* 95 (1990): 1032–50.

Forderhase, Nancy. "Limited Only by Earth and Sky: The Louisville Woman's Club and Progressive Reform, 1900–1910." *The Filson Club Quarterly* 59 (1985): 327–43.

Fortieth Anniversary Booklet of the South Carolina Federation of Colored Women's Clubs, 1909–1949. N.p., 1949.

Foster, Gaines. *Ghosts of the Confederacy: Defeat, the Lost Cause, and the Emergence of the New South*. New York: Oxford University Press, 1987.

Fox-Genovese, Elizabeth. *Within the Plantation Household: Black and White Women in the Old South*. Chapel Hill: University of North Carolina Press, 1988.

Frankel, Noralee, and Nancy S. Dye. *Gender, Class, Race, and Reform in the Progressive Era*. Lexington: University Press of Kentucky, 1991.

Franklin, Jimmie. "Black Southerners, Shared Experience, and Place: A Reflection." *Journal of Southern History* 60 (February 1994): 3–18.

Fraser, Walter. *Charleston! Charleston! The History of a Southern City*. Columbia: University of South Carolina Press, 1989.

Fredrickson, George M. *The Arrogance of Race: Historical Perspectives on Slavery, Racism, and Social Inequality*. Middletown, Conn.: Wesleyan University Press, 1988

Frederickson, Mary. "'Each One Is Dependent on the Other': Southern Churchwomen, Racial Reform, and the Process of Transformation, 1880–1940." In *Visible Women: New Essays on American Activism*, edited by Nancy Hewitt and Suzanne Lebsock. Urbana: University of Illinois, 1993, 296–324.

Freedman, Estelle. "Separatism as Strategy: Female Institution Building and American Feminism, 1870–1930." *Feminist Studies* 5 (1979): 512–29.

Friedman, Jean. *The Enclosed Garden: Women and Community in the Evangelical South, 1830–1900*. Chapel Hill: University of North Carolina Press, 1985.

Gaines, Kevin. *Uplifting the Race: Black Leadership, Politics, and Culture in the Twentieth Century*. Chapel Hill: University of North Carolina Press, 1996.

Gaston, Paul. *The New South Creed: A Study in Southern Mythmaking*. New York: Alfred A. Knopf, 1970.

Gatewood, Willard. *Aristocrats of Color: the Black Elite, 1880–1920*. Bloomington: Indiana University Press, 1990.

Gere, Anne Ruggles. *Intimate Practices: Literacy and Cultural Work in U.S. Women's Clubs, 1880–1920*. Urbana: University of Illinois Press, 1997.

Gere, Anne Ruggles, and Sarah R. Robbins. "Gendered Literacy in Black and White: Turn-of-the-Century African-American and European-American Club Women's Printed Texts." *Signs* 21 (1996): 643–78.

Giddings, Paula. *When and Where I Enter: The Impact of Black Women on Race and Sex in America*. New York: William Morrow, 1984.

Gilmore, Glenda Elizabeth. "Gender and Jim Crow: Sarah Dudley Pettey's Vision of the New South." *North Carolina Historical Review* 68 (1991): 261–85.

———. *Gender and Jim Crow: Women and the Politics of White Supremacy in North Carolina, 1896–1920*. Chapel Hill: University of North Carolina Press, 1996.

Giselle Roberts. *The Confederate Belle*. Columbia: University of Missouri Press, 2003.
Glassberg, David. *American Historical Pageantry: The Uses of Tradition in the Early Twentieth Century*. Chapel Hill: University of North Carolina Press, 1990.
Goldfield, David. *Still Fighting the Civil War: The American South and Southern History*. Baton Rouge: Louisiana State University Press, 2002.
Goodstein, Anita. "A Rare Alliance: African American and White Women in the Tennessee Elections of 1919 and 1920." *Journal of American History* 64 (1998): 219–46.
Gordon, Asa H. *Sketches of Negro Life and History in South Carolina*. N.p.: W. B. Conkey, 1929. Reprint, Columbia: University of South Carolina Press, 1971.
Gordon, Linda. "Black and White Visions of Welfare: Women's Welfare Activism, 1890–1945." *Journal of American History* 78 (1991): 559–90.
———, ed. *Women, the State, and Welfare*. Madison: University of Wisconsin Press, 1990.
Gordon, Lynn D. *Gender and Higher Education in the Progressive Era, 1890–1920*. New Haven, Conn.: Yale University Press, 1990.
Grantham, Dewey. *Southern Progressivism: The Reconciliation of Progress and Tradition*. Knoxville: University of Tennessee Press, 1983.
Gray, Dorothy Ann. "The Tangled Skein of Romanticism and Violence in the Old South: Southern Response to Abolitionism and Feminism, 1830–1861." Ph.D. diss., University of North Carolina, 1975.
Green, Elna C. *Southern Strategies: Southern Women and the Woman Suffrage Question*. Chapel Hill: University of North Carolina Press, 1997.
———. "Those Opposed: The Antisuffragists in North Carolina, 1900–1920." *North Carolina Historical Review* 67 (1990): 315–33.
Greenwood, Janette Thomas. *Bittersweet Legacy: The Black and White "Better Classes" in Charlotte, 1850–1910*. Chapel Hill: University of North Carolina Press, 1994.
Gulley, H. E. "Women and the Lost Cause: Preserving a Confederate Identity in the American Deep South." *Journal of Historical Geography* 19 (April 1993): 125–41.
Guy-Sheftall, Beverly. *Daughters of Sorrow: Attitudes Toward Black Women, 1880–1920*. Brooklyn, N.Y.: Carlson, 1990.
Hale, Grace Elizabeth. *Making Whiteness: The Culture of Segregation in the South, 1890–1940*. New York: Pantheon Books, 1998.
Hall, Jacquelyn Dowd. "The Mind That Burns in Each Body: Women, Woman Rape, and Racial Violence." In *Powers of Desire: The Politics of Sexuality*, edited by Ann Snitow and Christine Stansell. New York: Monthly Review Press, 1983, 328–49.
———. "Partial Truths: Writing Southern Women's History." In *Southern Women:*

Histories and Identities, edited by Virginia Bernhard. Columbia: University of Missouri Press, 1992, 11–29.

———. *Revolt Against Chivalry: Jesse Daniel Ames and the Women's Campaign Against Lynching.* New York: Columbia University Press, 1979.

———. "'You Must Remember This': Autobiography as Social Critique." *Journal of American History* 85 (September 1998): 439–65.

Hamilton, Tullia. "The History of the National Association of Colored Women." Ph.D. diss., Emory University, 1978.

Harlan, Louis R. *Separate and Unequal: Public School Campaigns and Racism in the Southern Seaboard States, 1901–1915.* Chapel Hill: University of North Carolina Press, 1958.

Hemmingway, Theodore. "Beneath the Yolk of Bondage: A History of Black Folk in South Carolina, 1900–1940." Ph.D. diss., University of South Carolina, 1976.

Hendricks, Wanda. *Gender, Race, and Politics in the Midwest: Black Club Women in Illinois.* Bloomington: Indiana University Press, 1998.

Hennig, Helen Kohn. *August Kohn: Versatile South Carolinian.* Columbia, S.C.: Vogue Press, 1949.

Hewitt, Nancy A. *Southern Discomfort: Women's Activism in Tampa, Florida, 1880s–1920s.* Urbana: University of Illinois Press, 2001.

Higginbotham, Evelyn Brooks. "African-American Women's History and the Metalanguage of Race." *Signs* 17 (1992): 151–74.

———. *Righteous Discontent: The Women's Movement in the Black Baptist Church, 1880–1920.* Cambridge, Mass.: Harvard University Press, 1993.

Hine, Darlene Clark, ed. *Black Women in America: An Historical Encyclopedia.* Vols. 1–2. Bloomington: University of Indiana Press, 1993.

———. "Rape and the Inner Lives of Black Women in the Middle West: Preliminary Thoughts on the Culture of Dissemblance." *Signs* 14 (Summer 1989): 912–20.

———. "'We Specialize in the Wholly Impossible': The Philanthropic Work of Black Women." In *Lady Bountiful Revisited: Women, Philanthropy, and Power,* edited by Kathleen D. McCarthy. New Brunswick, N.J.: Rutgers University Press, 1990.

Hine, Darlene Clark, and Anne Christie Farnham. "Black Women's Culture of Resistance and the Right to Vote." In *Women of the American South: A Multicultural Reader,* edited by Christie Anne Farnham. New York: New York University Press, 1997, 204–19.

Hobsbawm, Eric, ed. *The Invention of Tradition.* Cambridge, England: Cambridge University Press, 1983.

Holt, Thomas C. "Marking: Race, Race-making, and the Writing of History." *American Historical Review* 100 (February 1995): 1–20.

Hornsby, Benjamin F. *South Carolina Women: A Timeline.* Columbia: South Carolina Department of Archives, 1995.

Hoyt, Eleanor Hinton. "International Council of Women of the Darker Races: Historical Notes." *Sage* 3 (Fall 1986): 54–55.

Hudson, Janet. "From Constitution to Constitution, 1865–1895: South Carolina's Unique Stance on Divorce." *South Carolina Historical Magazine* 98 (January 1997): 75–96.

Hunt, Lynn. "Introduction: History, Culture, and Text." In *The New Cultural History*. Berkeley: University of California Press, 1989, 1–22.

Hunter, Jane Edna. *A Nickel and a Prayer*. Cleveland: Elli Kani, 1940.

Janiewski, Dolores. *Sisterhood Denied: Race, Gender, and Class in a New South Community*. Philadelphia: Temple University Press, 1986.

Johnson, Joan Marie. "'How Would I Live without Loulie?': Mary and Louisa Poppenheim, Activist Sisters in Turn-of-the-Century South Carolina." *Journal of Family History* 28 (October 2003): 561–77.

———. "The Shape of the Movement to Come: Women, Religion, and the Interracial Movement in 1920s South Carolina." In *"Warm Ashes": Issues in Southern History at the Dawn of the Twenty-First Century*. Columbia: University of South Carolina Press, 2003.

———. *Southern Women at Vassar: The Poppenheim Family Letters, 1882–1916*. Columbia: University of South Carolina Press, 2002.

———. "'This Wonderful Dream Nation!': Black and White South Carolina Women, and the Creation of the New South, 1898–1930." Ph.D. diss., University of California at Los Angeles, 1997.

Jones, Jacqueline. *Labor of Love, Labor of Sorrow: Black Women, Work, and the Family from Slavery to the Present*. New York: Basic Books, 1985.

Josey, E. J. *Handbook of Black Librarianship*. Littleton, Colo.: Libraries Unlimited, 1977.

Judson, Sarah Mercer. "Building the New South City: African-American and White Clubwomen in Atlanta, 1895–1930." Ph.D diss., New York University, 1997.

Kammen, Michael. *Mystic Chords of Memory: The Transformation of Tradition in American Culture*. New York: Alfred A. Knopf, 1991.

Kelley, Robin D. G. *Race Rebels: Culture, Politics, and the Black Working Class*. New York: The Free Press, 1994.

Kendrick, Ruby M. "'They Also Serve': The National Association of Colored Women, Inc." *Negro History Bulletin* 17 (1954): 171–75.

Kirby, Jack Temple. *Darkness at the Dawning: Race and Reform in the Progressive South*. Philadelphia: J. B. Lippincott, 1972.

Knupfer, Anne Meis. "'Toward a Tenderer Humanity and a Nobler Womanhood': African-American Women's Clubs in Chicago, 1890–1920." *Journal of Women's History* 7 (Fall 1995): 58–75.

Koonz, Claudia. *Mothers in the Fatherland: Women, the Family, and Nazi Politics*. New York: St. Martin's, 1987.

Kousser, J. Morgan. "Progressivism—For Middle Class Whites Only: North Carolina Education, 1880–1910." *Journal of Southern History* 46 (1980): 169–94.

Lasch-Quinn, Elisabeth. *Black Neighbors: Race and the Limits of Reform in the American Settlement House Movement, 1890–1945*. Chapel Hill: University of North Carolina Press, 1993.

Le Coq, Floss. "A Women's Clubs Legacy." *Sandlapper Magazine*, November 1979, 66–69.

Lebsock, Suzanne. *Free Women of Petersburg: Status and Culture in a Southern Town, 1784–1860*. New York: Norton, 1984.

Leloudis, James L. "School Reform in the New South: Women's Association for the Betterment of Public School Houses in North Carolina, 1902–1919." *Journal of American History* 49 (1983): 886–909.

Leonard, John, ed. *Woman's Who's Who of America, 1914–1915*. New York: American Commonwealth, 1914.

Lerner, Gerda, ed. *Black Women in White America: A Documentary History*. New York: Vintage Books, 1973.

———. "Early Community Work of Black Club Women." *Journal of Negro History* 59 (1974): 158–67.

Lindgren, James M. *Preserving the Old Dominion: Historic Preservation and Virginia Traditionalism*. Charlottesville: University of Virginia Press, 1993.

Link, William A. *The Paradox of Southern Progressivism, 1880–1930*. Chapel Hill: University of North Carolina Press, 1992.

Logan, Mary S. *The Part Taken by Women in American History*. Wilmington, Del.: Perry-Nalle, 1912. Reprint, New York: Arno Press, 1972.

Lowenthal, David. *The Past Is a Foreign Country*. Cambridge, England: Cambridge University Press, 1985.

Mack, Kibibi Voloria C. *Parlor Ladies and Ebony Drudges: African American Women, Class, and Work in a South Carolina Community*. Knoxville: University of Tennessee Press, 1999.

MacLean, Nancy. *Behind the Mask of Chivalry: The Making of the Second Ku Klux Klan*. New York: Oxford University Press, 1994.

———. "White Women and Klan Violence in the 1920s: Agency, Complicity and the Politics of Women's History." *Gender & History* 3 (Autumn 1991): 285–303.

Majors, M. A. *Noted Negro Women: Their Triumphs and Activities*. Chicago: Donohue Henneberry, 1893. Reprint, Freeport, N.Y.: Books for Libraries Press, 1971.

Mays, Benjamin E. *Born to Rebel: An Autobiography*. Athens: University of Georgia Press, 1971.

McArthur, Judith N. *Creating the New Woman: The Rise of Southern Women's Progressive Culture in Texas, 1893–1918*. Urbana: University of Illinois Press, 1998.

McCandless, Amy Thompson. "Anita Pollitzer: South Carolina Advocate for Equal Rights." *The Proceedings of the South Carolina Historical Society* (2000): 1–10.

McCluskey, Andrea Thomas. "'We Specialize in the Wholly Impossible': Black Women School Founders and Their Mission." *Signs* 22 (Winter 1997): 401–26.
Mennel, Robert M. *Thorns and Thistles: Juvenile Delinquents in the United States, 1825–1940*. Hanover, N.H.: University Press of New England, 1973.
Montgomery, Rebecca. "Lost Cause Mythology in New South Reform: Gender, Class, Race, and the Politics of Patriotic Citizenship." In *Negotiating Boundaries of Southern Womanhood: Dealing with the Powers That Be*, edited by Janet L. Coryell et al. Columbia: University of Missouri Press, 2000, 174–98.
Moore, John Hammond. *Columbia and Richland County: A South Carolina Community, 1740–1990*. Columbia: University of South Carolina Press, 1993.
Morrison, Toni. *Playing in the Dark: Whiteness and the Literary Imagination*. New York: Vintage Books, 1992.
Muncy, Robyn. *Creating a Female Dominion in American Reform, 1890–1935*. New York: Oxford University Press, 1991.
National Cyclopedia of American Biography. New York: J. T. White, 1930.
Neverdon-Morton, Cynthia. *Afro-American Women of the South and the Advancement of the Race, 1895–1925*. Knoxville: University of Tennessee Press, 1989.
Northington, Etta Belle. *A History of the Virginia Federation of Women's Clubs, 1907–1957*. Richmond: Virginia Federation of Women's Clubs, 1957.
Odem, Mary E. *Delinquent Daughters: Protecting and Policing Adolescent Female Sexuality in the United States, 1885–1920*. Chapel Hill: University of North Carolina Press, 1995.
Osterweis, Rollin, G. *The Myth of the Lost Cause, 1865–1900*. Hamden, Conn.: Archon Books, 1973.
Page, Thomas Nelson. *Negro: The Southerner's Problem*. New York: Scribner's, 1904.
Parrott, Angie. "'Love Makes Memory Eternal': The United Daughters of the Confederacy in Richmond, Virginia, 1897–1920." In *The Edge of the South: Life in Nineteenth Century Virginia*, edited by Edward L. Ayers and John C. Willis. Charlottesville: University of Virginia Press, 1991, 219–38.
Perkins, Linda M. "The Impact of the "Cult of True Womanhood' on the Education of Black Women." *Journal of Social Issues* 39 (1983): 17–28.
Peterkin, Julia. *Black April*. Indianapolis: Bobbs-Merrill, 1927.
Plum, Dorothy A. *The Magnificent Enterprise: A Chronicle of Vassar College*. Poughkeepsie, N.Y.: N.p., 1961.
Poppenheim, Louisa. "Woman's Work in the South." In *The South in the Building of the Nation*, vol. 10. Richmond: Southern History Publication Society, 1909.
Poppenheim, Mary Bouknight. "Bethany Hospital and Soldiers' Aid Association, Edgefield County, S.C.." In *South Carolina Women in the Confederacy*. Columbia: The State, 1905, 67–68.
———. "Personal Experiences." In *Women of the South in War Times*, edited by Matthew Page Andrews. Baltimore: Norman, Remington, 1920, 254–61.

Poppenheim, Mary B., et al. *A History of the United Daughters of the Confederacy.* Richmond: Garrett and Massie, 1938.
Potter, David. "The Historian's Use of Nationalism and Vice Versa." In *The South and Sectional Conflict.* Baton Rouge: Louisiana State University Press, 1968.
Powers, Bernard E. *Black Charlestonians: A Social History, 1820–1885.* Fayetteville: University of Arkansas Press, 1994.
Rabinowitz, Howard. *Race Relations in the Urban South, 1865–1885.* Urbana: University of Illinois Press, 1980.
Rable, George C. *Civil Wars: Women and the Crisis of Southern Nationalism.* Urbana: University of Illinois Press, 1989.
Reed, John Shelton. "The South: What Is It? Where Is It?" In *The South for New Southerners*, edited by Paul D. Escott. Chapel Hill: University of North Carolina Press, 1991.
Reid, John B. "'A Career to Build, a People to Serve, a Purpose to Accomplish': Race, Class, Gender, and Detroit's First Black Women Teachers, 1865–1916." In *"We Specialize in the Wholly Impossible": A Reader in Black Women's History*, edited by Darlene Clark Hine. Brooklyn, N.Y.: Carlson, 1995, 303–20.
Roberts, Giselle. *The Confederate Belle.* Columbia: University of Missouri Press, 2003.
Rodgers, Daniel T. "In Search of Progressivism." *Reviews in American History* 10 (1982): 113–32.
Roediger, David. *The Wages of Whiteness: Race and the Making of the American Working Class.* London: Verso, 1991.
Roth, Darlene Rebecca. *Matronage: Patterns in Women's Organizations, Atlanta, Georgia, 1890–1940.* Brooklyn, N.Y.: Carlson, 1994.
Rouse, Jacqueline Anne. *Lugenia Burns Hope: Black Southern Reformer.* Athens: University of Georgia Press, 1989.
Ruffins, Faith Davis. "'Lifting as We Climb': Black Women and the Preservation of African American History and Culture." *Gender and History* 6 (November 1994): 376–96.
Salem, Dorothy. *To Better Our World: Black Women in Organized Reform, 1890–1920.* Brooklyn, N.Y.: Carlson, 1990.
Sandage, Scott. "A Marble House Divided: The Lincoln Memorial, the Civil Rights Movement, and the Politics of Memory, 1939–1963." *Journal of American History* 80 (June 1993): 135–67.
Savage, Kirk. "The Politics of Memory: Black Emancipation and the Civil War Monument." In *Commemorations: The Politics of National Identity*, edited by John Gillis. Princeton, N.J.: Princeton University Press, 1994, 127–49.
Schwalm, Leslie. *A Hard Fight for We: Women's Transition from Slavery to Freedom in South Carolina.* Urbana: University of Illinois Press, 1997.
Scott, Anne Firor. *Making the Invisible Woman Visible.* Urbana: University of Illinois Press, 1984.

———. "Most Invisible of All: Black Women's Voluntary Organizations." *Journal of Southern History* 56 (February 1990): 3–22.

———. *Natural Allies: Women's Associations in American History*. Urbana: University of Illinois Press, 1991.

———. *The Southern Lady, From Pedestal to Politics, 1830–1930*. Chicago: University of Chicago Press, 1970.

Shaw, Stephanie. "Black Club Women and the Creation of the National Association of Colored Women." *Journal of Women's History* 3 (1991): 10–25.

———. *What a Woman Ought to Be and Do: Black Professional Women Workers During the Jim Crow Era*. Chicago: University of Chicago Press, 1996.

Silber, Nina. *The Romance of Reunion: Northerners and the South, 1865–1900*. Chapel Hill: University of North Carolina Press, 1993.

Simkins, Francis B. "Race Legislation in South Carolina Since 1865." *South Atlantic Quarterly* 20 (April 1921): 170–71.

———. *The Women of the Confederacy*. Richmond: Garrett and Massie, 1936.

Simms, Lois Averetta. *Profiles of African American Females in the Low Country of South Carolina*. Charleston, S.C.: Avery Research Center for African American History and Culture, 1992.

Simon, Bryant. "The Appeal of Cole Blease of South Carolina: Race, Class and Sex in the New South." *Journal of Southern History* 62 (February 1996): 57–86.

———. *A Fabric of Defeat: The Politics of South Carolina Millhands, 1910–1948*. Chapel Hill: University of North Carolina Press, 1998.

Sims, Anastasia. "Feminism and Femininity in the New South: White Women's Organization in North Carolina, 1883–1930." Ph.D. diss., University of North Carolina, 1985.

———. *The Power of Femininity in the New South: Women's Organizations and Politics in North Carolina, 1880–1930*. Columbia: University of South Carolina Press, 1997.

Sklar, Kathryn Kish. "Hull House in the 1890's: A Community of Women Reformers." *Signs* 10 (1985): 658–77.

Smith, Jessie Carney, ed. *Notable Black American Women*. New York: Gale Research, 1996.

The South in the Building of the Nation. Richmond: South Historical Publication Society, 1909.

Stevenson, Brenda. "Distress and Discord in Virginia Slave Families." In *In Joy and in Sorrow: Women, Family, and Marriage in the Victorian South, 1830–1900*, edited by Carol Bleser. New York: Oxford University Press, 1991.

Stine, Jean C., ed. *Contemporary Literary Criticism*. Detroit: Gale Research, 1985.

Storrs, Landon R. Y. "Gender and Sectionalism in New Deal Politics: Southern White Women's Campaign for Labor Reform." In *Searching for Their Places: Women in the South Across Four Centuries*, edited by Thomas H. Appleton, Jr., and Angela Boswell. Columbia: University of Missouri Press, 2003, 218–37.

Stowe, Steven M. *Intimacy and Power in the Old South: Ritual in the Lives of the Planters*. Baltimore: Johns Hopkins University Press, 1987.
Taylor, Antoinette Elizabeth. "South Carolina and the Enfranchisement of Women: The Early Years." *South Carolina Historical Society Magazine* 77 (April 1976): 115–26.
Taylor, William R. *Cavalier and Yankee: The Old South and the American National Character*. New York: George Braziller, 1961.
Terborg-Penn, Rosalyn. *African American Women in the Struggle for the Vote, 1850–1920*. Bloomington: Indiana University Press, 1998.
———. "Discrimination Against Afro-American Women in the Woman's Movement, 1830–1920." In *The Afro-American Woman: Struggles and Images*, edited by Sharon Harley and Rosalyn Terborg-Penn. Port Washington, N.Y.: Kennicat Press, 1978, 17–27.
Tetzlaff, Monica Maria. *Cultivating a New South: Abbie Holmes Christensen and the Politics of Race and Gender, 1852–1938*. Columbia: University of South Carolina Press, 2002.
Thelen, David. "Memory and American History." *Journal of American History* 75 (March 1989): 1117–29.
Thirteenth Census of the United States Taken in the Year 1910, vol. 4, Population, 1910, Occupational Statistics. Washington, D.C.: Government Printing Office, 1914.
Thomas, Mary Martha. "The Ideology of the Alabama Woman Suffrage Movement, 1890–1920." In *Southern Women: Histories and Identities*, edited by Virginia Bernhard. Columbia: University of Missouri Press, 1992, 108–28.
———. *The New Woman in Alabama: Social Reforms and Suffrage, 1890–1920*. Tuscaloosa: University of Alabama Press, 1992.
Tindall, George Brown. *South Carolina Negroes, 1877–1900*. Columbia: University of South Carolina Press, 1952.
Turner, Elizabeth Hayes. "'White-Gloved Ladies' and 'New Women' in the Texas Woman Suffrage Movement." In *Southern Women: Histories and Identities*, edited by Virginia Bernhard. Columbia: University of Missouri Press, 1992, 129–56.
———. *Women, Culture, and Community: Religion and Reform in Galveston, 1880–1920*. New York: Oxford University Press, 1997.
Ulmer, Barbara. "Virginia Durant Young: New South Suffragist." M.A. thesis, University of South Carolina, 1979.
Utsey, Walker Scott, ed. *Who's Who in South Carolina, 1934–1935*. Columbia: Current Historical Association, 1935.
Van Zelm, Antoinette. "Virginia Women as Public Citizens: Emancipation Days Celebrations and Lost Cause Commemorations, 1863–1890." In *Negotiating Boundaries of Southern Womanhood: Dealing with the Powers That Be*. Columbia: University of Missouri Press, 2000, 71–88.

Varon, Elizabeth R. *We Mean to Be Counted: White Women and Politics in Antebellum Virginia*. Chapel Hill: University of North Carolina Press, 1998.
Walker, Lillie S. "Black Librarians in South Carolina." In *The Black Librarian in the Southeast: Reminiscences, Activities, Challenges*. Durham: North Carolina Central University Press, 1980.
Wallace, David Duncan. *The History of South Carolina*, New York: American Historical Society, 1934.
―――. *South Carolina: A Short History, 1520–1948*. Columbia: University of South Carolina, 1961.
Washington, Margaret. "Club Work Among Negro Women." In *New Progress of a Race*, edited by J. W. Gibson. Atlanta: J. L. Nicholson, 1920.
Wedell, Marsha. *Elite Women and the Reform Impulse in Memphis, 1875–1915*. Knoxville: University of Tennessee Press, 1991.
Weiner, Marli F. *Mistresses and Slaves: Plantation Women in South Carolina, 1830–1880*. Urbana: University of Illinois Press, 1998.
Wells, Ida B. *Crusade for Justice: The Autobiography of Ida B. Wells*, edited by Alfreda M. Duster. Chicago: University of Chicago Press, 1972.
Wheeler, Marjorie Spruill. *New Women in the New South, The Leaders of the Woman Suffrage Movement in the Southern States*. New York: Oxford University Press, 1993.
White, Deborah Gray. "The Cost of Club Work, the Price of Black Feminism." In *Visible Women: New Essays on American Activism*, edited by Nancy Hewitt and Suzanne Lebsock. Urbana: University of Illinois, 1993, 247–69.
―――. *Too Heavy a Load: Black Women in Defense of Themselves*. New York: W. W. Norton, 1999.
Whites, Lee Ann. *The Civil War as a Crisis in Gender, Augusta, Georgia, 1860–1890*. Athens: University of Georgia Press, 1995.
―――. "The De Graffenried Controversy: Class, Race, and Gender in the New South." *Journal of Southern History* 54 (1988): 449–78.
Widener, Ralph. *Confederate Monuments: Enduring Symbols of the South and the War Between the States*. Washington, D.C.: Published by the author, 1982.
Wiebe, Robert. *The Search for Order, 1877–1920*. New York: Hill and Wang, 1967.
Williams, Fannie Barrier. "Club Movement Among Negro Women." In *Progress of a Race*, edited by J. W. Gibson. Atlanta: J. L. Nicholson, 1902, 197–231.
Williamson, Joel. *The Crucible of Race: Black and White Relations in the American South Since Emancipation*. New York: Oxford University Press, 1984.
Wilson, Charles Reagan. *Baptized in Blood: Religion of the Lost Cause, 1865–1920*. Athens: University of Georgia Press, 1980.
Wolcott, Victoria W. "'Bible, Bath, and Broom': Nannie Helen Burrough's National Training School and African-American Racial Uplift." *Journal of Women's History* 9 (Spring 1997): 88–110.
―――. *Remaking Respectability: African American Women in Interwar Detroit*. Chapel Hill: University of North Carolina Press, 2001.

Wood, Mary I. *The History of the General Federation of Woman's Clubs for the First Twenty-two Years of Its Organization*. New York: General Federation of Women's Clubs, 1912.
Woodward, C. Vann. *The Burden of Southern History*. Rev. ed. Baton Rouge: Louisiana State University Press, 1970.
———. *Origins of the New South, 1877–1913*. Baton Rouge: Louisiana State University Press, 1951.
———. *The Strange Career of Jim Crow*. 3rd ed. New York: Oxford University Press, 1974.
Wyatt-Brown, Bertram. *Southern Honor: Ethics and Behavior in the Old South*. New York: Oxford University Press, 1982.

Index

Adams, Dempie Anderson, 154
African Americans and Southern identity, 90–91, 96–104, 197–201
Amelia Pride Club, Rock Hill, 31–33, 37, 41, 43–44, 66, 68, 78, 112
American Political History, 42
Ames, Jessie Daniel, 80
Anderson, Marian, 29, 53, 169
Andrews, Anna, 172, 199
Avery Institute, Charleston, 14–16, 22, 46, 52–53

Barrett, Janie Porter, 56, 72, 92, 194
Bethune, Mary McLeod, 51, 54, 72–74, 92–96, 98–101, 103, 169, 195
Birnie, Charles, 13
Birnie, Richard, 13
Blease, Coleman, 143–44, 160, 169–70, 191, 200
Book Lovers Club, Charleston, 29, 171
Booker T. Washington Literary and Social Club, Georgetown, 47
Boykin, Cora S., 96
Boyle, Sarah Patton, 60
Brawley, Benjamin, 47
Brawley Book Club, Columbia, 47
Brooks, Mrs. R. T., 83, 183
Brown, Charlotte Hawkins, 54, 72, 82, 92–95, 98, 100, 181, 198
Brown, Hallie Quinn, 95
Burney, Minnie Melton, 11, 35, 213n34
Burroughs, Nannie Helen, 93–94
Butler, Susie Dart, 9, 51–53, 77, 96

Cain, Isabelle, 78, 164, 184, 186–88, 192
Calhoun, John C., 33, 37
Carey, Alice, 114, 170
Carter, Elizabeth, 94
Castalian Club, Rock Hill, 62, 145–46, 149, 150, 155–56
Century Club, Charleston, 9, 43, 66–67, 147
Charleston City Federation of Women's Clubs, 9, 20, 39–40, 146–47, 166–67
Charleston City Union. *See* Charleston City Federation of Women's Clubs
Charleston Female Seminary Alumnae Association, 147
Charleston Free Kindergarten Association, 95–96
Chautauqua Circle, Atlanta, Ga., 56
Child labor reform, 151–66
Childs, B. S., 112, 136
Christensen, Abbie Holmes, 75, 143
CIC. *See* Commission on Interracial Cooperation
Civic Club, Abbeville, 21
Civic Club, Charleston, 9, 142–43, 146
Civic League, Beaufort, 143
Claflin University, Orangeburg, 15, 50, 191
Clark, Septima, 16, 52, 214n56
Class status of clubwomen, 10–11, 13–15, 130–31, 153–57, 160–61, 173–76, 179–81, 194–201, 212n31, 213n47
Cleveland, Grover, 19
Clifford, Mary, 35

Clubwomen: and child labor reform, 151–66; and education reform, 41–43, 48, 65–66, 136–39, 169–72; and fund-raising, 172–73, 183–90; and gender roles, 17–23, 27; and homes for juvenile delinquents, 175–94; and industrial education, 66–67, 178–81, 190–92; and interracial cooperation, 67–84, 227n41; and kindergartens, 138–39, 156, 170–71; and Ku Klux Klan, 40–41; and libraries, 42, 53, 77, 139–41; and monuments, 44, 48–50; and race, 37–41, 57–59, 67–84, 107–24; and Reconstruction, 40; and slavery, 39–40; and social reform, 129–201; and Southern literature, 36–42; and study of history, 32–36, 46–48
Clyde, Florence Alberta, 15
Coleman, Hannah Hemphill, 20–21, 144–45, 215n78
Coleman, Lillian S., 120
Coleman, Ludie Merriam, 8, 39, 111, 139, 210n15
Commission on Interracial Cooperation (CIC), 13, 56, 61, 70–84, 183–84, 187
Conklin, Viola, 42
Cooley, Rossa, 66
Cooper, Dorcas, 11
Cox, Jeannette, 14–15, 51
Crosthwait, Mary, 72, 92
Culture Club, Columbia, 53, 192
Current Literature Club, Columbia, 11, 32, 37, 142

Daniels, F. E., 42
Daughters of the American Revolution (DAR), 9, 13, 34
Davis, Jefferson, 34–35, 43, 202
Denison, Dimies T. S., 118
Divorce, South Carolina clubwomen's stance on federal law concerning, 126–27
"Dixie," 33
Dooly, Isma, 115–16
Douglass, Frederick, 29, 45–48, 66
Dozier, James C., 186
Drake, Bessie, 77–78
Du Bois, W.E.B., 3, 29, 45–48, 83

Duke Foundation, 188
Dunbar, Paul Laurence, 46–47
Duncan, Bessie, 78, 151, 163–64

Education reform, 41–43, 48, 65–66, 136–39, 169–72
Educational background of clubwomen, 11–12, 15–16
Edwards, Johnette, 175
Eggleston, George, 39
Embley, Collin Robinson, 23
Evans, Emily, 20–21, 129, 150–51, 162–63

Fairwold Home for Delinquent Girls, 76, 78, 168–69, 181–201
Fant, Pearl, 150
Fields, Mamie Garvin, 15, 48–49, 50, 75, 95–96, 103, 171
Finlay, Bishop Kirkman G., 78, 183, 186–87
Freeman, Nell Duncan, 78, 184
Frost, Mary P., 38
Furman, Katherine, 78, 186

General Federation of Women's Clubs (GFWC), 1, 9–10, 65, 156, 159; founding of, 8; role of Southern women in, 3, 89–90, 104–7, 121–24; segregation of, 107–24; states' rights in, 124–28; and tuberculosis, 67
Gethers, Cora, 21, 174, 199–200
Gordon, Asa, 15–16, 170
Granger, Caroline, 38, 109, 114
Gray, Wil Lou, 140, 150–51, 170
Gridley, Mary P., 145, 155

Haskin, Sara Estell, 72
Haynes, Elizabeth Ross, 72
Henderson, Sara B., 9
Holmes, Louise Fordham, 76, 90, 194
Homes for juvenile delinquents, 175–94
Honer, Nina, 12
Hope, Lugenia Burns, 16, 54–56, 71–73, 81–82, 92–93, 95
Hopkins, Pauline, 119
Hughes, Virginia, 36–37, 69

Hunton, Addie, 98, 170
Hyde, Mrs. Charles, 39

Industrial education, 66–67, 178–81, 190–92
Intercollegiate Club, 9, 12
International Council of Women of the Darker Races, 14, 54–56
Irby, Julia, 68

Jennings, Maria Croft, 125, 135, 184
Johnson, Annie, 108–9, 115
Johnson, Bertha, 98
Johnson, Carrie Parks, 71–73
Judson, Bessie, 22
Judson, Ethel, 22

Kelly Alumnae Kindergarten Association, 139, 156
Kelly Free Kindergarten Association. *See* Kelly Alumnae Kindergarten Association
Keystone, 10, 20, 31–32, 35, 40, 42, 110–11, 145, 155
Kindergartens, 138–39, 156, 170–71
Kohn, August, 153
Kohn, Irene, 153
Ku Klux Klan, 28, 33, 40–41, 44, 197
Kyle, Alice J., 123

Ladies Memorial Association, Charleston, 9
Laney, Lucy, 72, 92
Lanier, Sidney, 33, 38
Lawton, Mamie, 22
Lee, Robert E., 33, 42–43, 56–57
Leevy, I. S., 78, 183, 186
Levy, Lela, 96
Levy, Maggie O., 172
Lewis, Lem, 171
Libraries, 42, 53, 77, 139–41
Lining, Ida, 12, 134–35
Lost Cause, 2–5, 25–30, 38–46, 56–59, 104–7, 129–36, 218n20
Louise Fordham Holmes Literary and Art Club, Charleston, 47
Lowe, Daisy Gordon, 99–100

Lowe, Rebecca, 104, 107–9, 114–15, 117, 164–65
Lumpkin, Katherine DuPre, 57

MacFeat, Minnie, 139
Magginis, Gertrude, 78
Manning, Leila, 11
Manning, Richard, 144
Marion Birnie Wilkinson Home for Girls. *See* Fairwold Home for Delinquent Girls
Mathews, Victoria Earle, 94
Matthews, Florence, 122
Mays, Benjamin, 14, 76, 80
Mazyck, Esther, 47
McClintock, Euphemia, 11, 213n34
McCrorey, Mary Jackson, 72, 92–93
McDuffie, Ella, 22
McFadyen, Irene, 153
McGowan, Clelia, 74–79, 184, 187–88, 190
McKissick, A. Foster, 152, 244n74
McKissick, Margaret Smythe, 11, 152–53, 176–78
Memminger Alumnae Association, Charleston, 147
Modern Priscilla Club, Charleston, 15, 171
Moorer, Lizelia A. Jenkins, 9, 22, 53, 90, 96, 194
Morrisette, Kate, 42
Morrison, Edna P., 51
Moton, Jennie, 72, 92
Munford, Mary, 135–36
Munsell, Bertha, 184
Murray, Emily Albertha, 9
Music Club, Abbeville, 21

NAACP, 51–52, 83
Napier, Nettie, 92
National Association of Colored Women (NACW), 169, 194–99; and African American history, 48; founding of, 9; and interracial cooperation, 72–73; Southern clubwomen and, 3, 89–90, 92–96, 99–104

National Notes, 80–81, 113–17
New Century Club, Columbia, 11, 34, 41, 43, 64, 78, 111–12, 146–48, 166
New Century Club, Johnston, 30
New Era Club, Spartanburg, 162
Nichols, Mrs. L. T., 140

Oglesby, Sarah, 15
Old Homestead Club, Darlington, 37, 40
Oliphant, Mary Simms, 51
Once a Week Club, Seneca, 8
One More Effort Club, Sumter, 169, 172
Orr, James L., 153, 161
Orr, Lillian Milner, 157
Ottley, Mrs. John K., 114–16
Outlook Club, 37–39
Over the Teacups Club, Darlington, 33, 42
Over the Teacups Club, Rock Hill, 11, 67, 155
Owings, Pauline, 11

Page, Thomas Nelson, 33, 37
Palmetto Leader, 21, 45, 48–50, 56, 186–87
Parker, Thomas, 76, 153
Patterson, Martha Orr, 30, 151, 153, 161, 176–78, 250n35
Pelzer Mill, 11, 152, 156
Perehelion Club, Rock Hill, 12, 18–19, 33, 43, 78
Peterkin, Julia Mood, 47
Phyllis Wheatley Club, Charleston, 14–15, 22, 46–47, 51–53, 76, 83, 171–73, 189
Pollitzer, Anita, 21
Pollitzer, Carrie, 21
Pollitzer, Mabel, 20
Poppenheim, Christie, 9–10, 146, 179
Poppenheim, Christopher, 10–11, 24–25, 34, 131
Poppenheim, Louisa Bouknight, 16, 204–5; author of book reviews in *Keystone*, 36, 39–40, 42, 64, 66; biography, 9–13, 30, 211n24; on child labor reform, 155–58; on clubwomen and Southern identity, 1–2, 34–36, 38, 42, 89, 104–7, 121–28, 131; Confederate lineage of, 34; on gender roles, 19; on industrial education, 179–80; and *Keystone*, 10, 36, 42; on race, 39–40, 62, 64–67, 69, 110, 112, 122–24; on social reform, 62, 67, 105, 139, 141–42, 145–47, 179–80; on Southern women and General Federation of Women's Clubs, 1–2, 89, 104–7, 110, 112, 121–28

Poppenheim, Mary Barnett: biography, 10–13, 30; Confederate lineage of, 34; on domestic servants, 68–69; on gender roles, 19; and *Keystone*, 10; on race, 68; on segregation of General Federation of Women's Clubs, 110; on Southern history, 36, 43, 106; and United Daughters of the Confederacy, 30, 35–36, 43; on women's rights, 12

Poppenheim, Mary Elinor, 24–25, 34–35
Progressive Club, Sumter, 172
Psychology Club, Charleston, 147

Recollections of a Rebel Surgeon and Other Sketches, 42
Reid, Rebecca, 80
Respectability, 21–22, 168, 173–75, 190–91, 194–201
Rhodes, Lilian J., 83, 98, 184
Roddey, Mary, 33
Rollins, Charlotte, 23
Rollins, Frances, 23
Rollins, Louisa, 23
Rowe, Etta Butler, 22, 53, 76, 92–93, 185–86, 192, 194
Ruffin, Josephine, 107–10, 116–18

Salmon, Lucy, 36
Saxon, Celia Dial, 9, 15, 76, 96, 184, 199, 214n58
Schureman, Catherine D., 116
Screven, Mary P., 154
Silone-Yates, Josephine, 81, 95, 118–19, 230n81
Singleton, Geneva, 15
Sligh, Mrs. Wilbur K., 19
Smith, Janie, 31
Smyth, Ellison, 152, 156

Social Reform, 4–5, 129–201. *See also* child labor reform; education reform; homes for juvenile delinquents; industrial education; kindergartens; libraries
Social Survey Club, Columbia, 149
South Carolina Audubon Society, 9
South Carolina Child Labor Committee (SCCLC), 157–58
South Carolina Equal Suffrage League, 21, 162
South Carolina Federation of Colored Women's Clubs (SCFCWC), 5, 13, 21, 29–30, 83, 206–7; and African American history, 44, 46–48, 55; and elitism, 175; and Fairwold Home for Delinquent Girls, 182–94; founding of, 9, 211n21; and interracial cooperation, 76–77; and respectability, 194–95, 198–201; and social reform, 168–70
South Carolina Federation of Women's Clubs (SCFWC), 2–3, 204–5; and child labor reform, 151–61; on divorce, 126–28; and education, 41–43, 65–66, 136–39; founding of, 8; and General Federation of Women's Clubs, 124–28; and home for delinquent boys, 175–81; and interracial cooperation, 77–79; and libraries, 42, 139–41; link to UDC, 30–32, 35, 132; and race, 62–63, 65–68, 77–79; and social reform, 129–42, 144–45, 148–67; and Southern identity, 41–43, 105–6, 132–35
South Carolina Kindergarten Association, Charleston, 139, 147
South Carolina Negro Business League, 13
South Carolina State College (later University), 13–14, 49, 51, 53, 94, 187, 191–92
South Carolina United Daughters of the Confederacy (SCUDC), 5, 8, 10, 35, 38, 74; link to women's clubs, 30–32; and slavery, 40
South Carolina Woman's Rights Association, 23
Southeast Branch of Vassar Alumnae Association, 9

Southeastern Federation of Women's Clubs, 73–74, 91, 95–96, 98–100, 103, 188, 193, 233n43
Southern Federation of Women's Clubs, 91, 96–99
Spears, Victoria, 172
Springs, Lena, 125–27, 159
Stokes, Ora Brown, 98
Stowe, Harriet Beecher, 37, 46
Sunlight Club, Orangeburg, 13–14, 22–23, 47, 53, 91, 95–96, 169, 171–73, 189, 192

Tanner Art Club, Florence, 170, 172
Taylor, Rebecca Stiles, 98–100, 103, 188, 233n44
Taylor, Susie King, 45–46
Terrell, Mary Church, 48, 95–96, 171, 174
Thomas, Edwina, 98
Thompson, Carrie, 48
Thursday Club, Columbia, 20, 148–49
Thursday Club, Greenville, 20
Thursday Club, Laurens, 150
Tillman, Ben, 200
Timrod, William Henry, 37–38
Turner, Viola Ford, 171

Uncle Tom's Cabin, 37, 45–46, 69
United Daughters of the Confederacy (UDC), 2–5, 8, 10, 12, 17–18, 63, 143, 145; link to women's clubs, 30–32; and Lost Cause, 25–29, 57–59, 203–5; and race, 40–41; and Southern identity, 40–46, 57–59, 203–5
Up-to-Date Club, Chester, 32

Vassar College, 12, 36, 121
Vincent, Belle, 76, 184
Visanska, Sarah, 19–20, 133–34, 138, 151–52, 155, 161, 166–67, 240–41n12
Voorhees College, 14

Walker, Maggie Lena, 92
Ward, May Alden, 122–23
Washington, Booker T., 29, 33, 47, 66, 68, 83, 180–81, 191

Washington, Josephine T., 99, 103
Washington, Margaret Murray, 16, 54–56, 72–73, 80–81, 83, 92, 94–97, 102, 120
Wednesday Club, Laurens, 20, 32
Wells, Ida B., 81, 119–20, 232n22
Wheatley, Phillis, 29, 46–47
White, Daisy, 30
White, Mrs. Joseph, 31
White, Rassie, 27
Wilkinson, Lula, 93
Wilkinson, Marion Birnie, 6, 9, 15–16, 169, 171, 206; and African American history, 53–56; biography, 13–14; education of, 15; and interracial cooperation, 56, 72, 74, 76, 80, 82–83; member of International Council of Women of the Darker Races, 54–56; member of Southern network of African American clubwomen, 54, 74, 91–96, 98; role in National Association of Colored Women, 72, 92–96, 101, 199; support for Fairwold Home for Delinquent Girls, 181–93; support for women's suffrage, 23
Wilkinson, Robert Shaw, 13–14, 74, 93, 189, 191–92
Williams, Fannie Barrier, 119
Willis, Azalea, 137
Women's suffrage, 18–21, 23
Woman's Christian Temperance Union, 71, 97
Women's Auxiliary of Episcopal Church, 77, 184
Women's League, Charleston, 97
Wright, Eloise, 30, 35

YWCA, 9, 13, 76, 92

Zimmerman, Geraldine, 101–2

NEW PERSPECTIVES ON THE HISTORY OF THE SOUTH
Edited by John David Smith

"In the Country of the Enemy": The Civil War Reports of a Massachusetts Corporal,
edited by William C. Harris (1999)

The Wild East: A Biography of the Great Smoky Mountains, by Margaret L. Brown (2000);
first paperback edition, 2001

*Crime, Sexual Violence, and Clemency: Florida's Pardon Board and Penal System
in the Progressive Era,* by Vivien M. L. Miller (2000)

*The New South's New Frontier: A Social History of Economic Development
in Southwestern North Carolina,* by Stephen Wallace Taylor (2001)

Redefining the Color Line: Black Activism in Little Rock, Arkansas, 1940–1970,
by John A. Kirk (2002)

The Southern Dream of a Caribbean Empire, 1854–1861, by Robert E. May (2002)

Forging a Common Bond: Labor and Environmental Activism during the BASF Lockout,
by Timothy J. Minchin (2003)

*Dixie's Daughters: The United Daughters of the Confederacy and the Preservation
of Confederate Culture,* by Karen L. Cox (2003)

*The Other War of 1812: The Patriot War and the American Invasion
of Spanish East Florida,* by James G. Cusick (2003)

*"Lives Full of Struggle and Triumph": Southern Women, Their Institutions
and Their Communities,* edited by Bruce L. Clayton and John A. Salmond (2003)

German-Speaking Officers in the United States Colored Troops, 1863–1867,
by Martin W. Öfele (2004)

Southern Struggles: The Southern Labor Movement and the Civil Rights Struggle,
by John A. Salmond (2004)

Radio and the Struggle for Civil Rights in the South, by Brian Ward (2004)

Luther P. Jackson and the Fight for Civil Rights by Michael Dennis (2004)

Southern Ladies, New Women: Race, Region, and Clubwomen in South Carolina, 1890–1930,
by Joan Marie Johnson (2004)

*"Don't Sleep With Stevens!:" The J. P. Stevens Campaign and the Struggle to Organize the South,
1963–08,* by Timothy J. Minchin (2005)

"The Ticket to Freedom": The NAACP and the Struggle for Black Political Integration,
by Manfred Berg (2005)

Joan Marie Johnson is visiting lecturer at Northeastern Illinois University in Chicago. She is editor of *Southern Women at Vassar: The Poppenheim Family Letters, 1882–1916* (2002).

www.ingramcontent.com/pod-product-compliance
Lightning Source LLC
Chambersburg PA
CBHW022105150426
43195CB00008B/280